Embedded Cryptography 1

SCIENCES

Computer Science,
Field Director – Jean-Charles Pomerol

Cryptography, Data Security,
Subject Head – Damien Vergnaud

Embedded Cryptography 1

Coordinated by
Emmanuel Prouff
Guénaël Renault
Matthieu Rivain
Colin O'Flynn

iSTE WILEY

First published 2025 in Great Britain and the United States by ISTE Ltd and John Wiley & Sons, Inc.

ISTE Ltd
27-37 St George's Road
London SW19 4EU
UK

www.iste.co.uk

John Wiley & Sons, Inc.
111 River Street
Hoboken, NJ 07030
USA

www.wiley.com

Library of Congress Control Number: 2024945145

British Library Cataloguing-in-Publication Data
A CIP record for this book is available from the British Library
ISBN 978-1-78945-213-6

ERC code:
PE6 Computer Science and Informatics
PE6_5 Security, privacy, cryptology, quantum cryptography

Contents

Preface

**Emmanuel Prouff[1], Guénaël Renault[2],
Matthieu Rivain[3], and Colin O'Flynn[4]**

[1] *LIP6, Sorbonne Université, Paris, France*
[2] *Agence nationale de la sécurité des systèmes d'information, Paris, France*
[3] *CryptoExperts, Paris, France*
[4] *Dalhousie University and NewAE Technology Inc, Halifax, Canada*

The idea for this project was born during a discussion with Damien Vergnaud. Damien had been asked to propose a series of volumes covering the different domains of modern cryptography for the SCIENCES series. He offered us the opportunity to take charge of the *Embedded Cryptography* books, which sounded like a great challenge to take on. In particular, we thought it was perfectly timely as the field was gaining increasing importance with the growing development of complex mobile systems and the Internet of Things.

The field of embedded cryptography, as a research domain, was born in the mid-1990s. Until that time, the evaluation of a cryptosystem and the underlying attacker model were usually agnostic of implementation aspects, whether the cryptosystem was deployed on a computer or on some embedded hardware like a smart card. Indeed, the attacker was assumed to have no other information than the final results of a computation and, possibly, the corresponding inputs. In this black box context, defining a cryptanalytic attack and evaluating resistance to it essentially consisted of finding flaws in the abstract definition of the cryptosystem.

In the 1990s, teams of researchers published the first academic results, highlighting very effective means of attack against embedded systems. These attacks were based on the observation that a system's behavior during a computation strongly depends on the values of the data manipulated (which was previously known and exploited by intelligence services). Consequently, a device performing

Embedded Cryptography 1,
coordinated by Emmanuel Prouff, Guénaël Renault,
Matthieu Rivain and Colin O'Flynn.

cryptographic computation does not behave like a black box whose inputs and outputs are the only known factors. The power consumption of the device, its electromagnetic radiation or its running time are indeed other sources that provide the observer with information on the intermediate results of the computation. Teams of researchers have also shown that it was possible to disrupt a computation using external energy sources such as lasers or electromagnetic pulses.

Among these so-called *physical attacks*, two main families emerge. The first gathers the (passive) side-channel attacks, including timing attacks proposed by Kocher (1996) and power analysis attacks proposed by Kocher et al. (1999), as well as the microarchitectural attacks that have considerably developed after the publication of the Spectre and Meltdown attacks in 2018 (Kocher et al. 2018). This first family of attacks focuses on the impact that the data manipulated by the system have on measurable physical quantities such as time, current consumption or energy dissipation related to state changes in memories. The second family gathers the (active) fault injection attacks, whose first principles were introduced by Boneh et al. (1997). These attacks aim to put the targeted system into an abnormal state of functioning. They consist, for example, of ensuring that certain parts of a code are not executed or that operations are replaced by others. Using attacks from either of these families, an adversary might learn sensitive information by exploiting the physical leakage or the faulted output of the system.

Since their inception, *side-channel attacks* and *fault injection attacks*, along with their countermeasures, have significantly evolved. Initially, the embedded systems industry and a limited number of academic labs responded with ad hoc countermeasures. Given the urgency of responding to the newly published attacks, these countermeasures were reasonably adequate at the time. Subsequently, the invalidation of many of these countermeasures and the increasing sophistication of attack techniques highlighted the need for a more formalized approach to security in embedded cryptography. A community was born from this observation in the late 1990s and gathered around a dedicated conference known as *cryptographic hardware and embedded systems* (CHES). Since then, the growth of this research domain has been very significant, resulting from the strong stake of the industrial players and the scientific interest of the open security issues. Nowadays, physical attacks involve state-of-the-art equipment capable of targeting nanoscale technologies used in the semiconductor industry. The attackers routinely use advanced statistical analyses or signal processing, while the defenders designing countermeasures call on concepts from algebra, probability theory or formal methods. More recently, and notably with the publication of the *Spectre* and *Meltdown* attacks, side-channel attacks have extended to so-called microarchitectural attacks, exploiting very common optimization techniques in modern CPUs such as out-of-order execution or speculative execution. Twenty-five years after the foundational work, there is now a large community of academic and industrial scientists dedicated to these problems. Embedded cryptography has gradually become a classic topic in cryptography and computer security, as illustrated by the increasing importance of this field in major cryptography and security conferences besides CHES, such as CRYPTO, Eurocrypt, Asiacrypt, Usenix Security, IEEE S&P or ACM CCS.

Pedagogical material

For this work, it seemed important to us to have both scientifically ambitious and pedagogical content. We indeed wanted this book to appeal not only to researchers in embedded cryptography but also to Master's students interested in the subject and curious to take their first steps. It was also important to us that the concepts and notions developed in the book be as illustrated as possible and therefore accompanied by a pedagogical base. In addition to the numerous illustrations proposed in the chapters, we have made pedagogical material available (attack scripts, implementation examples, etc.) to test and deepen the various concepts. These can be found on the following GitHub organization: https://github.com/embeddedcryptobook.

Content

This book provides a comprehensive exploration of embedded cryptography. It comprises 40 chapters grouped into nine main parts, and spanning three volumes. The book primarily addresses side-channel and fault injection attacks as well as their countermeasures. Part 1 of this volume is dedicated to *Software Side-Channel Attacks*, namely, timing attacks and microarchitectural attacks, primarily affecting software; whereas Part 2 is dedicated to *Hardware Side-Channel Attacks*, which exploit hardware physical leakages, such as power consumption and electromagnetic emanations. Part 3 focuses on the second crucial family of physical attacks against embedded systems, namely, *Fault Injection Attacks*.

A full part of the book is then dedicated to *Masking* in Part 1 of Volume 2, which is a widely used countermeasure against side-channel attacks and which has become an important research topic since their introduction in 1999. This part covers a variety of masking techniques, their security proofs and their formal verification. Besides general masking techniques, efficient and secure embedded cryptographic implementations are very dependent on the underlying algorithm. Consequently, Part 2, *Cryptographic Implementations*, is dedicated to the implementation of specific cryptographic algorithm families, namely, AES, RSA, ECC, and post-quantum cryptography. This part also covers hardware acceleration and constant-time implementations. Secure embedded cryptography needs to rely on secure hardware and secure randomness generation. In cases where hardware alone is insufficient for security, we must rely on additional software techniques to protect cryptographic keys. The latter is known as white-box cryptography. The next three parts of the book address those aspects. Part 3, Volume 2, *Hardware Security*, covers invasive attacks, hardware countermeasures and physically unclonable functions (PUF).

Part 1 of Volume 3 is dedicated to *White-Box Cryptography*: it covers general concepts, practical attack tools, automatic (gray-box) attacks and countermeasures as well as code obfuscation, which is often considered as a complementary measure to white-box cryptography. Part 2 is dedicated to *Randomness and Key Generation* in embedded cryptography. It covers both true and pseudo randomness generation as well as randomness generation for specific cryptographic algorithms (prime numbers for RSA, random nonces for ECC signatures and random errors for post-quantum schemes).

Finally, we wanted to include concrete examples of real-world attacks against embedded cryptosystems. The final part of this series of books contains those examples of *Real World Applications and Attacks in the Wild*. While not exhaustive, we selected representative examples illustrating the practical exploitation of the attacks presented in this book, hence demonstrating the necessity of the science of embedded cryptography.

Acknowledgments

This series of books results from a collaborative work and many persons from the embedded cryptography community have contributed to its development. We have tried to cover (as broadly as possible) the field of embedded cryptography and the many research directions related to this field. This has not been an easy task, given the dynamism and growth of the field over the past 25 years. Some experts from the community kindly shared their insights on the preliminary plan of the book, namely, Sonia Belaïd, Pierre-Alain Fouque, Marc Joye, Victor Lomné and Yannick Sierra. We would like to thank them for their insightful comments.

For each of the identified topics we wanted the book to cover, we have called upon expert researchers from the community, who have honored us by joining this project. The essence of this work is theirs. Dear Guillaume Barbu, Lejla Batina, Sonia Belaïd, Davide Bellizia, Florent Bernard, Begül Bilgin, Eleonora Cagli, Łukasz Chmielewski, Jessy Clédière, Brice Colombier, Jean-Sébastien Coron, Jean-Luc Danger, Lauren De Meyer, Cécile Dumas, Jean-Max Dutertre, Viktor Fischer, Pierre Galissant, Benedikt Gierlichs, Louis Goubin, Vincent Grosso, Sylvain Guilley, Patrick Haddad, Laurent Imbert, Ján Jančár, Marc Joye, Matthias Kannwischer, Stefan Katzenbeisser, Victor Lomné, José Lopes-Esteves, Ange Martinelli, Pedro Massolino, Loïc Masure, Nele Mentens, Debdeep Mukhopadhyay, Camille Mutschler, Ruben Niederhagen, Colin O'Flynn, Elisabeth Oswald, Dan Page, Pascal Paillier, Louisa Papachristodoulou, Thomas Peeters, Olivier Peirera, Thomas Pornin, Bart Preneel, Thomas Prest, Jean-René Reinhard, Thomas Roche,

Francisco Rodríguez-Henríquez, Franck Rondepierre, Eyal Ronen, Melissa Rossi, Mylene Rousselet, Sylvain Ruhault, Ulrich Ruhrmair, Sayandeep Saha, Patrick Schaumont, Sebastian Schrittwieser, Peter Schwabe, Richa Singh, Sergei Skorobogatov, François-Xavier Standaert, Petr Svenda, Marek Sys, Akira Takahashi, Abdul Rahman Taleb, Yannick Teglia, Philippe Teuwen, Adrian Thillard, Medhi Tibouchi, Mike Tunstall, Aleksei Udovenko, David Vigilant, Lennert Wouters, Yuval Yarom and Rina Zeitoun: thank you so much for the hard work!

To accompany these authors, we also relied on numerous reviewers who kindly shared their remarks on the preliminary versions of the chapters. Their behind-the-scenes work allowed us to greatly improve the technical and editorial quality of the books. We express our gratitude to them, namely, Davide Alessio, Sébastien Bardin, Sonia Belaïd, Eloi Benoist-Vanderbeken, Gaëtan Cassiers, Jean-Sebastien Coron, Debayan Das, Cécile Dumas, Julien Eynard, Wieland Fischer, Thomas Fuhr, Daniel Genkin, Dahmun Goudarzi, Eliane Jaulmes, Victor Lomné, Loïc Masure, Bart Mennink, Stjepan Picek, Thomas Pornin, Thomas Prest, Jurgen Pulkus, Michaël Quisquater, Thomas Roche, Franck Rondepierre, Franck Salvador, Tobias Schneider, Okan Seker, Pierre-Yves Strub, Akira Takahashi, Abdul Rahman Taleb, Mehdi Tibouchi, Aleksei Udovenko, Gilles Van Assche, Damien Vergnaud, Vincent Verneuil and Gabriel Zaid.

October 2024

References

Boneh, D., DeMillo, R.A., Lipton, R.J. (1997). On the importance of checking cryptographic protocols for faults. In *Proceedings of Eurocrypt'97*. Springer, Heidelberg, 1233, 37–51.

Kocher, P.C. (1996). Timing attacks on implementations of Diffie-Hellman, RSA, DSS, and other systems. In *Proceedings of CRYPTO'96*. Springer-Verlag, Heidelberg, 104–113.

Kocher, P.C., Jaffe, J., Jun, B. (1999). Differential power analysis. In *Proceedings of CRYPTO'99*. Springer-Verlag, Heidelberg, 1666, 388–397.

Kocher, P.C., Genkin, D., Gruss, D., Haas, W., Hamburg, M., Lipp, M., Mangard, S., Prescher, T., Schwarz, M., Yarom, Y. (2018). Spectre attacks. Exploiting speculative execution. *ArXiv* [Online]. Available at: http://arxiv.org/abs/1801.01203.

PART 1

Software Side-Channel Attacks

1

Timing Attacks

Daniel PAGE
University of Bristol, United Kingdom

Set within the context of cryptographic engineering, timing attacks are a class of side-channel attack: if the execution latency of some target operation depends on security-critical data, this may allow an attacker to leverage passive execution latency measurements in any attempt to recover said data. Timing attacks have a rich history, and, in part because variation in execution latency can arise from a wide range of sources, remain surprisingly stubborn. Although a known problem, they remain far from a solved problem as evidenced by related instances continuing to appear more than 20 years since initial publications on the topic. The aim of this chapter is to offer an introduction to that topic, covering *both* a set of foundational concepts from a more theoretical perspective *and* a set of example attacks and their mitigation (via countermeasures) from a more applied perspective. As a result, the content should enable you to understand and apply the concepts covered in a broader context, for example, within your own work, and beyond the specific, limited set of examples used.

1.1. Foundations

In this section, we focus on explanation of the central concepts. The aim, in fairly non-technical terms, is to first explain *what* a timing attack is, and then establish a terminology and model for characterizing and reasoning about them. Doing so offers a foundation, which we will then build on in section 1.2 through an investigation of more concrete, example attacks.

Embedded Cryptography 1,
coordinated by Emmanuel PROUFF, Guénaël RENAULT,
Matthieu RIVAIN and Colin O'FLYNN.

```
algorithm BUBBLE(X, n) begin
  do
    f ← false
    for i = 1 upto n − 1 do
      if X_{i−1} > X_i then
        X_{i−1} ↔ X_i
        f ← true
      end
    end
  while f = true
end
```

(a) A more abstract description of bubble sort, using pseudo-code

```c
void bubble( int* X, int n ) {
  bool f;

  do {
    f = false;

    for( int i = 0; i < n; i++ ) {
      if( X[ i - 1 ] > X[ i ] ) {
        int t            = X[ i - 1 ];
            X[ i - 1 ] = X[ i     ];
            X[ i     ] = t;

        f = true;
      }
    }
  }
  while( f == true );
}
```

(b) A more concrete description of bubble sort, using C source code

Figure 1.1. *Two descriptions of bubble sort*

1.1.1. *Execution latency in theory*

DEFINITION 1.1.– Given a computational process P, the term *execution latency* is a measure of the delay between P starting and finishing execution (whether it completes normally or is terminated abnormally).

We intentionally leave the *unit* of measurement undefined. That is, within different contexts it might be appropriate to use different units, for example, an abstract unit such as computational steps, a concrete, human-oriented unit such as seconds, or a concrete, machine-oriented unit such as clock cycles. If the unit relates to time in a meaningful way, then it is common to see execution *time* used synonymously with execution *latency*: both terms capture the idea that we measure how much time elapses between starting and finishing execution.

The bubble sort algorithm is conceptually simple, so is an appealing, generic example to use as a vehicle to explore this concept further. The algorithm, described in Figure 1.1(a) using pseudo-code, repeatedly iterates over an n-element input array X, comparing adjacent elements and swapping them in-place if they occur in the wrong order; this is repeated until the array is sorted, which we know is true when no more swaps are required.

So, given an input array, what is the execution latency of this algorithm? That is, how much time elapses between starting (using X and n as input) and finishing execution (meaning a sorted X is produced as output) of the algorithm? Analysis of computational complexity (or, more specifically, time complexity) offers one approach to providing an answer. Doing so gives a result in terms of abstract computational steps, focused on the problem size n. By using such analysis, we conclude that in the worst case *and* average case, the algorithm will perform $O(n^2)$ comparison operations and $O(n^2)$ swap operations; in the best case, the algorithm will perform $O(n)$ comparison operations and $O(1)$ swap operations.

DEFINITION 1.2.– The execution latency of a computational process P is termed *data dependent* if it depends on, and so may vary as a result of, the input data. Otherwise, it is termed *data independent*: this implies that the execution latency is the same, irrespective of the input data for every execution of P.

Two facts should be clear from our analysis of bubble sort. First, and more obviously, the *length* of X impacts the execution latency: in all cases, the number of steps will be greater for an X with many elements (i.e. larger n) than it will for an X with few elements (i.e. smaller n). Second, and less obviously, however, the *content* of X *also* impacts the execution latency: as suggested by the differing best and worse cases, the number of steps will be less for an X which is already (close to being) sorted than it will for an X, which is not. Either way, execution latency of the bubble sort algorithm would therefore be classified as data dependent.

1.1.2. *Execution latency in practice*

DEFINITION 1.3.– In concrete terms, data-dependent execution latency arises from (at least) the following cases: (1) *which operations are executed*, as determined by control-flow decisions made during execution; and (2) *how operations are executed*, or, put another way, what the execution latency of each executed operation is and whether or not it is data dependent.

Although instances of the first case can be identified within an abstract algorithm, instances of the second case are dependent on concrete details of an associated implementation and platform it is executed on. Conceptually at least, we could view this shift as including rather than (intentionally) excluding constant factors in analysis using computational complexity. Doing so is clearly imperative, because we ultimately aim to reason about concrete, real-world versus abstract, on-paper scenarios.

We can identify instances of both cases using Figure 1.1(b), which describes an implementation of bubble sort using C source code. For example, the `if` statement on line 8 represents an example of the first case: the flow of control is managed so lines 9–13 are either executed or not, depending on whether or not `X[ i - 1 ] > X[ i ]`. Likewise, the memory access implied by the expressions `X[ i - 1 ]` and `X[ i ]` on line 8 represents an example of the second case: the latencies of said accesses depend, for example, on the memory hierarchy (e.g. the existence and state of any caches that exist within it). More generally, the platform will optimize instruction execution; it may do so for both memory access *and* computational instructions (for example, although this implementation does not include any, shift, multiplication, and division instructions sometimes exhibit data-dependant execution latency). An implication of this fact is that robust analysis of data (in)dependence cannot arise from the (static) source code alone. The Instruction Set Architecture (ISA) said source code ultimate targets will typically only capture functional properties: how instructions will be (dynamically) executed, and therefore the behavioral properties of the platform (i.e. a specific micro-architectural implementation of that ISA), *also* need to be assessed.

1.1.3. *Attacks that exploit data-dependent execution latency*

In a sense, bubble sort is as efficient as it can be: it only performs the steps required to produce a correct output from an associated input by exiting the outer-loop as soon as no more swaps are required. Adopting a perspective where efficiency is the metric of interest, such an approach is clearly positive. In fact, do *any* negatives stem from it? If we adopt a different perspective where security is the (or at least a) metric of interest, the answer is yes.

Put simply, the fact that execution latency is data dependent implies some form of correlation: measuring the execution latency will provide information, of some form, about the data it depends on. Set in some scenario where an adversary has access to execution latency measurements, this can be hugely problematic. Specifically, consider a scenario where the data involved are security critical, for example, but without loss of generality, some cryptographic key material. Using bubble sort as an example starts to become tenuous at this point, so instead consider the following generic attack model:

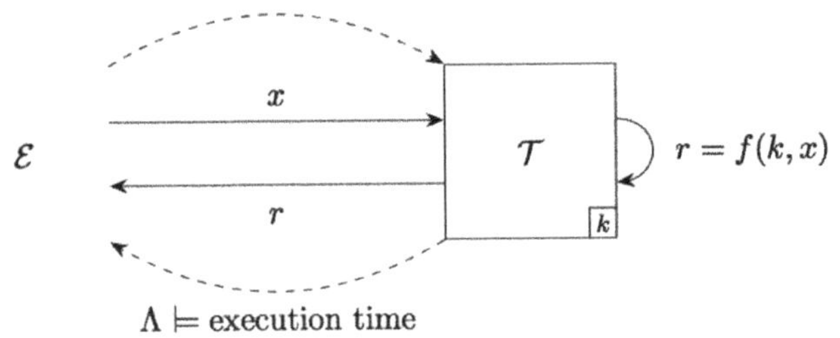

which helps fix various concepts and notation. $\mathcal{E}$ is using $\mathcal{T}$ to perform some computation f. Having first accepted an input x from $\mathcal{E}$, $\mathcal{T}$ computes and then provides $r = f(k, x)$ as output. $\mathcal{E}$ can also measure the execution latency associated with computation by $\mathcal{T}$, which we denote Λ. On the one hand, k *is* not and *should* not be known by $\mathcal{E}$. On the other hand, however, Λ may provide information about k if the execution latency of f is data dependent, and therefore may potentially be exploited in an attack aiming to recover it. This is the crux of a side-channel attack based on execution latency, or, less formally, a *timing attack*. We say that information about the security-critical data is leaked (or is leakage) through a side-channel represented by execution latency. Such attacks are potent, because, as a result of exploiting the additional information afforded by the side-channel, they can often be significantly more efficient than alternatives (e.g. traditional cryptanalysis).

Now focused on the topic of side-channel attacks, we need to address two important points regarding terminology. First, in relation to data (in)dependence, the term data are qualified by the fact that we almost always mean security-critical data. There is limited value in learning information about data we already know, for example, and so no implication for execution latency depending on it. So, from here on, read "data" as "security-critical data" unless otherwise stated. Second, it is very common to see the term constant-time (respectively, variable-time) used as a synonym for data-independent (respectively, data-dependent) execution latency in this context (already ignoring the clash vs. $O(1)$ in computational complexity). We avoid these terms, deeming data (in)dependence more reflective of what is actually intended. For example, the execution latency of a given algorithm *may* vary and need not reflect any *specific* constant: we only demand that it does *not* vary, and so is (some) constant with respect to security-critical data involved. Likewise, use of the term constant-time suggests execution time (or latency) is the *only* pertinent issue; in reality, and more generally, we need to address the challenge of data-dependent resource use (*both* in terms of which resources are used, *and* the length of time they are used for). We can find examples of this fact investigated in Chapter 2.

Having presented the high-level concept, we now refine various lower level details of our attack model. We do so in a piecemeal manner below, framing the discussion around a set of concise definitions which, in combination, help to explain and characterize specific attacks (such as those used as examples in section 1.2).

DEFINITION 1.4.– The attack strategy employed by $\mathcal{E}$ may be described as *differential* or *non-differential*.

At a high level, a non-differential attack will typically use few (even just one) execution latency measurements in isolation. In contrast, a differential attack will typically use many execution latency measurements in combination, for example, through analysis of when and how they differ as the result of data-dependent behavior by $\mathcal{T}$.

DEFINITION 1.5.– The attack strategy employed by $\mathcal{E}$ may be assessed, where relevant, in relation to either *efficacy* and/or *efficiency*.

Although exceptions might exist, efficacy is normally a binary assessment: either the attack by $\mathcal{E}$ is successful with respect to some stated aim or not. In contrast, there are many ways to assess efficient resource use by $\mathcal{E}$ during said attack. Focusing on time, for example, we might view the number of interactions with $\mathcal{T}$, the high-level, algorithm-related attack latency (e.g. stated in terms of computational complexity) or the low-level, implementation-related attack latency (e.g. stated in terms of wall-clock time), as indicative of how efficient $\mathcal{E}$ is.

DEFINITION 1.6.– If the interaction between $\mathcal{E}$ and $\mathcal{T}$ is direct, the attack is described as *local*; otherwise, if the interaction is indirect, the attack is described as *remote*.

There are other, reasonable ways to capture a similar concept, for example, using physical proximity (implying physical access) as the measure of localness. We opt for the above instead, because $\mathcal{E}$ and $\mathcal{T}$ may be in close physical proximity but *still* physically or logically isolated from each other; this would imply an indirect form of interaction. Either way, two points are important. First, although the attack model above at least *suggests* that $\mathcal{E}$ and $\mathcal{T}$ interact remotely, this is *not* a limitation. For example, $\mathcal{E}$ may leverage physical access to some device $\mathcal{T}$ in order to mount a local attack; $\mathcal{E}$ and $\mathcal{T}$ may be software processes (co-)resident and so executing locally on the same platform; $\mathcal{E}$ and $\mathcal{T}$ may be software processes resident and so executing on different platforms, interacting remotely via an intermediate network. Second, if/when a remote attack is feasible, this is often viewed as an advantage. For example, such an attack typically removes the need for physical access to $\mathcal{T}$, avoids any reliance on additional equipment (for example, see power- or EM-based side-channels) and allows attacks to be applied at greater scale (in the sense there are likely to be more accessible instances of $\mathcal{T}$ to attack).

DEFINITION 1.7.– From the perspective of $\mathcal{E}$, computation by $\mathcal{T}$ may be described as *synchronous* or *asynchronous*.

The synchronous case suggests that $\mathcal{E}$ knows or even *controls* when $\mathcal{T}$ starts or finishes execution; in contrast, the asynchronous case suggests that $\mathcal{T}$ operates independently from $\mathcal{E}$ (and, as a result, is often described as free-running). In the asynchronous case, one typically attempts to identify some form of trigger or reference event that indicates the start and/or finish of execution. Such an event might be observable via a secondary side-channel, or simply observation of when and how $\mathcal{T}$ interacts with external parties (such as $\mathcal{E}$) or resources (such as memory or peripheral devices).

DEFINITION 1.8.– The execution latency measurements taken by $\mathcal{E}$ are characterized by their *accuracy*, that is, how close the measured and actual execution latencies are, and *precision*, that is, how close two execution latency measurements for the same computation are. The former case typically relates to systematic error, for example, due to the impact of *quantization*; whereas the latter case typically relates to random error, for example, due to the impact of *noise*.

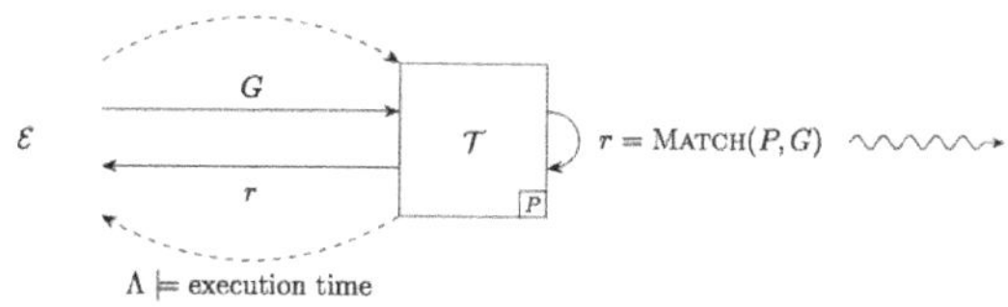


```
algorithm MATCH(P, G) begin
    if |P| ≠ |G| then
        return false
    end
    for i from 0 upto |G| − 1 do
        if P_i ≠ G_i then
            return false
        end
    end
    return true
end
```

(a) The attack model for Example 1.1, in section 1.2.1.

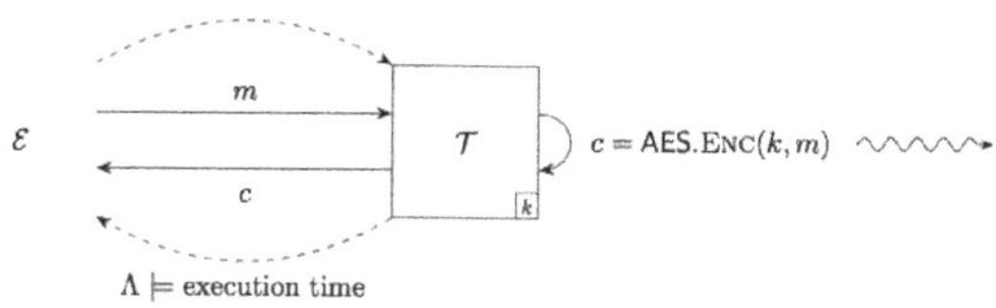


```
algorithm AES.ENC(k, m) begin
    rk ← k, rc ← 01_(16), s ← m
    s ← KEY-ADDITION(s, rk)
    for i = 1 upto Nr − 1 step +1 do
        s ← SUB-BYTES(s)
        s ← SHIFT-ROWS(s)
        s ← MIX-COLUMNS(s)
        (rk, rc) ← KEY-EXPANSION-STEP(rk, rc)
        s ← KEY-ADDITION(s, rk)
    end
    s ← SUB-BYTES(s)
    s ← SHIFT-ROWS(s)
    (rk, rc) ← KEY-EXPANSION-STEP(rk, rc)
    s ← KEY-ADDITION(s, rk)
    return s
end
```

(b) The attack model for Example 1.2, in section 1.2.2.

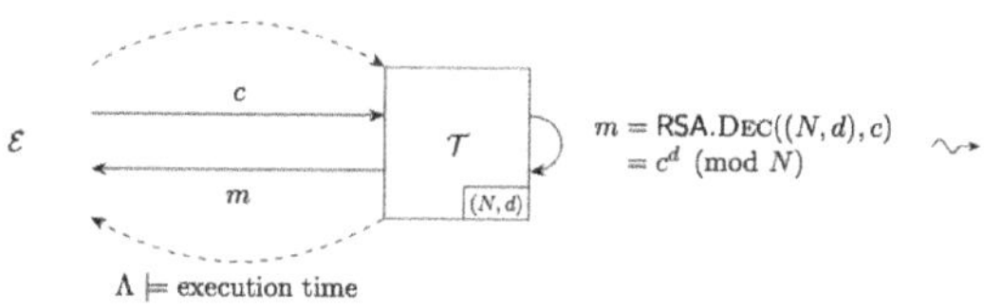


```
algorithm RSA.DEC((N, d), c) begin
    ĉ ← MONTMUL(c, ρ², N)
    r̂ ← MONTMUL(1, ρ², N)
    for i = |d| − 1 downto 0 do
        r̂ ← MONTMUL(r̂, r̂, N)
        if d_i = 1 then
            r̂ ← MONTMUL(r̂, ĉ, N)
        end
    end
    return MONTMUL(r̂, 1)
end
```

(c) The attack model for Example 1.3, in section 1.2.3.

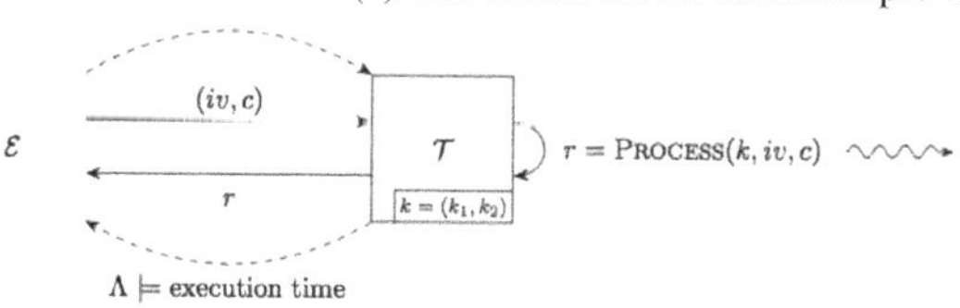


```
algorithm PROCESS(k, iv, c) begin
    m ∥ τ ∥ ρ = m' = AES-CBC.DEC(k_1, iv, c)
    if ρ is invalid then abort
    if HMAC-SHA-1.VER(k_2, m, τ) = false then abort
    r = f(m)
    return r
end
```

(d) The attack model for Example 1.4, in section 1.2.4.

Figure 1.2. *Attack models relating to the examples presented in section 1.2*

We deem any formal exploration of what noise *is* beyond our scope; it suffices to understand that noise will degrade accuracy and precision, in the sense that execution latency of the same computation within different interactions between $\mathcal{E}$ and $\mathcal{T}$ may differ (or fluctuate). The term Signal-to-Noise Ratio (SNR) is often used to capture the relative strength of the signal of interest, that is, the actual execution latency, versus any noise that causes the measured execution latency to differ. Both statistical and non-statistical techniques can typically be harnessed in an attempt to reduce or even remove noise, that is, yield higher SNR; examples include averaging and filtering. Doing so can be important, because, ultimately, SNR will typically have some impact on the efficiency and/or efficacy of most attacks.

1.2. Example attacks

In this section, we focus on application of the central concepts: the aim is to illustrate *how* timing attacks are mounted. Harnessing the foundation offered by section 1.1, we do so by considering a small set of examples each framed within a simple but plausible scenario; we structure each example in the same way by (1) defining the attack model, (2) analyzing the attack model, for example, to characterize the source of data dependence and then, finally, (3) presenting an attack based on said analysis.

1.2.1. *Example 1.1: an explanatory attack on password validation*

1.2.1.1. *Scenario*

Consider the attack model depicted in Figure 1.2(a): an adversary $\mathcal{E}$ interacts with a target device $\mathcal{T}$ that stores some embedded, security-critical data P (a password). When provided with input G (a guess at the password), $\mathcal{T}$ first performs the computation detailed by the algorithm MATCH (that is, string matching, or, more specifically password validation) and then responds with r as output. $\mathcal{E}$ can *also* measure the execution latency of computation performed by $\mathcal{T}$, so attempts to exploit this information with the aim of recovering P (implying, for example, it then gains access to $\mathcal{T}$).

1.2.1.2. *Analysis*

In the same way we reasoned about bubble sort, the MATCH algorithm is as efficient as it can be: as soon as it detects a mismatch between P and G, it immediately returns *false* rather than needlessly continuing. Such a mismatch can occur for two reasons. First, and resulting in execution of line 3, the mismatch might stem from the *length* of, that is, number of characters in, P and G: if $|P| \neq |G|$, then the two cannot match. Second, and resulting in execution of line 7, the mismatch might arise from the *content* of P and G: if $P_i \neq G_i$ for some i, then the two cannot match. This is termed early-abort behavior, and is possible when a special-case condition means the general-case algorithm need not be fully executed in order to provide correct output from the associated input. Viewed from the perspective of efficiency, this behavior is positive; when viewed from the perspective of security, the same behavior becomes negative; however, it means that the execution latency of MATCH is data dependent, that is, depends on P and G.

1.2.1.3. *Exploitation*

Assume, without loss of generality, that the set of valid characters is $A = \{$`'a'`, `'b'`, $\ldots$, `'z'`$\}$, and, specifically, that P = `"pencil"`, which means $|P| = 6$. The attack proceeds in two phases:

1) In this phase, the attack aims to recover $|P|$. To do so, we use a sequence of guesses:

$$G \in \langle \texttt{"a"}, \texttt{"aa"}, \texttt{"aaa"}, \texttt{"aaaa"}, \ldots \rangle$$

during interaction with $\mathcal{T}$, that is, the ith guess is $i + 1$ characters in length. The execution latency for guess G = `"aaaaaa"` will be longer than for the others because $|P| = |G|$; this means execution for it will progress into the loop, rather than early-abort at line 3. As such, identifying this G recovers $|P|$.

2) In this phase, the attack aims to recover P iteratively, that is, character-by-character. To recover P_i in iteration $i = 0$, we use a sequence of guesses:

$$G \in \langle \texttt{"aaaaaaa"}, \texttt{"baaaaaa"}, \texttt{"caaaaaa"}, \ldots, \texttt{"zaaaaaa"} \rangle$$

during interaction with $\mathcal{T}$, that is, the ith character cycles through all possibilities, while the others remain fixed. The execution latency for guess G = `"paaaaa"` will be longer than for the others, because $|P| = |G|$ and $P_0 = G_0$; this means execution will progress into loop iteration $i + 1 = 1$, rather than early-abort at line 7 in iteration $i = 0$. As such, G_0 = `'p'` is deemed correct in this guess, which we now fix. To recover P_i in iteration $i = 1$, we use a sequence of guesses:

$$G \in \langle \texttt{"paaaaaa"}, \texttt{"pbaaaaa"}, \texttt{"pcaaaaa"}, \ldots, \texttt{"pzaaaaa"} \rangle$$

during interaction with $\mathcal{T}$, that is, the ith character cycles through all possibilities, while the others remain fixed. The execution latency for guess G = `"peaaaa"` will be longer than for the others, because $|P| = |G|$, $P_0 = G_0$ and $P_1 = G_1$; this means execution will progress into loop iteration $i + 1 = 2$, rather than early-abort at line 7 in iteration $i = 1$. As such, G_1 = `'e'` is deemed correct in this guess, which we now fix. The attack continues in the same way for $0 \leq i < n$, until P is eventually fully recovered.

Since this is an explanatory attack, it is easy to assess it in terms of both efficacy and efficiency versus intuitive alternatives. For example, we could consider a brute-force attack: by essentially trying every n-character guess, this strategy assumes knowledge of n, requires $O(|A|^n)$ guesses and guarantees recovery of P. Or, we could consider a dictionary attack: by first constructing a dictionary of common (or likely) passwords $D = \{$`"password"`, `"qwerty"`, `"admin"`, $\ldots\}$ to use as guesses, this strategy does not assume knowledge of n, requires $O(|D|)$ guesses and does not guarantee recovery of P. In contrast, our side-channel attack does not assume knowledge of n, requires $O(|A| \cdot n)$ guesses and guarantees recovery of P; in a sense, the additional information allows it to offer greater efficiency than the brute-force attack *and* greater efficacy than the dictionary attack.

1.2.2. *Example 1.2: an attack on* `xtime`*-based AES*

1.2.2.1. *Scenario*

Assuming use of AES-128 throughout, consider the attack model depicted in Figure 1.2(b): an adversary $\mathcal{E}$ interacts with a target device $\mathcal{T}$, which stores some embedded, security-critical data k (an AES cipher key). When provided with input m (an AES plaintext), $\mathcal{T}$ first performs the computation detailed by the algorithm AES.ENC (i.e. AES encryption) and then responds with c (an AES ciphertext) as output. $\mathcal{E}$ can *also* measure the execution latency of computation performed by $\mathcal{T}$, so we attempted to exploit this information with the aim of recovering k.

1.2.2.2. *Analysis*

AES is an iterative block cipher based on an SP network; as one of three possible parameterizations, AES-128 uses a 16 byte cipher key and $b = 16$ byte block size. At a low level, it operates on elements in the finite field $\mathbb{F}_{2^8}$ realized as $\mathbb{F}_2[\mathbf{x}]/p(\mathbf{x})$, where $p(\mathbf{x}) = \mathbf{x}^8 + \mathbf{x}^4 + \mathbf{x}^3 + \mathbf{x} + 1$. A short-hand is often adopted for elements of this field, meaning, for example, $a(\mathbf{x}) = \mathbf{x}^4 + \mathbf{x} + 1 \equiv 13_{(16)}$, suggesting that each element can be represented by a byte (whose ith bit represents the ith coefficient). Elements of $\mathbb{F}_{2^8}$ are collected into (4×4)-element state and round key matrices; the ith row and jth column of such a matrix relating to round r is denoted $s_{i,j}^{(r)}$ and $rk_{i,j}^{(r)}$ respectively, with super- and/or subscripts omitted whenever irrelevant. The process of encryption initializes $s^{(0)} = m$ and $rk^{(0)} = k$, in both cases filling the left-hand matrix in a column-wise manner using content from the right-hand sequence of bytes.

$\mathcal{T}$ adopts an implementation strategy common in constrained platforms, targeting a balance that trades-off higher execution latency for lower memory footprint. This can be summarized as follows. First, it pre-computes the S-box: doing so implies it is realized using a table look-ups, rather than any computation. Second, it updates (or evolves) the cipher key, computing each round key during encryption rather than pre-computing them. Third, and finally, it uses the algorithm:

```
1 algorithm XTIME(a) begin
2 |   if a_7 = 1 then
3 |   |   return (a << 1) ⊕ 11B_(16)
4 |   else
5 |   |   return (a << 1)
6 |   end
7 end
```

to compute the multiplication-by-$\mathbf{x}$ operation, that is, $a(\mathbf{x}) \cdot \mathbf{x} \pmod{p(\mathbf{x})}$. On lines 3 and 5, the unconditional left-shift captures multiplication by $\mathbf{x}$. On line 3, however, the conditional XOR captures a reduction modulo $p(\mathbf{x})$; note that such a reduction is only required when $a_7 = 1$. Using this algorithm, it applies:

$$\text{MIX-COLUMN}\left(\begin{bmatrix} s_{0,j} \\ s_{1,j} \\ s_{2,j} \\ s_{3,j} \end{bmatrix}\right) = \begin{bmatrix} 02_{(16)} & 03_{(16)} & 01_{(16)} & 01_{(16)} \\ 01_{(16)} & 02_{(16)} & 03_{(16)} & 01_{(16)} \\ 01_{(16)} & 01_{(16)} & 02_{(16)} & 03_{(16)} \\ 03_{(16)} & 01_{(16)} & 01_{(16)} & 02_{(16)} \end{bmatrix} \times \begin{bmatrix} s_{0,j} \\ s_{1,j} \\ s_{2,j} \\ s_{3,j} \end{bmatrix}$$

$$= \begin{bmatrix} \texttt{xtime}(s_{0,j}) \oplus (\texttt{xtime}(s_{1,j}) \oplus s_{1,j}) \oplus s_{2,j} \oplus s_{3,j} \\ s_{0,j} \oplus \texttt{xtime}(s_{1,j}) \oplus (\texttt{xtime}(s_{2,j}) \oplus s_{2,j}) \oplus s_{3,j} \\ s_{0,j} \oplus s_{1,j} \oplus \texttt{xtime}(s_{2,j}) \oplus (\texttt{xtime}(s_{3,j}) \oplus s_{3,j}) \\ (\texttt{xtime}(s_{0,j}) \oplus s_{0,j}) \oplus s_{1,j} \oplus s_{2,j} \oplus \texttt{xtime}(s_{3,j}) \end{bmatrix}$$

to each jth column of the state within MIXCOLUMNS.

In summary, the execution latency of AES encryption is data dependent: this stems from the implementation strategy adopted, whereby the execution latency of `xtime` and therefore MIX-COLUMNS is data dependent.

1.2.2.3. *Exploitation*

The attack strategy aims to recover k iteratively, that is, byte-by-byte. Let k_j and m_j denote the jth byte of plaintext and cipher key, respectively. In any tth iteration of the attack, we aim to recover the target byte k_t based on the observation that, in the first MIX-COLUMNS invocation, the computation:

$$\texttt{xtime}(\text{S-BOX}(m_t \oplus k_t))$$

is performed at least once; we term this the target `xtime`. Doing so involves the following steps, parameterized by N and M:

1) Compute the $(256 \times N)$-element matrix $\mathcal{H}$ such that:

$$\mathcal{H}_{i,j} = \begin{cases} 1 \text{ if S-BOX}(i \oplus j)_7 = 1 \\ 0 \text{ if S-BOX}(i \oplus j)_7 = 0 \end{cases}$$

Across the rows, each $0 \leq i < 256$ captures a possible value of k_t; across the columns, each $0 \leq j < N$ captures a possible value of m_t (meaning $N = 256$ will consider *all* possible values). As such, each $\mathcal{H}_{i,j}$ captures whether or not the target `xtime` performs a conditional XOR for specific k_t and m_t.

2) Compute the $(N \times M)$-element matrix:

$$\mathcal{S}_{i,j} = \{\langle s_0, s_1, \ldots, s_{b-1}\rangle \mid s_k = i \text{if } k = t,\ s_k \text{is random if } k \neq t\}$$

of plaintexts. So, since all plaintexts in the ith row have the same tth byte, they all yield the same input to the target `xtime`. Let $\mathcal{R}_{i,j}$ denote the execution latency arising from encryption of $\mathcal{S}_{i,j}$, which we measure via interaction with $\mathcal{T}$, and $\bar{\mathcal{R}}_i$ denote the mean of execution latencies across the ith row of $\mathcal{R}$.

The idea is that, provided N and M are large enough, $\bar{\mathcal{R}}_i$ will reflect the target `xtime`, that is, it will be larger or smaller depending on whether or not the conditional XOR occurs. Put another way, with some probability of error, $\bar{\mathcal{R}}_i$ indicates the value of $\text{S-BOX}(i \oplus k_t)_7$. To recover k_t, we compare each $\bar{\mathcal{R}}$ with each $\mathcal{H}_i$, for example, using the Pearson correlation coefficient: the i which yields the strongest correlation indicates the value of k_t.

1.2.3. *Example 1.3: an attack on Montgomery-based RSA*

1.2.3.1. *Scenario*

Consider the attack model depicted in Figure 1.2(c): an adversary $\mathcal{E}$ interacts with a target device $\mathcal{T}$, which stores the embedded, security-critical data (N, d) (an RSA private key). When provided with input c (an RSA ciphertext), $\mathcal{T}$ first performs the computation detailed by the algorithm RSA.DEC (i.e. RSA decryption) and then responds with m (an RSA plaintext) as output. $\mathcal{E}$ can *also* measure the execution latency of computation performed by $\mathcal{T}$, so attempts to exploit this information with the aim of recovering d.

1.2.3.2. *Analysis*

$\mathcal{T}$ uses the left-to-right, binary (or square-and-multiply) exponentiation algorithm. Note that all modular squaring and multiplication operations, for example, in lines 4 and 6, are based on the use of Montgomery reduction. This requires pre-computation of ω and ρ from N, such that $\hat{x} = x \cdot \rho \pmod N$ then denotes the Montgomery representations of some x.

The execution latency of modular exponentiation is data dependent, because the execution of line 6 is conditional on d_i. An execution latency measurement may therefore allow us to infer how often line 6 is executed, and hence the Hamming weight of (or number of bits equal to 1 in) d. Beyond this, we need to analyze the MONTMUL algorithm as used to support the exponentiation algorithm. The steps involved are captured as follows:

```
algorithm MONTMUL(x, y, N) begin
    r ← x · y
    r ← (r + ((r · ω) mod ρ) · N)/ρ
    if r >= N then r ← r − N
    return r
end
```

where line 2 performs an integer multiplication, line 3 performs a Montgomery reduction, and then, finally, line 4 performs a conditional subtraction to fully reduce r modulo N. From this, we conclude that the execution latency of MONTMUL is also data dependent, because the execution of line 4 is dependent on both the operands x and y and the modulus N; as used to support exponentiation, this implies dependence on c (because it forms one of the operands), and, crucially, d (because it controls when, where and how MONTMUL is invoked).

1.2.3.3. *Exploitation*

The attack strategy aims to recover d iteratively, that is, bit-by-bit, working from the most-significant toward the least-significant bit. In any tth iteration of the attack, d is partially known and partially unknown, which we can depict as follows:

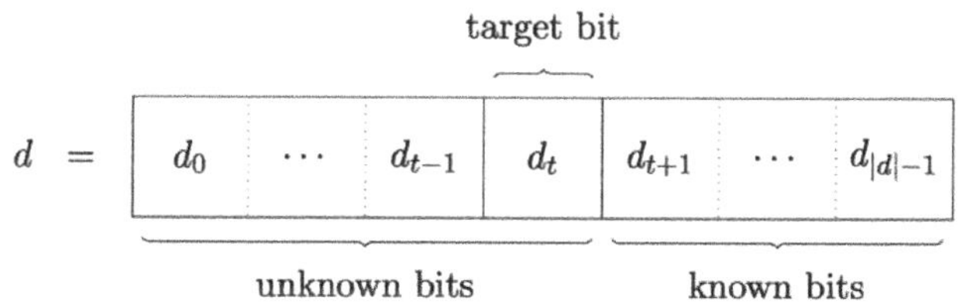

That is, we already know some more-significant bits of d (noting that it must be the case that some $d_{|d|-1} = 1$; otherwise $d = 0$) and so aim to recover the next less significant, as yet unknown target bit d_t. Let $c[k]$ denote some kth ciphertext, randomly selected modulo N for $0 \leq k < n$; for each such $c[k]$, we use (partial) knowledge of d to simulate a (partial) decryption as would be performed by $\mathcal{T}$. Doing so involves the following steps:

1) Start by setting $c = c[k]$, then simulating lines 2 and 3, that is, computing $\hat{c} \leftarrow \text{MONTMUL}(c, \rho^2, N)$ and $\hat{r} \leftarrow \text{MONTMUL}(1, \rho^2, N)$.

2) Step the simulation forward until we reach the start of loop iteration t (between lines 4 and 5). We can do so because d_i is known for $t < i < |d|$, meaning the simulation can perform exactly the same computation that $\mathcal{T}$ would.

3) Step the simulation forward until we reach the end of loop iteration t (between lines 8 and 9). We can do so because although d_i is unknown for $i = t$, we can fork the simulation to reflect guessing both possibilities:

a) for the simulation fork that guesses $d_i = 0$, line 6 is not executed so we do not update $\hat{r}$;

b) for the simulation fork that guesses $d_i = 1$, line 6 is executed so we update $\hat{r} \leftarrow \text{MONTMUL}(\hat{r}, \hat{c}, N)$.

4) Step the simulation forward until we reach the middle of loop iteration $t + 1$ (between lines 5 and 6). That is, we update $\hat{r} \leftarrow \text{MONTMUL}(\hat{r}, \hat{r}, N)$ and, in doing

so, record whether or not the conditional subtraction, that is, line 4 of MONTMUL, is executed.

5) Classify c by placing it into set:

$$\begin{array}{ll} \mathcal{S}_0 \text{ if the simulation fork guessed } d_i = 0 \text{ and no conditional subtraction is executed} \\ \mathcal{S}_1 \text{ if the simulation fork guessed } d_i = 0 \text{ and } \quad \text{conditional subtraction is executed} \\ \mathcal{S}_2 \text{ if the simulation fork guessed } d_i = 1 \text{ and no conditional subtraction is executed} \\ \mathcal{S}_3 \text{ if the simulation fork guessed } d_i = 1 \text{ and } \quad \text{conditional subtraction is executed} \end{array}$$

This means c is placed into exactly *two* sets: either $\mathcal{S}_0$ or $\mathcal{S}_1$ arising from the simulation fork that guessed $d_i = 0$, and either $\mathcal{S}_2$ or $\mathcal{S}_3$ arising from the simulation fork that guessed $d_i = 1$.

The idea is that we have intentionally constructed the sets so there should be a difference between the execution latency for the ciphertexts in $\mathcal{S}_0$ versus those in $\mathcal{S}_1$, and the ciphertexts in $\mathcal{S}_2$ versus those in $\mathcal{S}_3$. Under the assumption that conditional subtractions will occur more or less at random during exponentiation, ciphertexts in the latter will, on average, execute an extra conditional subtraction versus those in the former. However, only one of the guesses made by the simulation is actually correct, so that difference should only be evident in either the first or second case. Put another way, for the correct (respectively, incorrect) guess, the simulated computation will (respectively, will not) match the actual computation by $\mathcal{T}$; therefore, for the correct (respectively, incorrect) guess, the number of conditional subtractions that occur during exponentiation of ciphertexts in one set will differ from (respectively, be approximately equal to) those in the other set. So, let

$$\Lambda(\mathcal{S}_k) = \frac{1}{|\mathcal{S}_k|} \sum_{c \,\in\, \mathcal{S}_k} \Lambda(c)$$

denote the average execution latency of ciphertexts in set $\mathcal{S}_k$, where $\Lambda(c)$ denotes the execution latency for some ciphertext c: we measure this by interacting with $\mathcal{T}$. One of three cases will apply:

$$\begin{array}{lll} \text{abs}(\ \Lambda(\mathcal{S}_0) - \Lambda(\mathcal{S}_1)\ ) > \text{abs}(\ \Lambda(\mathcal{S}_2) - \Lambda(\mathcal{S}_3)\ ) & \Rightarrow & d_t = 0 \\ \text{abs}(\ \Lambda(\mathcal{S}_0) - \Lambda(\mathcal{S}_1)\ ) < \text{abs}(\ \Lambda(\mathcal{S}_2) - \Lambda(\mathcal{S}_3)\ ) & \Rightarrow & d_t = 1 \\ \text{abs}(\ \Lambda(\mathcal{S}_0) - \Lambda(\mathcal{S}_1)\ ) \simeq \text{abs}(\ \Lambda(\mathcal{S}_2) - \Lambda(\mathcal{S}_3)\ ) & & \end{array}$$

In the first (top) and second (middle) cases, the difference we expect will allow us to infer the value of d_t. In the third (bottom) case, however, the difference is too close to allow confident inference of d_t; this may be due to, for example, use of too small an n or the impact of noise.

Having recovered d_t, we proceed with the next, $(t+1)$th attack iteration and recover the next, $(t+1)$th bit of d in the same way; this continues until d is eventually fully recovered.

1.2.4. *Example 1.4: a padding oracle attack on AES-CBC*

1.2.4.1. *Scenario*

Assuming use of AES-128 throughout, consider the attack model depicted in Figure 1.2(d): an adversary $\mathcal{E}$ interacts with a target device $\mathcal{T}$, which stores the embedded, security-critical data k (some key material). When provided with input (iv, c), $\mathcal{T}$ first performs the computation detailed by the algorithm PROCESS, then responds with r as output. $\mathcal{E}$ obtains a ciphertext (iv^*, c^*), which is the encryption of some unknown plaintext m^* under k. It can *also* measure the execution latency of computation performed by $\mathcal{T}$, so attempts to exploit this information with the aim of recovering m^*.

1.2.4.2. *Analysis*

Let $x[i]_j$ denote the jth byte within the ith block of some n-block plaintext or ciphertext x; this means $0 \leq i < n$ and $0 \leq j < b$, assuming a b-byte block size.

At a high level, PROCESS can be described line-by-line as follows. Line 2 decrypts the ciphertext c, parsing the result m' as a plaintext m, some padding ρ and a tag τ. Then, line 3 checks whether ρ is valid, aborting if not; line 4 checks whether τ is valid, aborting if not; and, finally, line 5 processes m using some function f to produce r. At a low level, some further details are important: note that line 2 decrypts c using AES in Cipher Block Chaining (CBC) mode using the key k_1, and line 3 assumes τ is a SHA1-based HMAC Message Authentication Code (MAC) tag and checks validity accordingly using the key k_2. The padding scheme used to specify ρ is also important, but not detailed within the description of PROCESS. Although alternatives exist, assume a TLS-like scheme is used: let

$$\rho(\alpha) = \langle \underbrace{\alpha, \alpha, \ldots, \alpha}_{\alpha \text{byte(s)}}, \alpha \rangle$$

denote a valid padding sequence, which contains α byte(s) equal to α and then 1 compulsory byte equal to α, which records the total padding length. Note that if $m \parallel \tau$ is l bytes long, then $\rho = \rho(\, b - (l+1) \bmod b\,)$.

The execution latency of PROCESS is data dependent: if t_3 denotes the execution latency when $\mathcal{T}$ early-aborts on line 3 based on ρ, t_4 denotes the execution latency when $\mathcal{T}$ early-aborts on line 4 based on τ, and t_5 denotes the execution latency when $\mathcal{T}$ executes line 5, then, irrespective of their concrete values, $t_3 < t_4 < t_5$. In fact, we can focus on the ability to distinguish between these cases by defining a so-called padding oracle: for the scenario at hand, this would be something like:

$$\mathcal{O}(iv, c) = \begin{cases} \textbf{true} \text{ if AES-CBC.}\textsc{Dec}(k_1, iv, c) \text{has valid padding} \\ \textbf{false} \text{ if AES-CBC.}\textsc{Dec}(k_1, iv, c) \text{has invalid padding} \end{cases}$$

Doing so can be viewed as an abstraction of the underlying mechanism used to measure execution latency, thus separating it from the attack strategy.

1.2.4.3. *Exploitation*

Use of AES in CBC mode means that $\mathcal{T}$ will compute:

$$m'[i] = \text{AES.}\textsc{Dec}(k_1, c[i]) \oplus x_i$$

where

$$x_i = \begin{cases} iv & \text{if } i = 0 \\ c[i-1] & \text{if } i > 0 \end{cases}$$

for $0 \leq i < n$. The resulting plaintext m' is then parsed into the fields m, τ, and ρ, which we can depict as follows:

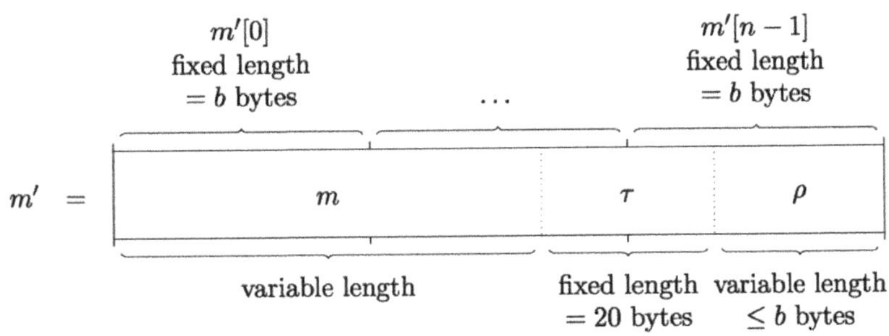

From this specific example, we can infer several more general facts. First, ρ will occur in $m'[n-1]$, that is, the last, $(n-1)$th block of m'. Second, although $|\rho|$ is unknown, we *do* know $|\rho| \leq b$ because the point of including it at all is to ensure $|m'| = 0 \pmod{b}$. Third, the definition of CBC mode means that:

$$m'[n-1] = \text{AES.}\textsc{Dec}(k_1, c[n-1]) \oplus x_i.$$

As such, by controlling x_i (meaning either iv or $c[n-2]$, depending on i), we can control $m'[n-1]$ and hence also the ρ then checked for validity by $\mathcal{T}$. For example, consider a two-block ciphertext c. If we construct an input (iv, c') where $c' = (c[0] \oplus \delta) \parallel c[1]$, for some δ, that is, $c'[0] = c[0] \oplus \delta$ and $c'[1] = c[1]$, then $\mathcal{T}$ will compute:

$$\begin{aligned} m'[0] &= \text{AES.DEC}(k_1, c'[0]) \oplus iv \\ &= \text{AES.DEC}(k_1, c[0] \oplus \delta) \oplus iv \\ m'[1] &= \text{AES.DEC}(k_1, c'[1]) \oplus c'[0] \oplus \delta \\ &= \text{AES.DEC}(k_1, c[1]) \oplus c[0] \oplus \delta \end{aligned}$$

That is, $\mathcal{T}$ will compute an m' where $m'[0]$ is randomized by and $m'[1]$ is controlled by the δ selected; since $m'[1]$ is the $(n-1)$th block in m', δ will also control ρ and hence the padding oracle result, that is,

$$\mathcal{O}(iv, (c[0] \oplus \delta) \parallel c[1]).$$

Based on these facts, and assuming again that $|c^*| = 2$, the attack proceeds in two phases:

1) In this phase, the attack strategy constructs a so-called "recover last byte(s)" oracle. First, select a random b-byte block δ and search for a value of δ_{b-1} such that:

$$\mathcal{O}(iv, (c^*[0] \oplus \delta) \parallel c^*[1]) = \textbf{true}.$$

Since the padding of m' is deemed to be valid, we know that one of:

$$\begin{array}{lclcl} m'[1]_{b-1} & = & m^*[1]_{b-1} \oplus \delta_{b-1} & = & \rho(0) \\ m'[1]_{b-2,\ldots,b-1} & = & m^*[1]_{b-2,\ldots,b-1} \oplus \delta_{b-2,\ldots,b-1} & = & \rho(1) \\ m'[1]_{b-3,\ldots,b-1} & = & m^*[1]_{b-3,\ldots,b-1} \oplus \delta_{b-3,\ldots,b-1} & = & \rho(2) \\ & \vdots & & \vdots & \end{array}$$

is true: however, we do not know *which* one. So, to recover one (or more) byte(s) of m', we need $|\rho|$, that is, the padding length. To recover it, start from $t = 0$ and alter (e.g. increment) δ_t. If

$$\mathcal{O}(iv, (c^*[0] \oplus \delta) \parallel c^*[1]) = \textbf{false},$$

then t marks the initial padding byte (because we just altered it, thus invalidating the padding) and implies that $|\rho| = b - t$; otherwise, increment t and try again.

2) In this phase, the attack strategy constructs a so-called "block decryption" oracle. As mentioned above, we have already recovered the most-significant $b - t$ bytes of m', that is, the *natural* padding: we therefore have:

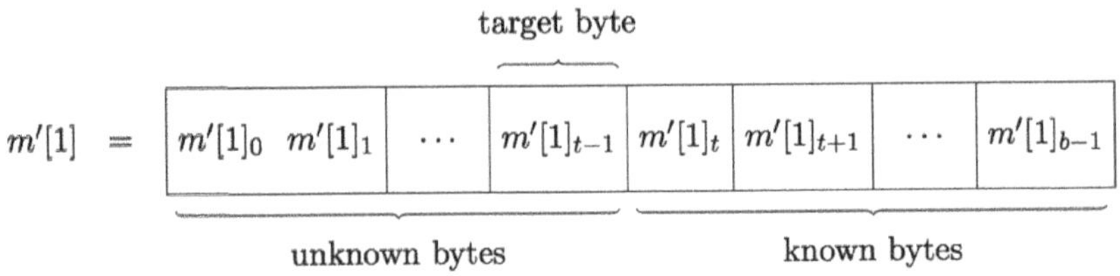

for some t where

$$m'[1]_{t,\ldots,b-1} = m^*[1]_{t,\ldots,b-1} \oplus \delta_{t,\ldots,b-1} = \rho(b-t-1).$$

To recover the next least-significant byte of $m'[1]$, we try to control δ so an *extended* padding is produced. To do so, we begin by incrementing the known padding bytes by setting $\delta_j = m'[1]_j \oplus (b-t)$ for $t \leq j < b$, and then we apply a similar strategy as above by searching for a value of δ_{t-1} such that the padding of m' is deemed valid: this recovers $m'[1]_{t-1}$. Then, we can iterate for each next least-significant byte to recover the whole of $m'[1]$ (and hence $m^*[1]$).

Of course, as described, this process is specific to recovery of $m'[1]$ and, even then, the case where $|c^*| = 2$. However, with minor alterations the same underlying concept generalizes to cater for recovery of any $m'[i]$ and for any $|c^*|$.

1.3. Example mitigations

Fundamentally, mitigating side-channel attacks based on execution latency can be achieved by preventing said execution latency being data dependent. Although true, this vastly understates the challenge in doing so, which is evidenced by a variety of points. For example, first, the basic properties of scale and complexity can be hugely challenging. On the one hand, there is a large design space of techniques to consider; on the other hand, they often need to be applied to and so integrated with a large, complex software code base that may be constrained, for example, with respect to requirements of some overarching protocol. Second, the underlying issue is evident in, and so potentially must be addressed at various levels of abstraction, for example, both at a high level, relating to the design algorithms, *and* at a low level, relating to their implementation, and, ultimately execution. Third, security may be *a* metric, not *the* metric of interest; there can be pressure to compromise on security in order to meet efficiency targets, for example, which demands carefully considered trade-offs.

Although, there is seldom a panacea for such challenges, (1) clear understanding of the context, constraints, problem and platform, and (2) well-informed selection and application of implementation techniques are centrally important in producing an outcome, which is fit for purpose. We can find a detailed treatment of relevant topics in Chapters 7 of Volume 2. For completeness, however, the following provides an illustrative overview of pertinent examples, framed around phases of a typical development cycle (implying iteration over said phases may be required).

1) *Design*: at a high(er) more abstract level, the first phase specifies a design for what will be implemented. Appropriate high-level choices will often have the largest impact from an efficiency perspective, and the same is true from a security perspective: care in this phase can make subsequent phases significantly easier.

Among many options, we might consider algorithm selection (in the context of ECC, e.g. use of the Montgomery ladder and/or complete addition formula), parameter selection (in the context of RSA, e.g. of ρ to remove conditional subtraction in Montgomery multiplication), techniques related to alternative representation of data (e.g. bit-slicing), techniques related to alternative computational models (e.g. based on URISC), approaches based on blinding (e.g. of an RSA private exponent), or approaches based on padding (e.g. to worst-case execution latency).

2) *Implementation*: at a low(er), more concrete level, the next phase implements what has been specified. Care with respect to how a high(er) level implementation is translated into a low-level instruction sequence by a tool chain, *and* how that instruction sequence is executed by the platform, is crucial. For example, note that many compiler optimizations intended to have a positive impact on efficiency *may* have a negative impact on security, e.g. by "un-doing" features intended to ensure data-independent execution latency.

Among many options, we might consider approaches based on control-flow linearization (or flattening) to yield straight-line code (e.g. software multiplexer gadgets, or via conditional-move instructions), approaches based on control-flow balancing, approaches that yield constant memory access patterns (e.g. within window-based modular exponentiation) and approaches that favor computation versus memory access (e.g. use of AES-NI versus look-ups into pre-computed S-box or T-table content).

3) *Evaluation*: in the final phase, we aim to evaluate what has been implemented, and, ideally, gather evidence and hence confidence that the associated execution latency is data independent.

Among many options, we might consider approaches based on (static) verification (including use of baseline assumptions, e.g. as provided by RISC-V `Zkt` pseudo-extension) and/or on (dynamic) experimentation (e.g. `ctgrind` and `dudec`).

1.4. Notes and further references

– Section 1.1. There are many good side-channel attack overviews. Anderson (2020) offers a accessible, general example with a range of historical context, while Koeune (2011) covers attacks based on execution latency specifically. The first publication related to such attacks was by Kocher (1996). Nearly a decade later, in Brumley and Boneh (2003) then expanded the scope by demonstrating remote applicability, that is, over a network. The same general concept has been further explored within numerous different scenarios, for example, by Schindler (2000), Aciiçmez et al. (2005) and Brumley and Tuveri (2011). The work of Kocher is seminal, which presents both specific attacks, for example, on RSA and DSA, *and* articulates the more general threat; we can make a strong argument that it represents the foundation of modern research on side-channel attacks. For example, it already notes that "*RAM cache hits can produce timing characteristics in implementations*" and thus identifies the more general challenge of data-dependent execution latency arising from the platform; the range of components studied along similar lines is vast, for example, including behavior of integer, such as Großschädl et al. (2010) and floating-point, such as Andrysco et al. (2015) and Kohlbrenner and Shacham (2017), instruction execution, plus wider, system-level components such as the C compiler (Kaufmann et al. 2016), the JIT compiler (Brennan et al. 2020) and the garbage collector (Pedersen and Askarov 2017).

Note that this chapter intentionally avoids coverage of so-called micro-architectural attacks, many of which are based on data-dependent execution latency in some way: Chapter 2 offers detailed coverage, but, for example, various related books such as Rebeiro et al. (2015) and surveys such as Ge et al. (2018) and Szefer (2019) may also be interesting. Also, although we adopted a focus on cryptographic examples, it is vital to stress the applicability of the same underlying concepts in other contexts: examples include recovery of key-stroke information (Song et al. 2001; Tey et al. 2013; Lipp et al. 2017; Balagani et al. 2018), recovery of resources associated with web-browsing (Felten and Schneider 2000; Kotcher et al. 2013; van Goethem et al. 2015), and traffic analysis (Murdoch and Danezis 2005; Wang et al. 2005). Likewise, it may be interesting to consider that data-dependent execution latency has *constructive* as well as *destructive* use-cases: examples include IP protection (Donda et al. 2015).

– Section 1.2.1. Among numerous explanatory examples, of side-channel attacks in general and those specifically based on execution latency, the presentation by Naccache and Tunstall (2000) is an often-cited instance. Although not strictly comparable to MATCH, it is interesting to note that the manual page for the C `memcmp` function warns "*[d]o not use `memcmp()` to compare security critical data, such as cryptographic secrets, because the required CPU time depends on the number of equal bytes*", and so hints at similar real-world behavior.

– Section 1.2.2. The attack description follows the study that of Koeune and Quisquater (1999), which predates the standardization of Advanced Encryption Standard (AES); although compatible in the scenario used, the authors consider then AES *candidate* Rijndael.

– Section 1.2.3. Rivest et al. (1978) introduced what we now know as the RSA public-key encryption scheme. This attack demands careful understanding of the associated implementation. As such, Gordon (1998) offers a general overview of exponentiation algorithms; Montgomery (1985) describes the eponymous Montgomery reduction technique, with Koç et al. (1996) surveying various implementation options for it. The attack strategy was already outlined by Kocher (1996), with further analysis later offered by Dhem et al. (1998). The attack description follows the latter, focusing on the second case they consider in Dhem et al. (1998), section 3.4, that is, attacking the modular squaring. Note that similar attacks are possible for other scenarios: examples include Mittmann and Schindler (2021), who consider Barrett (1987) reduction, and Bakhshi and Sadeghiyan (2007), who consider Blakley (1983) reduction.

– Section 1.2.4. This attack demands careful understanding of the associated implementation. As such, note that the components involved are all standardized in some way: see, for example, AES (2001), CBC mode (National Institute of Standards and Technology (NIST) 2001b, section 6.2), HMAC (2008) and the TLS-like padding scheme assumed (Dierks and Rescorla 2008, section 6.2.3.2). Set within a symmetric-focused scenario, the attack description follows that of Vaudenay (2002) (later generalized by Black and Urtubia 2002). A wide range of work has applied this approach to real-world targets: examples include Canvel et al. (2003) and Paterson and Yau (2004) and Yau et al. (2005), who consider it as applied to TLS- and ISO/IEC-based cases, respectively, Avoine and Ferreira (2018), who consider padding oracle attacks on a SCP02-compliant smart-card, and both Lucky 13 (AlFardan and Paterson 2013) and Lucky Microseconds (Albrecht and Paterson 2016), which represent further attacks on CBC-based encryption in (D)TLS. It is also important to acknowledge conceptually analogous alternatives set within an asymmetric-focused scenario: important examples include the attacks due to Bleichenbacher (1998) (see also Jager et al. (2012); Meyer et al. (2014); Böck et al. (2018); Ronen et al. (2019)) and later Manger (2001) (see also Strenzke (2010)).

– Section 1.3. Coverage of mitigation, or countermeasures, is challenging in the sense the topic is broad and diverse. From a software perspective only, in order to reduce the scope somewhat, an accessible starting point would be the "coding rules" for implementations maintained by Aumasson Github (n.d.a) and others. At a high level, data-dependent control-flow is supported by numerous, context-dependent approaches. For RSA, relevant examples include various work, for example, Walter (1999) and Hachez and Quisquater (2000), which considers elimination the data-dependent conditional subtraction in Montgomery multiplication. For ECC, relevant examples include use of complete formula, for example, as per Renes et al. (2016), and regular scalar multiplication based on the Montgomery ladder (Montgomery 1987) (thoroughly investigated by Joye and Yen (2003)); Joye (2004) and Oswald (2004) offer a general overview from destructive and constructive perspectives. At a low level, Molnar et al. (2006) propose the program counter security model, which is essentially a way to formally reason about data-dependent control-flow; such reasoning includes both checking for data-(in)dependence, and transformation of instruction sequences. Coppens et al. (2009) cover a range of related techniques for, for example, control-flow linearization, automation within an LLVM-based compiler back-end for x86 platforms.

It seems fair to say that, at least at the time of writing, tooling which supports (semi-)automatic analysis of implementations is limited but improving. As part of a wider survey, Barbosa et al. (2021), section IV present an overview; relevant examples can be categorized into static, for example, ct-verif (Almeida et al. 2016), FlowTracker (Rodrigues et al. 2016), MicroWalk (Wichelmann et al. 2018), SideTrail (Athanasiou et al. 2018) and FaCT (Cauligi et al. 2019) and dynamic, for example, `dudec` (Reparaz et al. 2017), `ctgrind` (Github n.d.b), Triggerflow (Gridin and Brumley 2019) and DATA (Weiser et al. 2018, 2020) cases.

1.5. References

Aciiçmez, O., Schindler, W., Koç, Ç. (2005). Improving Brumley and Boneh timing attack on unprotected SSL implementations. In *CCS '05: Proceedings of the 12th ACM Conference on Computer and Communications Security*, 139–146.

Albrecht, M.R. and Paterson, K.G. (2016). Lucky microseconds: A timing attack on amazon's s2n implementation of TLS. In *35th Annual International Conference on the Theory and Applications of Cryptographic Techniques*, Vienna, 622–643.

AlFardan, N.J. and Paterson, K.G. (2013). Lucky thirteen: Breaking the TLS and DTLS record protocols. In *2013 IEEE Symposium on Security and Privacy*, Berkeley, CA, 526–540.

Almeida, J.B., Barbosa, M., Barthe, G., Dupressoir, F., Emmi, M. (2016). Verifying constant-time implementations. In *Proceedings of the 25th USENIX Security Symposium*, Austin, 53–70.

Anderson, R. (2020). Side channels. In *Security Engineering: A Guide to Building Dependable Distributed Systems*, 3rd edition. Anderson, R. (edition). John Wiley & Sons, New York. doi: 10.5555/1373319.

Andrysco, M., Kohlbrenner, D., Mowery, K., Jhala, R., Lerner, S., Shacham, H. (2015). On subnormal floating point and abnormal timing. In *IEEE Symposium on Security and Privacy*, 623–639.

Athanasiou, K., Cook, B., Emmi, M., MacCarthaigh, C., Schwartz-Narbonne, D., Tasiran, S. (2018). SideTrail: Verifying time-balancing of cryptosystems. In *Verified Software. Theories, Tools and Experiments (VSTTE)*. Springer, Cham. doi: 10.1007/978-3-030-03592-1_12.

Avoine, G. and Ferreira, L. (2018). Attacking GlobalPlatform SCP02-compliant smart cards using a padding oracle attack. *IACR Transactions on Cryptographic Hardware and Embedded Systems*, 2018(2), 149–170 [Online]. Available at: https://tches.iacr.org/index.php/TCHES/article/view/878.

Bakhshi, B. and Sadeghiyan, B. (2007). A timing attack on Blakley's modular multiplication algorithm, and applications to DSA. *Applied Cryptography and Network Security*, 129–140.

Balagani, K.S., Conti, M., Gasti, P., Georgiev, M., Gurtler, T., Lain, D., Miller, C., Molas, K., Samarin, N., Saraci, E. et al. (2018). SILK-TV: Secret information leakage from keystroke timing videos. In *European Symposium on Research in Computer Security*, 263–280.

Barbosa, M., Barthe, G., Bhargavan, K., Blanchet, B., Cremers, C., Liao, K., Parno, B. (2021). SoK: Computer-aided cryptography. In *IEEE Symposium on Security and Privacy*, San Fransisco. doi: 10.1109/SP40001.2021.00008.

Barrett, P. (1987). Implementing the Rivest Shamir and Adleman public key encryption algorithm on a standard digital signal processor. In *Advances in Cryptology*, 311–323.

Black, J. and Urtubia, H. (2002). Side-channel attacks on symmetric encryption schemes: The case for authenticated encryption. In *Proceedings of the 11th USENIX Security Symposium*, 327–338.

Blake, I., Seroussi, G., Smart, N. (eds) (2004). *Advances in Elliptic Curve Cryptography*, 1st edition. Cambridge University Press, Cambridge. doi: 10.1017/CBO9780511546570.

Blakley, G. (1983). A computer algorithm for calculating the product AB modulo M. *IEEE Transactions on Computers*, 32(5), 497–500. doi: 10.1109/TC.1983.1676262.

Bleichenbacher, D. (1998). Chosen ciphertext attacks against protocols based on the RSA encryption standard PKCS #1. In *Advances in Cryptology – CRYPTO '98*, 1–12.

Böck, H., Somorovsky, J., Young, C. (2018). Return of Bleichenbacher's oracle threat (ROBOT). In *27th Usenix Security Symposium*, 817–849.

Brennan, T., Rosner, N., Bultan, T. (2020). JIT leaks: Inducing timing side channels through just-in-time compilation. In *Proceedings - 2020 IEEE Symposium on Security and Privacy*, 1207–1222.

Brumley, D. and Boneh, D. (2003). Remote timing attacks are practical. In *12th Usenix Security Symposium*.

Brumley, B.B. and Tuveri, N. (2011). Remote timing attacks are still practical. In *European Symposium on Research in Computer Security*, 355–371.

Canvel, B., Hiltgen, A.P., Vaudenay, S., Vuagnoux, M. (2003). Password interception in a SSL/TLS channel. In *Annual International Cryptology Conference*, 583–599.

Cauligi, S., Soeller, G., Johannesmeyer, B., Brown, F., Wahby, R., Renner, J., Grégoire, B., Barthe, G., Jhala, R., Stefan, D. (2019). FaCT: A DSL for timing-sensitive computation. In *Programming Language Design and Implementation (PLDI)*, June 22–26. ACM, Phoenix. doi: 10.1145/3314221.3314605.

Coppens, B., Verbauwhede, I., De Bosschere, K., De Sutter, B. (2009). Practical mitigations for timing-based side-channel attacks on modern x86 processors. In *Proceedings of the IEEE Symposium on Security and Privacy*, 45–60.

Dhem, J.-F., Koeune, F., Leroux, P.-A., Mestré, P., Quisquater, J.-J., Willems, J.-L. (1998). A practical implementation of the timing attack. In *Smart Card Research and Applications (CARDIS)*. Springer, Berlin, Heidelberg. doi: 10.1007/10721064_15.

Dierks, T. and Rescorla, E. (2008). The Transport Layer Security (TLS) protocol version 1.2. Internet Engineering Task Force (IETF) Request for Comments (RFC) 5246 [Online]. Available at: http://tools.ietf.org/html/rfc5246.

Donda, A.-T., Samarin, P., Samotyja, J., Lemke-Rust, K., Paar, C. (2015). Remote IP protection using timing channels. In *International Conference on Information Security and Cryptology*,

222–237.

Felten, E.W. and Schneider, M.A. (2000). Timing attacks on web privacy. In *Proceedings of the ACM Conference on Computer and Communications Security*, 25–32.

Ge, Q., Yarom, Y., Cock, D., Heiser, G. (2018).. A survey of microarchitectural timing attacks and countermeasures on contemporary hardware. *Journal of Cryptographic Engineering (JCEN)*, 8, 1–27. doi: 10.1007/s13389-016-0141-6.

Github (n.d.a). Cryptocoding [Online]. Available at: https://github.com/veorq/cryptocoding.

Github (n.d.b). Checking that functions are constant time with Valgrind [Online]. Available at: https://github.com/agl/ctgrind.

van Goethem, T., Joosen, W., Nikiforakis, N. (2015). The clock is still ticking: Timing attacks in the modern web. In *CCS '15: Proceedings of the 22nd ACM SIGSAC Conference on Computer and Communications Security*, 1382–1393.

Gordon, D. (1998). A survey of fast exponentiation methods. *Journal of Algorithms*, 27, 129–146. doi: 10.1006/jagm.1997.0913.

Gridin, I. and Brumley, C.G.N.T.B. (2019). Triggerflow: Regression testing by advanced execution path inspection. In *Detection of Intrusions and Malware, and Vulnerability Assessment (DIMVA)*. Springer, Cham. doi: 10.1007/978-3-030-22038-9_16.

Großschädl, J., Oswald, E., Page, D., Tunstall, M. (2010). Side-channel analysis of cryptographic software via early-terminating multiplications. In *International Conference on Information Security and Cryptology*, 176–192.

Hachez, G. and Quisquater, J.-J. (2000). Montgomery exponentiation with no final subtractions: Improved results. In *International Workshop on Cryptographic Hardware and Embedded Systems*, 293–301.

Jager, T., Schinzel, S., Somorovsky, J. (2012). Bleichenbacher's attack strikes again: Breaking PKCS#1 v1.5 in XML encryption. In *European Symposium on Research in Computer Security*, 752–769.

Joye, M. (2004). Defences against side-channel analysis. In *Advances in Elliptic Curve Cryptography*. Cambridge University Press, Cambridge. doi: 10.1017/CBO9780511546570.

Joye, M. and Yen, S.-M. (2003). The Montgomery powering ladder. In *International Workshop on Cryptographic Hardware and Embedded Systems*, 291–302.

Kaufmann, T., Pelletier, H., Vaudenay, S., Villegas, K. (2016). When constant-time source yields variable-time binary: Exploiting Curve25519-donna built with MSVC 2015. In *Cryptology and Network Security: 15th International Conference*, 573–582.

Koç, Ç.K., Acar, T., Kaliski, B. (1996). Analyzing and comparing Montgomery multiplication algorithms. *IEEE Micro*, 16(3), 26–33. doi: 10.1109/40.502403.

Kocher, P.C. (1996). Timing attacks on implementations of Diffie-Hellman, RSA, DSS, and other systems. In *Annual International Cryptology Conference*, 104–113.

Koeune, F. (2011). *Timing Attack*, 2nd edition. Springer, New York. doi: 10.1007/978-1-4419-5906-5.

Koeune, F. and Quisquater, J.-J. (1999). A timing attack against Rijndael. Technical Report CG-1999/1, Université catholique de Louvain.

Kohlbrenner, D. and Shacham, H. (2017). On the effectiveness of mitigations against floating-point timing channels. In *26th Usenix Security Symposium*, 69–81.

Kotcher, R., Pei, Y., Jumde, P., Jackson, C. (2013). Cross-origin pixel stealing: Timing attacks using CSS filters. In *CCS '13: Proceedings of the 2013 ACM SIGSAC Conference on Computer & Communications Security*, 1055–1062.

Lipp, M., Gruss, D., Schwarz, M., Bidner, D., Maurice, C., Mangard, S. (2017). Practical keystroke timing attacks in sandboxed JavaScript. In *22nd European Symposium on Research in Computer Security, Proceedings*. Springer-Verlag, Italy, 191–209.

Manger, J. (2001). A chosen ciphertext attack on RSA optimal asymmetric encryption padding (OAEP) as standardized in PKCS #1 v2.0. In *Annual International Cryptology Conference*, 230–238.

Meyer, C., Somorovsky, J., Weiss, E., Schwenk, J., Schinzel, S., Tews, E. (2014). Revisiting SSL/TLS implementations: New Bleichenbacher side channels and attacks. In *Proceedings of the 23rd USENIX Security Symposium*, San Diego, 733–748.

Mittmann, J. and Schindler, W. (2021). Timing attacks and local timing attacks against Barrett's modular multiplication algorithm. *Journal of Cryptographic Engineering (JCEN)*, 11(4), 369–397. doi: 10.1007/s13389-020-00254-3.

Molnar, D., Piotrowski, M., Schultz, D., Wagner, D. (2006). The program counter security model: Automatic detection and removal of control-flow side channel attacks. In *International Conference on Information Security and Cryptology*, 156–168.

Montgomery, P. (1985). Modular multiplication without trial division. *Mathematics of Computation*, 44(170), 519–521. doi: 10.1090/S0025-5718-1985-0777282-X.

Montgomery, P. (1987). Speeding the pollard and elliptic curve methods of factorization. *Mathematics of Computation*, 48(177), 243–264. doi: 10.1090/S0025-5718-1987-0866113-7.

Murdoch, S.J. and Danezis, G. (2005). Low-cost traffic analysis of tor. In *2005 IEEE Symposium on Security and Privacy*, 183–195.

Naccache, D. and Tunstall, M. (2000). How to explain side-channel leakage to your kids (invited talk). In *CHES 2000*, 229–230.

National Institute of Standards and Technology (NIST) (2001a). Advanced Encryption Standard (AES). Federal Information Processing Standard (FIPS) 197 [Online]. Available at: http://csrc.nist.gov.

National Institute of Standards and Technology (NIST) (2001b). Recommendation for Block Cipher Modes of Operation: Methods and Techniques. Special Publication 800-38A [Online]. Available at: http://csrc.nist.gov.

National Institute of Standards and Technology (NIST) (2008). The Keyed-Hash Message Authentication Code (HMAC) Federal Information Processing Standard (FIPS) 198 [Online]. Available at: http://csrc.nist.gov.

Oswald, E. (2004). Side-channel analysis. In *Advances in Elliptic Curve Cryptography*, 1st edition. Cambridge University Press, Cambridge. doi: 10.1017/CBO9780511546570.

Paterson, K.G. and Yau, A. (2004). Padding oracle attacks on the ISO CBC mode encryption standard. In *Cryptographers' Track at the RSA Conference*, 305–323.

Pedersen, M.V. and Askarov, A. (2017). From trash to treasure: Timing-sensitive garbage collection. In *2017 IEEE Symposium on Security and Privacy, SP 2017 – Proceedings*, 693–709.

Rebeiro, C., Mukhopadhyay, D., Bhattacharya, S. (2015). *Timing Channels in Cryptography*. Springer, Cham. doi: 10.1007/978-3-319-12370-7.

Renes, J., Costello, C., Batina, L. (2016). Complete addition formulas for prime order elliptic curves. In *Proceedings, Part I, of the 35th Annual International Conference on Advances in Cryptology — EUROCRYPT 2016*, 403–428.

Reparaz, O., Balasch, J., Verbauwhede, I. (2017). Dude, is my code constant time? In *Design, Automation & Test in Europe (DATE)*. IEEE, Lausanne. doi: 10.23919/DATE.2017.7927267.

Rivest, R.L., Shamir, A., Adleman, L.M. (1978). A method for obtaining digital signatures and public-key cryptosystems. *Communications of the ACM*, 21(2), 120–126.

Rodrigues, B., Fernando, M., Aranha, D. (2016). Sparse representation of implicit flows with applications to side-channel detection. In *International Conference on Compiler Construction (CC)*, ACM, New York, 110–120. doi: 10.1145/2892208.2892230.

Ronen, E., Gillham, R., Genkin, D., Shamir, A., Wong, D., Yarom, Y. (2019). The 9 lives of Bleichenbacher's CAT: New cache ATtacks on TLS implementations. In *2019 IEEE Symposium on Security and Privacy (SP)*, 435–452.

Schindler, W. (2000). A timing attack against RSA with the Chinese remainder theorem. In *International Workshop on Cryptographic Hardware and Embedded Systems*, 109–124.

Song, D.X., Wagner, D.A., Tian, X. (2001). Timing analysis of keystrokes and timing attacks on SSH. In *10th Usenix Security Symposium*, Washington, D.C.

Strenzke, F. (2010). Manger's attack revisited. In *International Conference on Information and Communications Security*, 31–45.

Szefer, J. (2019). Survey of microarchitectural side and covert channels, attacks, and defences. *Journal of Hardware and Systems Security*, 3(3), 219–234. doi: 10.1007/s41635-018-0046-1.

Tey, C.M., Gupta, P., Gao, D., Zhang, Y. (2013). Keystroke timing analysis of on-the-fly web apps. In *International Conference on Applied Cryptography and Network Security*, 405–413.

Vaudenay, S. (2002). Security flaws induced by CBC padding – Applications to SSL, IPSEC, WTLS... In *EUROCRYPT '02: Proceedings of the International Conference on the Theory and Applications of Cryptographic Techniques: Advances in Cryptology*, 534–546.

Walter, C. (1999). Montgomery exponentiation needs no final subtractions. *IEE Electronics Letters*, 35(21), 1831–1832. doi: 10.1049/el:19991230.

Wang, X., Chen, S., Jajodia, S. (2005). Tracking anonymous peer-to-peer VoIP calls on the Internet. In *CCS '05: Proceedings of the 12th ACM Conference on Computer and Communications Security*, 81–91.

Weiser, S., Zankl, A., Spreitzer, R., Miller, K., Mangard, S., Sigl, G. (2018). DATA – differential address trace analysis: Finding address-based side-channels in binaries. In *27th Usenix Security Symposium*, 603–620.

Weiser, S., Schrammel, D., Bodner, L., Spreitzer, R. (2020). Big numbers – Big troubles: Systematically analyzing nonce leakage in (EC)DSA implementations. In *29th Usenix Security Symposium*, 1767–1784.

Wichelmann, J., Moghimi, A., Eisenbarth, T., Sunar, B. (2018). MicroWalk: A framework for finding side channels in binaries. In *Annual Computer Security Applications Conference (ACSAC)*. doi: 10.1145/3274694.3274741.

Yau, A.K.L., Paterson, K.G., Mitchell, C.J. (2005). Padding oracle attacks on CBC-mode encryption with secret and random IVs. In *International Workshop on Fast Software Encryption*, 299–319.

2

Microarchitectural Attacks

Yuval YAROM
Ruhr University Bochum, Germany

In this chapter, we investigate a class of side-channel attacks that exploit the *microarchitecture* of the processor. Microarchitecture is the name for the set of components in the processor that implement the functionality it provides, that is, execute the instruction set. When multiple programs run on the same computer, they share the use of microarchitectural components. Such sharing is supposed to be transparent to the programs. However, because the state of many of these components affects execution speed, monitoring execution speed may leak information from one program to another. Microarchitectural side-channel attacks develop techniques for identifying and observing such leaked information.

2.1. Background

We first look at the main microarchitectural components and discuss how they interact with the software and improve its performance. We start with a discussion of the various caches that processors employ and continue to speculative, out-of-order execution.

2.1.1. *Memory caches*

Caches are small banks of fast memory that store recent results in order to provide them quickly if these results are needed again. The main caches in the processor store data retrieved from memory, exploiting the spatial and temporal locality that software often exhibits.

Embedded Cryptography 1,
coordinated by Emmanuel PROUFF, Guénaël RENAULT,
Matthieu RIVAIN and Colin O'FLYNN. © ISTE Ltd 2025.

In operation, the cache divides the address space into blocks, called *lines*, of a fixed size, which on most modern processors are 64 bytes. When the program requests memory, for example, using a load instruction, the processor searches the cache to see if the line that contains the requested address is in the cache. In a *cache hit*, when the line is cached, the processor uses the cached data. Conversely, in a *cache miss*, when the line is not cached, the processor needs to bring the data from the memory. In that case, the line is typically also stored in the cache for future use. Because the cache has a limited size, eventually some lines need to be evicted from the cache to make room for storing new lines. Most caches employ a variant of least recently used (LRU) replacement policy to decide which line to evict.

Modern processors use *set associative* caches, meaning that the cache is divided into a number of *sets*, where each set consists of a fixed number of *ways*. The number of ways in each set is also referred to as the cache associativity. Each memory line can be stored in only one of the sets of the cache, but can be stored in any of the ways of the cache set. In many cases, to map a memory line to a cache set, the processor just uses a sequence of bits from the address of the memory line as an index to the cache. However, some processors use more complex functions to map addresses to cache sets.

2.1.2. *Cache hierarchies*

To cater for multiple trade offs between cache speed and size, modern processors employ a hierarchy of caches, with caches at the top of the hierarchy (closer to the processor) being smaller but faster than caches lower in the hierarchy. Figure 2.1 shows an example of the cache hierarchy of a four-core Intel Core processor.

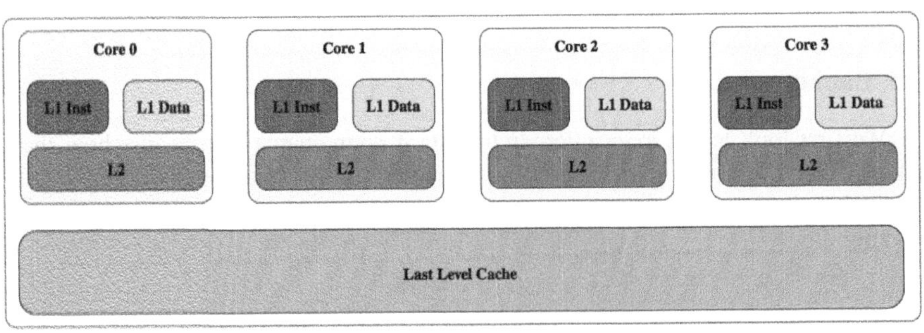

Figure 2.1. *The typical cache hierarchy of a four-core Intel processor. For a color version of this figure, see www.iste.co.uk/prouff/cryptography1.zip*

Each execution core includes three caches. Two L1 caches, one for storing data and the other for instructions (code), and an L2 cache, which is unified, that is, stores both data and instructions. All cores share a unified last level cache (LLC), whose size is several megabytes (the exact size depends on the processor model). The LLC in many Intel processor models is *inclusive*. That is, the contents of the LLC is a superset of the contents of the upper level caches. One implication of an inclusive cache is that when a cache line is evicted from the LLC, it must also be evicted from all of the L1 and L2 caches. Table 2.1 shows typical parameters for the caches in Intel processors.

Cache	Number of Sets	Associativity	Total Size	Latency
L1-D	64	8	32 KB	4 cycles
L1-I	64	8	32 KB	4 cycles
L2	512	8	256 KB	7 cycles
LLC	From 4096	12 or more	From 3 MB	28–32 cycles

Table 2.1. *Typical cache parameters for many Intel Core processors*

2.1.3. *Out-of-order execution*

To increase the utilization of the processor units, processors do not execute instructions in the order specified in the program. Instead, they can change the order of execution, as long as they ensure that the change does not affect the computation results. The processor core is typically divided into two main parts. The *front end* is responsible for reading the code of the program from memory, parsing it into instructions, and decoding them into a format that the processor uses for execution. In some processors, decoding includes translation into microcode, a set of elementary operations, called μops. In this chapter, we use the term "instruction" for both instructions and μops, ignoring the distinction between the two.

The *execution engine* receives a stream of instructions from the front end and routes them to the various execution units. The execution engine dispatches instructions for execution as soon as all of its arguments are available. Consequently, a young instruction can execute before an older instruction, that precedes it in the instruction stream, if the arguments of the younger instruction become available before those of the older instruction. The execution engine notifies the front end when instructions complete execution. The front end then retires instructions, committing their results to the state of the program. Instructions are only retired in their order in the program, maintaining the illusion of in-order execution.

Special handling is required when an instruction results in a trap, such as division by zero or illegal access to memory. To maintain the illusion of in-order execution, instead of handling the trap as soon as it is detected, the execution engine notifies the front end that the instruction causes a trap. The front end waits until all older instructions retire before handling the trap. It then squashes all instructions younger than the trapped instruction, ignoring any results they may have computed, and finally handles the trap. Instructions that are squashed after they were executed are often called transient instructions.

2.1.4. *Branch prediction*

Branches pose a challenge to out-of-order execution. If it takes time to compute the outcome of a branch, it may be desirable to start executing younger instructions that can be executed. However, before computing the branch outcome, the processor does not know where processing follows.

To address this challenge, when the front end encounters a branch, it tries to predict the outcome of the branch and proceed to process younger instructions based on the predicted outcome. Eventually, the execution engine executes the branch and compares the outcome to the prediction. If the prediction turns out to be correct, the program benefits from the early computation of younger instructions. Conversely, if the prediction turns out to be wrong, the front end squashes all mispredicted instructions and proceeds to issue instructions from the correct branch.

To predict branch outcomes, the processor maintains an array of dedicated caches that store the outcomes of recent branches. The two main caches are the branch target buffer (BTB) that stores the addresses that the branches branch to, aiming to predict indirect branches, and the branch history buffer (BHB) that predicts whether conditional branches will be taken or not.

2.1.5. *Other caches*

In addition to the main memory caches and the caches used for branch prediction, processors typically feature other caches. The translation lookaside buffer (TLB) is a dedicated cache that stores the results of recent translations of virtual addresses to physical addresses. The microcode cache is a front-end component that stores the results of recent translations of instructions to μops, reducing the overhead of such translation. Caching elements also exist outside the processor. For example, the row buffer in dynamic random access memory (DRAM) chips stores the contents of the most recently accessed memory row.

2.2. The Prime+Probe attack

This section discusses Prime+Probe, an attack technique that exploits the structure of the cache to leak information between processes that share the use of the cache. The attack consists of two main steps. In the prime step, the attacker completely fills one or more of the sets of the cache with its own data. In the probe step, the attacker measures the time it takes to access the data it previously used for filling the cache.

Between the two steps, the attacker gives the victim the opportunity to run and access memory. If the memory that the victim access is mapped to any of the cache sets that the attacker uses for the attack, victim access will evict some of the attacker's data. Hence, access during the probe step will incur delays due to cache misses, allowing the attacker to identify the cache sets that the victim has accessed.

2.2.1. *Prime+Probe on the L1 data cache*

As an example of a concrete Prime+Probe attack, we target the L1 data cache of a typical Intel Core processor. The L1 cache in these processors consists of 64 sets, each containing 8 or 12 cache lines, depending on the processor model. The size of each cache line is 64 bytes. To determine the cache set number that a memory address maps to, the processor uses bits 6–11 of the address.

For the rest of the example, we will assume that the L1 data cache is eight-way associative, that is, it has eight cache lines in each cache set. To fill a cache set, we need to find eight cache lines that map to it. A simple way to achieve that is to allocate a page-aligned cache-sized (32 KB) buffer, for example, using the `mmap` system call. Then, given a cache set $0 \leq s < 64$, the eight offsets $64 \cdot s + 4096 \cdot i$ for $0 \leq i < 8$ all map to cache set s. We use the term *eviction set* to refer to such a collection of memory locations that completely cover a cache set.

To prime a cache set, we can now read the contents of the eight memory locations in the eviction set. This will bring the eight locations into the cache and evict any other data from the same cache set. Technically, probing the cache set mainly requires measuring the time to access the same eviction set to check whether it is in the cache. However, due to out-of-order execution, a naive measurement is unlikely to achieve conclusive results.

To handle out-of-order execution, we need to first ensure that measured memory accesses are performed during the measured period. For that we use a fence instruction `lfence` before and after the measured sequence. The `lfence` instruction ensures that no younger instruction starts executing before all the instructions older than the `lfence` are committed. A second issue is that a memory miss delay may be masked due to concurrent, out-of-order execution. To overcome the issue, we need to introduce a dependency between memory accesses. A simple way is to create a linked list where each of the elements in the eviction set points to the next. When traversing the list, the processor has to wait for the data of one memory location before starting a load from the next. Consequently, the memory accesses execute sequentially, and the delay is not masked.

```
1 s0 = GETU32(in     ) ^ rk[0];
2 s1 = GETU32(in +  4) ^ rk[1];
3 s2 = GETU32(in +  8) ^ rk[2];
4 s3 = GETU32(in + 12) ^ rk[3];
5
6 /* round 1: */
7 t0 = Te0[s0>>24] ^ Te1[(s1>>16) & 0xff] ^ Te2[(s2 >>8) & 0xff] ^ Te3[s3 & 0xff] ^ rk[ 4];
8 t1 = Te0[s1>>24] ^ Te1[(s2>>16) & 0xff] ^ Te2[(s3 >>8) & 0xff] ^ Te3[s0 & 0xff] ^ rk[ 5];
9 t2 = Te0[s2>>24] ^ Te1[(s3>>16) & 0xff] ^ Te2[(s0 >>8) & 0xff] ^ Te3[s1 & 0xff] ^ rk[ 6];
10 t3 = Te0[s3>>24] ^ Te1[(s0>>16) & 0xff] ^ Te2[(s1 >>8) & 0xff] ^ Te3[s2 & 0xff] ^ rk[ 7];
```

Listing 2.1. *First encryption round of the T-table implementation of AES*

2.2.2. *Attacking T-table AES*

As an example, we will look at attacking an implementation of AES that uses T-tables. To recap, the T-tables in AES combine the effects of the sub-bytes, shift-rows, and mix-columns steps of the encryption. The implementation uses four T-tables, `Te0`, `Te1`, `Te2` and `Te3`. Each table consists of 256 entries of size 32 bits each. In each encryption round, the implementation XORs each state byte with the corresponding byte of the round key and uses the result to index one of the four T-tables. Thus, in each of the 10 rounds of AES-128, each T-table is accessed four times, to a total of 40 times over the encryption. Listing 2.1 shows the first round of the encryption. In lines 1–4 the code reads the plaintext and XORs it with the round key (stored in `rk`). Then, in lines 7–10, the code uses each byte of the state to index one of the four T-tables.

When attacking such an implementation, the adversary tries to learn information about the key by monitoring the cache access patterns. Specifically, the adversary first primes all of the cache sets of the L1 cache. The victim then performs one AES encryption with a known plaintext and an unknown key. Finally, the adversary performs the probe step of the attack to identify the cache sets accessed by the victim.

Clearly, if the adversary can determine which index in the T-tables is read at each step of the algorithm, they can recover the key. However, cache attacks have a limited resolution, both spatially and temporally. Specifically, the Prime+Probe attack has a cache-line resolution and cannot determine where within the cache line an access takes place. In the T-tables, each cache line includes 16 table entries. Consequently, the attacker can at best determine the most significant four bits of the accessed index.

Moreover, performing a cache attack takes time. During that time, the victim may perform several memory accesses. The Prime+Probe attack cannot determine the order of these memory accesses or the number of accesses to the same cache line. In our example, the victim performs a full encryption between the prime and the probe steps. Consequently, the adversary can determine which cache lines in the T-tables have been accessed during the encryption, but not the round in which the access happens.

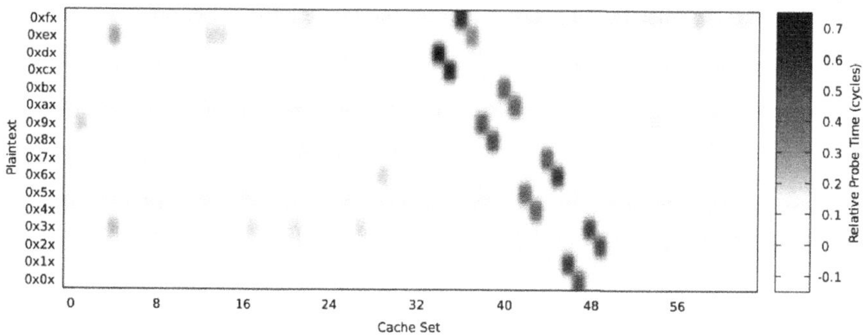

Figure 2.2. *Prime+Probe on AES. The shade indicates the relative probe time for cache set (X axis) and plaintext byte value (most significant four bits, Y axis). Darker shades indicate slower probe identifying the XOR of the plaintext and the key. For a color version of this figure, see www.iste.co.uk/prouff/cryptography1.zip*

To overcome the limited temporal resolution of Prime+Probe, we note that there is some probability that a cache line is not accessed at all during an encryption. Specifically, each T-table spans 16 cache lines and is accessed 40 times during an encryption. Thus, there is a probability of $\left(\frac{15}{16}\right)^{40} \approx 7.6\%$ that a specific cache line is not accessed at all during the encryption.

At the same time, the accessed indices are not random and are determined by the plaintext and the key. Hence, when encrypting multiple plaintexts that have the same value in one of the plaintext bytes, the same T-table index is accessed during the first round, and the cache line that contains it will always be accessed. Consequently, the average probe time of one specific cache set will be slower when fixing one plaintext byte than when using a random value.

Figure 2.2 shows the result of carrying out the Prime+Probe attack on 100,000 encryptions. The Y axis indicates the value of the four most significant bits of byte 6 of the plaintext. The X axis is the cache set. The shade indicates the difference between the average probe time of the cache set when the byte value has the indicated value in the four MSBs, compared to the average over all byte values.

As we can see, the average access time to most cache sets does not depend on the plaintext byte. However, cache sets 33–49 do show a plaintext-dependent access pattern, where for each group of plaintext values that have the same four MSBs, the probe time for one of the cache sets is slower by roughly 0.5 cycles, on average. We therefore hypothesize that T-table Te2, which is indexed by the 6th byte of the state, maps to these cache sets. By checking the ground truth, we can confirm the hypothesis.

When we check the relationship between the cache set that experiences slower probes and the four MSBs of the plaintext, we observe that plaintexts that start with bits 1101, that is, values 0xd0–0xdf, result in a slower probe of the first cache set that matches T-table `Te2`. This indicates that the cache set is always accessed when encrypting a plaintext with byte 6 in the range 0xd0–0xdf.

The index for accessing T-table `Te2` when processing byte 6 of the state, is computed by XORing byte 6 of the plaintext with byte 6 of the key. Hence, because the encryption always accesses the first cache set of `Te2` when the plaintext byte is in the range 0xd0–0xdf, we learn that the corresponding key byte is also in the same range 0xd0–0xdf. Comparing to the ground truth, where the byte is 0xd2, we can verify the data. We note that we could have used any other line in Figure 2.2, and get the same result.

Repeating the process for each of the 16 plaintext bytes, we learn 64 bits. To recover the rest of the key, we need to extend the attack to a second round. The process is quite similar. Specifically, given the known bits of the first round key bits, we can guess the remaining bits and predict which cache line accesses will happen in the second round. Correlating this information with the probe times we see will identify the correct guess and recover the key bits.

2.2.3. *Prime+probe on the LLC*

Because the L1 cache is not shared between cores, it cannot be used for cross-core attacks. Targeting the shared LLC allows such attacks, but requires more effort than an L1 attack due to the complexity of finding eviction sets. One cause of the issue is that the adversary uses virtual memory addresses, whereas the cache set is determined by the physical address. Bits 6–11, which encode the cache set in the L1, do not change when mapping virtual to physical addresses. However, the LLC has more cache sets than the L1, requiring more than six bits for addressing LLC cache sets. Bits 12 and above are not preserved during address translation. Consequently, the address translation process hides these bits from the attacker. Moreover, while the L1 uses the bits values as the cache set number, the Intel LLC uses an unpublished hash function.

A simple approach for finding eviction sets is to first find a set of candidate memory locations such that accessing all candidates evicts a *witness* memory location from the cache and then trims it to a minimal size. Algorithm 2.1 shows an example of this approach. The algorithm takes two inputs: a witness memory location w and a set of candidates for evicting w. Typically, these candidates will be chosen so that they match the known bits of the physical address of the witness. In lines 2–6, the algorithm expands the potential eviction set e, adding candidates until accessing the contents of e evicts the witness. The algorithm then tests each of the elements of the potential eviction set to check if they are required for evicting the witness. After removing all nonessential elements from the potential eviction set, only an eviction set for the witness remains.

Algorithm 2.1. Creating an eviction set for a witness line w

input : w: a witness line
input : c: a set of candidate memory lines for an eviction set for w
output: e: an eviction set for w

$e \leftarrow \{\}$
foreach $l \in c$ **do**
    $e \leftarrow e \cup \{l\}$
    if *evicts*(e, w) **then**
        break
end
foreach $l \in e$ **do**
    if *evicts*($e - \{l\}$, w) **then**
        $e \leftarrow e - \{l\}$
end
output e

The algorithm can be repeated to find all of the eviction sets for the LLC, allowing the adversary to perform cross-core Prime+Probe attacks. It should be noted that the attack only works if the LLC is inclusive. The reason is that evicting a line from a non-inclusive LLC does not necessarily evict it from the private L1 and L2 caches of the victim. Consequently, the attacker cannot observe victim accesses to lines evicted from the LLC. However, some processors use a cache directory to keep track of the coherency state of lines in the private caches of the cores. Evicting the directory entry also evicts the line from the private caches, allowing the attack.

2.2.4. *Variants of Prime+Probe*

Prime+Abort: Prime+Abort is a variant of the Prime+Probe attack, which exploits a property of the Intel Transactional Synchronization Extensions (TSX). In a nutshell, TSX is an extension of the x86 instruction set that supports sequences of instructions, called transactions, that are executed atomically. TSX relies on cached data to detect conflicting memory accesses during a transaction. Consequently, eviction of memory accessed during a transaction aborts the transaction.

In a Prime+Abort attack, the attacker starts a TSX transaction and accesses the elements of the eviction set of a cache set, completely filling the cache set. If the victim accesses memory in that cache set, the transaction aborts. The attacker detects the transaction abort and verifies that the abort cause is contention on resources to identify the victim access.

Prime+Abort provides two main advantages over the standard Prime+Probe attack. First, it does not rely on timing, reducing potential measurement errors. Second, unlike Prime+Probe, Prime+Abort does not poll the monitored cache set. Consequently, it achieves a higher temporal resolution. At the same time, Prime+Abort does have some limitations. In particular, the technique is unable to detect which of multiple cache sets is accessed. Moreover, due to security issues, TSX has been disabled in recent processors. Hence, the attack only works on older, unpatched processors.

Prime+Scope: the Prime+Scope attack takes advantage of the interplay between different levels of the cache hierarchy to improve the temporal resolution of the attack. The core idea in Prime+Scope is that when evicting a line from an inclusive LLC or from a cache directory, the line is also evicted from the attacker's L1 cache.

In the prime stage, the attacker fills the LLC cache set, which it monitors, with the contents of the eviction set. Instead of accessing the eviction set in an arbitrary order, the attacker uses a specific access pattern. The pattern is selected so that the LLC replacement candidate, that is, the cache line to be evicted next from the LLC, is also cached in the attacker's L1 cache. For the scope stage, the attacker repeatedly measures the access time to the LLC replacement candidate. Because the LLC replacement candidate is in the L1 cache, the access is fast. Moreover, because the access results in a cache hit, the L1 cache serves the access without notifying the LLC. Hence, the access does not affect the LLC replacement policy, and the LLC does not change the replacement candidate.

When the victim accesses a memory location that maps to the monitored cache set, the LLC needs to evict one of the cached lines and chooses the replacement candidate. Evicting the replacement candidate from the LLC also triggers an eviction from the attacker's L1 cache. Consequently, when the attacker next measures access time to this cache line, it experiences a cache miss in all cache levels, which results in a long access time, indicating a victim access. To resume the attack, the attacker now needs to reset the cache state by repeating the prime stage.

In the absence of victim access to the cache set, the scope stage of Prime+Scope only causes cache hits in the L1 cache. These are much faster than the accesses required to probe the cache set in Prime+Probe, allowing for an order of magnitude improvement in the temporal resolution of Prime+Scope compared to Prime+Probe.

Cache Occupancy Attack: instead of targeting specific cache sets, the cache occupancy variant of the Prime+Probe attack aims to measure the overall contention on the cache. For the attack, the attacker allocates a cache-sized buffer in memory and repeatedly measures the access time to all of the cache lines in the buffer. Each such measurement brings the whole buffer into the cache. Hence, the time to access the buffer correlates with the number of buffer cache lines evicted from the cache between consecutive measurements. When the victim performs more memory accesses, more cache lines will be evicted, and the measurement will be longer.

With the typical LLC size, each measurement takes hundreds and even thousands of microseconds. Consequently, the temporal resolution is significantly coarser than that of the Prime+Probe attack. Moreover, because the measurement covers the cache, the attacker does not learn about the addresses that the victim accesses, but only about the number of cache lines that the victim has accessed. Thus, the cache occupancy attack is typically used for coarse-grained events, such as detecting running applications and visited web sites. However, cache occupancy attacks against cryptographic schemes have also been demonstrated.

Due to its simplicity, the cache occupancy attack is very resilient. The attack can work in environments, such as web browsers, where the clock resolution is low. It can even work with alternative methods for measuring time, for example, using network latency. Furthermore, because the attack does not rely on a specific cache structure, it can overcome approaches for secure caches, designed to thwart the Prime+Probe attack.

2.3. The Flush+Reload attack

In this section, we discuss the Flush+Reload attack. Unlike Prime+Probe, which exploits the limited storage space in the cache, Flush+Reload exploits the adversary's ability to evict the cache lines it shares with the victim from the cache. Because it focuses on a specific cache line, rather than a cache set, the attack tends to be less noisy than Prime+Probe. However, the requirement for sharing memory limits the scenarios in which the attack is applicable.

2.3.1. *Attack technique*

To reduce the memory signature of the system, modern operating systems share memory between processes. One form of sharing is when an operating system maps the same library or program code to multiple processes. Another form of sharing is when an operating system or a virtual machine hypervisor coalesces pages with identical contents. As long as none of the sharing programs changes the contents of the shared pages, sharing reduces the combined memory requirements without affecting correctness. In the case of coalescing identical pages, the system typically uses copy-on-write semantics, where the system intercepts attempts by either process to modify the shared page and duplicates the contents to prevent modifications.

The cache does not distinguish between programs. Consequently, if one of the sharing processes accesses a shared memory line, the other process can experience a cache hit the first time it accesses the line. Conversely if a process evicts a shared line from the cache, it can cause a cache miss for the other process.

The Flush+Reload exploits this sharing of cache state. In the flush step, the adversary evicts a cache line from the cache, for example, using the x86 `clflush` instruction. After allowing the victim some time to execute, in the reload step the adversary measures the time it takes to load the line. If the victim has not accessed the line between the flush and the reload steps, the adversary witnesses a long reload time due to a cache miss. Otherwise, if the victim has accessed the line, the line is cached, and the reload time is shorter.

2.3.2. *Attacking square-and-multiply exponentiation*

As an example of using a Flush+Reload attack, we now use it against a victim that uses modular exponentiation, a core operation in multiple encryption schemes, such as RSA and ElGamal. Modular exponentiation takes three inputs: a base b, a modulus m and a secret exponent d. Its output is $b^d \bmod m$.

Algorithm 2.2. The square-and-multiply algorithm for modular exponentiation

input : base b, modulus m, and secret exponent $d = \sum_{i=0}^{n-1} d_i 2^i$
output: $b^d \bmod m$

$x \leftarrow 1$
for $i = n - 1$ **downto** *0* **do**
  $x \leftarrow x^2 \bmod m$
  if $d_i = 1$ **then**
    $x \leftarrow x \cdot b \bmod m$
end
return x

Algorithm 2.2 shows the square-and-multiply algorithm for performing modular exponentiation. The algorithm uses the representation of the exponent as an n-bit binary number, that is, $d = \sum_{i=1}^{n-1} d_i 2^i$, where $d_i \in \{0, 1\}$. It scans the exponent from the most significant to the least significant bit. For each bit, the algorithm squares an accumulator x and if the bit is set it multiplies the accumulator by the base b (all operations calculated modulo the modulus m). At the end of the algorithm, x contains the required result. The algorithm is used in several implementations of RSA and ElGamal encryption, for example, in version 1.4.13 of the GnuPG library.

When using Flush+Reload to attack such an implementation, the adversary monitors the memory lines that contain the code for the square and the multiply functions. That is, the adversary repeatedly flushes the two memory lines, waits a bit and reloads the lines while measuring the time to reload them. Figure 2.3 shows a sequence of such measurements. The X axis is the sample number and the Y axis shows the time it takes to access the monitored line at each sample. Low values indicate that the monitored line is in the cache, i.e. that which the code is executing.

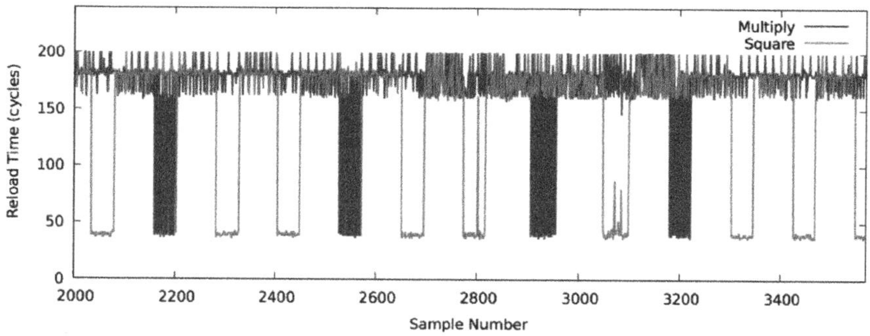

Figure 2.3. *Flush+Reload on the square-and-multiply implementation of modular exponentiation in GnuPG 1.4.13. Square followed by multiply indicates a bit 1, and square followed by another square indicates a bit 0. The exponent bits shown in this example are 10101100. For a color version of this figure, see www.iste.co.uk/prouff/cryptography1.zip*

When the exponent bit is one, the victim executes a square followed by a multiply. When the bit is zero, the victim only executes a square. In Figure 2.3, we see that a square operation took place between samples 2035 and 2079. This was followed by a multiply, at samples 2160–2200. Hence, we can conclude that the exponent bit that the victim processed between samples 2035 and 2200 was set. Conversely, the square operation between samples 2282 and 2327 is followed by another square operation (samples 2406–2449). Hence we conclude that the bit processed between samples 2282 and 2327 is clear. Following this logic, we can read the exponent bits processed in the window presented in Figure 2.3 and find that they are 10101100.

2.3.3. *Attack variants*

Several variants of the Flush+Reload attack have emerged using other primitives for either evicting the cache or measuring whether the target line is cached. The first such attack, Evict+Reload, targets the scenario of implementing the attack in non-x86 environment, where instructions for direct cache management are privileged and are not available to attack code executing in user-space. Instead of using `clflush` or an equivalent instruction, the adversary can use contention to evict the line from the cache. For that, the attacker needs an eviction set for the cache set in which the target cache line resides. Accessing this eviction set, as done for the prime step of the Prime+Probe attack, will load the eviction set to the cache, forcing eviction of any conflicting cache line, including the target cache line.

In the Flush+Flush variant, instead of measuring the time it takes to reload the target cache line, the adversary measures the time to flush it again. It turns out that the time it takes an Intel processor to execute the clflush instruction depends on whether the target memory line is cached or not. By measuring the flush time, the adversary both determines whether the line is cached and ensures that the line is no longer cached. Because there is no need for a separate reload step, the Flush+Flush attack has a higher temporal resolution than Flush+Reload. That is, the adversary can measure at a higher frequency. Moreover, in the Flush+Flush attack, the adversary does not trigger cache misses. Consequently, it is harder to detect an active Flush+Flush attack by monitoring the cache activity. On the down side, Flush+Flush shows much smaller timing differences than Flush+Reload, and the timing of the clflush instruction varies with the core that the attack code executes on. Consequently, the attack is noisier than Flush+Reload and is harder to execute in practice.

Last, the Prefetch+Prefetch attack exploits the cache coherency mechanism to achieve an effect similar to Flush+Reload. Cache coherency ensures that memory writes in one core are visible in all cores of the system. To maintain coherency, write operations in one core evict the target cache line from the private caches of all other cores, ensuring that future accesses in other cores get the updated contents of the cache line. To improve write performance, the x86 architecture provides a prefetchw instruction, which evicts a cache line from the private caches of *other* cores, in preparation for a write instruction in the executing core. The implementation of prefetchw on Intel processors does not check that the accessing user has write access to the target memory line. Consequently, prefetchw evicts the cache line from other cores even when the accessing process is only allowed to read the memory. Moreover, on many Intel processors, the time it takes to execute prefetchw depends on the coherence state of the target line. In particular, the time to execute prefetchw indicates whether another core has accessed the target memory line between successive invocations of prefetchw. Thus, the Prefetch+Prefetch is similar to Flush+Flush.

2.3.4. *Performance degradation attacks*

The temporal resolution of cache attacks limits the ability of the attacker to observe victim accesses. The attacks are typically performed in rounds that take hundreds to thousands of cycles each. In particular, Flush+Reload presents a trade-off between attack resolution and accuracy, showing a significant drop of accuracy when the time between the flush and the reload steps is less than 2,000 cycles.

A consequence of this limitation is that the attack cannot distinguish between successive victim accesses to the target memory line if the victim access frequency is higher than the sampling frequency of the attack. Performance degradation attacks aim to slow a victim down to reduce the access frequency and allow the attack to acquire the operation.

The core idea of the attack is to identify the victim code that executes between successive accesses to target memory addresses and flush this victim code from the cache. Repeated flushes of the victim code force the victim to incur a memory access delay when trying to execute the flushed code. The attack can slow down a tight loop by up to three orders of magnitude. For realistic scenarios, the attack typically achieves a slowdown of one to two orders of magnitude, allowing attacks in scenarios that are otherwise almost impossible.

A downside of the attack is that the slowdown is not uniform. Consequently, measurements in the presence of performance degradation tend to be noiser than otherwise.

2.4. Attacking other microarchitectural components

So far, we have looked at attacks that target data caches. In this section, we briefly discuss other microarchitectural components and how they can be exploited for attacks.

2.4.1. *Instruction cache*

Instead of targeting the data caches, an attacker can perform the Prime+Probe attack on one of the instruction caches. The attack typically reveals secret-dependent control flow, rather than secret dependent memory accesses, demonstrated in section 2.2.1.

The main difference between instruction-cache attacks and data-cache attacks is that instead of accessing the eviction sets, the attacker needs to execute code in the eviction set. Listing 2.2 shows an example of x86 code that performs the probe step in a Prime+Probe attack on an Intel L1 cache. The code first aligns the start of the function `L1IProbe()` to a page boundary (line 1). It then takes the current cycle count (line 3), records the clock reading in register `rsi` (line 4) and falls into a sequence of jump instructions that are 4,096 bytes apart. As discussed, the L1 cache has a cache line of 64 bytes and a total of 64 cache sets. Consequently, addresses that are a multiple of 4,096 bytes apart fall within the same L1 cache set. Finally, after visiting eight congruent addresses (for an 8-way cache), the code takes the current cycle count (line 19), subtracts the cycle count taken at the start of the function (line 20) and returns. The code in Listing 2.2 probes cache set 0. To target other cache sets, the attacker needs to offset the code within the page.

```
      .align 4096
L1IProbe:
      rdtscp
      mov %rax, %rsi
      jmp P2
      .align 4096
P2:   jmp P3
...
      .align 4096
P8:   rdtscp
      sub %rsi, %rax
      ret
```

Listing 2.2. *Probing the L1 Instruction Cache. For a color version of this listing, see www.iste.co.uk/prouff/cryptography1.zip*

Attacks on lower cache levels, such as the attacks in sections 2.2.3 and 2.3 target unified caches that cache both instruction and data. As demonstrated in section 2.3.2, such attacks can recover control flow. The main advantage that attacking the L1 instruction cache has over these attacks is that the temporal resolution is significantly higher. However, the results contain higher levels of noise, presenting a trade-off for the adversary. Moreover, the L1 instruction cache attack can only be applied within the same core, because the cache is private to the core.

2.4.2. *Branch prediction*

Another approach for retrieving the victim's control flow is to attack the branch predictor. Recall that the processor aims to predict future control flow based on past branch outcomes. The branch predictor itself consists of two main structures: the BTB, which predicts the address of a branch, and the BHB, which predicts whether the branch will be taken or not. On Intel processors, which tend to be popular research targets, conditional branches update the BTB only if the branch is taken. Consequently, attacks on the BTB can recover conditional branch outcomes, reducing the need for attacks on the BHB. Thus, here we focus on attacks that target the BTB.

Like other caches, the BTB is set associative and is therefore vulnerable to Prime+Probe attacks. However, unlike other caches, the BTB does not match the full address. Instead, it uses only some of the address bits (least significant 32 bits in most modern Intel processors). Hence a single BTB entry provides prediction to multiple *aliased* addresses. The main effect of aliasing on attacks is that only one prediction exists for aliased addresses. Hence, if we know the victim branch address, we can evict it from the BTB using an aliased branch, without a need for an eviction set.

2.5. Constant-time programming

The attacks on AES (section 2.2.2) and on modular exponentiation (section 2.3.2) represent the two main sources of leakage through microarchitectural side channels: secret dependent memory accesses and secret dependent control flow. *constant-time programming* is a coding paradigm that protects against such channels by preventing these forms of leakage. It also protects against timing leakage through instructions whose execution time depends on their arguments. This section presents the basics of constant-time programming.

2.5.1. *Constant-time select*

A core basic block for constant-time programming is the constant-time select operator, which provides a safe alternative to the conditional ternary operator in languages such as C. Specifically, the operator `ct_select(condition, true_val, false_val)` returns the result of the expression `condition ? true_val : false_val`. However, unlike the ternary operator, both values are evaluated, and the selection does not use any conditional control-flow instruction.

A straightforward implementation of `ct_select` is using conditional move instructions, such as the x86 instruction `CMOVcc`. These instructions move the source value to the destination if a condition is true. While efficient, the main drawbacks of these instructions are that they are machine dependent and there is no generic way of forcing their use in languages such as C.

```
int ct_select(int condition, int true_val, int false_val) {
  int mask;
  mask = condition ^ (condition - 1);
  mask = mask & ~condition;
  mask = mask >> (sizeof(int) * CHAR_BIT - 1);

  return (~mask & true_val) | (mask & false_val);
}
```

Listing 2.3. *An implementation of constant-time select for* `int` *values. For a color version of this listing, see www.iste.co.uk/prouff/cryptography1.zip*

A more generic approach is to use a mask whose value depends on the condition (all zero if the condition is true and all one if the condition is false). We can then calculate the result of `ct_select` using `(~mask & true_val) | (mask & false_val)`. In the case that `condition` is either 0 or 1, we can set `mask` to `condition - 1`. Listing 2.3 shows an implementation of `ct_select` for the general case, where any nonzero value indicates true. After line 3, the most significant bit of `mask` if `condition` is either zero or 0x80000000 (assuming 32 bit integers). Line 4 clears the most significant bit of `mask` if the most significant bit of `condition` is set. Hence, after line 4, the most significant bit of `mask` is set only if `condition` is 0, that is, false. Line 5 uses arithmetic shift to replicate most significant bit of `mask` to all of the bits, achieving the required value of all zero bits for true condition and all ones otherwise. The code can be adapted to other type sizes, as long as the size of the mask matches that of the values.

It should be noted that the code makes two assumptions on the C implementations. First, it assumes that language uses two's complement to represent negative numbers. Moreover, it assumes that the language uses arithmetic right shift for negative numbers. Both assumptions are not stipulated in the standard. Specifically the C (and C++) standards allow other negative number representations and state that right shift of negative numbers is an undefined behavior. However, in practice, the assumptions hold for all mainstream compilers and code similar to Listing 2.3 is common in cryptographic implementations.

2.5.2. *Eliminating secret-dependent branches*

As we have seen in Algorithm 2.2, when a program executes a branch whose condition depends on secret information, an adversary can use a side-channel attack to determine the condition and infer the secret information. Consequently, to protect against such attacks, constant-time programs avoid secret-dependent branches.

To eliminate secret-dependent branches, the program can always execute both the `then` block and the `else` block of the branch and use constant-time select to choose the required values for the variables. For example, Algorithm 2.3 shows the square-and-multiply-always algorithm, a constant-time version of Algorithm 2.2. As we can see, the `if` statement in the original algorithm (line 4 in Algorithm 2.2) has been removed. Instead, the multiplication is always executed, irrespective of the value of the exponent bit (line 4 Algorithm 2.3). The `ct_select` function in line 5 of Algorithm 2.3 replaces the value of x with the multiplication result if the current bit is set.

An important point to note is that `ct_select` should not be used for copying pointers. The reason is that subsequent dereferences of pointers selected with `ct_select` would result in memory accesses where the addresses depend on the secret condition. Instead, in the case of pointers, the program should use `ct_select` to deep-copy the structures that the pointers point to. Specifically, in Algorithm 2.3, the values of x and t will typically be represented using arrays. For a constant-time implementation, `ct_select` should be used to select each of the elements of the arrays.

Algorithm 2.3. The square-and-multiply-always algorithm for modular exponentiation

input : base b, modulus m, and secret exponent $d = \sum_{i=0}^{n-1} d_i 2^i$
output: $b^d \bmod m$

```
x ← 1
for i = n − 1 downto 0 do
    x ← x^2 mod m
    t ← x · b mod m
    x ← ct_select(d_i = 1, t, x)
end
return x
```

2.5.3. *Eliminating secret-dependent memory access*

Many implementations of cryptographic primitives include tables, where the choice of element to be accessed depends on secret data. We have seen one such example: the T-tables implementation of AES in Listing 2.1. To harden table access, constant-time programs need to access *all* possible memory addresses and use constant-time select to retain the correct value. Listing 2.4 shows an example of how this could be implemented for T-table access. In the listing, we have a function `ct_ttable` that takes an index `in` and a T-table `T` as arguments. The variable `rv`, which will hold the return value, is first initialized in line 2. Then, the function iterates over all possible values of `in` (line 4) and uses `ct_select` to choose between the previous value of `rv` and the value loaded from the table, based on whether the current index is the same as the input.

```
1 uint32_t ct_ttable(uint8_t in, uint32_t *T) {
2   uint32_t rv = 0ULL;
3
4   for (int i = 0; i < 256; i++)
5     rv = ct_select(i == in, T[i], rv);
6   return rv;
7 }
```

Listing 2.4. *An implementation of constant-time T-table access. For a color version of this listing, see www.iste.co.uk/prouff/cryptography1.zip*

2.6. Covert channels

So far, we have looked at microarchitectural side-channel attacks, where the attacker monitors the microarchitectural state of the processor to detect unintended leakage of victim execution patterns. Microarchitectural components can also be exploited to implement covert channels. In a covert channel, a *transmitter* (also referred to as a Trojan) seeks to send information to a *receiver* by using a medium that is not designed for communication.

Listing 2.5 shows an example of a cache-based covert channel that exploits the Flush+Reload technique. Specifically, the covert channel uses three functions: `cc_setup()`, `cc_transmit()`, and `cc_receive()`, to manipulate a shared array `probe_array` and transmit a single byte of data.

```
uint8_t probe_array[256 * 4096] = {1};

void cc_setup() {
  for (int i = 0; i < 256; i++)
    _mm_clflush(probe_array + i * 4096);
  _mm_mfence();
}

void cc_transmit(int value) {
  if (value < 0)
    return;
  volatile uint8_t *ptr = probe_array + value * 4096;
  uint8_t t = *ptr;
}

int cc_receive() {
  int junk = 0;
  _mm_mfence();

  for (int i = 0; i < 256; i++) {
    volatile uint8_t *ptr = probe_array + i * 4096;
    uint64_t start = __rdtscp(&junk);
    uint8_t v = *ptr;
    uint64_t latency = __rdtscp(&junk) - start;

    if (latency < THRESHOLD)
      return i;
  }
  return -1;
}
```

Listing 2.5. *Implementation of a cache-based covert channel. For a color version of this listing, see www.iste.co.uk/prouff/cryptography1.zip*

`cc_setup()` prepares the array for use by flushing 256 locations in the array from the cache (line 5). To transmit a byte, the transmitter invokes `cc_transmit()` (lines 9–14), which accesses one of the 256 locations flushed in the setup. Finally, to receive the value of the byte, the receiver invokes `cc_receive()` (lines 17–30), which reloads each of the 256 locations, returning the value that matches the first found in the cache.

2.7. Transient-execution attacks

Transient execution is a term for speculatively executing instructions only to squash them later when discovering they are not part of the nominal program execution. Transient execution, which is a natural outcome of out-of-order and speculative execution, does not change the architectural state of the processor, and is transparent to the executing program. However, it does leave footprints in the microarchitectural state of the processor. Transient-execution attacks aim at observing these footprints in order to bypass security checks and recover secret information. Specifically, in a transient execution attack, the adversary aims to cause the processor to transiently bypass a security test and transmit a secret value through a microarchitectural covert channel.

Transient-execution attacks are classified based on the main cause of transient execution which they exploit. Meltdown-type attacks exploit execution past an instruction that causes a trap, whereas Spectre-type attacks exploit transient execution caused by misspeculation. We first describe one variant of the Spectre attack and then proceed to Meltdown-type attacks.

2.7.1. *The Spectre attack*

The Spectre attack exploits transient-execution caused by branch misprediction to overcome software-enforced security boundaries. Listing 2.6 shows a proof of concept of a Spectre attack. The victim is the function `victim` (lines 1 to 5), which checks if `index` is in bounds, returning the contents from the array if it is, otherwise returning a constant 0. Note that in type-safe languages, such as JavaScript, this test is implicit in any array access.

The attack code is the function `spectre`. The code needs to set up the branch predictor so that the victim branch at line 2 mispredicts. To this aim, the attack code uses the function `victim_wrapper`, which calls `victim` after setting the branch history with a small loop (lines 9 and 10). The attack code calls `victim_wrapper` twice with an `index` value in range (lines 17 and 18), training the branch predictor that, for the history set in `victim_wrapper`, the branch condition is false.

```
1  int victim(uint64_t index) {
2    if (index >= array_len)
3      return -1;
4    return array[index];
5  }
6
7
8  int victim_wrapper(uint64_t index) {
9    for (int i = 0; i < 128; i++)
10     ;
11   return victim(index);
12 }
13
14
15 int spectre(int64_t index) {
16   volatile int junk = 0;
17   junk = victim_wrapper(0);
18   junk = victim_wrapper(0);
19
20   cc_setup();
21
22   _mm_clflush(&array_len);
23   _mm_mfence();
24   int rv = victim_wrapper(index);
25   cc_transmit(rv);
26
27   return cc_receive();
28 }
```

Listing 2.6. *The Spectre attack. For a color version of this listing, see www.iste.co.uk/prouff/cryptography1.zip*

The attack code then sets up a covert channel (line 20) and evicts the array length from the cache (line 22). It then calls the victim function with an index that is out of bounds (line 24). The branch at line 2 of the victim code aims to prevent array access with such an index. However, because the attacker evicted the array length from the cache, determining the branch condition requires a cache miss that takes a long time. During that time, the processor checks the BHB for a prediction. Based on the prior training that the condition is true (lines 17 and 18), the branch predictor mispredicts, and execution proceeds speculatively as if the branch condition were true.

During the resultant speculative execution, the processor first retrieves `array[index]`, which now is an arbitrary address, under the control of the attacker. The victim function returns this value, which is transmitted through the covert channel (line 25).

Eventually, the processor retrieves `array_len` from memory, computes the condition at line 2, and detects that the branch was mispredicted. The processor then terminates the speculative execution that started from the misprediction, and proceeds to the correct execution path, returning an error from `victim`. However, at this stage, the value that was speculatively retrieved from beyond the array bounds has already been transmitted through the covert channel. The attack code receives this value (line 27), returning the contents of memory that the victim function was not supposed to access.

The proof-of-concept code in this section demonstrates that an attacker can overcome software-based protections and recover secret data. Such protections are common in scenarios where untrusted code is running within a more trusted environment. For example, web browsers often execute JavaScript code that is downloaded from untrusted web sites. To allow safe execution of such code, the JavaScript runtime environment restricts the downloaded code to prevent its access to sensitive user data. The Spectre attack can overcome this protection.

Several variants of the Spectre attack have been suggested. These exploit different speculation mechanisms within the processors. Specifically, training the BTB to mispredict indirect branches can lead to arbitrary code execution, which can leak sensitive data, for example from an operating system kernel. Similarly, mistraining the return stack buffer, which predicts the addresses functions return to, has been exploited for attacks.

2.7.2. *Meltdown-type attacks*

Meltdown-type attacks exploit transient execution to overcome hardware-based protection mechanism. Recall that out-of-order execution may proceed past instructions that raise traps. In a Meltdown attack, the attacker issues a memory load from an address that is part of the operating system kernel. Typically, kernel addresses are mapped to all processes, but are protected against access from user-space code.

Accessing the kernel space raises a trap. However, until the trap is processed, younger instructions may execute. When the attack was discovered, if the accessed address was in the L1 cache, the processor performed the access transiently, allowing leaks of kernel data. Further research demonstrated that similar attacks can read other data that the processor handled, allowing a large number of attacks.

It should be noted that all of these attacks can be considered as processor bugs. Indeed, more recent versions of the processors include countermeasures for such attacks.

2.8. Summary

When multiple programs run on the same computer, they share the use of the microarchitectural components. When a program executes, it changes the state of the microarchitectural state, which, in turn, changes the performance of other programs. This creates a channel that can unintentionally leak information between programs. Such leaks can be exploited by attacks, such as Prime+Probe and Flush+Reload, to compromise the security of cryptographic implementations. To protect against such attacks, cryptographic implementations follow the constant-time paradigm, where the program avoids branches and memory accesses that depend on secret data.

Microarchitectural channels can be combined with speculative and out-of-order execution for mounting transient-execution attacks. In these attacks, transient instructions access data that the program is not allowed to access and transmit it through a microarchitectural channel. The Spectre attack exploits transient execution due to misspeculation to bypass software-based security boundaries. Similarly, Meltdown-type attacks exploit transient execution beyond traps to bypass hardware-enforced security checks.

2.9. Notes and further references

Ge et al. (2018) survey microarchitectural side-channel attacks and Lou et al. (2021) survey their application to cryptography. Canella et al. (2019b) survey transient-execution attacks. The two first attacks to exploit microarchitectural channels were published in 2002. Tsunoo et al. (2002) demonstrate a timing attack that exploits cache collisions in Misty (Matsui 1997), whereas Page (2002) suggests a theoretical attack on Data Encryption Standards (DES) (National Institute of Standards and Technology 1999) which use a trace of cache hits and misses.

– Section 2.2.1. The term Prime+Probe is due to Osvik et al. (2006), who develop the attack and propose using pointer chasing over a linked list to reduce noise due to out-of-order execution. Concurrently with them, Percival (2005) describes a very similar technique, but instead of following pointers, he uses arithmetic operations to create dependencies between memory accesses. Brasser et al. (2017) propose using performance counters instead of timing for the probe step and apply an attack against a genome indexing algorithm that uses hash tables. Last, Gulmezoglu et al. (2017) use both L1 and LLC attacks to detect applications in the cloud.

– Section 2.2.2. The attack in this section follows the approach of Osvik et al. (2006). Also, see this reference for information on the second round attack. Bonneau (2006) proposes a similar attack on the final round of AES, which can recover the full key in a single round. Similar attacks have been proposed against other table-based ciphers (Zhao and Wang 2010; Nguyen et al. 2012; Genkin et al. 2019; Chuengsatiansup et al. 2022).

– Section 2.2.3. The first Prime+Probe attacks on the LLC were published in 2015 (Irazoqui et al. 2015a; Liu et al. 2015). The attack has been demonstrated from browsers (Genkin et al. 2018) and across VMs (Ronen et al. 2018). Algorithm 2.1 is based on Liu et al. (2015). Vila et al. (2019) proposes a linear-time algorithm for finding eviction sets. Due to the importance of finding eviction sets for mounting attacks, several secure cache design aim to prevent this step (Werner et al. 2019; Tan et al. 2020; Saileshwar and Qureshi 2021). However, techniques for finding eviction sets for such caches have also been shown (Purnal et al. 2021b). Intel LLCs consist of multiple subcaches called slices. The processor uses a proprietary hash function to select the slice in which a memory location is cached. While the hash function is not public, several techniques for reverse engineering it have been published (Hund et al. 2013; Yarom et al. 2015; Maurice, et al. 2015a; Inci et al. 2016; McCalpin 2021).

– Section 2.2.4. Prime+Abort (Disselkoen et al. 2017) uses Intel TSX instead of probing. TSX has also been used for defending against cache attacks (Shih et al. 2017; Gruss et al. 2017). Prime+Scope is due to Purnal et al. (2021b). The first published cache occupancy attacks appeared in 2015 (Maurice et al. 2015b; Oren et al. 2015). The attack has been used for website fingerprinting (Shusterman et al. 2019, 2021). Cook et al. (2022) argue that cache contention is not the sole contributor for cache occupancy attacks and show that TLB shootdowns also contribute to the attack. Because they do not rely on eviction sets, cache occupancy attacks are effective against secure cache and can be used for attacking cryptographic implementations (Genkin et al. 2023).

– Section 2.3. Shared memory and cache flushes are the enabler of the Flush+Reload attack (Yarom and Falkner 2014; Gullasch et al. 2011). The attack has been applied in various contexts, including between processes, containers and VMs (Yarom and Falkner 2014; Zhang et al. 2014; Irazoqui et al. 2014), and against multiple cryptographic schemes (Benger et al. 2014; Irazoqui et al. 2014; Irazoqui et al. 2015b; Groot Bruinderink et al. 2016; Pessl et al. 2017). Zhang et al. (2016) propose an Arm implementation that uses system calls to overcome the absence of user-space flush instructions on Arm.

– Section 2.3.2. The demonstrated attack is based on Yarom and Falkner (2014).

– Section 2.3.3. Gruss et al. (2016) propose the Flush+Flush attack. Several works investigated improving its accuracy (Didier and Maurice 2021; Ding et al. 2022). The Evict+Reload technique is due to Gruss et al. (2015). Guo et al. (2022) propose the Prefetch+Prefetch attack among several techniques that exploit the prefetch instruction on Intel processors.

– Section 2.3.4. Allan et al. (2016) propose using cache flushes for performance degradation. Aldaya and Brumley (2022) observe that the technique is more effective within two hyperthreads of the same core.

– Section 2.4. Microarchitectural side-channel attacks targeting almost every component of the shared architecture have been proposed. We discuss attacks against the instruction cache (Aciiçmez and Schindler 2008; Aciiçmez et al. 2010; Zhang et al. 2012) and the branch predictors (Aciiçmez et al. 2006; Aciiçmez et al. 2007; Bhattacharya and Mukhopadhyay 2015; Evtyushkin et al. 2016, 2018). However attacks have also been demonstrated against translation lookaside buffers (Gras et al. 2018; Tatar et al. 2022), random number generators (Evtyushkin and Ponomarev 2016), interconnects (Wu et al. 2012; Paccagnella et al. 2021; Wan et al. 2022), prefetchers (Shin et al. 2018; Zhang et al. 2023b), memory ordering (Irazoqui et al. 2016; Moghimi et al. 2018; Islam et al. 2019), and many more (Aldaya et al. 2019; Kim et al. 2021; Puddu et al. 2021; Zhao et al. 2022; Rokicki et al. 2022).

– Section 2.5. The foundations for protecting cryptographic software from microarchitectural attacks were laid out together with the publication of the early attacks (Bernstein 2005; Osvik et al. 2006) and later formalized (Barthe et al. 2014). The NaCl library (Bernstein et al. 2012) is one of the first principled implementations of constant-time programming. Jancar et al. (2022) survey tools for enforcing constant-time programming and their use in practice.

– Section 2.6. The covert channel demonstrated in this paper is designed for use with transient-execution attacks. It is based on code from the Meltdown (Lipp et al. 2018) and Spectre (Kocher et al. 2019) papers. Transient-execution attacks exploiting other covert channels have been demonstrated, including port contention (Bhattacharyya et al. 2019), branch prediction (Chowdhuryy et al. 2020), and instruction timing (Zhang et al. 2023a). Outside transient-execution attacks, Ristenpart et al. (2009) use a cache-based covert channel to detect co-residency on a cloud server, and Maurice et al. (2017) investigate the bandwidth of covert channels.

– Section 2.7. Spectre (Kocher et al. 2019) and Meltdown (Lipp et al. 2018) are the first transient-execution attacks to be published. They were discovered in 2017 and publicly disclosed in early 2018. The distinction between Spectre-type and Meltdown-type attacks is due to Canella et al. (2019b). Xiong and Szefer (2021) survey transient-execution attacks and defenses.

– Section 2.7.1. The proof-of-concept code is based on the code in Kocher et al. (2019), with adaptations to use the covert channel from section 2.6 and the branch training of Röttger and Janc (2021). The code implements the Spectre V1 variant, also called Spectre-PHT (Canella et al. 2019b). Because the typical demo shows read out of array bounds, the variant is often referred to as "bounds check bypass". However, the same variant has been used in other scenarios, exploiting type confusion (Kirzner and Morrison 2021). Other variants exploit indirect branches (Kocher et al. 2019), the return stack buffer (Maisuradze and Rossow 2018; Koruyeh et al. 2018), and memory ordering speculation (Kiriansky and Waldspurger 2018).

– Section 2.7.2. The Meltdown attack (Lipp et al. 2018) is the prototype for a large number of Meltdown-type attacks, including Foreshadow (Van Bulck et al. 2018), microarchitectural data sampling (MDS) (van Schaik et al. 2019; Schwarz et al. 2019; Canella et al. 2019a), CrossTalk (Ragab et al. 2021), and others. These differ by the causes of traps and the type of information that leaks. Instead of leaking the data obtained from the trapped instruction, the Load Value Injection attack (Van Bulck et al. 2020) speculatively injects it into the victim execution, resulting in transient execution of arbitrary code within the victim.

2.10. References

Aciiçmez, O. and Schindler, W. (2008). A vulnerability in RSA implementations due to instruction cache analysis and its demonstration on OpenSSL. In *CT-RSA 2008*, Malkin, T. (ed.). Springer, Berlin, Heidelberg.

Aciiçmez, O., Koç, Ç.K., Seifert, J.-P. (2006). On the power of simple branch prediction analysis. Report 2006/351, Cryptology ePrint Archive [Online]. Available at: https://eprint.iacr.org/2006/351.

Aciiçmez, O., Koç, Ç., Seifert, J.-P. (2007). Predicting secret keys via branch prediction. In *CT-RSA 2007*, Abe, M. (ed.). Springer, Berlin, Heidelberg.

Aciiçmez, O., Brumley, B.B., Grabher, P. (2010). New results on instruction cache attacks. In *CHES 2010*, Mangard, S. and Standaert, F.-X. (eds). Springer, Heidelberg.

Aldaya, A.C. and Brumley, B.B. (2022). HyperDegrade: From GHz to MHz effective CPU frequencies. USENIX Security 2022 [Online]. Available at: https://www.usenix.org/system/files/sec22summer_aldaya.pdf.

Aldaya, A.C., Brumley, B.B., ul Hassan, S., García, C.P., Tuveri, N. (2019). Port contention for fun and profit. In *2019 IEEE Symposium on Security and Privacy*, San Francisco.

Allan, T., Brumley, B.B., Falkner, K.E., van de Pol, J., Yarom, Y. (2016). Amplifying side channels through performance degradation. In *ACSAC*. ACM, New York.

Barthe, G., Betarte, G., Campo, J.D., Luna, C.D., Pichardie, D. (2014). System-level non-interference for constant-time cryptography. In *ACM CCS 2014*, Ahn, G.-J., Yung, M., Li, N. (eds). ACM Press, New York.

Benger, N., van de Pol, J., Smart, N.P., Yarom, Y. (2014). "Ooh aah... just a little bit": A small amount of side channel can go a long way. In *CHES 2014*, Batina, L. and Robshaw, M. (eds). Springer, Berlin, Heidelberg.

Bernstein, D.J. (2005). Cache-timing attacks on AES. Paper, 2217245 [Online]. Available at: https://cr.yp.to/papers.html#cachetiming.

Bernstein, D.J., Lange, T., Schwabe, P. (2012). The security impact of a new cryptographic library. In *LATINCRYPT 2012*, Hevia, A. and Neven, G. (eds). Springer, Berlin, Heidelberg.

Bhattacharya, S. and Mukhopadhyay, D. (2015). Who watches the watchmen? Utilizing performance monitors for compromising keys of RSA on intel platforms. In *CHES 2015*, Güneysu, T. and Handschuh, H. (eds). Springer, Berlin, Heidelberg.

Bhattacharyya, A., Sandulescu, A., Neugschwandtner, M., Sorniotti, A., Falsafi, B., Payer, M., Kurmus, A. (2019). SMoTherSpectre: Exploiting speculative execution through port contention. In *ACM CCS 2019*, Cavallaro, L., Kinder, J., Wang, X., Katz, J. (eds). ACM Press, New York.

Bonneau, J. (2006). Robust final-round cache-trace attacks against AES. Report 2006/374, Cryptology ePrint Archive [Online]. Available at: https://eprint.iacr.org/2006/374.

Brasser, F., Müller, U., Dmitrienko, A., Kostiainen, K., Capkun, S., Sadeghi, A. (2017). Software grand exposure: SGX cache attacks are practical. In *WOOT*. USENIX Association, Berkeley.

Canella, C., Genkin, D., Giner, L., Gruss, D., Lipp, M., Minkin, M., Moghimi, D., Piessens, F., Schwarz, M., Sunar, B., Van Bulck, J., Yarom, Y. (2019a). Fallout: Leaking data on meltdown-resistant CPUs. In *ACM CCS 2019*, Cavallaro, L., Kinder, J., Wang, X., Katz, J. (eds). ACM Press, New York.

Canella, C., Van Bulck, J., Schwarz, M., Lipp, M., von Berg, B., Ortner, P., Piessens, F., Evtyushkin, D., Gruss, D. (2019b). A systematic evaluation of transient execution attacks and defenses. In *USENIX Security 2019*, Heninger, N. and Traynor, P. (eds). USENIX Association, Berkeley.

Chowdhuryy, M.H.I., Liu, H., Yao, F. (2020). BranchSpec: Information leakage attacks exploiting speculative branch instruction executions. In *ICCD*. IEEE, Hartford.

Chuengsatiansup, C., Genkin, D., Yarom, Y., Zhang, Z. (2022). Side-channeling the Kalyna key expansion. In *CT-RSA 2022*, Galbraith, S.D. (ed.). Springer, Berlin, Heidelberg.

Cook, J., Drean, J., Behrens, J., Yan, M. (2022). There's always a bigger fish: A clarifying analysis of a machine-learning-assisted side-channel attack. In *ISCA*. ACM Press, New York.

Didier, G. and Maurice, C. (2021). Calibration done right: Noiseless Flush+Flush attacks. In *DIMVA*, Bilge, L., Cavallaro, L., Pellegrino, G., Neves, N. (eds). Springer, Cham.

Ding, R., Zhang, Z., Zhang, X., Gongye, C., Fei, Y., Ding, A.A. (2022). A cross-platform cache timing attack framework via deep learning. In *DATE*. IEEE, Antwerp.

Disselkoen, C., Kohlbrenner, D., Porter, L., Tullsen, D.M. (2017). Prime+abort: A timer-free high-precision L3 cache attack using intel TSX. In *USENIX Security 2017*, Kirda, E. and Ristenpart, T. (eds). USENIX Association, Berkeley.

Evtyushkin, D. and Ponomarev, D.V. (2016). Covert channels through random number generator: Mechanisms, capacity estimation and mitigations. In *ACM CCS 2016*, Weippl, E.R., Katzenbeisser, S., Kruegel, C., Myers, A.C., Halevi, S. (eds). ACM Press, New York.

Evtyushkin, D., Ponomarev, D.V., Abu-Ghazaleh, N.B. (2016). Jump over ASLR: attacking branch predictors to bypass ASLR. In *MICRO*. IEEE, Taipei.

Evtyushkin, D., Riley, R., Abu-Ghazaleh, N.B., Ponomarev, D. (2018). BranchScope: A new side-channel attack on directional branch predictor. In *ASPLOS*. ACM Press, New York.

Ge, Q., Yarom, Y., Cock, D., Heiser, G. (2018). A survey of microarchitectural timing attacks and countermeasures on contemporary hardware. *Journal of Cryptographic Engineering*, 8(1), 1–27.

Genkin, D., Pachmanov, L., Tromer, E., Yarom, Y. (2018). Drive-by key-extraction cache attacks from portable code. In *ACNS 18*, Preneel, B. and Vercauteren, F. (eds). Springer, Berlin, Heidelberg.

Genkin, D., Poussier, R., Sim, R.Q., Yarom, Y., Zhao, Y. (2019). Cache vs. key-dependency: Side channeling an implementation of pilsung. *IACR TCHES*, 2020(1), 231–255.

Genkin, D., Kosasih, W., Liu, F., Trikalinou, A., Unterluggauer, T., Yarom, Y. (2023). CacheFX: A framework for evaluating cache security. In *ASIACCS 23*. ACM Press, New York.

Gras, B., Razavi, K., Bos, H., Giuffrida, C. (2018). Translation leak-aside buffer: Defeating cache side-channel protections with TLB attacks. In *USENIX Security 2018*, Enck, W. and Felt, A.P. (eds). USENIX Association, Berkeley.

Groot Bruinderink, L., Hülsing, A., Lange, T., Yarom, Y. (2016). Flush, gauss, and reload – A cache attack on the BLISS lattice-based signature scheme. In *CHES 2016*, Gierlichs, B. and Poschmann, A.Y. (eds). Springer, Berlin, Heidelberg.

Gruss, D., Spreitzer, R., Mangard, S. (2015). Cache template attacks: Automating attacks on inclusive last-level caches. In *USENIX Security 2015*, Jung, J. and Holz, T. (eds). USENIX Association, Berkeley.

Gruss, D., Maurice, C., Wagner, K., Mangard, S. (2016). Flush+Flush: A fast and stealthy cache attack. In *DIMVA*, Caballero, J., Zurutuza, U., Rodríguez, R. (eds). Springer, Cham.

Gruss, D., Lettner, J., Schuster, F., Ohrimenko, O., Haller, I., Costa, M. (2017). Strong and efficient cache side-channel protection using hardware transactional memory. In *USENIX Security 2017*, Kirda, E. and Ristenpart, T. (eds). USENIX Association, Berkeley.

Gullasch, D., Bangerter, E., Krenn, S. (2011). Cache games – Bringing access-based cache attacks on AES to practice. In *2011 IEEE Symposium on Security and Privacy*. Oakland.

Gulmezoglu, B., Eisenbarth, T., Sunar, B. (2017). Cache-base application detection in the cloud using machine learning. Report 2017/245, Cryptology ePrint Archive [Online]. Available at: https://eprint.iacr.org/2017/245.

Guo, Y., Zigerelli, A., Zhang, Y., Yang, J. (2022). Adversarial prefetch: New cross-core cache side channel attacks. In *2022 IEEE Symposium on Security and Privacy*. San Francisco.

Hund, R., Willems, C., Holz, T. (2013). Practical timing side channel attacks against kernel space ASLR. In *NDSS 2013*. IEEE, Berkeley.

Inci, M.S., Gülmezoglu, B., Irazoqui, G., Eisenbarth, T., Sunar, B. (2016). Cache attacks enable bulk key recovery on the cloud. In *CHES 2016*, Gierlichs, B. and Poschmann, A.Y. (eds). Springer, Berlin, Heidelberg.

Irazoqui, G., Inci, M.S., Eisenbarth, T., Sunar, B. (2014). Wait a minute! A fast, cross-VM attack on AES. In *RAID*, Stavrou, A., Bos, H., Portokalidis, G. (eds). Springer, Cham.

Irazoqui, G., Eisenbarth, T., Sunar, B. (2015a). S$A: A shared cache attack that works across cores and defies VM sandboxing – and its application to AES. In *2015 IEEE Symposium on Security and Privacy*. San Jose.

Irazoqui, G., Inci, M.S., Eisenbarth, T., Sunar, B. (2015b). Lucky 13 strikes back. In *ASIACCS 15*, Bao, F., Miller, S., Zhou, J., Ahn, G.-J. (eds). ACM Press, New York.

Irazoqui, G., Eisenbarth, T., Sunar, B. (2016). Cross processor cache attacks. In *ASIACCS 16*, Chen, X., Wang, X., Huang, X. (eds). ACM Press, New York.

Islam, S., Moghimi, A., Bruhns, I., Krebbel, M., Gülmezoglu, B., Eisenbarth, T., Sunar, B. (2019). SPOILER: Speculative load hazards boost rowhammer and cache attacks. In *USENIX Security 2019*, Heninger, N. and Traynor, P. (eds). USENIX Association, Berkeley.

Jancar, J., Fourné, M., Braga, D.D.A., Sabt, M., Schwabe, P., Barthe, G., Fouque, P.-A., Acar, Y. (2022). "They're not that hard to mitigate": What cryptographic library developers think about timing attacks. In *2022 IEEE Symposium on Security and Privacy*. San Francisco.

Kim, J., Jang, H., Lee, H., Lee, S., Kim, J. (2021). UC-Check: Characterizing micro-operation caches in x86 processors and implications in security and performance. In *MICRO*. ACM Press, New York.

Kiriansky, V. and Waldspurger, C.A. (2018). Speculative buffer overflows: Attacks and defenses. *arXiv/1807.03757*, 12.

Kirzner, O. and Morrison, A. (2021). An analysis of speculative type confusion vulnerabilities in the wild. In *USENIX Security 2021*, Bailey, M. and Greenstadt, R. (eds). USENIX Association, Berkeley.

Kocher, P., Horn, J., Fogh, A., Genkin, D., Gruss, D., Haas, W., Hamburg, M., Lipp, M., Mangard, S., Prescher, T. et al. (2019). Spectre attacks: Exploiting speculative execution. In *2019 IEEE Symposium on Security and Privacy*. San Francisco.

Koruyeh, E.M., Khasawneh, K.N., Song, C., Abu-Ghazaleh, N.B. (2018). Spectre returns! Speculation attacks using the return stack buffer. In *WOOT*. USENIX Association, Berkeley.

Lipp, M., Schwarz, M., Gruss, D., Prescher, T., Haas, W., Fogh, A., Horn, J., Mangard, S., Kocher, P., Genkin, D. et al. (2018). Meltdown: Reading kernel memory from user space. In *USENIX Security 2018*, Enck, W. and Felt, A.P. (eds). USENIX Association, Berkeley.

Liu, F., Yarom, Y., Ge, Q., Heiser, G., Lee, R.B. (2015). Last-level cache side-channel attacks are practical. In *2015 IEEE Symposium on Security and Privacy*. San Jose.

Lou, X., Zhang, T., Jiang, J., Zhang, Y. (2021). A survey of microarchitectural side-channel vulnerabilities, attacks, and defenses in cryptography. *Computing Surveys*, 54(6), 1–37.

Maisuradze, G. and Rossow, C. (2018). ret2spec: Speculative execution using return stack buffers. In *ACM CCS 2018*, Lie, D., Mannan, M., Backes, M., Wang, X. (eds). ACM Press, New York.

Matsui, M. (1997). New block encryption algorithm MISTY. In *FSE'97*, Biham, E. (ed.). Springer, Berlin, Heidelberg.

Maurice, C., Le Scouarnec, N., Neumann, C., Heen, O., Francillon, A. (2015a). Reverse engineering Intel last-level cache complex addressing using performance counters. In *Research in Attacks, Intrusions, and Defenses. RAID 2015*, Bos, H., Monrose, F., Blanc, G. (eds). Springer, Berlin, Heidelberg.

Maurice, C., Neumann, C., Heen, O., Francillon, A. (2015b). C5: Cross-cores cache covert channel. In *DIMVA*, Almgren, M., Gulisano, V., Maggi, F. (eds). Springer, Cham.

Maurice, C., Weber, M., Schwarz, M., Giner, L., Gruss, D., Boano, C.A., Mangard, S., Römer, K. (2017). Hello from the other side: SSH over robust cache covert channels in the cloud. In *NDSS 2017*. The Internet Society, San Diego.

McCalpin, J. (2021). Mapping addresses to L3/CHA slices in Intel processors. ACELab Technical Report, University of Texas at Austin, Austin [Online]. Available at: https://repositories.lib.utexas.edu/handle/2152/86210.

Moghimi, A., Eisenbarth, T., Sunar, B. (2018). MemJam: A false dependency attack against constant-time crypto implementations in SGX. In *CT-RSA 2018*, Smart, N.P. (ed.). Springer, Berlin, Heidelberg.

National Institute of Standards and Technology (1999). FIPS PUB 46-3 data encryption standard (DES). Standard, NIST, Gaithersburg [Online]. Available at: https://csrc.nist.gov/files/pubs/fips/46-3/final/docs/fips46-3.pdf.

Nguyen, P.H., Rebeiro, C., Mukhopadhyay, D., Wang, H. (2012). Improved differential cache attacks on SMS4. In *Inscrypt*, Kutyłowski, M. and Yung, M. (eds). Springer, Berlin, Heidelberg.

Oren, Y., Kemerlis, V.P., Sethumadhavan, S., Keromytis, A.D. (2015). The spy in the sandbox: Practical cache attacks in JavaScript and their implications. In *ACM CCS 2015*, Ray, I., Li, N., Kruegel, C. (eds). ACM Press, New York.

Osvik, D.A., Shamir, A., Tromer, E. (2006). Cache attacks and countermeasures: The case of AES. In *CT-RSA 2006*, Pointcheval, D. (ed.). Springer, Berlin, Heidelberg.

Paccagnella, R., Luo, L., Fletcher, C.W. (2021). Lord of the ring(s): Side channel attacks on the CPU on-chip ring interconnect are practical. In *USENIX Security 2021*, Bailey, M. and Greenstadt, R. (eds). USENIX Association, Berkeley.

Page, D. (2002). Theoretical use of cache memory as a cryptanalytic side-channel. Report 2002/169, Cryptology ePrint Archive [Online]. Available at: https://eprint.iacr.org/2002/169.

Percival, C. (2005). Cache missing for fun and profit. In *BSDCan 2005*, Ottawa, CA [Online]. Available at: https://www.daemonology.net/papers/htt.pdf.

Pessl, P., Bruinderink, L.G., Yarom, Y. (2017). To BLISS-B or not to be: Attacking strong swan's implementation of post-quantum signatures. In *ACM CCS 2017*, Thuraisingham, B.M., Evans, D., Malkin, T., Xu, D. (eds). ACM Press, New York.

Puddu, I., Schneider, M., Haller, M., Capkun, S. (2021). Frontal attack: Leaking control-flow in SGX via the CPU frontend. In *USENIX Security 2021*, Bailey, M. and Greenstadt, R. (eds). USENIX Association, Berkeley.

Purnal, A., Giner, L., Gruss, D., Verbauwhede, I. (2021a). Systematic analysis of randomization-based protected cache architectures. In *2021 IEEE Symposium on Security and Privacy*. San Francisco.

Purnal, A., Turan, F., Verbauwhede, I. (2021b). Prime+scope: Overcoming the observer effect for high-precision cache contention attacks. In *ACM CCS 2021*, Vigna, G. and Shi, E. (eds). ACM Press, New York.

Ragab, H., Milburn, A., Razavi, K., Bos, H., Giuffrida, C. (2021). CrossTalk: Speculative data leaks across cores are real. In *2021 IEEE Symposium on Security and Privacy*. San Francisco.

Ristenpart, T., Tromer, E., Shacham, H., Savage, S. (2009). Hey, you, get off of my cloud: Exploring information leakage in third-party compute clouds. In *ACM CCS 2009*, Al-Shaer, E., Jha, S., Keromytis, A.D. (eds). ACM Press, New York.

Rokicki, T., Maurice, C., Botvinnik, M., Oren, Y. (2022). Port contention goes portable: Port contention side channels in web browsers. In *ASIACCS 22*, Suga, Y., Sakurai, K., Ding, X., Sako, K. (eds). ACM Press, New York.

Ronen, E., Paterson, K.G., Shamir, A. (2018). Pseudo constant time implementations of TLS are only pseudo secure. In *ACM CCS 2018*, Lie, D., Mannan, M., Backes, M., Wang, X. (eds). ACM Press, New York.

Röttger, S. and Janc, A. (2021). A Spectre proof-of-concept for a Spectre-proof web [Online]. Available at: https://security.googleblog.com/2021/03/a-spectre-proof-of-concept-for-spectre.html.

Saileshwar, G. and Qureshi, M.K. (2021). MIRAGE: Mitigating conflict-based cache attacks with a practical fully-associative design. In *USENIX Security 2021*, Bailey, M. and Greenstadt, R. (eds). USENIX Association, Berkeley.

van Schaik, S., Milburn, A., Österlund, S., Frigo, P., Maisuradze, G., Razavi, K., Bos, H., Giuffrida, C. (2019). RIDL: Rogue in-flight data load. In *2019 IEEE Symposium on Security and Privacy*. San Francisco.

Schwarz, M., Lipp, M., Moghimi, D., Van Bulck, J., Stecklina, J., Prescher, T., Gruss, D. (2019). ZombieLoad: Cross-privilege-boundary data sampling. In *ACM CCS 2019*, Cavallaro, L., Kinder, J., Wang, X., Katz, J. (eds). ACM Press, New York.

Shih, M.-W., Lee, S., Kim, T., Peinado, M. (2017). T-SGX: Eradicating controlled-channel attacks against enclave programs. In *NDSS 2017*. The Internet Society, San Diego.

Shin, Y., Kim, H. C., Kwon, D., Jeong, J.-H., Hur, J. (2018). Unveiling hardware-based data prefetcher, a hidden source of information leakage. In *ACM CCS 2018*, Lie, D., Mannan, M., Backes, M., Wang, X. (eds). ACM Press, New York.

Shusterman, A., Kang, L., Haskal, Y., Meltser, Y., Mittal, P., Oren, Y., Yarom, Y. (2019). Robust website fingerprinting through the cache occupancy channel. In *USENIX Security 2019*, Heninger, N. and Traynor, P. (eds). USENIX Association, Berkeley.

Shusterman, A., Agarwal, A., O'Connell, S., Genkin, D., Oren, Y., Yarom, Y. (2021). Prime+probe 1, JavaScript 0: Overcoming browser-based side-channel defenses. In *USENIX Security 2021*, Bailey, M. and Greenstadt, R. (eds). USENIX Association, Berkeley.

Tan, Q., Zeng, Z., Bu, K., Ren, K. (2020). PhantomCache: Obfuscating cache conflicts with localized randomization. In *NDSS 2020*. The Internet Society, San Diego.

Tatar, A., Trujillo, D., Giuffrida, C., Bos, H. (2022). TLB;DR: Enhancing TLB-based attacks with TLB desynchronized reverse engineering. In *USENIX Security 2022*, Butler, K.R.B. and Thomas, K. (eds). USENIX Association, Berkeley.

Tsunoo, Y., Tsujihara, E., Minematsu, K., Miyauchi, H. (2002). Cryptanalysis of block ciphers implemented on computers with cache. In *ISITA*, Walter, C.D., Koç, Ç.K., Paar, C. (eds). Springer, Berlin, Heidelberg.

Van Bulck, J., Minkin, M., Weisse, O., Genkin, D., Kasikci, B., Piessens, F., Silberstein, M., Wenisch, T.F., Yarom, Y., Strackx, R. (2018). Foreshadow: Extracting the keys to the Intel SGX kingdom with transient out-of-order execution. In *USENIX Security 2018*, Enck, W. and Felt, A.P. (eds). USENIX Association, Berkeley.

Van Bulck, J., Moghimi, D., Schwarz, M., Lipp, M., Minkin, M., Genkin, D., Yarom, Y., Sunar, B., Gruss, D., Piessens, F. (2020). LVI: Hijacking transient execution through microarchitectural load value injection. In *2020 IEEE Symposium on Security and Privacy*. San Francisco.

Vila, P., Köpf, B., Morales, J.F. (2019). Theory and practice of finding eviction sets. In *2019 IEEE Symposium on Security and Privacy*. San Francisco.

Wan, J., Bi, Y., Zhou, Z., Li, Z. (2022). MeshUp: Stateless cache side-channel attack on CPU mesh. In *2022 IEEE Symposium on Security and Privacy*. San Francisco.

Werner, M., Unterluggauer, T., Giner, L., Schwarz, M., Gruss, D., Mangard, S. (2019). ScatterCache: Thwarting cache attacks via cache set randomization. In *USENIX Security 2019*, Heninger, N. and Traynor, P. (eds). USENIX Association, Berkeley.

Wu, Z., Xu, Z., Wang, H. (2012). Whispers in the hyper-space: High-speed covert channel attacks in the cloud. In *USENIX Security 2012*, Kohno, T. (ed.). USENIX Association, Berkeley.

Xiong, W., Szefer, J. (2021). Survey of transient execution attacks and their mitigations. *Computing Surveys*, 54(3), 1–36.

Yarom, Y. and Falkner, K. (2014). FLUSH+RELOAD: A high resolution, low noise, L3 cache side-channel attack. In *USENIX Security 2014*, Fu, K. and Jung, J. (eds). USENIX Association, Berkeley.

Yarom, Y., Ge, Q., Liu, F., Lee, R.B., Heiser, G. (2015). Mapping the intel last-level cache. Report 2015/905, Cryptology ePrint Archive [Online]. Avalable at: https://eprint.iacr.org/2015/905.

Zhang, Y., Juels, A., Reiter, M.K., Ristenpart, T. (2012). Cross-VM side channels and their use to extract private keys. In *ACM CCS 2012*, Yu, T., Danezis, G., Gligor, V.D. (eds). ACM Press, New York.

Zhang, Y., Juels, A., Reiter, M.K., Ristenpart, T. (2014). Cross-tenant side-channel attacks in PaaS clouds. In *ACM CCS 2014*, Ahn, G.-J., Yung, M., Li, N. (eds). ACM Press, New York.

Zhang, X., Xiao, Y., Zhang, Y. (2016). Return-oriented flush-reload side channels on ARM and their implications for android devices. In *ACM CCS 2016*, Weippl, E.R., Katzenbeisser, S., Kruegel, C., Myers, A.C., Halevi, S. (eds). ACM Press, New York.

Zhang, Z., Barthe, G., Chuengsatiansup, C., Schwabe, P., Yarom, Y. (2023a). Ultimate SLH: Taking speculative load hardening to the next level. In *USENIX Security 2023*. USENIX Association, Berkeley.

Zhang, Z., Tao, M., O'Connell, S., Chuengsatiansup, C., Genkin, D., Yarom, Y. (2023b). BunnyHop: Exploiting the instruction prefetcher. In *USENIX Security 2023*. USENIX Association, Berkeley.

Zhao, X. and Wang, T. (2010). Improved cache trace attack on AES and CLEFIA by considering Cache miss and S-box misalignment. Report 2010/056, Cryptology ePrint Archive [Online]. Available at: https://eprint.iacr.org/2010/056.

Zhao, Z.N., Morrison, A., Fletcher, C.W., Torrellas, J. (2022). Binoculars: Contention-based side-channel attacks exploiting the page walker. In *USENIX Security 2022*, Butler, K.R.B. and Thomas, K. (eds). USENIX Association, Berkeley.

PART 2

Hardware Side-Channel Attacks

3

Leakage and Attack Tools

Davide BELLIZIA[1] and Adrian THILLARD[2]

[1]*Independent researcher, Italy*

[2]*Ledger, Paris, France*

3.1. Introduction

Informative physical leakages have been a primary concern in the design and the implementation of systems processing sensitive information, as it has been widely demonstrated that they provide a huge attack surface for malicious adversaries. When an inherent physical emission can be related to data (or more generally, to operations) manipulated by a secure device, the emission becomes a *side-channel*. Clearly, side-channel analysis and attacks have assumed a primary role in the cryptographic community in the last 20 years, since they do not require expensive equipment to be performed/mounted. In this chapter, we will first introduce the physics behind most common side-channels, discussing what the root causes are that generate informative leakages through measurable emissions and how to capture them. Next, we discuss common and generic models used in side-channel analysis, and we conclude with a brief review of main platforms and tools available for investigating side-channel attacks, focusing on open-hardware and/or open-source ones.

3.2. Data-dependent physical emissions

As the first paper regarding the exploitation of informative physical emission was published 1996 by Paul Kocher, the cryptographic community has started to increasingly intensify the effort in investigating *side-channel analysis* to recover

Embedded Cryptography 1,
coordinated by Emmanuel PROUFF, Guénaël RENAULT,
Matthieu RIVAIN and Colin O'FLYNN.

information from computational systems. In this section, we discuss the physics behind most common side-channels, such as power consumption and electromagnetic emissions.

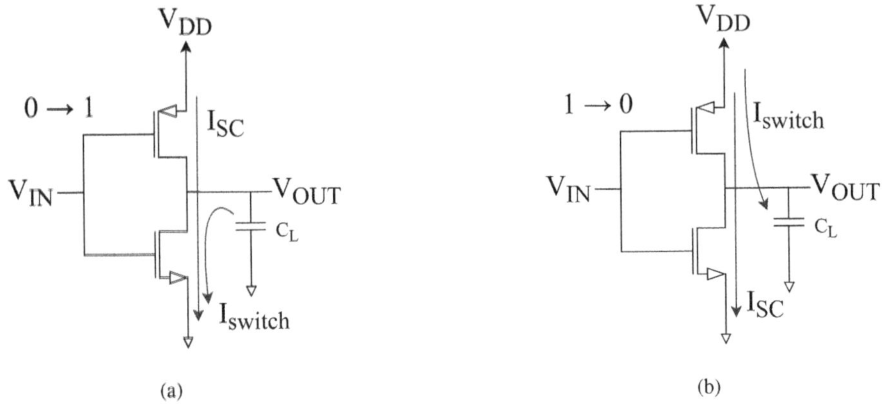

Figure 3.1. *Dynamic currents in a CMOS inverter gate due to* $0 \rightarrow 1$ *(a) and* $1 \rightarrow 0$ *(b) input transitions. For a color version of this figure, see www.iste.co.uk/prouff/cryptography1.zip*

3.2.1. *Dynamic power*

The dynamic power consumption of a complementary metal-oxide-semiconductor (CMOS) circuit is defined as the fraction of the total power that is due to charge/discharge events (switching) in a logic circuit. As suggested by its name, the dynamic power consumption is related to the dynamic behavior of a CMOS circuit, as shown in Figures 3.1 and 3.2. The dynamic component of the overall power consumption is given by the sum of two main components:

$$P_{dyn} = P_{SC} + P_{switch} \quad [3.1]$$

where P_{SC} is the *short-circuit power* and P_{switch} is the *switching power*.

The *short-circuit power* is due to non-ideal effects in CMOS gates. By construction, each CMOS gate is composed of a PMOS pull-up network, which is responsible in providing a charging path for the output capacitance to V_{DD}, and a NMOS pull-down network, which allows the output capacitance to discharge toward ground. Depending on the combination of input values, only one network at a time is connected to its respective power rail, and, in general, no direct path between V_{DD} and ground exists. Nevertheless, since real signals have finite rise and fall times, during transitions of the output state of a cell, both pull-up and pull-down networks provide a resistive path between the power rails for a short time, as shown in Figure 3.2. When this situation occurs, an impulse of current is drawn from V_{DD} directly to ground. We refer to this current as the *short-circuit current* i_{SC}. This phenomenon is usually observable for both output transitions. The associated *short-circuit power* consumed in a period of elaboration T is expressed as follows:

$$P_{SC} = \frac{1}{T} \cdot \int_0^T V_{DD} i_{SC}(t)dt \qquad [3.2]$$

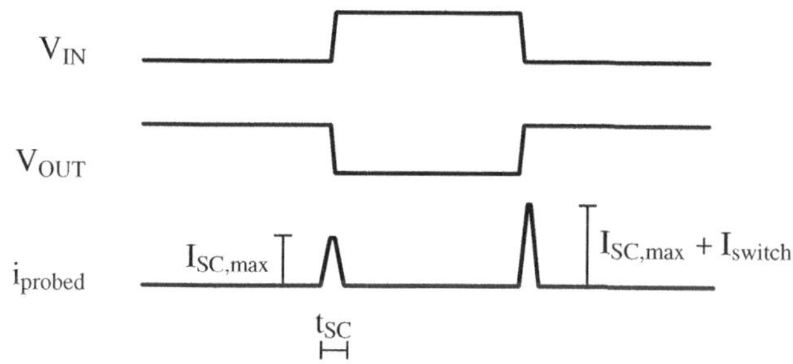

Figure 3.2. *Current consumption in a CMOS inverter (seen from V_{DD})*

If we assume that short-circuit current in a CMOS gate is a triangular shaped pulse with base t_{SC} and height $I_{SC,max}$, the short-circuit power can also be expressed as follows:

$$P_{SC} = \frac{V_{DD} \cdot t_{SC} \cdot I_{SC,max} \cdot \alpha_T}{T} \qquad [3.3]$$

where α_T is the *switching activity* of the gate that represents the probability that a transition of a net occurs within a clock period T. As it is clear, P_{SC} depends linearly on the operating frequency and the switching activity as well as on the power supply voltage. The *switching* power represents the most important component in dynamic consumption, as it directly relates to charge/discharge events of the output capacitance of a CMOS gate, as well to its output value. In the $0 \rightarrow 1$ transition, the output capacitance is charged to V_{DD} through the pull-up network that provides a resistive path, while the ground rail is isolated as the pull-down network is disabled. The current absorbed due to this charging event is provided from the power rail. During the opposite transition $1 \rightarrow 0$, the pull-down network offers a resistive path from the output note to ground. The output capacitance discharges toward the ground, and no extra current is absorbed from V_{DD} in this case. The average switching power can be expressed similarly to the short-circuit power, adopting one period of elaboration as reference time window. For each possible j configuration of inputs, with $j = 1, ..., N$, we can express the jth *switching power* of the circuit as:

$$P^j_{switch} = \frac{1}{T}\int_0^T V_{DD} \cdot i^j_{switch} dt = V^2_{DD} \cdot f_{CLK} \cdot C_L \cdot Pr^j_{0\to1} \qquad [3.4]$$

where $Pr^j_{0\to1}$ is the probability that a $0 \to 1$ output transition occurs for the given jth input combination in T and C_L is the output load capacitance. If we define the switching activity α_T as $\sum_{j=1}^{N} Pr^j_{0\to1}/N$, we can define the average *switching power* as:

$$P_{switch} = \frac{1}{N}\sum_{j=1}^{N} P^j_{switch} = V^2_{DD} \cdot C_L \cdot f_{CLK} \cdot \alpha_T \qquad [3.5]$$

It is clear from equations [3.3] and [3.5] that the activity of a CMOS circuit is tightly coupled with the dynamic power consumption of the circuit itself. This aspect is clearly critical from a security perspective, as it represents a source of information leakage for a malicious adversary that could eavesdrop information by monitoring the instantaneous power consumption of a CMOS circuit. Without loss of generality, we can observe that the power consumption absorbed by a CMOS inverter can represent a valuable source of information leakage, as it provides information about its input/output state, as reported in Table 3.1. This behavior is not restricted to a CMOS inverter but can be generalized to more complicated gates and circuits, as widely discussed in literature.

Transition	Dynamic power	Static power
$0 \to 0$	0	$P_{static,0}$
$0 \to 1$	P_{SC}	$P_{static,1}$
$1 \to 0$	$P_{SC} + P_{switch}$	$P_{static,0}$
$1 \to 1$	0	$P_{static,1}$

Table 3.1. *Power consumption of a CMOS inverter gate observed from the V_{DD} rail*

3.2.2. *Static power*

With the aggressive down-scaling of CMOS technologies, geometrical features of transistors in integrated circuits have been reduced into the nanometer scale, and several second-order effects such as reverse bias-pn junction leakage, sub-threshold leakage, drain-induced barrier lowering (DIBL) and threshold voltage (V_{TH}) roll-off are no longer negligible as source of static power absorption. Their role in the power budget of integrated circuits has started to become a non-secondary concern in the design of new devices, especially for dependable applications. It has been widely demonstrated in many security and non-security works how static power in CMOS circuits is correlated with processed data, and clearly it represents a concrete side-channel to recover sensitive information from cryptographic implementations. Among aforementioned physical effects that impact on the generation on parasitic static currents, sub-threshold leakage I_{sub} is the most representative in deep-scaled technologies (<100 nm). I_{sub} in a MOS transistor depends on several factors, and a comprehensive model of this current is given by:

$$I_{sub} \approx K \cdot \frac{W}{L} \cdot e^{\frac{V_{GS}-(V_{TH}-\eta V_{DS}+\gamma V_{SB})}{n V_T}} \cdot \left(1 - e^{\frac{-V_{DS}}{V_T}}\right) \qquad [3.6]$$

where W and L are the gate width and length, respectively; V_{GS}, V_{DS} and V_{SB} denote the gate-source voltage, the drain-source voltage and the source-body voltage. K, η and γ are technology-dependent constants and V_T is the thermal voltage given by:

$$V_T = \frac{kT}{q} \qquad [3.7]$$

where k is the Boltzmann's constant, T is the absolute temperature and q is the electrical charge of the electron.

It is worth noting that from a digital perspective, the input state of a transistor, and more generally of a gate, has impact on such power absorption component. Research activity dealing with the relationship between the static power consumption and input state of circuits has been triggered by the necessity to reduce the power requirement, especially in battery-operated devices implemented with deep-scaled devices, where idle time may represent a huge portion of the lifecycle of the device itself. Starting from 2007, also security-related works have shown that it is possible to exploit this correlation to extract and recovery sensitive data, leading to a novel class of side-channel methodologies denoted as *leakage power analysis* (LPA), also referred to as *attack exploiting static power* (AESP). In most common cases, the overall static power of a CMOS circuit can be approximated easily with linear models (e.g. Hamming Weight) of data at its input.

Compared to the dynamic case, static power analysis is characterized by a different adversarial model. In particular, a major difference is represented by the fact that measuring static power consumption requires that the adversary has the ability to control the clock signal, with the additional ability to stop it freely, as shown in

Figure 3.3. This assumption is widely used in this specific context, and a recent work (see notes and further references) has shown that this requirement may be relaxed in some scenarios; eventually, it is required that the target intermediate variable is stable for *enough* time to be exploited.

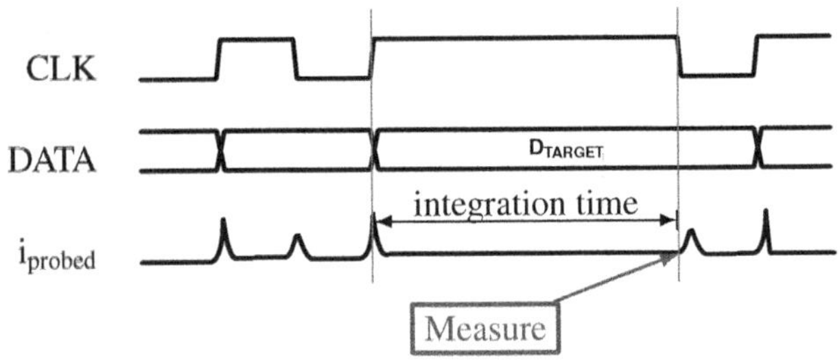

Figure 3.3. *Static power measurement by stopping the clock signal CLK. For a color version of this figure, see www.iste.co.uk/prouff/cryptography1.zip*

3.2.3. *Electro-magnetic emissions*

Clearly, power consumption is a direct consequence of currents flowing through an integrated circuit, but it is not the only (measurable) one. It has to be noted that a current flowing through a wire generates a magnetic field. The Biot–Savart's law describes the magnetic field $d\vec{B}$ at a distance r due to an element $d\vec{l}$ of wire carrying a stationary current I as follows:

$$d\vec{B} = \frac{\mu_0}{4\pi} \cdot I \cdot \frac{d\vec{l} \times \vec{r}}{r^3} \qquad [3.8]$$

where μ_0 is the magnetic permeability of free space (we are assuming no medium between the current-carrying wire and the observation point) and $\vec{r}$ is the vector specifying the distance between the wire element and the observation point P. Assuming that we measure the magnetic field with a simple coil loop probe (we assume a single turn probe for simplicity), any variation of the current in time will induce a voltage at the loop's opening expressed as follows:

$$V_{loop} = -\frac{d\phi}{dt} = \int_{surface} \vec{B} \cdot d\vec{A} \qquad [3.9]$$

where ϕ is the magnetic flux through the loop and A is its surface. As the Biot–Savart's law gives an inverse-cubic relation of the measured magnetic field with the distance, it is clear that the closer the probe is to the source of current flowing, the stronger the signal. From a side-channel perspective, variations in the magnetic field surrounding an integrated circuit due to its activity may provide useful information to a malicious adversary, and *near-field* measurements are usually required. In addition, a non-static magnetic field induces variations in the electric field, due to Maxwell's equations, and, therefore, it is common to refer to this side-channel analysis methodology as *electro-magnetic analysis* (EMA).

From the discussion above, we can observe that the EMA offers some different advantages compared to power analysis. In CMOS-integrated circuits, current peaks are usually observed during data transitions, as shown above, and they are characterized by very steep transients. Hence, the derivative of these peaks is quite high, and measurable in the proximity of the area where a data transition occurs. These aspects have important consequences (that hold in general):

– It is possible to find a relationship between data transitions and changes in the magnetic field, leading to an informative side-channel leakage.

– In many cases, the presence of this informative leakage may suggest where the data transition occurs in a "spatial" sense.

Compared to the power side-channel, which, in general, gives to the adversary a "general view" of the activity of the integrated circuit, the electromagnetic emission may provide useful information about where the leakage is generated.

3.2.4. *Other sources of physical leakages*

Power consumption and electromagnetic emissions are the most explored side-channels in the physical security literature in nearly two decades. Clearly, these physical emissions are not the only ones that have been exploited to recover useful information and sensitive data from integrated circuits and processing systems.

One of the most noteworthy side-channels is represented by the execution time, leading to *timing analysis*. In general, when the execution flow of an application is data dependent, the execution time of the application itself provides information regarding processed data. The classical example is the school-book implementation of the modular exponentiation (also called *square-and-multiply*) used for Diffie–Hellmann and RSA private-key operations that has been documented in the seminal work of Paul Kocher from 1996. In this simple, but yet explicative, example, bits of the key directly impact on which operation is performed, as shown in Algorithm 3.1.

As it is clear, monitoring the execution time, the bits of the key can be inferred and the secret can be revealed. Clearly, this methodology can be applied to a plethora of other algorithms, such as elliptic curve cryptography ones.

Algorithm 3.1. Square-and-Multiply

Input: $M, n, k = (k_{w-1}, k_{w-2}, ..., k_0)$
Output: $C = M^k \mod n$
$C = 1$
for $j = w-1, w-2, ..., 0$ **do**
  $C = C^2 \mod n$ **if** $k_j = 1$ **then**
    $C = C \cdot M \mod n$
return C

The physics behind CMOS-integrated circuits offers a number of possibilities to extract sensitive information. When a MOS transistor is conducting, carriers gain kinetic energy due to the source-drain electric field. This electric field is not uniform, and it is very intense in the region nearby the drain, where the energy of the carrier can be released as a photon. It has to be noted that this release is more dominant in n-type transistors due to the higher mobility of the electrons[1]. Therefore, this luminescence in CMOS technology may lead to a data-dependent behavior similar to power consumption, implying the existence of a side-channel. As integrated circuits are usually made up of layers of interconnecting metals, this photonic emission is hardly observable from the top-side of a device. A good spot to observe such emission may be the back-side of the chip, which usually needs to be firstly de-capsulated, meaning that the passivation layer has to be removed, and thinned, in order to reduce the filtering effect offered by the silicon substrate, as it absorbs wavelength shorter than silicon's band-gap energy. For this analysis methodology, mainly near-infrared (NIR) photons are used to extract information. In general, optical side-channels offer advantages similar to EMA, meaning that they also include the *locality* feature to the observed leakage, but frequently require expensive equipment (e.g. lasers and detectors).

Also, acoustic waves emitted from devices while operating has been used as a side-channel. A simple example comes from the activity of the cooling fan of a CPU. When the CPU performs heavy operations, it is straightforward to assume that its temperature raises from the idle condition, leading to the fan spinning at a higher rate to compensate the excessive heat. This dependency can be exploited to recover the operation flow and key bits. Similarly to the simple modular exponentiation case, for algorithms that have a tight coupling between operation flow and processed data, the the acoustic side-channel is an eligible attack vector, also leading to remote probing with directional microphones. We remark that these kinds of side-channel usually offer very limited bandwidth, which is usually in the range of tens of kilohertz, and its applicability is limited compared to power and EM emissions.

1 Electrons are carriers in n-type transistors.

3.3. Measuring a side-channel

Capturing information by means of side-channel is not trivial. This important step in the evaluation (or in the attack) of a device is critical under many points of view, as it carries hard to quantify risks of security overstatement. Clearly, noisy or badly designed measurement setups may lead evaluators to conclude that their implementations or their devices are less informative than what they actually are, hence, providing a false sense of assurance. However, this important aspect of the physical security has not been thoroughly investigated in literature, and only a few works discuss the impact it has on the overall level of security of devices (see notes and further references). In this section, we discuss the importance of the "measuring act". In particular, we recall the basic power analysis measurement setup and give further details about probing methods for power and EM analysis.

3.3.1. *Power analysis setup*

We refer to the heterogeneous system devoted to capture and record side-channel observations as a *measurement setup*. In Figure 3.4, we show a typical power analysis measurement setup model. We motivate this particular choice by observing that power consumption is one of the most popular side-channel among the physical security community, and the classical measurement setup for power analysis shares a common "ground" with others. A bit more precisely, the current absorbed by the device under test (DUT) is first monitored by a probe, which has the role to convert the current signal into a voltage signal. This signal can then be amplified using a *preamplifier stage* in order to increase its magnitude, mitigate noise in the measurements and improve electrical characteristics for the following blocks. At the end of the so-called measurement chain, a digital storage oscilloscope (DSO) samples and quantizes the analog voltage signal, converting it into a specific digital representation. Usually, the sampling operation is started by a trigger event (or a trigger signal), in order to synchronize different measurements and ease the analysis/exploitation of the observed side-channel. The choice of these components and how they interact with each other impact (e.g. impedance mismatch, saturation of analog front-ends and undersampling) sensibly on the final outcome of the practical side-channel security evaluation of a leaking implementation.

3.3.2. *Probes and probing methodologies*

One of the most critical part of a side-channel measurement setup is represented by the probe. As discussed above, the probe has the role to convert the side-channel observation into a voltage signal, and from an electronic point of view, it can be considered as the first block in the measurement chain. In this section, we discuss this critical "block" in the measurement chain. More in details, we introduce the two main techniques to measure power consumption for power analysis, and we give some general characteristics regarding electromagnetic probes.

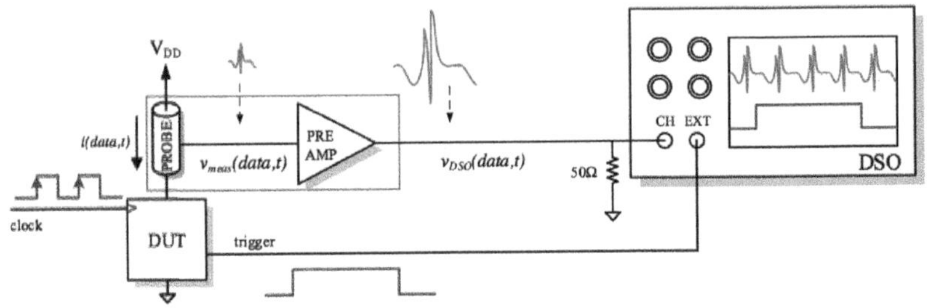

Figure 3.4. *Generic power analysis setup model. For a color version of this figure, see www.iste.co.uk/prouff/cryptography1.zip*

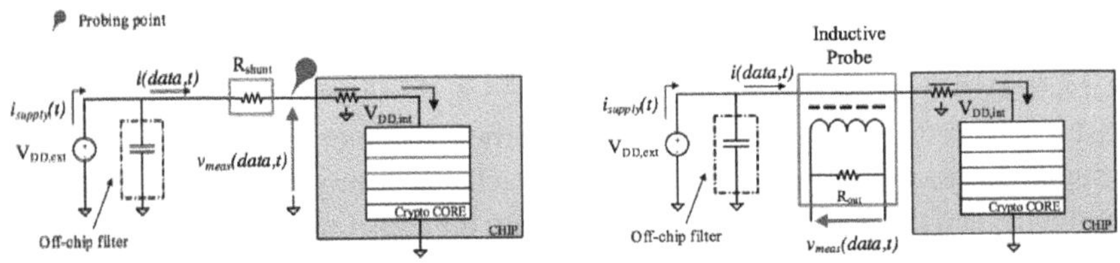

(a) (b)

Figure 3.5. *Probing methodologies for power analysis measure: shunt resistor (a) and inductive probing (b). For a color version of this figure, see www.iste.co.uk/prouff/cryptography1.zip*

3.3.2.1. *Shunt resistor*

The current absorption of the DUT is simply measured as a voltage burden across a resistor, as shown in Figure 3.5(a), exploiting Ohm's law:

$$v_{meas}(data, t) = -i(data, t)R_{drop} \qquad [3.10]$$

where R_{drop} is the value of the *probing* resistor, $v_{meas}(data, t)$ is the voltage measured across the resistor and $i(data, t)$ is the current absorbed by the DUT. Intuitively, the higher the value of R_{drop}, the higher the signal will be, but the larger the voltage burden across it. In this condition, the DUT may experience some malfunctioning (e.g. brown reset and impossibility to boot). In addition, the shunt resistor acts also as a thermal noise generator, for which the magnitude of the power spectral density increases linearly with the value of the resistor.

3.3.2.2. *Inductive probe*

An inductive probe is a current transformer where the input circuit (the line the evaluator/adversary wants to probe) acts as a primary coil, and its output (e.g. input of the preamplifier stage or DSO's analog front-end) corresponds to the secondary coil. Therefore, based on the mutual inductance between the two coils of the current transformer, the inductive probe can sense the current in the primary coil and generate a proportional current in the secondary coil. If the secondary coil is terminated on a resistance, a voltage signal proportional to the sensed current on the primary coil is generated on the output of the probe. Usually, the output voltage signal is given as follows:

$$v_{meas}(data, t) = i_{data,t} \cdot TZ_{R_{out}} \qquad [3.11]$$

where $TZ_{R_{out}}$ is the transimpedence of the probe on the output impedance (a typical output impedance is 50Ω). The probed line and the oscilloscope are galvanically isolated, since there is no electrical connection between them. On the other hand, the mutual inductance introduces a small inductive parasitic on the probed circuit. Ensuring that the lead wire that is used to monitor the current absorbed by the DUT is short (most cases, $\sim$5cm is sufficient), the introduced parasitic is practically negligible, ensuring a clean probing of the power consumption. We must point out that probing with the inductive method has a drawback in the case of an evaluator/adversary wanting to observe a very low frequency spectrum (50 kHz). Since the probe acts as a transformer, the bandwidth between the DC and lower cut-off frequency of the probe is rejected. On the other hand, with this probing technique, it is not possible to monitor static power consumption, since low frequency signals are cut-off (DC up to 100 kHz).

3.3.2.3. *Electro-magnetic probes*

Probes and probing methodology are even more critical in measurement setups for EM analysis, due to the nature of weaker signals involved. As discussed above, EM emissions allow evaluators/adversaries to collect information in a localized area of the DUT (which may extend to the printed circuit board on which it is mounted). In most common settings, the antenna is placed as close as possible to the DUT to minimize the influence from a non-targeted area of the chip and thus reducing unwanted *algorithmic* noise, and decapsulation of the silicon die is sometimes required to improve the quality of the signal. Intuitively, the analysis of EM emissions of deep-scaled technologies, where geometrical features are shrunk down to the nanometer scale and integrated circuits tend to be more *dense*, may benefit from shorter resolution antennas.

3.4. Leakage modeling

3.4.1. *Mathematical modeling*

Side-channel traces are measurements of physical phenomena occurring within the targeted device. While we described the electronic origins of these leakages in the previous section, a mathematical model is required in order to gain a sound understanding of exactly how these traces relate to the data being manipulated.

State of the art models rely on two basic hypotheses:

– *Only computation leaks*: every time any data Z is used to perform any computation $f(Z)$ in the executed algorithm, this computation can leak and hence be measured. However, anytime any data are not processed by the algorithm, it will not leak and hence will not appear on side-channel measurements.

– *Additive noise*: for any data Z being processed, the leakage can be written as the sum of a deterministic function of Z and a random noise. This noise can come from many sources, such as the measurement of unrelated physical phenomena in the target, or the accuracy of our setup, probes, scopes, filters, etc.

To summarize, a side-channel trace L can be seen as a sequence of points l each representing some computation on some data. Each of these points can be modeled as a sum $l = m(Z) + \mathcal{N}$, where m is some deterministic function on the manipulated data Z and $\mathcal{N}$ is a random noise.

In the following, we will propose specific instantiations for the deterministic model m and random noise $\mathcal{N}$. All of the following models are close approximations of some real physical behavior.

3.4.1.1. *Hamming weight model*

In order to get an informal intuition of a realistic choice for the deterministic part m, we propose to consider an 8-bit register, preloaded at a null value.

0	0	0	0	0	0	0	0

Now, let us consider that a value $Z = 0b10011100$ is moved into this register. This operation induces the modification of some bits of the register. As stated in the previous section, and summarized in Table 3.1, each of these modifications imply some energy ϵ.

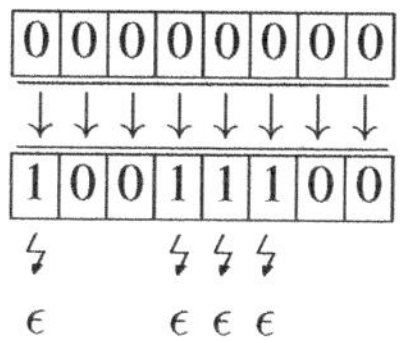

A perfect measure of the physical phenomenon associated with this operation would therefore equal 4ϵ. A simple generalization to any value Z would induce a measure of ϵ times the number of set bits of Z. This latter notion is called the Hamming weight of Z and is denoted $HW(Z)$. Hence, we can set $m = HW$, and determinate that:

$$l = \epsilon \cdot HW(Z) + \mathcal{N}. \qquad [3.12]$$

3.4.1.2. *Hamming distance model*

The Hamming distance model considers that registers are not preloaded at the null value, and that successive values erase each other. As an illustration, let us consider the register loaded with a value $Z = 0b10011100$.

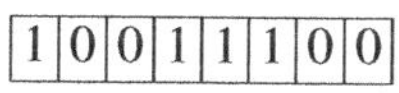

Now, let us consider that a value $Z' = 0b11000011$ is moved into this register. This operation induces the modification of some bits of the register, and each of these modifications imply some energy ϵ.

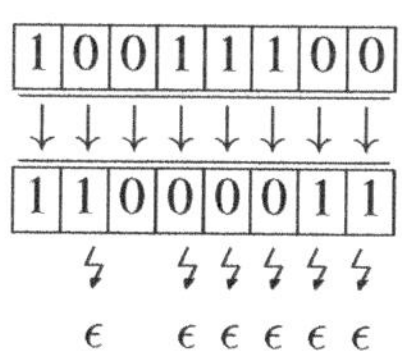

A perfect measure of the physical phenomenon associated with this operation would hence be 6ϵ. A simple generalization to any values Z, Z' would induce a measure of ϵ times the number of differing bits of Z and Z'. This later notion is called the Hamming distance of Z and is denoted $HD(Z, Z')$. Note that this can also be computed using the Hamming weight: $HD(Z, Z') = HW(Z \oplus Z')$. Hence, we can set $m = HD$, and determinate that:

$$l = \epsilon \cdot HD(Z, Z') + \mathcal{N}. \qquad [3.13]$$

In most cases, the literature simplifies Hamming weight and Hamming distance models by considering that $\epsilon = 1$. This simplification is most of the time done without loss of generality, since the statistical tools and proofs are invariant with respect to linear factors. Depending on the model, it allows us to write: $l = HW(Z) + \mathcal{N}$ or $l = HD(Z, Z') + \mathcal{N}$.

3.4.1.3. *Weighted sum of bits*

We can increase the complexity of the model by relaxing the assumption that every bit leaks the same value ϵ, and, instead, consider that a modification of each bit of index i will induce a different energy ϵ_i.

By using the assumption of a register preloaded to a null value, and the move of the value $Z = 0b10011100$.

0	0	0	0	0	0	0	0

Now, let us consider that a value $Z = 0b10010100$ is moved into this register. Once again, this operation induces the modification of some bits of the register, and each of these modifications imply some energy ϵ.

0	0	0	0	0	0	0	0
↓	↓	↓	↓	↓	↓	↓	↓
1	0	0	1	0	1	0	0
ϟ			ϟ		ϟ		
ϵ_0			ϵ_3		ϵ_5		

Generalizing to any value Z, written in binary $(z_0, z_1, z_2, z_3, z_4, z_5, z_6, z_7)$, the leakage would then be:

$$l = \sum_{i=0}^{7} \epsilon_i z_i + \mathcal{N}. \qquad [3.14]$$

3.4.1.4. *Polynomial model*

We can yet again increase the complexity by relaxing the linear assumption and consider *coupling* effects, that is, the modification of several bits at the same time can have a nonlinear effect. The deterministic part of the leakage is hence considered as a polynomial of degree $d \leq 8$ in the bits $(z_0, z_1, z_2, z_3, z_4, z_5, z_6, z_7)$, with associated energies $\epsilon_i, \epsilon_{i,j}, \epsilon_{i,j,k} \dots$

For example, a polynomial model of degree $d = 2$ would be:

$$l = \sum_{i=0}^{7} \epsilon_i z_i + \sum_{i=0,j=0;i!=j}^{7,7} \epsilon_{i,j} z_i z_j + \mathcal{N}. \qquad [3.15]$$

Contrary to the case of Hamming weight or Hamming distance, the weighted sum of bits models and polynomial model often require the estimation of the values ϵ_i. This estimation can be costly, especially when the degree of the polynomial is high. This drawback sometimes prevents attackers from using this approach in practical settings, but is a model of choice for designers aiming at gaining a solid understanding of their device.

3.4.1.5. *Noise*

Most literature model the random noise as following a normal distribution. This assumption stems from the observation that the noise is actually the sum of several physical phenomena occurring in the device, as well as some unpredictable error due to the model. Applying a strong version of the central limit theorem, we know that the sum of these independent random variables converges toward a normal distribution.

This model has been observed to match experiments quite well.

3.4.2. *Signal-to-noise ratio*

As underlined by the mathematical modeling, any point of the side-channel measurement contains some information about some data Z, but it also contains a certain amount of noise. Statistical tools can help to quantify this information, find relevant points of interest and validate a model.

The most commonly used tool is the *signal-to-noise ratio* (SNR). For any point l, SNR computes a ratio between the estimated signal and noise in the following way:

$$SNR(l, Z) = \frac{V[E[l|Z]]}{E[[V[l|Z]]]}, \qquad [3.16]$$

where E and V, respectively, denote the expectation and variance.

In practice, the expectation and variance are estimated because of a large number of acquired traces.

In order to validate a model m, the SNR can trivially be adapted and computed as:

$$SNR(l, m(Z)) = \frac{V[E[l|m(Z)]]}{E[[V[l|m(Z)]]]}. \qquad [3.17]$$

As an example, we will compute different SNRs on the following curve, which represents the beginning of an AES:

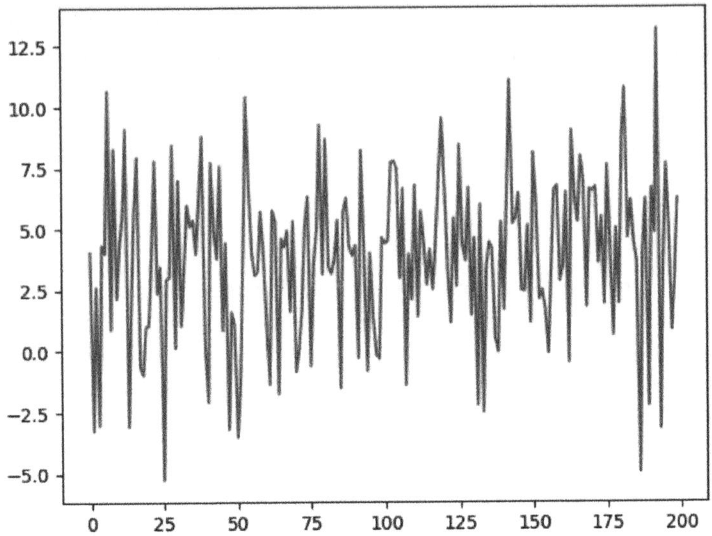

Figure 3.6. *Example side-channel trace: beginning of an AES*

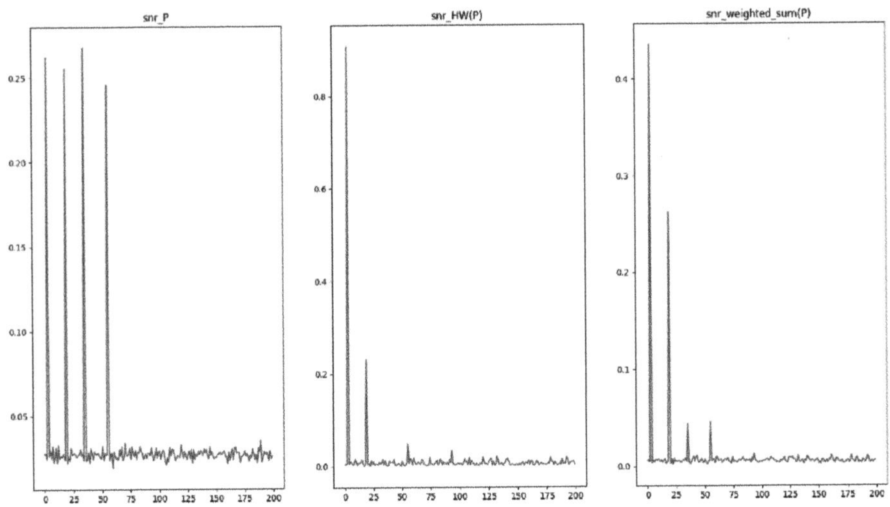

Figure 3.7. *Example side-channel trace: SNR results. Left to right: plaintext, Hamming weight of plaintext, some weighted sum of bits*

The SNR results, shown in Figure 3.7, have been computed on one byte of the plaintext, on its Hamming weight and on an arbitrarily weighted sum of its bits.

From these results, we can draw some preliminaries conclusions. Four points strongly depend on the plaintext; among those, the first one is the most informative, and the last two do not seem to really relate to the plaintext, but more likely to some bijective function of it (e.g. an SBOX). The most promising model seems to be the Hamming weight.

3.4.3. *Open source boards*

Several boards are commercially available to perform side-channel measurements. We hereafter describe some of them, available at least partially in open source and/or open hardware. An illustration of these boards can be seen in Figure 3.8.

Figure 3.8. *Three boards described in this chapter. From the top and clockwise: ChipWhispererPro, LEIA and Scaffold. For a color version of this figure, see: www.iste.co.uk/prouff/cryptography1.zip*

3.4.3.1. *ChipWhisperer*

Developed by NewAE Technology, ChipWhisperer comes in different flavors: Nano, Lite or Pro.

In each case, ChipWhisperer is a complete open source toolchain for learning about side-channel attacks and fault injection on embedded devices and validating the resistance of these devices. In particular, ChipWhisperer focuses on power analysis. Some versions also enable voltage and clock glitching attacks, which briefly disrupt a device's power or clock to cause unintended behavior.

More information about ChipWhisperer can be found at: https://chipwhisperer.readthedocs.io/en/latest/.

3.4.3.2. *ChipWhisperer Nano*

The ChipWhisperer Nano is the lowest cost platform for performing side-channel power analysis attacks in training and educational environments. It comes with a STM32F030F4P6 built-in target that can be cut and replaced by other external targets. Note that 8-bit ADC with 20 MS/s sampling rate and fixed-gain front-end allows measurements of on-board and some external targets.

3.4.3.3. *ChipWhisperer Lite*

The ChipWhisperer Lite is fully open source (hardware, software, firmware and FPGA code). It integrates hardware for performing power analysis measurement, device programming, glitching, serial communication and an example target that can be loaded with cryptographic algorithms. The single-board version comes in two variants: Atmel XMEGA or STM32F3 Arm target. The capture and target side can be broken apart and connected to other targets. Note that 10-bit ADC with 105 MS/s sampling rate, combined with up to +55 dB gain amplifier, allow for the measurement of small signals.

3.4.3.4. *ChipWhisperer Pro*

The ChipWhisperer Pro has been designed to remain compatible with existing ChipWhisperer Lite interfaces, but adds new features thanks to a larger internal FPGA. It has a larger internal and adds a streaming mode for huge captures at slower speeds, plus a pattern-based trigger for working with real hardware targets. Programmers for XMEGA (PDI) and STM32Fx (serial bootloader) targets are built-in. Note that 10-bit ADC with 105 MS/s sampling rate, combined with up to +55 dB gain amplifier, allow for the measurement of small signals.

3.4.3.5. *LEIA*

Developed by H2Lab, LEIA is targeted toward smart cards targets. It is an open hardware and open source device designed for educational and evaluation purposes. It implements a fully controlled ISO7816 stack with a dedicated custom hardware platform to acquire measurements for SCA characterization. The LEIA board is made up of two main parts: a STM32 MCU that contains the firmware handling the ISO7816-3 stack, and the ISO7816-3 connector that communicates with the target smart card (i.e. handling the physical connection) and is isolated with optocouplers for clean measurements. Having a fully controlled ISO7816 stack allows us to position precise triggers at dedicated events (sending an APDU, receiving the response, etc.), which helps to get synchronized traces of power consumption activity. Low-level access to the ISO7816-3 protocol also allows us to explore interesting paths such as smart cards conformity checks, etc.

More information about LEIA can be found at: https://h2lab.org/devices/leia/boards_leia/.

3.4.3.6. *Scaffold*

Developed by Ledger, Scaffold is an open source, open hardware electronic motherboard designed to quickly setup, instrument and test circuits. The board can be controlled through USB using a Python3 API, enabling easy development of tests. The FPGA architecture runs at 100 MHz and embeds many peripherals: UART, I2C, ISO7816, SPI, power supply controllers, delay and pulse generators with 10 ns resolution, chaining modules for advanced triggering, and clock generator with glitching feature. The board also integrates an 11X analog amplifier with 200 MHz bandwidth for power measurement. The on-board shunt resistor can be tuned from 0 to 100 ohms. Scaffold is able to operate from 1.5 to 3.3 V devices: power supplies and I/O bank voltage can be tuned thanks to adjustable voltage regulators. Scaffold is also fault-injection friendly, and embeds four special I/Os able to generate 5 V pulses, which are compatible with ALPhANOV PDM laser sources.

More information about Scaffold can be found at: https://github.com/Ledger-Donjon/scaffold.

3.4.4. *Open source libraries for attacks*

Several open source projects allow for the statistical treatment of side-channel data, from simple manipulation of the traces, computation of SNRs, to more evolved attacks that we will describe in the following chapters. We propose hereafter to shortly present some of these open source tools.

3.4.4.1. *Daredevil*

Daredevil is a library, part of the *Side-Channel Marvels* developed by Philippe Teuwen in C++. It allows us to perform (higher-order) correlation power analysis.

Daredevil can be downloaded at: https://github.com/SideChannelMarvels/Daredevil/.

3.4.4.2. *Jlsca*

Jlsca is a library developed by several Riscure's employees in Julia. It allows for the computation of lots of side-channel analyses and trace processing.

Julia can be downloaded at: https://github.com/Riscure/Jlsca.

3.4.4.3. *Lascar*

Lascar is a library developed by Ledger in python. It allows for the computation of lots of side-channel analyses and trace processing. It mainly relies on packages numba, numpy and scipy.

Lascar can be downloaded at: https://github.com/Ledger-Donjon/lascar.

3.4.4.4. *SCALib*

SCALib is a library developed by Université Catholique de Louvain. It is especially focused on an advanced side-channel attack called SASCAgraph, which combines information on several intermediate values to recover the secret key.

SCALib can be downloaded at: https://scalib.readthedocs.io/en/latest/index.html.

3.4.4.5. *SCAred*

SCAred is a library developed by eShard in python with a C extension for signal processing. It allows for the computation of lots of side-channel analyses and trace processing. It mainly relies on packages cython, numba, numpy, scipy, as well as estraces, an eShard library for manipulating side-channel traces.

SCAred can be downloaded at: https://gitlab.com/eshard/scared.

3.5. Notes and further references

– Section 3.2.1. The first publication that formally defines the side-channel as a concrete cryptographic attack class has been published by Kocher (1996). One of the reference books for side-channel analysis, and in particular power analysis, is Mangard et al. (2007).

– Section 3.2.2. Static power consumption has been the target of many works in literature, as it involves technological problems (Halter and Najm 1997; Narendra and Chandrakasan 2005), as well as security issues (Bellizia et al. 2017; Karimi et al. 2019; Bellizia et al. 2021b). A more accurate sub-threshold current's model (see equation [3.6]) is reported in Narendra and Chandrakasan (2005). A formal definition of the AESP is reported in Bellizia et al. (2017). In Moos (2019), how the requirement regarding the ability of the adversary to stop the clock to measure the static power can be relaxed in some scenarios.

– Section 3.2.3. Quisquater and Samyde formally define the Electro-Magnetic Analysis for the first time in 2001 (Quisquater and Samyde 2001).

– Section 3.2.4. In the seminal paper by Kocher (1996), the existence of the data-dependence in the execution time of several public-key cryptographic primitives is exploited to retrieve key material. More details regarding the emission of photons within conductive state of MOS transistors are reported in Villa et al. (1995). An example of an acoustic attack against RSA implementations running on laptops is detailed in Genkin et al. (2014).

– Section 3.3. The reader interested in learning more about the impact of the design of the measurement setup on the overall security level of devices is referred to the following papers: Guilley et al. (2011); Merino Del Pozo and Standaert (2017); Wittke et al. (2018); Moos et al. (2020) and Bellizia et al. (2021b). As this aspect is very relevant to evaluate the security level of devices, we also advise the ISO/IEC 20082-1 and ISO/IEC 20082-2 as further readings.

– Section 3.3.2.1. A variant of the shunt resistor methodology presented in this chapter is also described in the IEC 61967-4 standard.

– Section 3.3.2.3. In the field of electromagnetic analysis, several works have discussed about the importance on the choice of the probe (Mulder 2010; Wittke et al. 2018), remarking how this aspect is strictly fundamental to the outcome of the evaluation. In addition to characteristics like sensitivity and bandwidth, antennas for near-field probing are usually categorized according to their spatial features, such as resolution (usually given in μm).

– Section 3.4.1. The *Only Computation Leaks* assumption was introduced by Micali and Reyzin (2004).

– Section 3.4.3.1. The ChipWhisperer boards have notably been used by Joe Grand to glitch and successfully recover more than US$2 million in funds in a hardware wallet (Grand 2022).

– Section 3.4.3.5. The Leia board has notably been used by the Swedish Royal Instute of Technology to recover the key of USIM cards (Brisfors et al. 2020).

– Section 3.4.3.6. The Scaffold board has notably been used by Ledger to break PIN verifications on hardware wallets (Guillemet et al. 2019; Pedro 2020).

3.6. References

Bellizia, D., Bongiovanni, S., Monsurrò, P., Scotti, G., Trifiletti, A. (2017). Univariate power analysis attacks exploiting static dissipation of nanometer CMOS VLSI circuits for cryptographic applications. *IEEE Trans. Emerg. Top. Comput.*, 5(3), 329–339. doi: 10.1109/TETC.2016.2563322.

Bellizia, D., Sala, R.D., Scotti, G. (2021a). SC-DDPL as a countermeasure against static power side-channel attacks. *Cryptogr.*, 5(3), 16.

Bellizia, D., Udvarhelyi, B., Standaert, F.-X. (2021b). Towards a better understanding of side-channel analysis measurements setups. In *20th Smart Card Research and Advanced Application Conference, CARDIS*. Springer, Cham.

Brisfors, M., Forsmark, S., Dubrova, E. (2020). How deep learning helps compromising USIM. In *19th Smart Card Research and Advanced Application Conference, CARDIS*. Springer, Cham.

Genkin, D., Shamir, A., Tromer, E. (2014). RSA key extraction via low-bandwidth acoustic cryptanalysis. In *Advances in Cryptology – CRYPTO 2014*, Garay, J.A. and Gennaro, R. (eds). Springer, Berlin.

Grand, J. (2022). How I hacked a hardware crypto wallet and recovered $2 million [Online]. Available at: https://www.youtube.com/watch?v=dT9y-KQbqi4.

Guillemet, C., Pedro, M.S., Servant, V. (2019). Breaking trezor one with side channel attacks [Online]. Available at: https://donjon.ledger.com/Breaking-Trezor-One-with-SCA/.

Guilley, S., Maghrebi, H., Souissi, Y., Sauvage, L., Danger, J.-L. (2011). Quantifying the quality of side-channel acquisitions. In *COSADE 2011*. Springer, Berlin.

Halter, J. and Najm, F. (1997). A gate-level leakage power reduction method for ultra-low-power cmos circuits. In *Proceedings of CICC 97 – Custom Integrated Circuits Conference*. IEEE, Santa Clara.

International Organization For Standardization (2019). IT security techniques: Test tool requirements and test tool calibration methods for use in testing non-invasive attack mitigation techniques in cryptographic modules – Part 1: Test tools and techniques. ISO/IEC 20082-1.

International Organization For Standardization (2020). IT security techniques: Test tool requirements and test tool calibration methods for use in testing non-invasive attack mitigation techniques in cryptographic modules – Part 2: Test calibration methods and apparatus. ISO/IEC 20082-2.

Karimi, N., Moos, T., Moradi, A. (2019). Exploring the effect of device aging on static power analysis attacks. *IACR Transactions on Cryptographic Hardware and Embedded Systems*, 2019(3), 233–256 [Online]. Available at: https://tches.iacr.org/index.php/TCHES/article/view/8295.

Kocher, P.C. (1996). Timing attacks on implementations of Diffie-Hellman, RSA, DSS, and other systems. In *Advances in Cryptology – CRYPTO'96*, Koblitz, N. (ed.). Springer, Heidelberg.

Mangard, S., Oswald, E., Popp, T. (2007). *Power Analysis Attacks – Revealing the Secrets of Smart Cards*. Springer, New York.

Merino Del Pozo, S. and Standaert, F.-X. (2017). Getting the most out of leakage detection: Statistical tools and measurement setups hand in hand. In *COSADE 2017: 8th International Workshop on Constructive Side-Channel Analysis and Secure Design*, Guilley, S. (ed.). Springer, Heidelberg.

Micali, S. and Reyzin, L. (2004). Physically observable cryptography (extended abstract). In *TCC 2004: 1st Theory of Cryptography Conference*, Naor, M. (ed.). Springer, Heidelberg.

Moos, T. (2019). Static power SCA of sub-100nm CMOS ASICs. *IACR Transactions on Cryptographic Hardware and Embedded Systems*, 2019(3), 202–232 [Online]. Available at: https://tches.iacr.org/index.php/TCHES/article/view/8294.

Moos, T., Moradi, A., Richter, B. (2020). Static power side-channel analysis: An investigation of measurement factors. *IEEE Trans. Very Large Scale Integr. Syst.*, 28(2), 376–389.

Mulder, E.D. (2010). Electromagnetic techniques and probes for side-channel analysis on cryptographic devices. PhD Thesis, KU Leuven, Belgium.

Narendra, S.G. and Chandrakasan, A. (2005). *Leakage in Nanometer CMOS Technologies*. Springer-Verlag, Berlin.

Pedro, M.S. (2020). Keepkey hardware wallet under the scope [Online]. Available at: https://donjon.ledger.com/keepkey-side-channel-attack/.

Quisquater, J. and Samyde, D. (2001). Electromagnetic analysis (EMA): Measures and counter-measures for smart cards. In *Smart Card Programming and Security: International Conference on Research in Smart Cards, E-smart 2001, Cannes, France, September 19–21, 2001. Proceedings*, Attali, I. and Jensen, T.P. (eds). Springer, Berlin.

Villa, S., Lacaita, A.L., Pacelli, A. (1995). Photon emission from hot electrons in silicon. *Phys. Rev. B*, 52, 10993–10999.

Wittke, C., Kabin, I., Klann, D., Dyka, Z., Datsuk, A., Langendoerfer, P. (2018). Horizontal DEMA attack as the criterion to select the best suitable EM probe. Cryptology ePrint Archive, Report 2018/1181 [Online]. Available at: https://eprint.iacr.org/2018/1181.

4

Supervised Attacks

Eleonora CAGLI[1] and Loïc MASURE[2]

[1] *CEA-Leti, Université Grenoble Alpes, France*

[2] *LIRMM, CNRS, Université de Montpellier, France*

This chapter and the next one present two classes of threat models that are considered in side-channel attacks (SCA), namely, *supervised* and *unsupervised* attacks. In the latter scenario, the attacker leverages some assumptions on the leakage modeling that was discussed in Chapter 3. Unfortunately, such assumptions are not always verified in reality, which may leave the attack somewhat sub-optimal. On the other hand, supervised attacks aim at trading off as much physical assumption as possible by leveraging a preliminary physical characterization of the leakage. By allowing for instantiating (almost) worst-case scenarios, such powerful threat models have encountered great success since their introduction in the early 2000s, and still remain a *must* in the SCA practitioner's toolbox.

4.1. General framework

4.1.1. *The profiling ability: a powerful threat model*

Suppose that, as part of an attack, Eve needs to guess a chunk[1] of a secret key used in one of the cryptographic primitives implemented in a target device $\mathcal{T}$. Eve

1 Usually, side-channel attacks enable an adversary to use a *divide-and-conquer* strategy, by targeting each chunk of a whole secret, independently from the others. Hence, in this chapter, we will only focus on the recovery of one chunk of secret.

Embedded Cryptography 1,
coordinated by Emmanuel PROUFF, Guénaël RENAULT, Matthieu RIVAIN and Colin O'FLYNN.

does not know how the device behaves physically. That is, once Eve acquired some SCA traces (e.g. power consumption and EM emanation), she has no idea about the relationship between the physical measurements and the handled sensitive variable values. This implies that she is not able to interpret the SCA traces and exploit them to reveal the underlying encryption key. The theoretical leakage models described in Chapter 3 seem unsatisfactory. If only she had a way to collect traces under a known encryption key... Now, Eve will not likely be able to acquire traces ad libitum on $\mathcal{T}$, since modern secure devices may include security mechanisms that avoid such a use case, and anyway, she does not know the value of the key she tries to recover!

However, Eve really wants her attack to succeed, so she tries to find a way to circumvent this problem. She remembers that she has a very good friend working at the foundry manufacturing her target device, and persuades him to steal a prototype of the target device in the developers' office, and to give it to her. Hopefully for Eve, this device, which we denote by $\mathcal{C}$, not only behaves similarly to her target but also has additional functionalities: for debugging purposes, developers may have a full control on the encryption key. Moreover, other security mechanisms, such as the ones limiting the number of acquisitions in a row, are disabled on the clone device $\mathcal{C}$. This asset may help Eve to improve her knowledge of the physical behavior, and thereby increase her chances of success – or at least to assess whether her actual target is worth the means she is willing to devote.

This kind of threat scenario, where a clone device is available to perform a preliminary characterization phase of the target, is called a *profiling attack*. We may notice that profiling attacks require non-trivial means from Eve – for example, a list of well-chosen good friends. Nevertheless, such a scenario is not that unrealistic. Nowadays, the lifecycle of an electronic device is highly partitioned, with different entities as hardware, firmware and software designers/developers, foundries, personalization agents and final users. A security flaw may exist in the process applied to produce a secure electronic device[2]. In the remaining sections of this chapter, we will mostly consider this worst-case scenario, since it allows for strong security guarantees – although at the cost of a somewhat pessimistic assessment of the target weaknesses. We discuss hereafter some notions of profiling attack.

The clone device: as explained in Eve's threat model, we make two main assumptions regarding the device on which Eve gets trained.

First, we assume that Eve may have full control on the stolen device $\mathcal{C}$. We say that it is an *open sample*. Concretely, when Eve runs $\mathcal{C}$, she not only knows the inputs

2 These potential flaws are, by the way, always analyzed, as well as SCA-related threats, during a normalized evaluation process, such as the one defined in the ISO/IEC 15408 norm (Common Criteria).

of the cryptographic primitive (initial states, plaintexts, secret key and even random nonces if the implementation is non-deterministic), but may also choose their values. We may even assume that Eve has access to any specification about the algorithm, that is, by knowing which are the security mechanisms used in the implementation, and may choose to disable them. In other words, the only unknown parameter from Eve is the physical leakage behavior occurring during the execution of the primitive.

Second, we assume that $\mathcal{C}$ behaves perfectly like the true target device $\mathcal{T}$ to break. We say that $\mathcal{C}$ is a *clone* device of $\mathcal{T}$. Since the leakages may be assumed to be non-deterministic, the outcomes of the attack performances should be the same against $\mathcal{C}$ and $\mathcal{T}$. Naturally, this assumption sounds somewhat unrealistic, since nowadays technology production processes are prone to small imprecision, always insignificant with respect to the functionality of the produced devices, but that influences the leakage, making it device dependent. Intuitively, if $\mathcal{T}$ differs from the clone, then the attack performance is always negatively degraded. Nevertheless, this bias in the security assessment turns out to be particularly useful for evaluators when considering worst-case scenarios: it suffices to simulate a side-channel attack on $\mathcal{C}$ to infer a lower bound on the security level of $\mathcal{T}$, without considering a discrepancy between both devices.

The training phase – the attack phase: the way a profiling attack is mounted is sketched in Figure 4.1. Eve first characterizes the leakage behavior on the clone device, conducting a so-called *training phase*, depicted on the left part of Figure 4.1. In this first step of the profiling attack, Eve queries the clone device $\mathcal{C}$ with some chosen pairs of plaintexts and keys $(p_1, k_1), \ldots, (p_{N_C}, k_{N_C})$, so that she can measure the corresponding leakages $\boldsymbol{x}'_1, \ldots, \boldsymbol{x}'_{N_C}$. Leakages measures are traces that contain several time samples. They are thus represented by vectors of D components. Then, Eve can use this knowledge to build a so-called *distinguisher* $\mathcal{D}\,()$ that will be defined in section 4.1.2. Eve will use $\mathcal{D}\,()$ to realize the *attack phase* in itself, depicted on the right of Figure 4.1. In this second step, Eve does not know the fixed encryption key $k^\star$, so she queries the target device $\mathcal{T}$ with some chosen plaintexts $q_1, \ldots, q_{N_a}$, and measures in return the leakages $\boldsymbol{x}_1, \ldots, \boldsymbol{x}_{N_a}$, with the hope that the overall knowledge acquired over the clone $\mathcal{C}$ and the target $\mathcal{T}$ can lead her to guess the actual value of $k^\star$.

The unbounded acquisition power: regardless of how the training and the attack phases are done, intuitively, the more measurements acquired, the higher the chances of Eve guessing the right value of the encryption key $k^\star$. While the target device $\mathcal{T}$ could have some protection mechanisms that prevent Eve from using as many measurements as desired on the target $\mathcal{T}$, she can deactivate these mechanisms on the clone device $\mathcal{C}$. As a result, we usually assume that Eve may acquire and process an *unbounded* number of traces N_C over $\mathcal{C}$. While having an unbounded amount of data is naturally impossible, acquiring as many traces as desired is nevertheless realistic. As an order of magnitude, we may think that the number of training traces that can be acquired within a few days typically reaches up to 10^8 for symmetric and asymmetric cryptography. Naturally, any real-life attacker or evaluator will operate with bounded powers. This means that a bounded amount of data drawn from a leakage distribution cannot perfectly depict the whole distribution in itself. This necessarily results in some performance loss compared to the optimal attack that Eve will try to minimize.

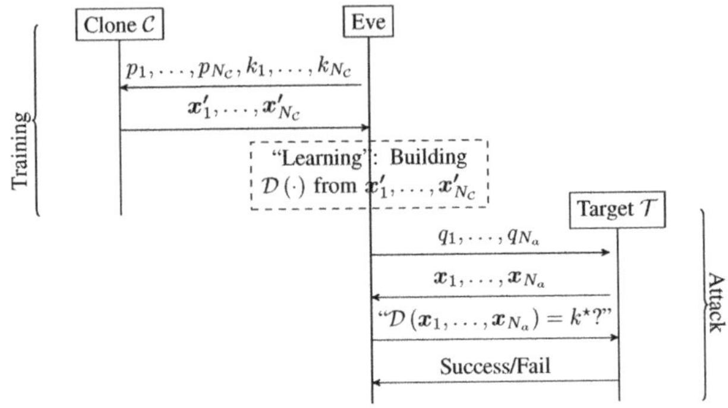

Figure 4.1. *Supervised attack scenario*

> **Exercise 4.1.** Suppose that Eve wants to break a symmetric cryptographic primitive hardware implementation requiring 300 processor clock cycles on a target device running at a 150 MHz clock frequency. The oscilloscope is assumed to have a sampling rate of 5 GS/s, and needs a time $0.1\ \mu$s at the end of each acquisition to store each time sample of the performed measurement on a computing server. How long will the acquisition last if the number of acquired traces is 10^7? (solution: about 2.8 h). How big must be the storage on the computing server, assuming that each time sample is encoded onto a byte? (solution: about 93 GB). What happens when replacing the symmetric primitive by an asymmetric one running, requiring 30,000 clock cycles? (about 11.6 days and 9 TB).

4.1.2. *Maximum likelihood distinguisher*

Let us now explain how Eve can leverage the knowledge of the leakages observed during the training phase in order to efficiently succeed in the attack phase. Eve would like to build an algorithm that takes those attack traces as an input – along with their corresponding plaintexts – and returns the guessed secret key. More precisely, the algorithm would return a list of hypothetical values of the secret key in decreasing order of preference. Such an algorithm is called a *distinguisher*. It is built during the training phase, then used during the attack phase to infer on the secret key of the device under attack. There exist several distinguishers in the SCA literature, and some of these will be covered by Chapter 5. However, here, we are interested in whether there exists an optimal distinguisher. We consider that the optimal distinguisher is the one that, given an amount of traces N_a acquired on the true target $\mathcal{T}$, maximizes the probability that the first hypothetical key returned by the distinguisher coincides with the actual key used during encryption.

The existence of an optimal distinguisher is addressed by the following fundamental result. Before introducing it, we need to define the concept of *sensitive intermediate computation* – or *sensitive variable.* A sensitive variable Z is a random variable depending both on a public data P known by Eve, and on the secret key K to guess: $Z = \mathrm{Comp}(P, K)$. In the remaining sections of this chapter, we will assume that any leakage observed by Eve during the training phase or the attack phase depends on a sensitive variable. Making inference on the variable Z should be sufficient to retrieve the secret key; thus, Z will represent the actual target of the side-channel attack. Throughout this chapter, and without any loss of generality, we assume that without knowing the secret key k nor any side information, Z is uniformly distributed over $\{0, \ldots, B-1\}$. As an example, if Z is a b -bit variable, $B = 2^b$.

THEOREM 4.1.– Let $\mathcal{S}_\mathcal{T} = \{(\boldsymbol{x}_1, q_1), \ldots, (\boldsymbol{x}_{N_a}, q_{N_a})\}$ be a set of N_a attack traces observed on the target device $\mathcal{T}$, with their corresponding public plaintext. Let $Z = \mathrm{Comp}(P, K)$ be a sensitive variable. Then, if Z is uniformly distributed, the optimal distinguisher is the *maximum likelihood distinguisher*:

$$\mathcal{D}(\mathcal{S}_\mathcal{T}) = \operatorname*{argsort}_k \sum_{i=1}^{N_a} \log \Pr(\boldsymbol{X} = \boldsymbol{x}_i | Z_i = \mathrm{Comp}(q_i, k)) . \qquad [4.1]$$

Additionally to being the optimal distinguisher, the maximum likelihood distinguisher has other interesting properties. We say that it is an *additive* distinguisher: the scores – that is, the sums in equation [4.1] for each value of k – to compare between each hypothetical value k of the secret key is a sum of individual scores computed independently for each trace. This carries two advantages.

First, we said that Eve's training phase consisted of building a distinguisher, namely, an algorithm taking as an input a given N_a of traces and returning a hypothetical key. If Eve considers building the maximum likelihood distinguisher, her training is reduced to building an algorithm that takes as an input only *one* trace, and outputs one score for each hypothetical value of the secret key. This is arguably a much simpler task.

Second, the maximum likelihood distinguisher output merely depends on the number of traces N_a used for the online attack. In particular, Eve may work incrementally: if she is not satisfied with her attack, she may simply reiterate it with more traces by adding the scores computed on the new traces to the scores previously computed for each hypothetical key k. This process can be done without having to run the distinguisher again from scratch. Such a feature is particularly interesting for evaluators, when estimating the minimal value N_a required to reach a given probability of success. This estimation may be efficiently conducted by incrementing N_a until reaching the desired probability.

From unbounded to bounded acquisition power: we have seen that Eve's attack may be reduced to compute some scores based on the conditional distribution $\Pr(\boldsymbol{X} \mid Z)$. However, we assumed that Eve does not know this probability distribution. Instead, she may estimate it during the training phase, thanks to the traces acquired on the clone device $\mathcal{C}$. A naive way to do that would be to estimate the conditional distribution with its *empirical* distribution where for any $\boldsymbol{x}$, the probability is estimated by the frequency of the event "$\boldsymbol{X} = \boldsymbol{x} \mid Z = z$" in the *training set* $\mathcal{S}_\mathcal{C} = \{(\boldsymbol{x}'_1, z_1), \ldots, (\boldsymbol{x}'_{N_\mathcal{C}}, z_{N_\mathcal{C}})\}$, where $z_i = \text{Comp}(p_i, k_i)$, for all $1 \leq i \leq N_\mathcal{C}$. However, this is a highly inefficient way. Not only using the empirical distribution cannot work if the leakage distribution is not discrete, but even if the leakage $\boldsymbol{X}$ is discrete, the empirical distribution suffers from the so-called *curse of dimensionality*. Intuitively, letting D stand for the input trace dimensionality, whereas, B stands for the number of possible values that Z may take. it means that in order for the empirical distribution to be accurate enough, the amount $N_\mathcal{C}$ of profiling traces that Eve needs to acquire should scale exponentially with the input dimensionality D and the output dimensionality B. This is barely affordable for any real-world adversary.

The link between supervised attacks and machine learning: thankfully, the curse of dimensionality can be circumvented by using the so-called *parametric* approach. It consists of assuming that the true distribution belongs (or at least is "close") to a given family $\mathcal{H}$ of parametric functions. Each model m in $\mathcal{H}$ takes a leakage as an input and returns a vector of scores aiming at emulating $\Pr(\boldsymbol{X} = \boldsymbol{x} \mid Z = z)$ for each value of z. Then, a *learning algorithm* $\mathcal{A}$ is asked to select a model candidate m from $\mathcal{H}$ that seems to "fit the best" the data $\mathcal{S}_\mathcal{C}$ observed by Eve during the acquisition phase, with the hope that the fitting of the model returned by $\mathcal{A}$ generalizes well to the whole true leakage distribution. Adopting the machine learning paradigm allows us to leverage the wide literature from this research field. That is why in this chapter, we use the terminology of *supervised attacks* to denote an adversary that builds her distinguisher using the supervised learning paradigm[3]. The remaining sections of this chapter will give an overview of machine learning techniques for supervised attacks, that is, what kind of prior knowledge and learning algorithm to use, depending on Eve's powers.

Generative versus discriminative: let us first discuss what kind of probability distribution Eve must estimate. Equation [4.1] refers to a so-called *generative* model $\Pr(\boldsymbol{X} \mid Z)$: it considers modeling the causality relationship between the sensitive

3 We stress that profiling attacks are not necessarily supervised attacks, and conversely. As an example, it is possible to emulate supervised attacks without having to use a clone device. Some examples in this respect will be reviewed in Chapter 5.

intermediate computation Z (the cause) and the corresponding leakage $\boldsymbol{X}$ (the consequence). The advantage of generative models is to be interpretable for the practitioner and may allow us to draw some links with some physical behavior of the target $\mathcal{T}$ which was reviewed in Chapter 3. To provide an example, if for some values of the sensitive target variable sharing the same Hamming weight, denoted HW, the parameters describing the generative model are roughly the same, then it may be a clue that the Hamming weight leakage model discussed in Chapter 3 actually holds for the target device, that is, $\boldsymbol{X} = \mathsf{HW}(Z) + \epsilon$, for some noise ϵ independent of Z. Accordingly, this may provide the developer with some insights to iteratively improve the security of the target device. That is why such models are often preferred by developers and evaluators.

However, this also has some drawbacks. Indeed, the sensitive intermediate computation Z is not likely to be the unique cause affecting the observation of the leakage. Consequently, building a generative model comes with the risk of spending a lot of effort (in terms of computational and acquisition complexity) in modeling some aspects of the physical behavior – for example, loading of public and non-sensitive data – which may not depend on the actual value of Z, thereby being non necessary to make a discrepancy. For adversaries with truly malicious intents, that is, only aiming at recovering the secret chunk, the generative approach might not be well suited. That is why we may embrace another approach for estimating the probability distribution using the following lemma.

LEMMA 4.1.– Assuming that the prior distribution of Z is uniform, the maximum likelihood distinguisher may be rephrased as follows:

$$\mathcal{D}(\mathcal{S}_{\mathcal{T}}) = \underset{k}{\operatorname{argsort}} \sum_{i=1}^{N_a} \log \Pr\left(Z_i = \operatorname{Comp}\left(p_i, k\right) | \boldsymbol{X}_i = \boldsymbol{x}_i\right). \qquad [4.2]$$

Exercise 4.2. Using Bayes' theorem, verify the equivalence between 4.2 and 4.1.

Contrary to equations [4.1] and [4.2] rather refers to a so-called *discriminative* model. Instead of attempting to model how the value of Z affects the observed leakage $\boldsymbol{X}$, a discriminative model aims at focusing only on how some aspects of the observed leakage allow for making a discrepancy between different observed values of the sensitive intermediate computation Z. In practice, since the adversary only needs to guess the underlying intermediate computation behind the observed leakage, regardless of the whole leakage model, discriminative models are often more straightforward.[4] Nonetheless, both generative and discriminative approaches present

4 This idea is well summarized by Vapnik (1998): *"When solving a given problem, try to avoid a more general problem as an intermediate step"*.

some advantages, and thus deserve to be considered. This is why we present some examples of both approaches and discuss their own advantages and weaknesses.

4.2. Building a model

We now present some ways to build models used by Eve to feed the maximum likelihood distinguisher. In each case, we specify the subset $\mathcal{H}$ denoting the prior knowledge, along with the corresponding learning algorithm $\mathcal{A}$.

4.2.1. *Generative model via Gaussian templates*

We start by introducing *Gaussian templates*. This is a generative model, assuming that the leakage $\boldsymbol{X}$ follows a (multivariate) Gaussian distribution, whose mean vector μ_z and covariance matrix Σ_z both depend on the value z of the underlying sensitive intermediate computation. Concretely, the learning algorithm $\mathcal{A}$ is the following: Eve groups her acquisitions on the clone device $\mathcal{C}$ by value of Z, and for each class, estimate μ_z with the empirical mean $\widehat{\mu}_z$, and Σ_z with the empirical covariance matrix $\widehat{\Sigma}_z$. The probability function returned by $\mathcal{A}$ is then given by:

$$\Pr(\boldsymbol{X} = \boldsymbol{x}|Z) \approx \frac{1}{(2\pi)^{D/2}|\widehat{\Sigma}_z|^{1/2}} e^{-\frac{1}{2}(\boldsymbol{x}-\widehat{\mu}_z)^\intercal \widehat{\Sigma}_z^{-1}(\boldsymbol{x}-\widehat{\mu}_z)}. \quad [4.3]$$

Gaussian templates are efficient models, as long as the trace dimensionality (i.e. the number of time samples considered in each trace) remains low (typically around $D \leq 10$). However, when the dimensionality increases, some computational complexity overheads may appear. As an example, for computing equation [4.3], the empirical covariance matrices $\widehat{\Sigma}_z$ must be all invertible, which is not satisfied if there is one hypothetical value z for which the number of traces acquired on the clone device is less than D. In other words, the minimum number of traces acquired on $\mathcal{C}$ is $B \cdot D$.

Moreover, provided that the empirical covariance matrices are all invertible, computing the inverse results in a $\mathcal{O}\left(B \cdot D^3\right)$ run-time complexity, which may quickly become prohibitive. To circumvent those computational caveats, we discuss hereafter two solutions: a linear discriminant analysis (shared covariance matrix) and a naive Bayes estimator (diagonal covariance matrix). A third solution consists of priorly performing a selection of a few time samples, or another dimensionality reduction of side-channel traces, using one of the techniques discussed in section 4.3.

> **Practical Exercise 4.3.** Let us consider the ASCADv1-variable dataset. Targeting the proposed variable (i.e. the third byte of the AES state after SubByte operation), how many time samples must be selected in order to ensure that all covariance matrices are invertible (as

many time samples as the minimal number of traces per class minus 1...703)? How many of them must be discarded? When keeping such a maximal number of time samples, what is the complexity of the covariance matrix inversion?

Shared covariance matrix (linear discriminant analysis)[5]: Eve may additionally assume that the parameters characterizing the noise in the leakage model are all the same (homoscedasticity hypothesis). For Gaussian templates, the noise parameter is materialized by the covariance matrices Σ_z. The resulting empirical covariance matrix is then estimated by taking the average of the covariance matrices $\widehat{\Sigma}_z$, over all the hypothetical values that the sensitive intermediate computation Z may take:

$$\widehat{\Sigma} = \frac{1}{B} \sum_z \widehat{\Sigma}_z. \qquad [4.4]$$

This technique is known as the *shared covariance* – or pooled covariance – trick. It allows us to address the two shortcomings of Gaussian templates listed before. First, the necessary condition regarding the required number of traces for having invertible covariance matrices is decreased from $B \cdot D$ to D. Second, there is now only one covariance matrix to invert, which decreases the run-time complexity from $\mathcal{O}\left(B \cdot D^3\right)$ to $\mathcal{O}\left(D^3\right)$. In return, Eve may lose some distinguishing information which could be contained in the different covariance matrices[6].

Diagonal covariance matrix: Eve may assume otherwise that the covariance matrix is diagonal, meaning that all the time samples in the trace leak independently from each other. This assumption is also known in machine learning as a so-called *naive Bayes* estimator. Here, Eve's task is reduced to estimate only $B \cdot D$ variance terms, corresponding to the diagonal coefficients of the covariance matrices $\widehat{\Sigma}_z$, instead of $B \cdot D^2$ coefficients in regular Gaussian templates. Accordingly, the matrix inversion is also more efficient, since inverting all the diagonal matrices may be done in $B \cdot D$ operations, instead of $B \cdot D^3$.

Practical Exercise (in notebook) 4.4. Get familiar with Gaussian templates variants by performing complete attacks against AES algorithm.

5 In machine learning, the term linear discriminant analysis (LDA) refers as well to a classification tool based on Gaussian assumption and shared covariance matrix. Nevertheless, a common abuse is done, and widely accepted in the SCA domain, to refer to LDA as a dimensionality reduction technique to apply before later classification. This will be clarified in section 4.3.

6 In particular, this makes Gaussian templates attacks with shared covariance matrix ineffective against some counter-measures such as masking, which will be detailed in Chapter 7 of this volume and Part 1 of Volume 2.

4.2.2. Discriminative model via logistic regression

So far in section 4.2.1, we have seen some examples of generative models. We now consider studying discriminative models. To understand why such models may be useful, let us first consider Gaussian templates with shared covariance matrix that we introduced before. Like in equation [4.2], we may use Bayes' theorem to convert the generative model to a discriminative one. It follows that, if the prior distribution of Z is uniform, the conditional posterior probability may be expressed as:

$$\Pr(Z = z | \boldsymbol{X} = \boldsymbol{x}) = \frac{\exp(-A^\star_z \boldsymbol{x})}{\sum_{z' \in \mathcal{Z}} \exp(-A^\star_{z'} \boldsymbol{x})}, \qquad [4.5]$$

for some matrix $A^\star = (A^\star_0, \ldots, A^\star_{B-1})^\intercal \in \mathbb{R}^{B \times D}$ to estimate that depends on the mean vectors μ_z and on the shared covariance matrix Σ, as it is asked in the following exercise.

> **Exercise 4.5.** Show that the matrix $A^\star$ is a function φ of the mean vectors μ_z and of the shared covariance matrix Σ.

Such a model is called *logistic regression* or *generalized linear model* as well, since equation [4.5] can be seen as a nonlinear function σ of the linear mapping $\boldsymbol{x} \mapsto A^\star \cdot \boldsymbol{x}$, and where

$$\sigma(\boldsymbol{y}) = \frac{1}{\sum_{i=0}^{B-1} e^{\boldsymbol{y}[i]}} \left(e^{\boldsymbol{y}[0]}, \ldots, e^{\boldsymbol{y}[B-1]}\right)^\intercal, \quad \boldsymbol{y} = (\boldsymbol{y}[0], \ldots, \boldsymbol{y}[B-1])^\intercal [4.6]$$

is the so-called *softmax* function. To see this, observe Figure 4.2 (left) where two Gaussian distributions with the same covariance matrix are depicted, for $D = 2, B = 2$. Over the contours are depicted the dashed curves verifying the equation $\Pr(Z = 0 | \boldsymbol{X} = \boldsymbol{x}) = \alpha$, for some α ranging from 10^{-4} to $1 - 10^{-4}$. As we can see, these curves are plane, emphasizing the linear nature of the discriminative model, despite the (highly) nonlinear nature of the generative model counter-part.

As a result, the logistic regression model can be seen as a generalization of the Gaussian template with shared covariance matrix. Notice that the latter criterion is necessary: Figure 4.2 (right) depicts the same situation as in Figure 4.2 (left), but with different covariance matrices. It can be noticed that the dashed curves are no longer plane. Moreover, the discriminative model of logistic regression is known to be more resilient than the generative model of LDA, if the true leakage distribution does not exactly follow a Gaussian distribution.

How to estimate the matrix $A^\star$ in equation [4.5]? Whereas the generative approach with Gaussian templates with shared covariance matrix would estimate the matrix $A^\star$ using the empirical mean vectors $\widehat{\mu}_z$ and empirical covariance $\widehat{\Sigma}$, the discriminative approach tackles the problem another way around. It considers the matrix $A^\star$ as the solution of an optimization problem, where the goal is to minimize a *loss function* quantifying the dissimilarity between the probability distribution given by equation [4.5] and the true probability distribution. Since the latter one is unknown, it is estimated by using the training set $\mathcal{S}_{\mathcal{C}}$. The *cross-entropy* may be used to quantify such a dissimilarity. In general, the *cross-entropy* between two probability distributions p and q is defined as:

$$H(p, q) = -\mathbb{E}_p[\log q]. \qquad [4.7]$$

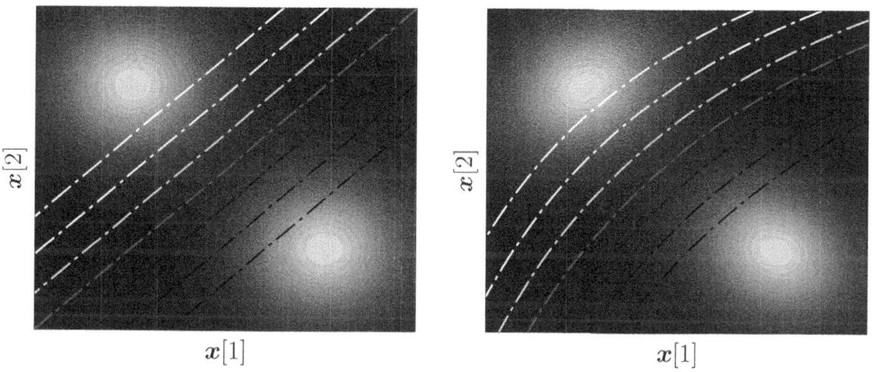

Figure 4.2. *Example of Gaussian distributions for $B = 2, D = 2$. The contours denote the marginal distribution of the generative model. The dashed lines denote the level lines of the discriminative model $\Pr(Z = 0|\boldsymbol{X} = \boldsymbol{x})$ (ranging from 10^{-4} to $1 - 10^{-4}$). Left: shared covariance matrix. Right: non-shared covariance matrix. For a color version of this figure, see www.iste.co.uk/prouff/cryptography1.zip*

Let q be the probability distribution given in equation [4.5] and let p_i stand for a fixed trace in the training set $(\boldsymbol{x}'_i, z_i) \in \mathcal{S}_{\mathcal{C}}$ the trivial distribution on $\{0, \ldots B-1\}$ such that $p(z_i) = 1$. In this case, the cross-entropy reduces to:

$$\begin{aligned} H(p_i, q) &= -\log\left(\frac{\exp\left((A_{z_i} \cdot \boldsymbol{x}'_i)\right)}{\sum_{z' \in \mathcal{Z}} \exp\left(A_{z'} \cdot \boldsymbol{x}'_i\right)}\right) \\ &= A_{z_i} \cdot \boldsymbol{x}'_i - \log\left(\sum_{z' \in \mathcal{Z}} \exp\left(A_{z'} \cdot \boldsymbol{x}'_i\right)\right) \end{aligned}$$

Taking the average, or equivalently the sum, over the whole training set $\mathcal{S}_C$, the optimization problem is therefore defined as follows:

$$A^\star \approx \widehat{A} = \underset{A}{\operatorname{argmin}} \sum_{(\boldsymbol{x}'_i, z_i) \in \mathcal{S}_C} H(p_i, q). \qquad [4.8]$$

Solving the minimization of equation [4.8] is a well-defined problem, as it can be verified that the function to minimize is convex.

Exercise 4.6. Show that for logistic regression, the loss function to minimize is convex.

Convex optimization problems have nice properties. In particular, the empirical solution $\widehat{A}$ is *consistent*, that is, the performances of the model obtained with $\widehat{A}$ quickly converge toward the performances that we would have got using the true solution $A^\star$ when the amount of training data tends toward infinity. Nevertheless, the latter convergence is slightly slower than what we could have by estimating $A^\star$ with $\varphi\left(\{\widehat{\mu}_z\}_z, \widehat{\Sigma}\right)$. This fact emphasizes that there is intrinsically a trade-off between using a model relying on lighter assumptions, and therefore less likely to make mistakes for an adversary with unbounded acquisition capacities, and a model relying on stronger assumptions but more efficient from the perspective of the acquisition complexity. Generally speaking, this trade-off is common to any supervised learning problem.

Exercise (in notebook) 4.7. Practical application of logistic regression, with scikit-learn python library.

4.2.3. *From logistic regression to neural networks*

Now we have seen how the Gaussian noise assumption could be relaxed by using logistic regression, we may wonder to what extent we may weaken even more our prior bias when tackling side-channel analysis. In this section, we present a rather general approach, leveraging *deep neural networks* (DNNs). The idea can be synthesized as follows: recall that with logistic regression, the output probability was computed as a function of the following shape: $\Pr(Z = z|\boldsymbol{X} = \boldsymbol{x}) \approx \sigma(\widehat{A} \cdot \boldsymbol{x})$, where σ is the softmax function defined in equation [4.6], such that the overall model is a generalized linear model. Even if generalized linear models are easy to use, they are prone to modelize linear phenomena, which cannot encompass any kind of leakage distribution that Eve may encounter. To address this limitation, an intuitive idea is to replace the matrix-vector product inside the softmax function by a mapping $\mathbb{R}^D \to \mathbb{R}^B$ that could describe a wider class of leakage distributions. This is where *neural networks* come into play.

Generally speaking, a neural network can be seen as a directed acyclic computation graph. The computation graph has D input nodes – one for each dimension of the input leakage – and B output nodes – one for each hypothetical value of Z. Each node aims at representing a *neuron*. A neuron takes as inputs the values of one (or several) other neurons, and returns as an output a real value that can be then passed as an input to one (or several) other neurons. More precisely, if the vector $\boldsymbol{x} \in \mathbb{R}^d$ denotes the d input values of a neuron, the latter one computes as an output value a so-called *ridge* function, that is, a function of the type $f(\boldsymbol{x}) = g(\boldsymbol{x}^\intercal \cdot \theta)$, for some nonlinear function $g : \mathbb{R} \to \mathbb{R}$, and some $\theta \in \mathbb{R}^d$. The function g is often called the *activation* function, and θ is often referred to as the *parameter* (a.k.a. *weights*) of the neuron. In a sense, θ replaced the matrix A in the generalized linear model. Likewise, we refer to the shape of the graph, along with the nature of each activation function, as the *architecture* of the neural network, whereas we refer to the list of parameters describing all elementary functions as Θ.

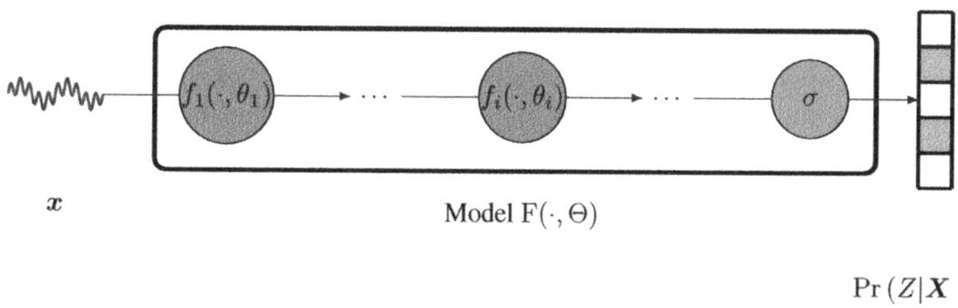

Figure 4.3. *A sketch of MLP. For a color version of this figure, see www.iste.co.uk/prouff/cryptography1.zip*

Among the plethora of architectures, we focus hereafter on the most generic one, called *multi-layer perceptron* (MLP), and sketched in Figure 4.3. Here, the neurons are partitioned and organized as *layers*. In an MLP, each neuron of a layer takes as input all the neurons of the previous layer. An MLP has at least two layers. One is formed by all the input nodes of the neural network, and another layer is formed by all the output nodes. All the remaining layers are often called the *hidden* (or intermediate) layers. An interesting property of MLPs made of at least one hidden layer is that they are *universal* approximators: under mild assumptions, for any leakage model, there exists a one-hidden-layer MLP that approximates the conditional probability distribution $\Pr(Z|\boldsymbol{X})$ up to any arbitrary precision. It generally suffices to increase the dimensionality of the output of the hidden layer. This property makes MLPs candidates of choice for SCA. Remarkably, this property allows MLPs to be more resilient than other models to the presence of some *counter-measures* that a designer may include in the implementation, including the *masking* counter-measure, which will be reviewed in Chapter 1 of Volume 2[7].

The setting of the parameters can be done similarly to the setting of the matrices in logistic regression: the adversary can set their values by solving an optimization problem, using a loss function similar to the one considered in equation [4.8], by replacing the matrix A by the parameters Θ as a decision variable. Usually, the loss function is differentiable with respect to the parameter vector Θ but is no longer convex, due to the nonlinearity of the activation functions. This makes optimizing the loss function for MLPs – and for any other DNN – theoretically hard, but surprisingly efficient in practice. Usually, the optimization is done thanks to a gradient descent, since the gradient of the loss function with respect to each decision variable can be efficiently computed for DNNs, thanks to the so-called *backward propagation* algorithm. Whereas the setting of the parameters can thus be done quite efficiently, it does not imply that the optimized DNN results in an appropriate model. Indeed, if the architecture of the DNN has not been properly designed, it may be impossible to approximate the desired leakage model. The design of an architecture consists of the choice of a quite high number of parameters, the so-called *hyper-parameters*. Different from the *parameters*, an efficient optimization algorithm for the *hyper-parameters* does not exist and they are practically chosen arbitrarily, or following some heuristics. Hyper-parameters for MLPs include the number of layers, the number of neurons for each layer, the nature of the activation function, etc. The design space of neural network architectures is therefore prone to a combinatorial blow-up. Moreover, some hyper-parameters related to the optimization phase (or *training*) have to be set: the proper variant of the gradient descent algorithm, the geometrical length of the step performed through the gradient-opposite direction (the so-called *learning rate*). It is important to remark that while optimizing a neural network, it is much more efficient to compute the loss function, and its gradient, only onto a small set of traces at the time, and apply a step in the opposite-gradient direction for each of such mini-batches evaluation. The size of the batches, named *batch-size*, and the number of *epochs* (evaluations onto the whole dataset) are also important hyper-parameters of the optimization procedure. It may also be important to apply some *regularization* techniques or to perform a so-called *early-stopping*, a stop of the optimization algorithm by monitoring certain parameters, to prevent the *over-fitting* (phenomenon briefly discussed in section 4.3). Such techniques also come with some hyper-parameters which need to be fixed by hand by the adversary.

7 In section 1.3.2 of Chapter 12, we will see that to defeat masking, some *combination functions* must be computed. These functions can be automatically approximated by an MLP from the raw traces of a masked implementation.

Exercise (in notebook) 4.8. Practical application of MLP, with tensorflow.keras.

4.3. Controlling the dimensionality

So far in section 4.2, we have seen several models to estimate the conditional probability distribution, either from a generative perspective, or from a discriminative one. In any case, it deals with estimating a mapping $\mathbb{R}^D \to \mathbb{R}^B$, where D stands for the input trace dimensionality, whereas B stands for the number of possible values that Z may take. Intuitively, the higher D and B, the higher the amount $N_{\mathcal{C}}$ of traces measured during the profiling phase, in order to keep the estimated models accurate enough. To be more precise, $N_{\mathcal{C}}$ must scale linearly (or even polynomially for some classes of models) with D and B. This is far better than for non-parametric models, where we mentioned in section 4.1.2 that the curse of dimensionality required $N_{\mathcal{C}}$ to scale exponentially with D and B. Still, it may be hard to comply with this requirement, due to the potential high dimensionality D of side-channel leakages. If this requirement is not met, any learning algorithm may be prone to the so-called *over-fitting*: a phenomenon in which the model learns the training data *by heart*. This is very regrettable, because a model that has over-fitted on training data, does not generalize its results over new unseen data: Eve cannot succeed her attack against the true target with an over-fitted model.

A very intuitive way to deal with finite traces and high-dimensional data is to control the effective value of the input dimensionality D, and/or the value of the output dimensionality B. The latter approach is rather specific to the field of side-channel analysis, and is thoroughly studied in Chapter 3. In the remainder of this section, we will focus on the former approach. Most of the time, the raw side-channel traces have high dimensionality – typically thousands or even millions of time samples – whereas only a tiny fraction of them may be informative about a secret variable to target. These informative points are called *Points of Interest* (PoI). On the other hand, given the continuous nature of the sampled side-channel signals, it is realistic to assume that the information that PoIs bring is somehow redundant, and may be extracted into some smaller sized form. The problem of performing an opportune *dimensionality reduction* goes hand in hand with the research of PoIs: a convenient dimensionality reduction should enhance the contribution of such PoIs, while reducing or nullifying the one provided by non-interesting points.

In the remaining sections of this chapter, we introduce one method for each approach, namely, the signal-to-noise ratio (SNR) in section 4.3.1 for the PoIs selection, and Fisher's linear discriminant analysis in section 4.3.2 for the dimensionality reduction.

4.3.1. *Points of interest selection with signal-to-noise ratio*

A way to localize such PoIs is the sample-wise computation of the so-called SNR. The SNR is a metric that is computed for each time sample t in the trace as follows:

$$\mathrm{SNR}(t) = \frac{\mathrm{Var}(\vec{\mu}_z(t))}{\mathbb{E}[\vec{\varrho}_z(t)]}, \qquad [4.9]$$

where, for $(\boldsymbol{x}'_i, z_i) \in \mathcal{S}_C$, N_C^z denotes the number of training traces belonging to the z class, and $\vec{\mu}_z = \frac{1}{N_C^z} \sum_{i:\, Z_i = z} \boldsymbol{x}'_i$ and $\vec{\varrho}_z = \frac{1}{N_C^z - 1} \sum_{i:\, Z_i = z} (\boldsymbol{x}'_i - \vec{\mu}_z)^2$ respectively stand for the empirical mean and the empirical variance (taken over all the values of Z) of the leakage distribution at time sample t.

To illustrate how useful the SNR can be, let us take an example in the simplest case, namely where $D = 1$, and $B = 2$, as depicted in Figure 4.4.

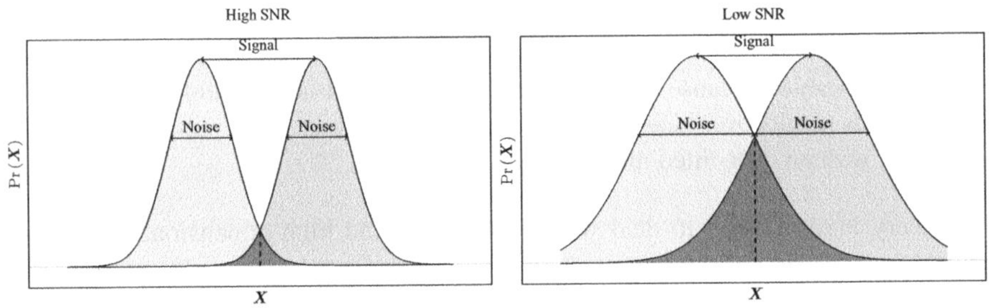

Figure 4.4. *Principle of an SNR (relative scale for the y-axes). Left: a high SNR means a small red area, hence a low probability of error. Right: a low SNR means a wide red area, hence a high probability of error. For a color version of this figure, see www.iste.co.uk/prouff/cryptography1.zip*

Here, two distributions, one blue and one green, are depicted, along with their noise – how spread each distribution is – and their signal – how "shifted" both distributions are with respect to each other. If an adversary wants to distinguish whether a leakage has been drawn from the green distribution or the blue one, then they could apply the maximum likelihood distinguisher (for one trace instead of N_a) by predicting that any leakage at the right of the dashed black vertical line (a.k.a. the so-called *decision surface*) would belong to the blue distribution, whereas any leakage at the left of the decision surface would belong to the green distribution. Therefore, the red area under the curve coincides with the probability of error in that prediction. Some standard results in information theory allow us to link the probability of error (the red area) by a function of the SNR.

Exercise 4.9. Assume that the green and blue distributions in Figure 4.4 are Gaussians of means respectively μ_0, μ_1 and of common standard deviation σ, and that those parameters are known by Eve.

1) Prove that the probability of distinguishing whether *one* leakage has been drawn from the blue distribution or the green one is a function of $\sqrt{\text{SNR}}$, where $\text{SNR} = \frac{(\mu_1 - \mu_0)^2}{\sigma^2}$.

2) Verify that when the two leakage distributions coincide (i.e. $\text{SNR} = 0$), the success rate equals $1/2$, and when $\Delta \to \infty$, the success rate tends toward 1.

3) Extend the previous case by assuming that N_a independent leakages have been drawn, either from the blue distribution or from the green one. Show that the probability of distinguishing is a function of $\sqrt{N_a} \cdot \sqrt{\text{SNR}}$.
Verify the results with numerical simulations available on:
https://colab.research.google.com/drive/10y9DwHABxfFDn8Uj6lrZEUKsbz6pPzbD.

In other words, the SNR allows the adversary/evaluator to guess how a time sample t in the leakage helps in distinguishing between two values of the sensitive intermediate computation Z; or said inversely, the SNR helps the evaluator in guessing whether they can ignore a given time sample without losing much information about the target secret. That is why the SNR is a popular tool for evaluators.

The limits of SNR: we have seen that an evaluator can conclude from a high SNR value that a time sample should be kept as a PoI. Since we are seeking in this section to reduce the dimensionality of the trace, it is tempting to conclude the converse, namely that a time sample with a low SNR could be ignored. Unfortunately, this converse is not true, as the SNR quantifies how informative the time samples are, *independently* of the others. In other words, by computing the SNR, we are disregarding how informative several time samples observed *jointly* are. In an extreme case, we will see in the next chapters that there could be some leakage distributions such that each time sample has a null SNR while both time samples are jointly highly informative, because of some counter-measures.

Exercise (in notebook) 4.10. Compute the SNR related to the first byte of SubByte output on *ASCAD-v1-variable* dataset.

4.3.2. *Fisher's linear discriminant analysis*

We have seen in section 4.3.1 how the SNR could be useful for the PoIs selection. We now explain how to handle the dimensionality reduction, thanks to Fisher's LDA. There is a reason why the terminology of Fisher's LDA is close to LDA, the other name of the Gaussian template with shared covariance. To see this, observe again the dashed lines in Figure 4.2 (left) denoting the domains with equal value of $\Pr(Z = 0 \mid \boldsymbol{X} = \boldsymbol{x})$. Recall that since the discriminative model is a generalized linear model, these curves are lines – or hyperplanes if D ranges in a higher dimensionality. In other words, it does not change the output of the model if the leakage is projected onto the linear subspace orthogonal to the dashed lines, that is to say, the linear subspace spanned by the segment between the two centroids. Likewise, we may generalize this idea to more than two classes: it suffices to project the traces onto the linear subspace spanned by all the centroids, that is, the subspace spanned by the eigen-vectors of the so-called *inter-class scatter matrix*:

$$\mathbf{S}_{\mathsf{signal}} = \sum_{z \in \mathcal{Z}} N_C^z (\vec{\mu}_z - \mu_{\boldsymbol{x}})(\vec{\mu}_z - \mu_{\boldsymbol{x}})^{\mathsf{T}}, \qquad [4.10]$$

with non-zero eigenvalues. Interestingly, the dimensionality of this subspace no longer depends on the input dimensionality D, but is rather upper bounded by $B - 1$ in the worst-case. Still, this may not be sufficient as the number of classes may be high, for example, for an 8 -bit target, $B - 1 = 255$, and Eve may want to decrease further the dimensionality for practical reasons, while keeping as much informative leakage as possible in order to make a discrepancy between the B different distributions. What can Eve do in that case? Instead of keeping the non-zero eigen-values of $\mathbf{S}_{\mathsf{signal}}$, she can project the traces on the linear subspace spanned by the *largest* eigen-vectors of the matrix $\mathbf{S}_{\mathsf{noise}}^{-1} \cdot \mathbf{S}_{\mathsf{signal}}$ where:

$$\mathbf{S}_{\mathsf{noise}} = \sum_{z \in \mathcal{Z}} \sum_{\substack{i=1 \\ z_i = z}}^{N_C} (\boldsymbol{x}_i - \vec{\mu}_z)(\boldsymbol{x}_i - \vec{\mu}_z)^{\mathsf{T}}, \qquad [4.11]$$

is the so-called *intra-class scatter matrix*. Intuitively, the matrix product $\mathbf{S}_{\mathsf{noise}}^{-1} \cdot \mathbf{S}_{\mathsf{signal}}$ may be seen as a generalization of the SNR reviewed in section 4.3.1.

Exercise 4.11. Assume that $N_C \ll D$. How many eigenvectors of the scatter matrices can we expect to get, at most?

Exercise 4.12. Simulate realizations of two bi-dimensional Gaussian variables and perform LDA (classification of new samples under Gaussian hypothesis with shared covariance matrix) and Fisher linear discriminant dimensionality reduction using scikit-learn python library.

4.4. Building de-synchronization-resistant models

All the techniques that have been described up to now in this chapter are efficient in contexts where acquisitions are perfectly synchronous, that is, when the same phenomena during the execution of the implementation happens at the same time samples, from one observed leakage to another. However, this assumption is fairly strong, and traces may be misaligned. This may happen for many reasons. To keep one in mind, exactly because it affects statistical tools for side-channel analysis, injecting some desynchronization on purpose is a classical and widespread countermeasure. Misalignment may be achieved in several ways (e.g. by hardware clock jitter or software random delay interrupt).

Unfortunately, the efficiency of the models we have presented so far drops when applied to misaligned traces. To understand why, let us simply focus on side-channel traces which include a single PoI localized at a time sample $t^\star$, surrounded by non-informative fully-noisy points. A desynchronization makes the PoI move, so that its position γ becomes randomly distributed in an unknown way: $\gamma \sim \Gamma$ such that $\mathbb{E}[\Gamma] = t^\star$. The time sample $t^\star$ will thus assume the relevant leakage value only when $\gamma = t^\star$, whereas it will be considered as a fully noisy point otherwise. While the expected value of the trace in $t^\star$ is still the same, and in particular, still class dependent, its SNR level is as much lower as higher the variance of Γ is. The number of profiling traces required to keep the SNR of the PoIs higher than the ground noise level – that is, to allow the PoIs to be detectable – raises in a linear way with respect to the Γ standard deviation. In the same way as the SNR, Gaussian templates, LDA, logistic regressors and MLPs suffer from misalignment. Anyway, the amount of information leaked by the device is not lower. It is simply spread over as many points as the range of Γ. Indeed, all the points of such a range acquire a statistical dependency from the sensitive variable, actually becoming PoIs. An optimal attack strategy should combine all those PoIs in order to retrieve the global amount of information. Performing an engineering realignment strategy may be a solution. In cases where realignment is not feasible, convolutional neural networks (CNNs) may come to help. For this reason, they are introduced in this section.

CNNs allow us to learn shift-invariant features, that is, characteristics of the traces for which the position is not discriminant, that are thus able to stay efficient in the presence of desynchronization. They are neural networks that differ from MLPs by the presence in their architecture of two additional types of layers: the *convolutional layer* and the *pooling layer*, two operations that replace the vector inner product $\boldsymbol{x} \cdot \theta$ inside the activation functions g.

The *convolutional layer* is a linear layer that acts by computing a series of convolutions between an input and one or several *filters*, a.k.a. *kernels*. A schematic representation of a (one-dimensional) convolutional layer is given in Figure 4.5. Filters, depicted in blue, are matrices of trainable weights for which the input features are locally multiplied. To apply a convolutional layer to an input of size $D \times V$, where the value of V is typically 1 when the input is the side-channel trace (first layer), n_{filter} filters of size $W \times V$ (where W is called *kernel size*) are slid over the length dimension of the input. The filters form a window which defines a linear transformation of $W \times V$ consecutive points of the data into new matrices of size

$1 \times n_{\text{filter}}$. The fact that the same filters are locally repeatedly multiplied across the input is responsible for the *shift-covariant* character of the convolutional layer – that is, applying a convolutional layer to a shifted input results in the same output, up to the same shift. Intuitively, we can figure that, once trained, each convolutional filter is specialized in the extraction of a particular pattern, wherever the pattern is localized in the input.

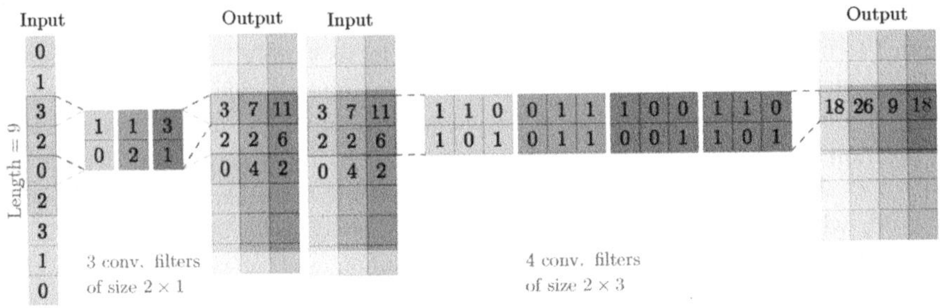

Figure 4.5. *Two convolutional layers. Left:* $W = 2, V = 1, n_{\text{filter}} = 3$, stride $= S = 1$, padding $= P = 0$. *Right:* $W = 2, V = 3, n_{\text{filter}} = 4$. *For a color version of this figure, see www.iste.co.uk/prouff/cryptography1.zip*

The length dimension of the output of a convolutional layer depends on several parameters – for example, the input length, the filter size and other parameters that the interested reader may find by solving the following exercise. In the most common configuration, the length dimension of the output is set to remain the same as the input, so that the size of the output is $D \times n_{\text{filter}}$.

Exercise 4.13. Get familiar with the one-dimensional convolutional layer parameters.

1. **Stride.** The stride parameter expresses in number of units the amount of movements the filters perform while sliding across the input. It constitutes a form of subsampling.

a) Observe the first convolutional layer of Figure 4.5. The filter size is $W = 2$ and no padding is applied to the input. The stride in the figure is equal to 1, that is, the filter moves by one unit before applying again. What is the temporal dimension of the output? Why?

b) What would be the temporal dimension of the output if the filter size would have been $W = 3$?

c) What would be the temporal dimension of the output with a stride equal to 2? And with a stride equal to 3?

d) Observe that if stride equals 3, some input samples do not contribute to the output. This leads to an unreasonable information loss. For that reason, it is more natural to take stride smaller than ....

e) Let D be the temporal size of the input, W the filter size and S the stride; express the temporal size of the output in absence of padding (solution: $\lfloor \frac{D-W}{S} + 1 \rfloor$).

2. **Padding.** In Figure 4.5, it may be observed that the top and bottom temporal samples of the inputs are multiplied only once by the $W = 2$-sized filters, and in particular, are never multiplied by both the filter components. In order to allow for more space for the filter to cover the input, a padding may by applied. The most common padding is the so-called *zero padding*, obtained by concatenating p zeros at the beginning and at the end of the time axis. The P parameter is commonly fixed following two strategies, known as *full padding* and *same padding*.

f) In *full padding*, $P = W - 1$, so every possible partial or complete superposition of the filter on the input is taken into account. Using such a padding always enlarges the temporal dimension. For the first convolutional layer of Figure 4.5, what would be the temporal dimension of the output if a full padding was applied? (solution: 10)

g) Let D be the temporal size of the input, and W the filter size; express the temporal size of the output in presence of a full padding and with a unit stride ($S = 1$) (solution: $D + W - 1$).

h) Let D be the temporal size of the input, W the filter size and S the stride. Express the temporal size of the output in presence of a full padding (solution: $\lfloor \frac{D+W-2}{S} + 1 \rfloor$).

i) In *same padding*, the size of the padding is chosen in such a way that the temporal dimension of the output is the same as the one of the input. Observe the first convolutional layer of Figure 4.5. Verify that no matter the size of the padding P, it is not possible to obtain an output with temporal dimension equal to 9.

j) Assume now that the filter size is $W = 3$ instead of $W = 2$. Which value must take P in order to obtain a *same padding*? (solution: $P = 1$).

k) Let us consider a convolutional layer with stride $S = 1$ and odd filter size $W = 2K + 1$. Which value must take P in order to obtain a *same padding*? The reader may deduce that it is in general a good idea to choose odd sizes for convolutional filters in order to gain the control of the output size by means of a *same padding* (solution: $P = K$).

l) Express the temporal dimension of the output of a generic convolutional layer, with filter size K, stride S, padding P, applied to an input of dimensional size equal to D (solution: $\lfloor \frac{D+2P-W}{S} + 1 \rfloor$).

The *pooling layer* is a nonlinear layer that reduces the spatial size. Since the size of the data is enlarged after the application of several convolutional filters, pooling layers are introduced to keep the data complexity under control while stacking several convolutional layers. To apply a pooling layer, the input data is split into contiguous patches of a given size – say u, along the temporal dimension. Then, a *sub-sampling* function is applied on each patch. Usually, the sub-sampling extracts the averaged or maximum value of its input entries. A schematic example of a maximum value-based pooling layer is depicted in Figure 4.6. By construction, the pooling layer is mostly *shift-invariant*: when applying such a layer on a shifted input, the output merely changes – up to side effects, depending on the pooling size u. In contrast with convolutional layers, the pooling layer does not contain any trainable parameters.

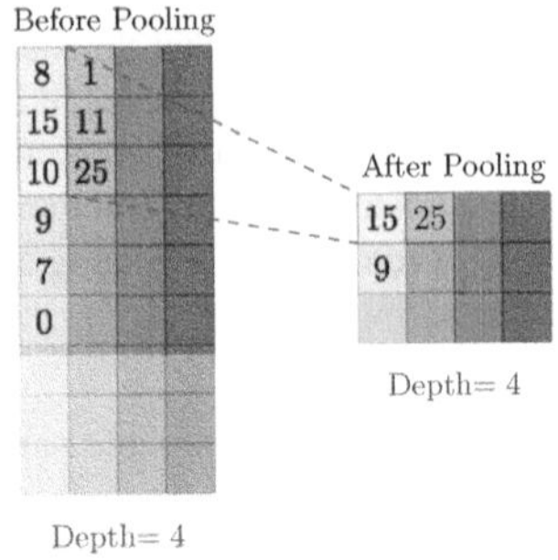

Figure 4.6. *A Max Pooling layer. For a color version of this figure, see www.iste.co.uk/prouff/cryptography1.zip*

Exercise 4.14. A pooling layer is defined by parameters that are totally analogous to those of a convolutional layer: the filter size W, the stride S and the padding P.

a) It is very common to choose W and S in such a way that the filter totally spans the input space, without overlapping. What it the relationship between W and S which guarantees such a property? (solution: $W = S$).

b) It is unusual to apply a padding to a pooling layer. Express the temporal dimension of the output of a generic pooling layer, with filter size K, stride S, padding $P = 0$, applied to an input of dimensional size equal to D (solution: $\lfloor \frac{D-W}{S} + 1 \rfloor$).

Both convolutional and pooling layers can be seen as a particular case of dense layer from an MLP with some particular constraints on the weights. Therefore, the set of models covered by CNNs is a subset of models covered by MLP. This means that the prior knowledge of CNN is strictly stronger than that of MLPs.

4.5. Summary of the chapter

This chapter now comes to its end, and we have presented several ways for Eve to model the leakage distribution in order to feed her distinguisher, and thereby to efficiently recover the secret key embedded in the target device. An exhaustive and detailed list of the whole spectrum of models which could be used for supervised attacks is beyond the scope of this introductory chapter. Nevertheless, and as a synthesis of what has been reviewed here, we present in Figure 4.7 several models, sorted with respect to the prior bias they require, and their sample complexity – that is, how their performance scales with the number of traces acquired on the clone device $N_{\mathcal{C}}$. It is noticeable that at the extreme of the generative models spectrum, we may find autoencoders (AE), which are unsupervised variants of MLPs and CNNs, and even some *non-parametric* models, like the kernel density estimator (KDE). Those models are quite powerful, in the sense that they merely require any prior bias, but as a drawback they are very prone to the curse of dimensionality[8]. With all these tools in hand, Eve is now ready to select the best way to mount her supervised attacks, depending on her means.

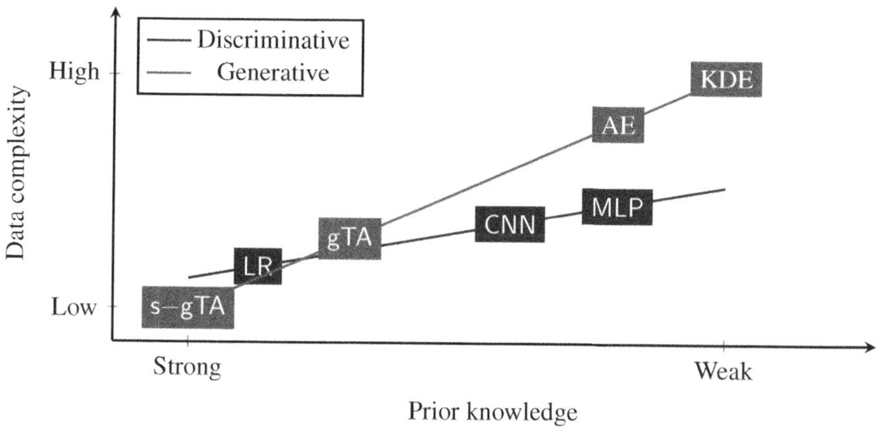

Figure 4.7. *Synthesis of generative and discriminative models, and their complexity:* gTA *(resp.* s–gTA*) stands for Gaussian templates (resp. with shared covariance matrix).* LR *stands for the logistic regression. For a color version of this figure, see www.iste.co.uk/prouff/cryptography1.zip*

4.6. Notes and further references

– In section 4.1.1, we explained the reasons why it makes sense, especially in a security evaluation context, to assume the clone $\mathcal{C}$ behaves exactly like the actual target $\mathcal{T}$. The problem related to potential discrepancy between $\mathcal{C}$ and $\mathcal{T}$ is a so-called *portability issue*, and is assessed in several domains where machine learning is applied. In SCA, some recent publications discuss such an issue (Bhasin et al. 2020).

– The optimality of the maximum likelihood distinguisher has been stated by Heuser et al. (2014). It extends a well-known result in learning theory, under the name of Bayes' classifier (Shalev-Shwartz and Ben-David 2014, p. 25).

8 Hence, the terminology "non-parametric", although correct, is somewhat misleading: it may be tempting to believe that the more parameters, the more complex the model, and hereupon non-parametric models might require very few traces in the training phase. Unfortunately, non-parametric models often require much more traces in the training phase to reach a satisfying performance. The reason is that such models are mostly prone to the curse of dimensionality.

– Vapnik's quote is taken from his monograph (Vapnik 1998).

– Historically, supervised attacks have been introduced by Chari et al. (2003) in their seminal paper *Template Attacks*, where they introduced Gaussian templates, also known in the machine learning terminology as *Quadratic Discriminant Analysis* (QDA). Template attacks have been generalized under the terminology of *profiling* attacks. Since this terminology carries the legacy prone of SCA to use generative models, we rather use the – more general – term of *supervised* attacks here.

– Beside Gaussian templates, machine learning has been progressively adopted in supervised attacks since the early 2010s; first with *Random Forest*and *Support Vector Machines* (Lerman et al. 2013, 2014, 2015), then with Deep Neural Networks (Martinasek and Zeman 2013; Martinasek et al. 2016). Later, Maghrebi and Cagli paved the way toward the use of CNNs to deal with de-synchronized leakages (Cagli et al. 2017).

– Beside Convolutional Neural Networks, in order to deal with the desynchronization issue, a research track investigates about techniques for side-channel analysis in the frequency domain. The interested reader may refer to the thesis of Gabriel Destouet for a complete bibliography and some modern insights (Destouet 2022).

– The use of shared covariance matrix for Gaussian templates has been proposed by Choudary and Kuhn (2013). It draws some tight links with LDA.

– Efron made a comparative study between Gaussian templates with shared covariance matrix, and logistic regression, in the case of two classes (Efron 1975).

– The reader interested in the universal approximation theorem may refer to Allan Pinkus' (1999) survey.

– The loss function presented in equation [4.8] is the most used in SCA. Nevertheless, over the past few years, the choice of alternative loss has become vivid research topic, and many proposals have been done in literature, for example, Zaid et al. (2021).

– The back-propagation algorithm, its advantages and inconvenients are part of a more general field of study called *automatic differentiation*. The interested reader may refer to the survey of Baydin et al. (2017).

– The reader interested in neural networks in general may refer to Goodfellow's textbook about general purpose deep learning (Goodfellow et al. 2016). In the particular application case of SCA, the interested reader may refer to the respective theses of the authors of this chapter (Cagli 2018; Masure 2020); or the survey of Picek et al. (2022).

4.7. References

Baydin, A.G., Pearlmutter, B.A., Radul, A.A., Siskind, J.M. (2017). Automatic differentiation in machine learning: A survey. *J. Mach. Learn. Res.*, 18, 153:1–153:43 [Online]. Available at: http://jmlr.org/papers/v18/17-468.html.

Bhasin, S., Chattopadhyay, A., Heuser, A., Jap, D., Picek, S., Ranjan, R. (2020). Mind the portability: A warriors guide through realistic profiled side-channel analysis. In *NDSS 2020-Network and Distributed System Security Symposium*, 1–14.

Cagli, E. (2018). Feature extraction for side-channel attacks (Extraction de caractéristiques pour les attaques par canaux auxiliaires). PhD Thesis, Sorbonne University, Paris [Online]. Available at: https://tel.archives-ouvertes.fr/tel-02494260.

Cagli, E., Dumas, C., Prouff, E. (2017). Convolutional neural networks with data augmentation against jitter-based countermeasures: Profiling attacks without pre-processing. In *CHES 2017*, Fischer, W. and Homma, N. (eds). Springer, Heidelberg.

Chari, S., Rao, J.R., Rohatgi, P. (2003). Template attacks. In *CHES 2002*, Kaliski Jr., B.S., Çetin Kaya. K., Paar, C. (eds). Springer, Heidelberg.

Choudary, O. and Kuhn, M.G. (2013). Efficient template attacks. In *CARDIS*. Springer, Cham.

Destouet, G. (2022). Ondelettes pour le traitement des signaux compromettants. PhD Thesis, Grenoble Alpes University, Grenoble [Online]. Available at: https://tel.archives-ouvertes.fr/tel-03758771.

Efron, B. (1975). The efficiency of logistic regression compared to normal discriminant analysis. *Journal of the American Statistical Association*, 70(352), 892–898 [Online]. Available at: http://www.jstor.org/stable/2285453.

Goodfellow, I.J., Bengio, Y., Courville, A.C. (2016). *Deep Learning: Adaptive Computation and Machine Learning*. MIT Press, Cambridge [Online]. Available at: http://www.deeplearningbook.org/.

Heuser, A., Rioul, O., Guilley, S. (2014). Good is not good enough: Deriving optimal distinguishers from communication theory. In *CHES 2014*, Batina, L. and Robshaw, M. (eds). Springer, Heidelberg.

Lerman, L., Medeiros, S.F., Bontempi, G., Markowitch, O. (2013). A machine learning approach against a masked AES. In *CARDIS*. Springer, Cham.

Lerman, L., Bontempi, G., Markowitch, O. (2014). Power analysis attack: An approach based on machine learning. *Int. J. Appl. Cryptogr.*, 3(2), 97–115.

Lerman, L., Poussier, R., Bontempi, G., Markowitch, O., Standaert, F. (2015). Template attacks vs. machine learning revisited (and the curse of dimensionality in side-channel analysis). In *COSADE*. Springer, Cham.

Martinasek, Z. and Zeman, V. (2013). Innovative method of the power analysis. *Radioengineering*, 22, 586–594.

Martinasek, Z., Dzurenda, P., Malina, L. (2016). Profiling power analysis attack based on MLP in DPA contest V4.2. In *39th International Conference on Telecommunications and Signal Processing, TSP 2016*, June 27–29. IEEE, Vienna. doi: 10.1109/TSP.2016.7760865.

Masure, L. (2020). Towards a better comprehension of deep learning for side-channel analysis (Vers une meilleure compréhension de l'apprentissage profond appliqué aux attaques par observations). PhD Thesis, Sorbonne University, Paris [Online]. Available at: https://tel.archives-ouvertes.fr/tel-03651269.

Picek, S., Perin, G., Mariot, L., Wu, L., Batina, L. (2022). Sok: Deep learning-based physical side-channel analysis. *ACM Comput. Surv.* doi: 10.1145/3569577.

Pinkus, A. (1999). Approximation theory of the mlp model in neural networks. *Acta Numerica*, 8, 143–195.

Shalev-Shwartz, S. and Ben-David, S. (2014). *Understanding Machine Learning – From Theory to Algorithms*. Cambridge University Press, Cambridge [Online]. Available at: http://www.cambridge.org/de/academic/subjects/computer-science/pattern-recognition-and-machine-learning/understanding-machine-learning-theory-algorithms.

Vapnik, V. (1998). *Statistical Learning Theory*. John Wiley & Sons, New York.

Zaid, G., Bossuet, L., Dassance, F., Habrard, A., Venelli, A. (2021). Ranking loss: Maximizing the success rate in deep learning side-channel analysis. *IACR TCHES*, 2021(1), 25–55 [Online]. Available at: https://tches.iacr.org/index.php/TCHES/article/view/8726.

5
Unsupervised Attacks

Cécile DUMAS
CEA-Leti, Université Grenoble Alpes, France

This chapter covers side channel attacks during execution of the targeted embedded cryptographic implementation, when such signals are obtained solely from the evaluated product via auxiliary channels. In contrast to the supervised attacks described in the previous chapter, these attacks are referred to as *unsupervised attacks*.

5.1. Introduction

5.1.1. *Supervised attacks*

The attacker considered in Chapter 4 possessed a clone device $\mathcal{C}$ of the targeted component $\mathcal{T}$ (or a replica of the targeted code), the secrecy of which they could control in order to obtain signals comparable to those acquired on $\mathcal{T}$. In this supervised scenario, summarized in Figure 4.1, the signals resulting from the execution of $\mathcal{C}$ could be labeled because of the full knowledge of the data manipulated by the $\mathcal{C}$ code. Data labeling enables the characterization of the leaks relative to the data. Then, using this characterization, called *profiling*, additional, unlabeled signals from the execution of $\mathcal{T}$ were analyzed for secret data.

Imagining a supervised scenario, where the attacker has significant control over the data on a $\mathcal{C}$ replica and infinite means establishing leakage profiling, allows us to envisage the worst-case scenario. Studying this type of scenario is important, as the

Embedded Cryptography 1,
coordinated by Emmanuel PROUFF, Guénaël RENAULT,
Matthieu RIVAIN and Colin O'FLYNN.

resistance of an implementation to these powerful attacks guarantees the security of the system in all cases.

However, these attacks are not entirely realistic, since they are only accessible to attackers with a high attack potential. Indeed, the existence of a controllable $\mathcal{C}$ replica of the targeted component or code is not always guaranteed, or difficult to obtain due to confidentiality constraints. While the risk to these attackers is critical, the threat is potentially relatively low. Conversely, if no controllable $\mathcal{C}$ replica is needed to exploit leaks in an implementation, even an attacker with a low attack potential will be able to compromise the security of a product. Such a flaw will be accessible to a larger number of individuals, increasing the scope of the repercussions. It is therefore important to assess the resistance of a cryptographic implementation to *unsupervised attacks*, which are more accessible and therefore less costly.

Unsupervised attacks, which appeared upstream of supervised attacks at the end of the 20th century, operate on the same principles, except that they rely solely on signals acquired from the target component $\mathcal{T}$. The attacker knows the target implementation and its inputs/outputs, but has no information on the internal data, which are secret; the attacker's action is therefore reduced to the attack phase, where, as explained in Chapter 4, the attacker must make hypotheses about the value of sensitive data. In order to classify the different hypotheses, the attacker uses a *distinguisher* that assigns a score to each key hypothesis. If the correct key hypothesis has the highest score, the attack is considered successful.

What is more, an attacker will only have a limited number of traces at his disposal. The resistance of a product must therefore be assessed in a specific context, taking into account the restrictions of use and the possibilities of the attacker. As in the previous chapter, we consider the number of traces used by the attacker to be a quantitative criterion for the attack carried out.

5.1.2. *Unsupervised attacks*

An attacker has access to a component (the *target* $\mathcal{T}$) that performs a cryptographic calculation, from which the attacker intends to recover the secret key used. Whether or not the attacker can choose the input messages for the calculation, it is assumed that the attacker knows the plaintext, or failing that, can read the output ciphertext. In parallel with the calculation, signals emitted by the component are measured, usually with an oscilloscope. Once the acquisitions have been completed, the attacker performs statistical analyses to find the value of the key.

The signals measured are the *attack traces* and are denoted as $(\mathbf{x}_i)_{i\in\{1,\ldots,N_a\}}$. The trace $\mathbf{x}_i \in \mathcal{X}^D$, of length D, is acquired during the computation time of a cryptographic function $\mathbf{C}$, with a known (or encrypted) plaintext $p_i \in \mathcal{P}$ and an unknown piece of fixed key $k^\star \in \mathcal{K}$ as input. This piece of key, referred to hereafter simply as *key*, is the attacker's target. The output of the calculation $\mathbf{C}$ is called *sensitive data* and is generally denoted $z = \mathbf{C}(p, k)$ for any plaintext p and key k. In order to find the secret key, the attacker will make hypotheses k about its true value $k^\star$. It is therefore important to have a countable $\mathcal{K}$ of possibilities. Classically, in the case of a key byte, this set has 256 values. The true calculation of the sensitive data with plaintext p and $k^\star$ is $z^\star = \mathbf{C}(p, k^\star)$.

The set of traces and their plain text $\{(\mathbf{x}_1, p_1), \ldots, (\mathbf{x}_{N_a}, p_{N_a})\}$ corresponds to the set $\mathcal{S}_\mathcal{T}$ in Figure 5.1, which summarizes the principle of unsupervised attacks and illustrates the notations used later.

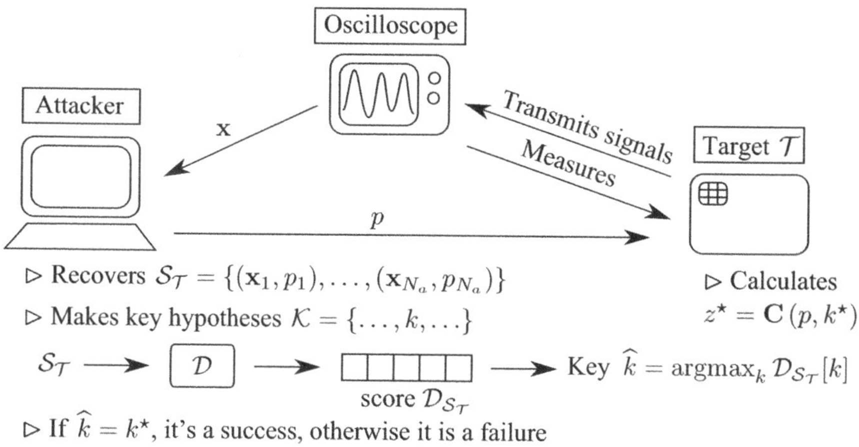

Figure 5.1. *Principle of an unsupervised attack*

From a statistical point of view, we consider that the values $p_i \in \mathcal{P}$ for $i \in \{1, \ldots, N_a\}$ are realizations of the random variable P, the vectors $\mathbf{x}_i \in \mathcal{X}^D$ for $i \in \{1, \ldots, N_a\}$ are realizations of the random vector $\mathbf{X}$, and the values $z_i = \mathbf{C}(p_i, k) \in \mathcal{Z}$ for $i \in \{1, \ldots, N_a\}$, with $p_i \in \mathcal{P}$ and $k \in \mathcal{K}$, are realizations of the random variable Z; as the value k is generally fixed, we can use the notation Z_k to distinguish the random variables $\mathrm{Z}_{k^\star} = \mathbf{C}(\mathrm{P}, k^\star)$ and $\mathrm{Z}_k = \mathbf{C}(\mathrm{P}, k)$ for $k \neq k^\star$.

The expectation and variance of a random variable X are denoted $\mathbb{E}[\mathrm{X}]$ and $\mathrm{Var}(\mathrm{X})$, respectively. For a function f, the expectation of $f(\mathrm{X})$ under the distribution of X is denoted $\underset{\mathrm{X}}{\mathbb{E}}[f(\mathrm{X})]$. The covariance of two random variables X and Y is denoted $\mathrm{Cov}(\mathrm{X}, \mathrm{Y})$. The corresponding empirical mean, variance and covariance are denoted $\overline{\mathrm{X}}$, $\langle \mathrm{X}^2 \rangle$ and $\langle \mathrm{X}, \mathrm{Y} \rangle$, respectively.

The data $(z_i)_{i\in\{1,\dots,N_a\}}$ are said to be sensitive, as knowledge of them provides information about the secret key $k^\star$ and reduces its entropy. They are therefore a prime target for an attacker. In the case of symmetrical cryptographic algorithms, the attacker will typically target the output of an S-box. For example, in the case of AES, this output is encoded on 8 bits, so $0 \leq z_i \leq 2^8 - 1$ for $i \in \{1, \dots, N_a\}$. As the encoding induces a finite data size, the variable Z is discrete. Generally speaking, if the encoding is on n bits, Z belongs to the finite set $\mathcal{Z} = \{0, \dots, 2^n - 1\}$.

The random vector $\mathbf{X}$ is also considered discrete, since it is derived from a measurement via an oscilloscope with limited memory depth: $\mathbf{X} \in \mathcal{X}^D$ with $\mathcal{X}$ a finite set of size generally between 256 and 2^{16}. However, as it represents a signal of a physical nature, the $\mathbf{X}$ vector can be extended to continuous values, with $\mathcal{X} = \mathbb{R}$.

The objective of the attacks studied here is to recover the secret $k^\star$ using the $\mathcal{S}_\mathcal{T}$ set of N_a traces. To rank the different key hypotheses, the attacker uses a distinguisher $\mathcal{D}$ which, applied to $\mathcal{S}_\mathcal{T}$, assigns a score to each key hypothesis. The best score is denoted as $\widehat{k}$ and is worth $\mathrm{argmax}_{k\in\mathcal{K}}\, \mathcal{D}_{\mathcal{S}_\mathcal{T}}[k]$. If the correct key hypothesis has the best score, that is, if $k^\star = \widehat{k}$, the attack is considered successful. Other notions of success can be defined, and will be discussed in Chapter 6. As the number of traces required to successfully complete an attack is limited, it is interesting to consider as an efficiency criterion the minimum number of traces $N_a^\star$, necessary to achieve success with a certain probability.

5.1.3. *How to attack without profiling?*

The absence of profiling means that, unlike supervised attacks (see Chapter 4), experiments cannot be used to directly estimate a possible generative or discrimative model. To compensate for this absence, with a minimum of efficiency, it is necessary to have a priori knowledge about the acquired traces and use more adapted attack methods. This a priori knowledge is based on the attacker's assumptions about leaks and is intended to replace the profiling and learning phase of Figure 4.1 in the previous chapter, as shown in Figure 5.2. Some assumptions made by the attacker are quite reasonable, while others may be very far from reality. The effectiveness of a given attack method will obviously be influenced by the quality of this information a priori, more or less realistic, but it will also depend on the method chosen and its ability to deal with the inaccuracies introduced by overly restrictive assumptions. For this reason, this chapter presents several methods, whose effectiveness will depend on the nature of the acquired traces.

Chapter 3 provides several leakage models that describe the shape of acquired traces, relating signal magnitude to the data being manipulated. In order to inject a priori knowledge easily, we define a deterministic leakage model δ that depends only on the sensitive data and gives an intuition about the shape of its leakage. The $\mathbf{x}[t]$ value of a trace at a time t is split into two components: $\mathbf{x}[t] = \delta(z) + \mathbf{b}[t]$, with:

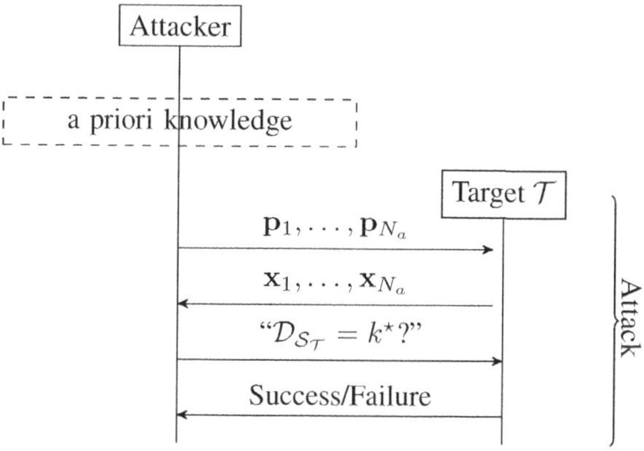

Figure 5.2. *Scenario of an unsupervised attack*

– A deterministic component δ that depends on the algorithm, the other variables it handles, the way they are processed, the experiment conditions, etc. More generally, it depends on the random variable corresponding to the sensitive data Z and any fixed, non-random data. The function $\delta(\mathrm{Z})$ represents an instantaneous model of Z, so it does not depend on time.

– A random time component $\mathbf{b}[t]$ realization of a random variable $\mathbf{B}[t]$, such that $\mathbf{b} = \mathbf{x} - \delta(z)$ is a vector of dimension D. This second component may depend on Z in the general case.

If the assumptions made about the random variable $\mathbf{B}[t]$ are identical at each instant t, the modeling can be simplified to univariate modeling: we assume that at each instant of the trace: $x = \delta(z) + b$, where x and b are, respectively, the realizations of the random variables X and B. Univariate modeling is used by univariate attacks, which apply this single model to the entire trace, as opposed to multivariate attacks, which use multivariate modeling, different at each instant.

In the following, we will consider that a model $\mathbf{m}$ represents the trace $\mathbf{x}$ at certain times $t \in \{t_1, \ldots, t_D\}$ according to a key hypothesis k and is written $\mathbf{m}_k[t] = \delta(\mathbf{C}(p,k)) + \mathbf{b}[t]$ or vectorially:

$$\mathbf{m}_k = \boldsymbol{\delta}(\mathbf{C}(p,k)) + \mathbf{b}$$

by denoting $\boldsymbol{\delta}(z)$ the constant vector of size D of value $\delta(z)$. In the univariate case, it simplifies to $m_k = \delta(\mathbf{C}(p,k)) + b$.

In the next section, we present appropriate attack methods based on the model used to describe the acquired traces, that is, on the assumptions the attacker makes about δ

and **B**. These methods are characterized by the use of a context-sensitive distinguisher (as seen in Chapter 4 and redefined by Definition 3.1).

5.2. Distinguishers

The aim of this section is to define a general framework within which to study attack methods using distinguishers based on known statistical tools.

In order to retrieve the secret $k^\star$, the attacker has a family of models $(\mathbf{m}_k)_{k \in \mathcal{Z}}$ parameterized by a hypothesis k made on the secret and a set of traces $(\mathbf{x}_i)_{i \in \{1,\dots,N_a\}}$, which can be partitioned according to the value of k so that each trace is assigned a value $z_i = \mathbf{C}(p_i, k)$. From a statistical point of view, we consider the random vector $\mathbf{X}$, the parameter k on which the random variable Z_k depends, and the model $\mathbf{m}_k$.

The attacker's sole objective is to find $k^\star$ efficiently, that is, by minimizing the number of traces acquired. Knowing the distribution law of the traces, the likelihood of a model with the traces, or even just the nature of the relationship between the traces and the various models does not really interest the attacker. The attacker just needs a tool to distinguish the true secret from the wrong hypotheses. For this reason, a number of statistical tools can be used as distinguishers to select the most probable k hypothesis.

DEFINITION 5.1. DISTINGUISHER.– Let $\mathcal{S}_\mathcal{T}$ be a set of attack traces associated with clear texts. A *distinguisher* $\mathcal{D}$ is a function from $\mathcal{S}_\mathcal{T}$ to a *score vector* in $\mathbb{R}^{|\mathcal{K}|}$:

$$\mathcal{D} : \mathcal{S}_\mathcal{T} \mapsto \begin{pmatrix} \vdots \\ \mathcal{D}_{\mathcal{S}_\mathcal{T}}[k] \\ \vdots \end{pmatrix}. \qquad [5.1]$$

For a $\mathcal{D}$ distinguisher to be effective, the difference between the scores $\mathcal{D}_{\mathcal{S}_\mathcal{T}}[k^\star] - \mathcal{D}_{\mathcal{S}_\mathcal{T}}[k]$ must be positive for any k hypothesis and high enough for a bad $k \neq k^\star$ key hypothesis. In this way, the score for the right hypothesis stands out from the other scores.

> COMPREHENSION EXERCISE 5.1.– Let $\mathcal{S}_\mathcal{T}$ be a set of attack traces. It is assumed that a $\mathcal{D}$ distinguisher returns the following score vector: $\mathcal{D}^1_{\mathcal{S}_\mathcal{T}} = (0, 10, 3, 5, 6, 2, 3, 1)^\intercal$. What is the size of $\mathcal{K}$? If the value of key $k^\star$ is 0, is the attack successful? Same questions for $\mathcal{D}^2_{\mathcal{S}_\mathcal{T}} = (10, 9, 3, 5)^\intercal$, $\mathcal{D}^3_{\mathcal{S}_\mathcal{T}} = (10, 10, 3, 5)^\intercal$ and $\mathcal{D}^4_{\mathcal{S}_\mathcal{T}} = (10, 10)^\intercal$.

The following sections describe the use of different statistical tools:

– As mentioned in Chapter 4, likelihood is used to describe the plausibility of the parameter k for a model $\mathbf{m}$, given the observation of realizations of $\mathbf{X}$. This tool is presented in section 5.3.

– Mutual information quantifies the dependence between the random variables $\mathbf{X}$ and Z. This tool is presented in section 5.4.

– The correlation coefficient quantifies the linear dependence between the random variables $\mathbf{X}$ and Z. This tool is presented in section 5.5.

5.3. Likelihood distinguisher

5.3.1. *Distinguisher definition*

Initially, we will be looking to use the methods seen in Chapter 4 based on the likelihood distinguisher.

As a reminder, for a given plaintext p and trace $\mathbf{x} \in \mathcal{X}^D$, the likelihood $\mathcal{L}$ of a fixed parameter $k \in \mathcal{K}$ is the function that associates to it the probability that $\mathbf{X}$ is equal to $\mathbf{x}$ knowing Z is equal to $\mathbf{C}(p,k)$, that is: $\mathcal{L} : k \mapsto \Pr(\mathbf{X} = \mathbf{x} | \mathrm{Z} = z = \mathbf{C}(p,k))$. The attacker expects it to be maximal for a good key hypothesis.

In order to calculate the probability, we need to make some hypotheses about the distribution of $\mathbf{B}$. The usual hypothesis is that $\mathbf{B}$ follows a normal distribution. This is the following hypothesis, already introduced in the previous chapter in section 4.2.1.

ASSUMPTION 5.1. GAUSSIAN NOISE.– For a given value z, the random vector $(\mathbf{B} | \mathrm{Z} = z)$ follows a normal distribution $\mathcal{N}(\boldsymbol{\mu}_{z,\mathbf{B}}, \boldsymbol{\Sigma}_{z,\mathbf{B}})$, with $\boldsymbol{\mu}_{z,\mathbf{B}}$ a vector of dimension D and $\boldsymbol{\Sigma}_{z,\mathbf{B}}$ a matrix of dimension $D \times D$.

It allows us to express the probabilities $\Pr(\mathbf{X} = \mathbf{x} | \mathrm{Z} = z)$ for any z using the probability density function of the normal distribution. Unfortunately, without profiling, it is not possible to estimate the parameters of these distributions. The idea is therefore to define a variant of the distinguisher based on a new likelihood function for the parameter k that incorporates the model $\mathbf{m}_k$, since this is also parameterized by k. For a given plaintext p and trace $\mathbf{x} \in \mathcal{X}^D$, this likelihood function is defined by $L : k \in \mathcal{Z} \mapsto \Pr(\mathbf{m}_k = \mathbf{x} | \mathrm{Z} = \mathbf{C}(p,k))$. We therefore have:

$$
\begin{aligned}
L(k) &= \Pr(\mathbf{m}_k = \mathbf{x} | \mathrm{Z} = \mathbf{C}(p,k)) \\
&= \Pr(\boldsymbol{\delta}(\mathbf{C}(\mathrm{P},k)) + \mathbf{B} = \mathbf{x} | \mathrm{Z} = \mathbf{C}(p,k)) \\
&= \Pr(\boldsymbol{\delta}(\mathrm{Z}) + \mathbf{B} = \mathbf{x} | \mathrm{Z} = z)
\end{aligned}
$$

Since the random vector $(\boldsymbol{\delta}(\mathrm{Z}) | \mathrm{Z} = z)$ is constant, the random vector $(\boldsymbol{\delta}(\mathrm{Z}) + \mathbf{B} | \mathrm{Z} = z)$ follows the normal distribution with mean vector $\boldsymbol{\delta}(z) + \boldsymbol{\mu}_{z,\mathbf{B}}$ and covariance matrix $\boldsymbol{\Sigma}_{z,\mathbf{B}}$, where $z = \mathbf{C}(p,k)$.

In order to determine the function δ and the parameters $\boldsymbol{\mu}_{z,\mathbf{B}}$ and $\boldsymbol{\Sigma}_{z,\mathbf{B}}$, we will see in the next section that, due to the absence of profiling traces, it is necessary to add hypotheses about the leakage model. Once the model parameters have been defined (using only the attack traces), the attacker uses the distinguisher associated with the likelihood function L, and more precisely with twice the logarithm to simplify the formula. It is denoted $\mathcal{D}^{ll}_{\mathcal{S}_\mathcal{T}}$ (*ll* for *log-likelihood*) and defined for a hypothesis k by:

$$\begin{aligned}\mathcal{D}^{ll}_{\mathcal{S}_\mathcal{T}}[k] &= 2 \times \log\left(\sqrt{(2\pi)^D} \cdot L(k)\right)\\ &= 2 \times \log\left(\sqrt{(2\pi)^D} \cdot \prod_i \frac{\exp\left(-\frac{1}{2}\boldsymbol{\Delta}_i^\intercal \boldsymbol{\Sigma}_{z_i,\mathbf{B}}^{-1}\boldsymbol{\Delta}_i\right)}{\sqrt{(2\pi)^D \cdot \det \boldsymbol{\Sigma}_{z_i,\mathbf{B}}}}\right)\\ &= 2 \times \left(\sum_i \log\left(\det \boldsymbol{\Sigma}_{z_i,\mathbf{B}}\right)^{-1/2} - \frac{1}{2}\sum_i \left(\boldsymbol{\Delta}_i^\intercal \boldsymbol{\Sigma}_{z_i,\mathbf{B}}^{-1}\boldsymbol{\Delta}_i\right)\right)\\ &= -\sum_i \log\left(\det \boldsymbol{\Sigma}_{z_i,\mathbf{B}}\right) - \sum_i \left(\boldsymbol{\Delta}_i^\intercal \boldsymbol{\Sigma}_{z_i,\mathbf{B}}^{-1}\boldsymbol{\Delta}_i\right)\end{aligned}$$

where $\boldsymbol{\Delta}_i = \mathbf{x}_i - \boldsymbol{\delta}(z_i) - \boldsymbol{\mu}_{z_i,\mathbf{B}}$ and $z_i = \mathbf{C}(p_i, k)$.

From this definition follows a simpler distinguisher in the case where $\boldsymbol{\Sigma}_{z,\mathbf{B}}$ does not depend on z. This is a homoscedasticity hypothesis defined as follows:

ASSUMPTION 5.2. NOISE HOMOSCEDASTICITY.– The random vectors $(\mathbf{B}\,|\,\mathrm{Z} = z)_{z\in\mathcal{Z}}$ have a common covariance matrix equal to $\boldsymbol{\Sigma}_\mathbf{B}$, which is the covariance matrix of the random vector $\mathbf{B}$.

Since under this hypothesis the term $\det \boldsymbol{\Sigma}_\mathbf{B}$ does not depend on Z, the new distinguisher obtained is the following:

$$\mathcal{D}^{homo}_{\mathcal{S}_\mathcal{T}}[k] = -\sum_i \left((\mathbf{x}_i - \boldsymbol{\delta}(z_i) - \boldsymbol{\mu}_{z_i,\mathbf{B}})^\intercal \boldsymbol{\Sigma}_\mathbf{B}^{-1}(\mathbf{x}_i - \boldsymbol{\delta}(z_i) - \boldsymbol{\mu}_{z_i,\mathbf{B}})\right)$$

In the univariate case ($D = 1$), the two previous distinguishers also simplify:

$$\begin{aligned}\mathcal{D}^{ll}_{\mathcal{S}_\mathcal{T}}[k] &= -\sum_i \log \sigma^2_{z_i,\mathrm{B}} - \sum_i \left(\Delta_i \sigma^{-2}_{z_i,\mathrm{B}} \Delta_i\right)\\ &= -\sum_i \log \sigma^2_{z_i,\mathrm{B}} - \sigma^{-2}_{z_i,\mathrm{B}} \sum_i \Delta_i^2\end{aligned}$$

where $\mu_{z,\mathrm{B}}$ and $\sigma^2_{z,\mathrm{B}}$ are the conditional mean and variance and $\Delta_i = x_i - \delta(z_i) - \mu_{z_i,\mathrm{B}}$.

And:

$$\mathcal{D}_{\mathcal{S}_\mathcal{T}}^{homo}[k] = -\sum_i (x_i - \delta(z_i) - \mu_{z_i,\mathbf{B}})^2$$

Note that this last distinguisher is that of the least-squares method.

COMPREHENSION EXERCISE 5.2.– Let a set of traces (x_i) be acquired with a plaintext p_i and a fixed key $k^\star$, both of one bit, such that a trace at each instant can be modeled by $x_i = p_i \times k^\star + b_i$, knowing that P follows a uniform distribution and B follows a normal distribution $\mathcal{N}(0, 1)$.

Which distinguisher is the attacker using? If the attacker decides to define $\delta(z) = p + k$, what will the distinguisher scores be?

5.3.2. *Determining Gaussian model parameters*

The choice of function δ and parameters $\boldsymbol{\mu}_{z,\mathbf{B}}$ and $\Sigma_{z,\mathbf{B}}$ for $z = \mathbf{C}(p,k)$ is a delicate step, as it conditions the effectiveness, or even the success, of the attack. Assuming noise homoscedasticity (Assumption 5.2) and using the distinguisher $\mathcal{D}_{\mathcal{S}_\mathcal{T}}^{homo}$ in the univariate case allows us to reasonably restrict the number of parameters. Indeed, the closer the modeling is to reality, the less noise will vary according to the sensitive data. In this case, we can assume the independence of B and Z.

ASSUMPTION 5.3. NOISE INDEPENDENCE.– The random variables **B** and Z are independent.

Note: If this hypothesis holds, for any $z \in \mathcal{Z}$ we have $\boldsymbol{\mu}_{z,\mathbf{B}} = \boldsymbol{\mu}_\mathbf{B}$ and $\Sigma_{z,\mathbf{B}} = \Sigma_\mathbf{B}$.

Furthermore, without the profiling phase, the determination of Points of Interest is more hazardous. In this case, the maximum likelihood distinguisher uses the method of least squares, which is also the most efficient estimator for linear regression in the case where errors are independent and identically distributed. It is then interesting to combine the two estimates to obtain a distinguisher that finds both the right model and the right parameters. To do this, simply define δ as a linear function of z or as a linear combination of descriptive functions of z. The study of models provides us with two possible modeling examples: Hamming weight leakage of z or bit weighted leakage of z. The use of the former is detailed in the following, while the use of the latter is described in section 5.3.4.

5.3.3. *Linear leakage model for sensitive data*

The following model assumes that the trace depends linearly on a known function φ at a given instant.

ASSUMPTION 5.4. LINEAR MODEL.– The trace x is linear as a function φ of the sensitive data z and is modeled by $m_k = \alpha \cdot \varphi(z) + b$, where α is a constant and b represents noise.

With Gaussian noise (Assumption 5.1) and independent of Z (Assumption 5.3), the model is rewritten as $m_k = \beta_0 + \beta_1\varphi(z) + b$, such that the noise B follows a normal distribution with mean zero.

The function φ can be, for example, the Hamming weight of z. With knowledge of the secret $k^\star$, it is possible to calculate $z_i^\star = \mathbf{C}(p, k^\star)$ and $\varphi(z_i^\star)$ for each trace x_i, then find β_0 and β_1 by linear regression, minimizing the error $\sum_i b_i^2 = \sum_i (x_i - \beta_0 - \beta_1\varphi(z_i^\star))^2$. Conversely, knowing β_0 and β_1, we can find the secret $k^\star$ by maximizing $\mathcal{D}_{\mathcal{ST}}^{homo}[k] = -\sum_i (x_i - \beta_0 - \beta_1\varphi(z_i))^2$. The idea is to find the secret $k^\star$, β_0 and β_1 by maximizing $\mathcal{D}_{\mathcal{ST}}^{homo}[k]$. For this, we denote $\overline{\varphi(\mathrm{Z}_k)}$ and $\overline{\mathrm{X}}$ the empirical means, $\langle \varphi(\mathrm{Z}_k)^2 \rangle$ and $\langle \mathrm{X}^2 \rangle$ the empirical variances and $\langle \varphi(\mathrm{Z}_k),\mathrm{X} \rangle$ the empirical covariance of $\varphi(\mathrm{Z}_k)$ and X calculated on N_a samples, and we calculate β_0 and β_1, as a function of k fixed, using classic linear regression formulas:

$$\beta_1 = \frac{\sum_i (\varphi(z_i) - \overline{\varphi(\mathrm{Z}_k)}) \cdot (x_i - \overline{\mathrm{X}})}{\sum_i (x_i - \overline{\mathrm{X}})^2} = \frac{\langle \varphi(\mathrm{Z}_k),\mathrm{X} \rangle}{\langle \mathrm{X}^2 \rangle}$$

$$\beta_0 = \overline{\mathrm{X}} - \beta_1 \cdot \overline{\varphi(\mathrm{Z}_k)}$$

The distinguisher $\mathcal{D}_{\mathcal{ST}}^{homo}$ is therefore rewritten as follows:

$$\begin{aligned}
\mathcal{D}_{\mathcal{ST}}^{homo}[k] &= -\sum_i (x_i - \beta_0 - \beta_1\varphi(z_i))^2 \\
&= -\sum_i \left(x_i - \overline{\mathrm{X}} + \beta_1 \cdot \overline{\varphi(\mathrm{Z}_k)} - \beta_1\varphi(z_i)\right)^2 \\
&= -\sum_i \left(x_i - \overline{\mathrm{X}} - \beta_1 \cdot \left(\varphi(z_i) - \overline{\varphi(\mathrm{Z}_k)}\right)\right)^2 \\
&= -N_a \left(\langle \mathrm{X}^2 \rangle - 2\beta_1 \cdot \langle \varphi(\mathrm{Z}_k),\mathrm{X} \rangle + \beta_1^2 \cdot \langle \varphi(\mathrm{Z}_k)^2 \rangle\right)
\end{aligned}$$

Since the empirical variance $\langle \mathrm{X}^2 \rangle$ of X does not depend on k, this distinguisher is now equivalent to:

$$\begin{aligned}
&2\beta_1 \cdot \langle \varphi(\mathrm{Z}_k),\mathrm{X} \rangle - \beta_1^2 \cdot \langle \varphi(\mathrm{Z}_k)^2 \rangle \\
&= \frac{2(\langle \varphi(\mathrm{Z}_k),\mathrm{X} \rangle)^2}{\langle \mathrm{X}^2 \rangle} - \frac{(\langle \varphi(\mathrm{Z}_k),\mathrm{X} \rangle)^2 \cdot \langle \varphi(\mathrm{Z}_k)^2 \rangle}{\langle \mathrm{X}^2 \rangle^2}
\end{aligned}$$

which is equivalent to the following distinguisher denoted as $\mathcal{D}^{ls}_{\mathcal{S}_\mathcal{T}}$ (*ls* for *least squares*):

$$\mathcal{D}^{ls}_{\mathcal{S}_\mathcal{T}}[k] = (\langle\varphi(\mathrm{Z}_k),\mathrm{X}\rangle)^2 \cdot \left(2 \cdot \langle\mathrm{X}^2\rangle - \langle\varphi(\mathrm{Z}_k)^2\rangle\right) \quad [5.2]$$

The second term $2 \cdot \langle\mathrm{X}^2\rangle - \langle\varphi(\mathrm{Z}_k)^2\rangle$ could also be ignored if the variances of the random variables $(\varphi(\mathrm{Z}_k))_{k\in\mathcal{K}}$ are equal. This assumption, whose interest is purely computational, is an assumption of homoscedasticity between $\delta(\mathrm{Z}_k)$ and Z_k:

ASSUMPTION 5.5. HOMOSCEDASTICITY OF δ.– The variance of the random variable $\delta(\mathrm{Z}_k)$ is identical for all $k \in \mathcal{K}$.

The validity of this assumption is discussed in section 5.6. However, it should not be forgotten that an attacker's main objective is to minimize N_a such that the distinguisher $\mathcal{D}^{ls}_{\mathcal{S}_\mathcal{T}}$ always returns the correct key assumption $k^\star$. Under these conditions, even if the assumption is valid, using the true value of the variance instead of an empirical estimate slightly modifies the definition of the distinguisher as N_a decreases.

5.3.4. *Linear leakage model for sensitive data bits*

The preceding linear model can be extended to a binary description of the sensitive data, in the case where the bits of the sensitive data contribute independently to the leakage of z:

ASSUMPTION 5.6. BITWISE LINEAR MODEL.– The trace x is linear in each of the n bits $z^{(1)} \dots z^{(n)}$ of the sensitive data z and is modeled by $m_k = \boldsymbol{\beta}[0] + \sum_j z^{(j)}\boldsymbol{\beta}[j] + b$, where $\boldsymbol{\beta}$ is a vector of dimension $n+1$ and b is noise.

With Gaussian noise (Assumption 5.1) and independent of Z (Assumption 5.3), the noise B follows a normal distribution and is independent of Z, so its mean is constant. Thanks to the existence of the constant term $\boldsymbol{\beta}[0]$, the mean can be considered zero.

The use of this model leads to an attack called a *linear regression attack* (LRA). As the errors b follow the same normal distribution with mean zero, the same idea as in the previous section is followed: the aim is to find both the secret $k^\star$ and the vector $\boldsymbol{\beta}$ by maximizing $\mathcal{D}^{homo}_{\mathcal{S}_\mathcal{T}}[k]$. The matrix $\boldsymbol{M}_k$ of dimension $N_a \times (n+1)$ is defined using the bit values of $z_i = \mathbf{C}(p_i, k)$ as follows:

$$\boldsymbol{M}_k = \begin{pmatrix} \vdots & \vdots & & \vdots \\ 1 & z_i^{(1)} & \dots & z_i^{(n)} \\ \vdots & \vdots & & \vdots \end{pmatrix}$$

The traces x_i are rearranged into a vector of size N_a: $\mathbf{v} = (\ldots, x_i, \ldots)^\mathsf{T}$ so as to estimate the $n+1$ linear regression coefficients by the following vector formula:

$$\boldsymbol{\beta} = (\boldsymbol{M}_k^\mathsf{T} \cdot \boldsymbol{M}_k)^{-1} \cdot \boldsymbol{M}_k^\mathsf{T} \cdot \mathbf{v}$$

The distinguisher $\mathcal{D}_{\mathcal{S}_\mathcal{T}}^{homo}$ is therefore rewritten as follows:

$$\begin{aligned}
\mathcal{D}_{\mathcal{S}_\mathcal{T}}^{lra}[k] &= -\sum_i (x_i - \boldsymbol{\beta}[0] - \sum_j z^{(j)} \boldsymbol{\beta}[j])^2 \\
&= -\sum_i (x_i - (\boldsymbol{M}_k \cdot \boldsymbol{\beta})[i])^2 \\
&= -(\mathbf{v} - \boldsymbol{M}_k \cdot \boldsymbol{\beta})^\mathsf{T} \cdot (\mathbf{v} - \boldsymbol{M}_k \cdot \boldsymbol{\beta}) \\
&= -(\mathbf{A}_k \cdot \mathbf{v})^\mathsf{T} \cdot \mathbf{A}_k \cdot \mathbf{v} \\
&= -\mathbf{v}^\mathsf{T} \cdot \mathbf{A}_k^\mathsf{T} \cdot \mathbf{A}_k \cdot \mathbf{v}
\end{aligned}$$

where $\mathbf{A}_k = \mathbf{I} - \boldsymbol{M}_k \cdot (\boldsymbol{M}_k^\mathsf{T} \cdot \boldsymbol{M}_k)^{-1} \cdot \boldsymbol{M}_k^\mathsf{T}$ with $\mathbf{I}$ the identity matrix. $\mathbf{A}$ depends only on p_i and k. This matrix can be pre-calculated if we know the p_i. Otherwise, it is always possible to simplify the matrix $(\boldsymbol{M}_k^\mathsf{T} \cdot \boldsymbol{M}_k)^{-1}$ of size $(n+1) \times (n+1)$, assuming uniformity and bit independence of Z whatever the value of k. To do this, we replace it with the following the matrix $\boldsymbol{S}$:

$$\boldsymbol{S} = \frac{1}{N_a} \begin{pmatrix}
n+1 & -2 & \cdots & \cdots & \cdots & -2 \\
-2 & 4 & 0 & \cdots & \cdots & 0 \\
\vdots & 0 & \ddots & \ddots & & \vdots \\
\vdots & \vdots & \ddots & \ddots & \ddots & \vdots \\
\vdots & \vdots & & \ddots & \ddots & 0 \\
-2 & 0 & \cdots & \cdots & 0 & 4
\end{pmatrix}$$

We will then use the matrix $\mathbf{A}_k = \mathbf{I} - \boldsymbol{M}_k \cdot \boldsymbol{S} \cdot \boldsymbol{M}_k^\mathsf{T}$.

> COMPREHENSION EXERCISE 5.3.– Show that $\boldsymbol{S}$ is the inverse matrix of $\boldsymbol{M}_k^\mathsf{T} \cdot \boldsymbol{M}_k$ if the bits of Z are uniform and independent.

5.3.5. *Conclusion*

In this section, we have defined several distinguishers based on the use of likelihood. Several assumptions are necessary in order to define distinguishers that can be computed using attack traces alone. Assuming the noise to be Gaussian (Assumption 5.1) allows the maximum likelihood to be reformulated, while Assumption 5.2 of noise homoscedasticity allows it to be simplified. If the leakage model and noise parameters are not fully known, we have proposed two univariate methods (Assumptions 5.4 and 5.6) to use these distinguishers by considering an independent noise (Assumption 5.3) and combining the search for secrecy with linear regression. This technique also makes it possible to use other types of modeling. Moreover, the normality constraint can be relaxed by combining linear regression with the least squares method. Furthermore, the distinguishers presented above can be extended to the multivariate case if Points of Interest are known and/or if the modeling can be extended to several instants of the trace.

The disadvantage of using these distinguishers remains the choice of model, which influences noise independence. If the modeling of the deterministic part of the signal is not correct, the noise resulting from this modeling will actually depend on the sensitive data. Under these conditions, the effectiveness of distinguishers in recovering the secret may diminish and is no longer guaranteed.

Maximum likelihood is a parametric estimation tool based on parametric laws, such as the leakage models considered here as functions of the normal law. However, fixing the family of the joint distribution of **X** and Z greatly restricts the space of possibilities and reinforces the constraint of correct model choice. The next section relaxes this constraint by using non-parametric estimation methods.

5.4. Mutual information

The aim of this section is to study the mutual information tool that quantifies the dependence between the random variables **X** and Z.

5.4.1. *Information theory*

The entropy of a discrete random variable Z, denoted $\mathsf{H}(Z)$, quantifies the uncertainty that exists on the value of a realization of Z. It is defined by:

$$\mathsf{H}(Z) \triangleq -\sum_{z\in\mathcal{Z}} \Pr(Z = z) \log_2 \Pr(Z = z)$$

The entropy of a variable represents the number of binary questions required to guess its value. It is a theoretical measure of the amount of uncertainty.

The joint entropy of a pair of random variables and the conditional entropy are naturally defined in the same way by considering the associated joint and conditional probabilities.

The joint entropy of Z and $\mathbf{X}$ is defined by:

$$\mathsf{H}(Z, \mathbf{X}) \triangleq - \sum_{(z,\mathbf{x})\in(\mathcal{Z},\mathcal{X}^D)} \Pr(Z = z, \mathbf{X} = \mathbf{x}) \log_2 \Pr(Z = z, \mathbf{X} = \mathbf{x})$$

Let $\mathbf{x} \in \mathcal{X}^D$ be a realization of $\mathbf{X}$, then the conditional entropy of Z knowing $\mathbf{X} = \mathbf{x}$ is defined by:

$$\mathsf{H}(Z|\mathbf{X} = \mathbf{x}) \triangleq - \sum_{z\in\mathcal{Z}} \Pr(Z = z|\mathbf{X} = \mathbf{x}) \log_2 \Pr(Z = z|\mathbf{X} = \mathbf{x})$$

This value depends on the observation $\mathbf{x}$, so we can generalize with the definition of the conditional entropy of a discrete random variable Z knowing the random vector $\mathbf{X}$:

$$\mathsf{H}(Z|\mathbf{X}) \triangleq \mathbb{E}_{\mathbf{X}}[\mathsf{H}(Z|\mathbf{X} = \mathbf{x})]$$

Conditional entropy quantifies the uncertainty remaining on Z once $\mathbf{X}$ is fully known. It is always smaller than the unconditional entropy of Z (when $\mathbf{X}$ is not known): $\mathsf{H}(Z|\mathbf{X}) \leq \mathsf{H}(Z)$ with equality if and only if Z and $\mathbf{X}$ are independent, since in this case knowledge of $\mathbf{X}$ does not reduce the uncertainty on Z.

The notion of independence between Z and $\mathbf{X}$ therefore appears in this equality and is measured by mutual information:

DEFINITION 5.2. MUTUAL INFORMATION.– Let the random vector $\mathbf{X} \in \mathcal{X}^D$ with $\mathcal{X}$ be a finite set and the random variable $Z \in \mathcal{Z}$. The mutual information between $\mathbf{X}$ and Z is defined by:

$$\mathsf{MI}(Z; \mathbf{X}) \triangleq \mathsf{H}(Z) - \mathsf{H}(Z|\mathbf{X})$$

This definition takes several forms thanks to the property $\mathsf{H}(Z|\mathbf{X}) = \mathsf{H}(Z, \mathbf{X}) - \mathsf{H}(\mathbf{X})$, which also highlights the symmetrical nature of mutual information: $\mathsf{MI}(Z; \mathbf{X}) = \mathsf{MI}(\mathbf{X}; Z)$.

5.4.2. *Distinguisher*

Mutual information analysis (MIA) is an attack that uses the mutual information between the traces $\mathbf{X}$ and the sensitive data obtained Z. From the relation $\mathsf{MI}(\mathrm{Z};\mathbf{X}) = \mathsf{H}(\mathrm{Z}) + \mathsf{H}(\mathbf{X}) - \mathsf{H}(\mathrm{Z},\mathbf{X})$, we define the following distinguisher:

$$\mathcal{D}^{mi}_{\mathcal{S}_\mathcal{T}}[k] = \mathsf{MI}(\mathrm{Z}_k;\mathbf{X}) \quad [5.3]$$

$$= \sum_{\mathbf{x}}\sum_{z} \Pr(\mathrm{Z}_k = z, \mathbf{X} = \mathrm{x}) \log_2 \frac{\Pr(\mathrm{Z}_k = z, \mathbf{X} = \mathrm{x})}{\Pr(\mathrm{Z}_k = z)\cdot \Pr(\mathbf{X} = \mathrm{x})} \quad [5.4]$$

Depending on the formula used to calculate $\mathsf{MI}(\mathrm{Z}_k;\mathbf{X})$, this distinguisher can take several forms:

$$\mathcal{D}^{mi}_{\mathcal{S}_\mathcal{T}}[k] = \mathsf{MI}(\mathrm{Z}_k;\mathbf{X}) = \mathsf{H}(\mathrm{Z}_k) - \mathsf{H}(\mathrm{Z}_k\,|\,\mathbf{X}) \quad [5.5]$$

$$= \mathsf{MI}(\mathbf{X};\mathrm{Z}_k) = \mathsf{H}(\mathbf{X}) - \mathsf{H}(\mathbf{X}\,|\,\mathrm{Z}_k) \quad [5.6]$$

COMPREHENSION EXERCISE 5.4.– Demonstrate equality [5.4].

For the distinguisher $\mathcal{D}^{mi}_{\mathcal{S}_\mathcal{T}}$ to be effective, its score must be higher for the correct key hypothesis $k = k^\star$. Now, the difference between the scores $\mathcal{D}^{mi}_{\mathcal{S}_\mathcal{T}}[k^\star] - \mathcal{D}^{mi}_{\mathcal{S}_\mathcal{T}}[k]$ for any k is (from equation [5.6]):

$$\mathcal{D}^{mi}_{\mathcal{S}_\mathcal{T}}[k^\star] - \mathcal{D}^{mi}_{\mathcal{S}_\mathcal{T}}[k] - \mathsf{H}(\mathbf{X}) - \mathsf{H}(\mathbf{X}\,|\,\mathrm{Z}_{k^\star}) - \mathsf{H}(\mathbf{X}) + \mathsf{H}(\mathbf{X}\,|\,\mathrm{Z}_k)$$
$$= \mathsf{H}(\mathbf{X}\,|\,\mathrm{Z}_k) - \mathsf{H}(\mathbf{X}\,|\,\mathrm{Z}_{k^\star})$$

The effectiveness of the distinguisher $\mathcal{D}^{mi}_{\mathcal{S}_\mathcal{T}}$ is therefore assured as soon as the traces follow the following assumption.

ASSUMPTION 5.7. UNCERTAINTY A PRIORI.– The knowledge of a wrong key hypothesis $k \in \mathcal{K}$ does not reduce the uncertainty of the traces any more than the actual value: $\mathsf{H}(\mathbf{X}\,|\,\mathrm{Z}_k) \geq \mathsf{H}(\mathbf{X}\,|\,\mathrm{Z}_{k^\star})$.

This assumption holds true when the noise is independent of the sensitive data (Assumption 5.3). Indeed, as $\mathbf{X} = \delta(\mathrm{Z}_{k^\star}) + \mathbf{B}$ with independent $\mathrm{Z}_{k^\star}$ and $\mathbf{B}$, the term $\mathsf{H}(\mathbf{X}\,|\,\mathrm{Z}_{k^\star})$ simplifies:

$$\mathsf{H}(\mathbf{X}\,|\,\mathrm{Z}_{k^\star}) = \mathsf{H}(\delta(\mathrm{Z}_{k^\star}) + \mathbf{B}\,|\,\mathrm{Z}_{k^\star}) = \mathsf{H}(\mathbf{B}\,|\,\mathrm{Z}_{k^\star}) = \mathsf{H}(\mathbf{B})$$

Since the addition of knowledge cannot increase uncertainty, we have:

$$\begin{aligned}\mathsf{H}(\mathbf{X}|\mathrm{Z}_k) &\geq \mathsf{H}(\mathbf{X}|\mathrm{Z}_k,\mathrm{Z}_{k^\star}) \geq \mathsf{H}(\delta(\mathrm{Z}_{k^\star})+\mathbf{B}|\mathrm{Z}_k,\mathrm{Z}_{k^\star})\\ &\geq \mathsf{H}(\mathbf{B}) = \mathsf{H}(\mathbf{X}|\mathrm{Z}_{k^\star})\end{aligned}$$

So a good key hypothesis maximizes the distinguisher's score. However, there is no guarantee that other assumptions will not also maximize scores. The next section studies the case where it is possible to invert the function $\mathbf{C}$.

5.4.3. *Bijectivity*

For a fixed $k \in \mathcal{K}$, the function $p \mapsto \mathbf{C}(p,k)$ is assumed to be bijective, with the reciprocal function $z \mapsto \mathbf{C}^{-1}(z,k)$.

If we study the difference between the scores $\mathcal{D}^{mi}_{\mathcal{S}_\mathcal{T}}[k^\star] - \mathcal{D}^{mi}_{\mathcal{S}_\mathcal{T}}[k]$ for any k from the formula [5.5], we have:

$$\begin{aligned}\mathcal{D}^{mi}_{\mathcal{S}_\mathcal{T}}[k^\star] - \mathcal{D}^{mi}_{\mathcal{S}_\mathcal{T}}[k] &= \mathsf{H}(\mathrm{Z}_{k^\star}) - \mathsf{H}(\mathrm{Z}_{k^\star}|\mathbf{X}) - \mathsf{H}(\mathrm{Z}_k) + \mathsf{H}(\mathrm{Z}_k|\mathbf{X})\\ &= \mathsf{H}(\mathrm{Z}_{k^\star}) - \mathsf{H}(\mathrm{Z}_k) + \mathsf{H}(\mathrm{Z}_k|\mathbf{X}) - \mathsf{H}(\mathrm{Z}_{k^\star}|\mathbf{X})\end{aligned} \qquad [5.7]$$

As the function $\mathbf{C}$ is bijective, for each key hypothesis k, we can associate with each value z, a unique plaintext $p \in \mathcal{P}$ and a unique value $z^\star$ such that $p = \mathbf{C}^{-1}(z,k)$ and $z^\star = \mathbf{C}(p,k^\star)$. Thus, we have:

$$\begin{aligned}\Pr(\mathrm{Z}_k = z|\mathbf{X}=\mathrm{x}) &= \Pr(\mathrm{P}=p|\mathbf{X}=\mathrm{x})\\ &= \Pr(\mathbf{C}(\mathrm{P},k^\star) = z^\star|\mathbf{X}=\mathrm{x})\\ &= \Pr(\mathrm{Z}_{k^\star} = z^\star|\mathbf{X}=\mathrm{x})\end{aligned}$$

Consequently, the distributions of $(\mathrm{Z}_k \mid \mathbf{X})$ and $(\mathrm{Z}_{k^\star} \mid \mathbf{X})$ are identical and $\mathsf{H}(\mathrm{Z}_k|\mathbf{X}) = \mathsf{H}(\mathrm{Z}_{k^\star}|\mathbf{X})$ for any k. Similarly, $\mathsf{H}(\mathrm{Z}_k) = \mathsf{H}(\mathrm{Z}_{k^\star})$, which cancels out equation [5.7] and results in $\mathcal{D}^{mi}_{\mathcal{S}_\mathcal{T}}[k^\star] = \mathcal{D}^{mi}_{\mathcal{S}_\mathcal{T}}[k]$ for any k.

When $\mathbf{C}$ is bijective, it is therefore necessary to apply a non-injective function φ to Z_k and use the following distinguisher:

$$\mathcal{D}^{mia}_{\mathcal{S}_\mathcal{T}}[k] = \mathsf{MI}(\varphi(\mathrm{Z}_k);\mathbf{X})$$

In the case where $\mathbf{C}$ is not bijective, taking the identity for φ is a very generic choice. But in the opposite case, we are once again faced with the dilemma of making the right choice to find a model that does not reduce the effectiveness of the attack. Indeed, suppose we have a model φ and a distinguisher $\mathcal{D}$, such that for $\mathcal{S}_\mathcal{T}$, the distinguisher returns the best score for the correct key $k^\star$. Let us denote k' the lowest ranked key and define the model $\varphi' : z \mapsto \varphi'(z) = \varphi(\mathbf{C}\left(\mathbf{C}^{-1}\left(z, k^\star\right), k'\right))$. The same distinguisher $\mathcal{D}$ applied to the same traces $\mathcal{S}_\mathcal{T}$ will return k' as the best score.

This example shows the importance of choosing the function φ whose application will inevitably reduce mutual information: $\mathsf{MI}\left(\varphi(\mathrm{Z}); \mathbf{X}\right) \leq \mathsf{MI}\left(\mathrm{Z}; \mathbf{X}\right)$. Since the image set of φ is smaller, its application to Z leads to a loss of information. To limit this, we can either use a leakage model, such as the Hamming weight, and calculate the mutual information between the assumed leakage of Z and the acquired trace, or minimize the loss, for example, by deleting a single bit from Z.

5.4.4. *Probability calculation*

Calculating the distinguisher $\mathcal{D}^{mia}_{\mathcal{S}_\mathcal{T}}[k]$ for all key assumptions k requires calculating the probabilities $\Pr\left(\mathrm{Z}_k = z, \mathbf{X} = \mathbf{x}\right)$ and $\Pr\left(\mathbf{X} = \mathbf{x}\right)$ from N_a attack traces $\mathbf{x}_i$ and associated plaintext p_i. Probabilities $\Pr\left(\mathrm{Z}_k = z\right)$ can be calculated more simply from key hypotheses and plaintexts.

Since the random vector $\mathbf{X}$ is made up of D variables in $\mathcal{X}$ and the set $\mathcal{X}$ is finite but possibly large, estimating the probability $\Pr\left(\mathrm{Z} = z, \mathbf{X} = \mathbf{x}\right)$ can be complex due to the large number of possible values $(z, \mathbf{x})$. For simplicity, we restrict ourselves here to the univariate case, but it is possible to extend the methods presented below to the multivariate case.

In the case where $\mathcal{X}$ is small (if X is a byte, for example), the probability $\Pr\left(\mathrm{Z} = z, \mathrm{X} = x\right)$ (respectively, $\Pr\left(\mathrm{X} = x\right)$) can be estimated by calculating the frequencies of occurrence of the pair of values (z, x) (respectively, of the value x):

$$\begin{aligned}\Pr\left(\mathrm{Z} = z, \mathrm{X} = x\right) &= \frac{\left|\{i | (z_i, x_i) = (z, x)\}\right|}{N_a} \\ &= \frac{\left|\{i | \mathbf{C}\left(p_i, k\right) = z, x_i = x\}\right|}{N_a}\end{aligned}$$

If $\mathcal{X}$ is larger, or if the number of traces is insufficient to have enough occurrences of the pair (z, x), calculating frequencies of appearance will give a distorted estimate of probability. In this case, a histogram calculation will allow under-represented value classes to be grouped together.

The histogram method defines a set of N_c value classes for X of approximately identical widths.

The probability $\Pr(\mathrm{Z} = z, \mathrm{X} \in c_j)$ (respectively, $\Pr(\mathrm{X} \in c_j)$) can then be estimated by calculating the frequencies of occurrence in each class of the pair of values (z, x) (respectively, of the value x):

$$\Pr(\mathrm{Z} = z, \mathrm{X} \in c_j) = \frac{|\{i | z_i = z, x_i \in c_j\}|}{N_a} = \frac{|\{i | \mathbf{C}(p_i, k) = z, x_i \in c_j\}|}{N_a}$$

The number of probabilities to be estimated for $\Pr(\mathrm{Z}, \mathrm{X})$ is thus reduced from $|\mathcal{Z}| \times |\mathcal{X}|$ to $|\mathcal{Z}| \times |\varphi(\mathcal{Z})|$.

The distinguisher formula naturally extends to:

$$\mathcal{D}_{\mathcal{S}_\mathcal{T}}^{mia}[k] = \sum_{j,z} |c_j| \Pr(\mathrm{Z} = z, \mathrm{X} \in c_j) \log_2 \frac{\Pr(\mathrm{Z} = z, \mathrm{X} \in c_j)}{\Pr(\mathrm{Z} = z) \cdot \Pr(\mathrm{X} \in c_j)}$$

TRAINING EXERCISE.– From the training traces provided, calculate the values of the mutual information distinguisher for each key hypothesis using the histogram method.

One way of generalizing this probability calculation is to consider X as a continuous random variable. The signal before the measurement is physical in nature, so we can assume that the finiteness of the set $\mathcal{X}$ is artificial and due to the approximation of the oscilloscope when recording the value. In reality, it is reasonable to consider that X can take an infinite number of values in $\mathbb{R}$. Calculating its probability density is certainly more complex, but potentially more accurate than using the approximate values returned by the oscilloscope.

To estimate the probability density, a kernel method can be used to smooth the estimation and eliminate artificial discretization.

Kernel estimation of the probability in x consists of averaging for any observed value of X a kernel function K centered on x, generally a statistical law density, as follows:

$$\Pr(\mathrm{Z} = z, \mathrm{X} = x) = \frac{1}{N_a h} \sum_i K\left(\frac{x - x_i}{h}\right)$$

where K and h are two parameters to be defined:

– the kernel function K, which defines the form of the smoothing. Here, as the objective is to recover the physical signal, the choice of a normal distribution density seems consistent:

$$K : u \mapsto K(u) = \frac{1}{\sqrt{2\pi}} \exp\left(-\frac{1}{2}u^2\right)$$

– the bandwidth h, which influences the smoothness.

The distinguisher integral is then calculated by decomposing the interval $\mathcal{X}$ by N_c pieces c_j centered at x_j of equal size.

$$\mathcal{D}_{\mathcal{S}_\mathcal{T}}^{mia}[k] = \sum_{j,z} |c_j| \Pr(\mathrm{Z} = z, \mathrm{X} = x_j) \log_2 \frac{\Pr(\mathrm{Z} = z, \mathrm{X} = x_j)}{\Pr(\mathrm{Z} = z) \cdot \Pr(\mathrm{X} = x_j)}$$

The number of points for calculating the integral N_c should be chosen as small as possible, so that the size of the pieces is much smaller than h.

In the end, we can see that the number of traces N_a must be sufficient to efficiently estimate the $|\mathcal{Z}| \times |\varphi(\mathcal{Z})|$ probabilities, that is, $N_a \gg |\mathcal{Z}| \times |\varphi(\mathcal{Z})|$.

5.4.5. *Conclusion*

In this section, we have defined a distinguisher based on the mutual information between traces and a model applied to sensitive data. The assumptions concerning the non deterministic part are quite flexible, since if the noise is not independent of the sensitive data (Assumption 5.3 is not valid), it may be sufficient to assume that the uncertainty on the traces does not decrease more with the knowledge of a wrong key hypothesis than with its real value (Assumption 5.7). The choice of sensitive data and the associated model is not trivial. At the very least, the model must not be bijective, but there is no guarantee that it will be effective in the general case. The more realistic the upstream information provided by the model, and the more specific to the secret, the better the distinguisher will be able to differentiate between wrong hypotheses and the right key.

We have seen several methods for calculating the probability density involved in the distinguisher formula. The quantity of probabilities to be calculated requires a fairly large number of traces, which can reduce the effectiveness of the attack if this number is insufficient.

On the other hand, the advantage is that it is possible to remain multivariate by considering random vectors as random variables in higher dimensional spaces, but it is then necessary to manage the curse of dimensionality.

Since it seems essential to provide upstream information, the following sections present distinguishers based on presumptions about the nature of the relationship between traces and sensitive data.

5.5. Correlation

We saw in section 5.3 that under Gaussian noise (Assumption 5.1) the maximum likelihood method is equivalent to least squares in the univariate case. Combined with linear regression, the associated distinguisher enables us to find the secret, but also to estimate the parameters of the regression line, which is superfluous for the attacker's purposes. If the relationship between two variables is approximately linear (Assumption 5.4), correlation is the preferred statistical tool for assessing their linear dependency.

5.5.1. *Linear relationship – CPA*

If the relationship between $\mathbf{X}$ and Z is linear, the model $\mathbf{m}_k = \boldsymbol{\delta}(\mathbf{C}(p,k)) + \mathbf{b}$ is reformulated thanks to the existence of a vector $\boldsymbol{\alpha}$ and a function φ, such that at any instant t : $\mathbf{m}_k[t] = \boldsymbol{\alpha}[t] \cdot \varphi(\mathbf{C}(p,k)) + \mathbf{b}[t] = \boldsymbol{\alpha}[t] \cdot \varphi(z) + \mathbf{b}[t]$. The idea is to calculate the correlation between $\mathbf{X}$ and $\varphi(\mathrm{Z}_k)$ for any key assumption k. Since the value of $\boldsymbol{\alpha}[t]$ is not useful and since $\varphi(\mathrm{Z}_k)$ is not time dependent, this is a univariate attack, so we can simplify the modeling to $m_k = \alpha \cdot \varphi(z) + b$.

Correlation power analysis (CPA) is an attack that uses correlation as a distinguisher.

$$\begin{aligned}\mathcal{D}_{\mathcal{S}_T}^{cpa}[k] &= \frac{\left|\mathrm{Cov}\left(\mathrm{X}, \varphi(\mathrm{Z}_k)\right)\right|}{\sigma(\mathrm{X}) \cdot \sigma\left(\varphi(\mathrm{Z}_k)\right)} \\ &= \frac{\left|\mathbb{E}\left[\mathrm{X} \cdot \varphi(\mathrm{Z}_k)\right] - \mathbb{E}\left[\mathrm{X}\right] \cdot \mathbb{E}\left[\varphi(\mathrm{Z}_k)\right]\right|}{\sigma(\mathrm{X}) \cdot \sigma\left(\varphi(\mathrm{Z}_k)\right)}\end{aligned}$$

where $\sigma(\cdot)$ represents the standard deviation of a random variable and $|\cdot|$ denotes the absolute value.

When the key hypothesis is correct, there is a linear relationship, so the correlation will not be zero. As it can be positive or negative, it is necessary to consider the absolute value.

But for the correlation-based distinguisher to find the right key, it is necessary to make an assumption about the variable B whose dependence on Z must be restricted (otherwise the relationship between Z and X would no longer be linear in nature). To guarantee the adequacy of the model, we assume that B is a noise independent from Z (Assumption 5.3).

Under this assumption, the covariance is rewritten as:

$$\begin{aligned}\mathrm{Cov}\left(\mathrm{X},\varphi(\mathrm{Z}_k)\right) &= \mathrm{Cov}\left(\alpha\cdot\varphi(\mathrm{Z}_{k^\star})+\mathrm{B},\varphi(\mathrm{Z}_k)\right)\\ &= \alpha\mathrm{Cov}\left(\varphi(\mathrm{Z}_{k^\star}),\varphi(\mathrm{Z}_k)\right)+\mathrm{Cov}\left(\mathrm{B},\varphi(\mathrm{Z}_k)\right)\\ &= \alpha\mathrm{Cov}\left(\varphi(\mathrm{Z}_{k^\star}),\varphi(\mathrm{Z}_k)\right)\end{aligned}$$

For a good key assumption, the covariance simplifies to:

$$\mathrm{Cov}\left(\mathrm{X},\varphi(\mathrm{Z}_{k^\star})\right) = \alpha\mathrm{Cov}\left(\varphi(\mathrm{Z}_{k^\star}),\varphi(\mathrm{Z}_{k^\star})\right) = \alpha\mathrm{Var}\left(\varphi(\mathrm{Z}_{k^\star})\right)$$

The difference between the squared scores for $k^\star$ and any k is:

$$\begin{aligned}&\mathcal{D}^{cpa}_{\mathcal{S}_\mathcal{T}}[k^\star]^2 - \mathcal{D}^{cpa}_{\mathcal{S}_\mathcal{T}}[k]^2\\ &= \frac{\left(\alpha\mathrm{Var}\left(\varphi(\mathrm{Z}_{k^\star})\right)\right)^2}{\mathrm{Var}\left(\mathrm{X}\right)\cdot\mathrm{Var}\left(\varphi(\mathrm{Z}_{k^\star})\right)} - \frac{\left(\alpha\mathrm{Cov}\left(\varphi(\mathrm{Z}_{k^\star}),\varphi(\mathrm{Z}_k)\right)\right)^2}{\mathrm{Var}\left(\mathrm{X}\right)\cdot\mathrm{Var}\left(\varphi(\mathrm{Z}_k)\right)}\\ &= \frac{\alpha^2\left(\mathrm{Var}\left(\varphi(\mathrm{Z}_{k^\star})\right)\cdot\mathrm{Var}\left(\varphi(\mathrm{Z}_k)\right)-\mathrm{Cov}\left(\varphi(\mathrm{Z}_{k^\star}),\varphi(\mathrm{Z}_k)\right)^2\right)}{\mathrm{Var}\left(\mathrm{X}\right)\cdot\mathrm{Var}\left(\varphi(\mathrm{Z}_k)\right)}\end{aligned}$$

According to the Cauchy–Schwarz inequality:

$$\mathrm{Cov}\left(\varphi(\mathrm{Z}_{k^\star}),\varphi(\mathrm{Z}_k)\right)^2 \leq \mathrm{Var}\left(\varphi(\mathrm{Z}_{k^\star})\right)\cdot\mathrm{Var}\left(\varphi(\mathrm{Z}_k)\right)$$

So a good key assumption maximizes the distinguisher scores. If another key assumption k also maximizes scores, this means that $\mathrm{Cov}\left(\varphi(\mathrm{Z}_{k^\star}),\varphi(\mathrm{Z}_k)\right)^2 = \mathrm{Var}\left(\varphi(\mathrm{Z}_{k^\star})\right)\cdot\mathrm{Var}\left(\varphi(\mathrm{Z}_k)\right)$. This constraint is equivalent to the existence of a linear relationship between $\varphi(\mathrm{Z}_k)$ and $\varphi(\mathrm{Z}_{k^\star})$.

COMPREHENSION EXERCISE 5.5.– Let a set of traces (x_i) be acquired with a uniform plaintext p_i and a fixed key $k^\star$, both of a single bit, such that a trace at each instant can be modeled by $x_i = p_i \oplus 1 \oplus k^\star + b_i$, knowing that P follows a uniform distribution and B is independent of Z. Compare the distinguisher scores in the case where the attacker defines $\varphi(\mathrm{Z}_k) = p \oplus k$.

Apart from this constraint, the choice of the function φ is left entirely to the attacker's discretion. Hamming's weight (or distance) is a classic and often gives good results. However, if the function φ is poorly defined, the square of the covariance $\mathrm{Cov}\left(\varphi(\mathrm{Z}_{k^\star}), \varphi(\mathrm{Z}_k)\right)^2$ will be far from the perfect value $\mathrm{Var}\left(\varphi(\mathrm{Z}_{k^\star})\right) \cdot \mathrm{Var}\left(\varphi(\mathrm{Z}_k)\right)$ and the inequality $\mathrm{Cov}\left(\mathrm{X}, \varphi(\mathrm{Z}_k)\right) \leq \mathrm{Cov}\left(\mathrm{X}, \varphi(\mathrm{Z}_{k^\star})\right)$ may not be verified.

The distinguisher formula can be simplified in theory, since the ranking of scores for any k will not be influenced by the variance of traces in the denominator, which does not depend on the key assumption. Moreover, if the homoscedasticity of the function φ is verified, the variance $\mathrm{Var}\left(\varphi(\mathrm{Z}_k)\right)$ is identical for all k (Assumption 5.5) and could be suppressed in the distinguisher expression, which is now expressed using only the covariance term:

$$\mathcal{D}^{cov}_{\mathcal{S}_\mathcal{T}}[k] = \mathrm{Cov}\left(\mathrm{X}, \varphi(\mathrm{Z}_k)\right) \qquad [5.8]$$

However, if we want to compare several distinguishers with each other, for example along each instant of the trace, or for different models, it is worth keeping the Pearson coefficient formula, which gives results normalized between $[-1, 1]$.

TRAINING EXERCISE.– From the training traces provided, calculate the correlation distinguisher values for each key hypothesis.

5.5.2. *Equivalence*

Here, we compare the CPA distinguisher with the least squares distinguisher presented in equation [5.2]. As a reminder, to ensure the effectiveness of this univariate attack, the deterministic part is assumed to be linear in Z (Assumption 5.4) and independent of noise (Assumption 5.3), which in this particular case follows a normal distribution (Assumption 5.1). This distinguisher is simplified by replacing the empirical values by their respective moments as follows:

$$\begin{aligned}\mathcal{D}^{ls}_{\mathcal{S}_\mathcal{T}}[k] &= (\langle \varphi(\mathrm{Z}_k),\mathrm{X}\rangle)^2 \cdot \left(2 \cdot \langle \mathrm{X}^2\rangle - \langle \varphi(\mathrm{Z}_k)^2\rangle\right)\\ &\approx \left(\mathrm{Cov}\left(\varphi(\mathrm{Z}_k), \mathrm{X}\right)\right)^2 \cdot \Big(2 \cdot \mathrm{Var}\left(\mathrm{X}\right) - \mathrm{Var}\left(\varphi(\mathrm{Z}_k)\right)\Big)\end{aligned}$$

However, in the case where the homoscedasticity of the function φ is verified, the variance $\mathrm{Var}\left(\varphi(\mathrm{Z}_k)\right)$ is identical for any key hypothesis k (Assumption 5.5). The distinguisher $\mathcal{D}^{ls}_{\mathcal{S}_\mathcal{T}}$ is therefore equivalent to $\mathrm{Cov}\left(\varphi(\mathrm{Z}_k), \mathrm{X}\right)^2$, which is equivalent to the simplified CPA distinguisher $\mathcal{D}^{cov}_{\mathcal{S}_\mathcal{T}}$ given in equation [5.8]. This confirms that the normality constraint on noise can be relaxed in this context. The least-squares distinguisher is therefore a special case of CPA.

5.5.3. *Conclusion*

This section presents the CPA distinguisher based on the correlation between two random variables. This distinguisher assumes the existence of a linear relationship between the sensitive data and the traces, which translates into the independence of noise and sensitive data (Assumption 5.3). Today, CPA is the most widely used tool for univariate attacks, with a simple weight or Hamming distance model. There are several reasons for this popularity.

The first thing to note is the low computational complexity of the distinguisher compared to other tools.

Second, historically, the first methods were special cases of CPA. The latter will therefore be considered as a generalization rather than a new attack.

CPA does require a model, but only the existence of a linear relationship with this model is evaluated. In many cases, it is even possible to escape from the linear case, since we are not looking for a perfect correlation, but rather a better correlation for the right key hypothesis. This also explains the popularity of the Hamming weight model, in which all bits leak equivalently: it represents a median choice within the family of functions based on bit leakage.

5.6. A priori knowledge synthesis

This section groups together the various assumptions on the data, used by an unsupervised attack, encountered in the previous sections. To avoid confusion with key hypotheses, we will call an *assumption* a hypothesis that is not necessarily easy to verify, such as the nature of the acquired signals, for example, and *property* a hypothesis that is easily verifiable, such as the uniformity of clear texts.

The introduction of these assumptions stems from the difficulties involved in defining a very general leakage model.

The first difficulty concerns the choice of sensitive data likely to leak throughout the trace. This choice depends on both the algorithm and the resolution of the trace. In the extreme case where the trace represents the entire execution of a hardware AES in a single instant, the sensitive data could be any data dependent on the key. On the other hand, in the case of a long trace which, for example, describes in multiple instants all the stages of a modular exponentiation where the exponent is processed bit by bit, the choice of Z brings more or less complexity: the sensitive data can be just one bit, whose leakage is more or less instantaneous, or a 32-bit word in a modular multiplication, whose leakage is repeated in many instants throughout the multiplication. The choice of sensitive data therefore places emphasis on certain moments when it is manipulated.

Moreover, the choice of δ also influences the temporal dimension of the modeling. For example, if Z is a byte at the input of a byte permutation, two different leakage models could be defined at the input and output of the permutation. The definition of δ therefore implies very particular instants.

We saw in section 5.3 two models that are classically chosen for δ:

– Linear model (Assumption 5.4): the trace x is linear as a function φ of the sensitive data z and is modeled by $m_k = \alpha \cdot \varphi(z) + b$, where α is a constant and b represents noise.

– Bitwise linear model (Assumption 5.6): the trace x is linear in each of the n bits $z^{(1)} \dots z^{(n)}$ of the sensitive data z and is modeled by $m_k = \boldsymbol{\beta}[0] + \sum_j z^{(j)} \boldsymbol{\beta}[j] + b$, where b is the noise.

These models work quite well, but they can lack generality.

For example, if the trace in one instant represents a calculation that depends on several random variables, then the deterministic function δ will not model the whole calculation, but only the part relating to the sensitive data Z in isolation. The other Z leaks in combination with the other variables will be contained in **B**. For example, if the sensitive data are a byte at the input of the AES, it will be used with the other bytes in the column to calculate the output.

Apart from the very particular instants linked to δ, the modeling introduces a bias more or less dependent on Z. However, if the random variables **B** and Z are dependent, it may be difficult to characterize **B**. To avoid this, it may be advantageous to assume that **B** is noise unrelated to the sensitive data:

NOISE INDEPENDENCE (Assumption 5.3).– The random variables **B** and Z are independent.

For the reasons given above, this assumption is not necessarily realistic, especially in the multivariate case, because of the biases possibly introduced by the modeling. If possible, it would be advantageous to restrict the modeling to only those instants when noise independence is verified. In the univariate case, the assumption of independence of B and Z is reasonable if there is an instant when the deterministic component δ correctly models the leakage of Z; indeed, independence will be effective at this instant. Whether independence (Assumption 5.3) is verified will have to be studied on a case-by-case basis.

COMPREHENSION EXERCISE 5.6.– Let $\mathbf{x}$ be a trace of dimension 3, such that $\mathbf{x}[0] = z^\star$, $\mathbf{x}[1] = z^\star + k^\star$ and $\mathbf{x}[2] = p$. We wish to model each instant by the univariate model defined by $m_k = (\mathbf{C}(p,k)) + b = z + b$. Under what conditions does this modeling follow Assumption 5.3 of noise independence?

If this is not the case, it is also possible to consider the following assumption, weaker than that of independence, which corresponds to a poor choice of δ:

A PRIORI UNCERTAINTY (Assumption 5.7).– The knowledge of a wrong key hypothesis $k \in \mathcal{K}$ does not reduce the uncertainty of the traces any more than the actual value: $\mathsf{H}(\mathbf{X} \mid \mathrm{Z}_k) \geq \mathsf{H}(\mathbf{X} \mid \mathrm{Z}_{k^\star})$.

In some cases, we can simply be satisfied with a variance (or covariance in the multivariate case) that is independent of the sensitive data. This assumption of homoscedasticity is implied by that of independence, but is less restrictive:

NOISE HOMOSCEDASTICITY (Assumption 5.2).– The random vectors $(\mathbf{B} \mid \mathrm{Z} = z)_{z \in \mathcal{Z}}$ have a common covariance matrix equal to $\Sigma_{\mathbf{B}}$, which is the covariance matrix of the random vector **B**.

Finally, in addition to the dependence between **B** and Z, we need to make some assumptions about the distribution of **B**. The usual assumption is that **B** follows a normal distribution:

GAUSSIAN NOISE (Assumption 5.1).– For a given value z, the random vector $(\mathbf{B} \mid \mathrm{Z} = z)$ also follows a normal distribution $\mathcal{N}(\boldsymbol{\mu}_{z,\mathbf{B}}, \Sigma_{z,\mathbf{B}})$.

A final classical assumption concerns the deterministic part of the model, for which a homoscedasticity condition between $\delta(\mathrm{Z})$ and Z may be necessary.

HOMOSCEDASTICITY OF δ (Assumption 5.5).– The variance of the random variable $\delta(\mathrm{Z}_k)$ is identical for all $k \in \mathcal{K}$.

This assumption depends solely on the choice of δ and the definition of the sensitive data, that is, the function **C**. In cryptography, particularly symmetrical cryptography, if the input is uniform, we observe uniformity of the sensitive data. We define a first property on the uniformity of P:

PROPERTY 5.1. UNIFORMITY OF P.– The random variable P is uniform.

This property may not be verified if the attacker does not control the inputs. We also define the following property:

PROPERTY 5.2. EDS PROPERTY OF A FUNCTION.– A function $f : \mathcal{P} \times \mathcal{K} \to \mathcal{A}$ has the EDS property (for *Equal Distributions under different Subkeys*), if when P is uniform the distributions of the variables $f(\mathrm{P}, k)$ are identical for all values $k \in \mathcal{K}$.

The EDS property is verified by the or-exclusive operator $\oplus$, classically used in symmetric cryptography.

LEMMA 5.1.– The function $\oplus$ has the EDS property.

Indeed, for all a and b, $\Pr(\mathrm{P} \oplus k_1 = a) = \Pr(\mathrm{P} = a \oplus k_1) = \Pr(\mathrm{P} = b)$ since P is uniform. So taking $b = a \oplus k_2$, we have $\Pr(\mathrm{P} \oplus k_1 = a) = \Pr(\mathrm{P} \oplus k_2 = a)$. Finally, this last lemma allows us to construct other functions with the EDS property:

LEMMA 5.2.– If the function $f : \mathcal{P} \times \mathcal{K} \to \mathcal{A}$ has the EDS property, then for any function $g : \mathcal{A} \to \mathcal{B}$, the composite function $g \circ f$ has the EDS property.

For all a, $\Pr(g(f(\mathrm{P}, k_1)) = a) = \sum_b \Pr(f(\mathrm{P}, k_1) = b) \cdot \Pr(g(b) = a)$. Since f has the EDS property, for all b, $\Pr(f(\mathrm{P}, k_1) = b) = \Pr(f(\mathrm{P}, k_2) = b)$. So for all a, $\Pr(g(f(\mathrm{P}, k_1)) = a) = \sum_b \Pr(f(\mathrm{P}, k_2) = b) \cdot \Pr(g(b) = a) = \Pr(g(f(\mathrm{P}, k_2)) = a)$.

COMPREHENSION EXERCISE 5.7.– Show that the Hamming weight function at the output of an AES S-box has the EDS property, although it is not bijective. Is this true for DES? Why is this?

Therefore, if **C** is a function of $p \oplus k$, it will have the EDS property, as will any f of **C**.

Under P uniformity, the EDS property allows us to calculate a mean and variance common to all key assumptions, since the distributions are identical.

LEMMA 5.3.– If **C** has the EDS property and P is uniform, then Assumption 5.5 is verified.

COMPREHENSION EXERCISE 5.8.– Demonstrate Lemma 5.3.

The various assumptions and properties are summarized in Table 5.1.

5.7. Conclusion on statistical tools

The distinguishers studied in the previous sections all have their advantages and disadvantages, but their use essentially depends on the assumptions made about the nature of the traces and the possibility of establishing a coherent leakage model.

As the attacker has no profiling capability, it is unrealistic to assume that they know exactly how sensitive data are leaked. A model, more or less accurate and more or less correct, will always be required.

Name	Definition	Concerns	Implied by
Gaussian noise	Assumpt. 5.1	**B**	
Noise homoscedasticity	Assumpt. 5.2	**B** and **C**	Assumpt. 5.3
Noise independence	Assumpt. 5.3	**B** and **C**	
Linear model	Assumpt. 5.4	δ	
Homoscedasticity of δ	Assumpt. 5.5	δ	Prop. 5.1 and 5.2
Bitwise linear model	Assumpt. 5.6	δ	
Uncertainty a priori	Assumpt. 5.7	**B** and **C**	Assumpt. 5.3
Uniformity of P	Prop. 5.1	P	
EDS property of **C**	Prop. 5.2	**C**	

Table 5.1. *Synthesis of classic assumptions and properties*

If the predicted model is linear, CPA is an attack that requires few assumptions and has low computational complexity. The use of likelihood will be of interest in the case of a linear model in each of the bits. In other cases, MIA is an appropriate tool.

If several models are being considered, or if the model depends on unknown parameters, it is also possible to combine several attacks on all models or all parameters, in order to find the optimal model for the effectiveness of a particular attack, be it CPA, likelihood or MIA.

TRAINING EXERCISE.– Using the training traces provided, compare the distinguisher values for each LRA, MIA and CPA attack. Are these attacks successful in recovering the key? On average, how many traces are needed to achieve at least a 99% success rate?

Table 5.2 summarizes all the distinguishers discussed in the previous sections.

Name	Distinguisher	Section	Assumpt.	Model	Multivariate	Complexity
Likelihood	$\mathcal{D}^{ll}_{\mathcal{S}_\mathcal{T}}$	5.3.1	5.1	Necessary	Possible	++
Likelihood	$\mathcal{D}^{homo}_{\mathcal{S}_\mathcal{T}}$	5.3.1	5.1, 5.2	Necessary	Possible	+
Least squares	$\mathcal{D}^{ls}_{\mathcal{S}_\mathcal{T}}$	5.3.3	5.1, 5.3, 5.4	Linear	Not	-
LRA	$\mathcal{D}^{lra}_{\mathcal{S}_\mathcal{T}}$	5.3.4	5.1, 5.3, 5.6	Linear (bits)	Not	+
MIA	$\mathcal{D}^{mia}_{\mathcal{S}_\mathcal{T}}$	5.4.2	5.7	Non bijective	Possible	+++
CPA	$\mathcal{D}^{cpa}_{\mathcal{S}_\mathcal{T}}$	5.5.1	5.3, 5.4	Linear	Not	-

Table 5.2. *Summary of the characteristics of the distinguishers used for unsupervised attacks*

5.8. Exercise solutions

Exercise 5.1. *Let $\mathcal{S}_\mathcal{T}$ be a set of attack traces. It is assumed that a $\mathcal{D}$ distinguisher returns the following score vector: $\mathcal{D}^1_{\mathcal{S}_\mathcal{T}} = (0, 10, 3, 5, 6, 2, 3, 1)^\intercal$. What is the size of $\mathcal{K}$? If the value of key $k^\star$ is 0, is the attack successful? Same questions for $\mathcal{D}^2_{\mathcal{S}_\mathcal{T}} = (10, 9, 3, 5)^\intercal$, $\mathcal{D}^3_{\mathcal{S}_\mathcal{T}} = (10, 10, 3, 5)^\intercal$ and $\mathcal{D}^4_{\mathcal{S}_\mathcal{T}} = (10, 10)^\intercal$.*

– $\mathcal{D}^1_{\mathcal{S}_\mathcal{T}}$ is the vector of scores for a set of eight possible values for $\mathcal{K}$. The key found is the second (with a value of 1), not the first (with a value of 0), so the attack was unsuccessful.

– $\mathcal{D}^2_{\mathcal{S}_\mathcal{T}}$ is the vector of scores for a set of four possible values for $\mathcal{K}$. The key found is the first (of value 0), so the attack is successful.

– $\mathcal{D}^3_{\mathcal{S}_\mathcal{T}}$ is the vector of scores for a set of four possible values for $\mathcal{K}$. Two keys are found: the first (of value 0) and the second (of value 1), so the attack is not successful, but the entropy per bit of the key has decreased from 2 to 1.

– $\mathcal{D}^4_{\mathcal{S}_\mathcal{T}}$ is the vector of scores for a set of 2 possible values for $\mathcal{K}$. No keys were found, so the attack was unsuccessful.

Exercise 5.2. *Let a set of traces (x_i) be acquired with a plaintext p_i and a fixed key $k^\star$, both of one bit, such that a trace at each instant can be modeled by $x_i = p_i \times k^\star + b_i$, knowing that* P *follows a uniform distribution and* B *follows a normal distribution $\mathcal{N}(0, 1)$.*

Which distinguisher is the attacker using? If the attacker decides to define $\delta(z) = p + k$, what will the distinguisher scores be?

This is a univariate case, where the variances of B do not depend on Z, so we use $\mathcal{D}^{homo}_{\mathcal{S}_\mathcal{T}}$.

$$\begin{aligned}
\mathcal{D}^{homo}_{\mathcal{S}_\mathcal{T}}[k] &= -\sum_i (x_i - \delta(z_i) - \mu_{z_i,\mathrm{B}})^2 \\
&= -\sum_i (p_i \times k^\star + b_i - p_i - k - 0)^2 \\
&= -\sum_i (p_i(k^\star - 1) - k + b_i)^2 \\
&= -\sum_i (p_i(k^\star - 1) - k)^2 - \sum_i (b_i)^2 - 2\sum_i b_i(p_i(k^\star - 1) - k)) \\
&= -\sum_i (p_i(k^\star - 1) - k)^2 - N_a \cdot 1 - 0 \\
&= -(k^\star - 1)^2 \sum_i (p_i)^2 - \sum_i (k)^2 + 2k(k^\star - 1)\sum_i (p_i) - N_a \\
&= -(k^\star - 1)^2 \frac{N_a}{2} - N_a k^2 + 2k(k^\star - 1)\frac{N_a}{2} - N_a \\
&= -(k^\star - 1)^2 \frac{N_a}{2} - N_a k^2 + k(k^\star - 1)N_a - N_a
\end{aligned}$$

We have the following two cases:

$$\begin{aligned}
k^\star = 0 &\implies \mathcal{D}^{homo}_{\mathcal{S}_\mathcal{T}}[0] = -\frac{3N_a}{2} \;>\; \mathcal{D}^{homo}_{\mathcal{S}_\mathcal{T}}[1] = -\frac{7N_a}{2} \\
k^\star = 1 &\implies \mathcal{D}^{homo}_{\mathcal{S}_\mathcal{T}}[0] = -N_a \;>\; \mathcal{D}^{homo}_{\mathcal{S}_\mathcal{T}}[1] = -2N_a
\end{aligned}$$

We observe that the key is not found if it is worth 1.

Exercise 5.3. *Show that $\boldsymbol{S}$ is the inverse matrix of $\boldsymbol{M}_k^\intercal \cdot \boldsymbol{M}_k$ if the bits of Z are uniform and independent.*

We have:

$$\boldsymbol{M}_k^{\mathsf{T}} \cdot \boldsymbol{M}_k = \begin{pmatrix} 1 & z_1^{(1)} & \dots & z_1^{(n)} \\ \vdots & \vdots & & \vdots \\ 1 & z_{N_a}^{(1)} & \dots & z_{N_a}^{(n)} \end{pmatrix} \cdot \begin{pmatrix} 1 & \dots & 1 \\ z_1^{(1)} & \dots & z_{N_a}^{(1)} \\ \vdots & & \vdots \\ z_1^{(n)} & \dots & z_{N_a}^{(n)} \end{pmatrix}$$

$$= N_a \begin{pmatrix} 1 & \overline{Z^{(1)}} & \dots & \dots & \dots & \overline{Z^{(n)}} \\ \overline{Z^{(1)}} & \overline{Z^{(1)}Z^{(1)}} & \overline{Z^{(1)}Z^{(2)}} & \dots & \dots & \overline{Z^{(1)}Z^{(n)}} \\ \vdots & \overline{Z^{(2)}Z^{(1)}} & \ddots & \ddots & & \vdots \\ \vdots & \vdots & \ddots & \ddots & \ddots & \vdots \\ \vdots & \vdots & & \ddots & \ddots & \overline{Z^{(n-1)}Z^{(n)}} \\ \overline{Z^{(n)}} & \overline{Z^{(n)}Z^{(1)}} & \dots & \dots & \overline{Z^{(n)}Z^{(n-1)}} & \overline{Z^{(n)}Z^{(n)}} \end{pmatrix}$$

$$= N_a \begin{pmatrix} 1 & \frac{1}{2} & \cdots & \cdots & \cdots & \frac{1}{2} \\ \frac{1}{2} & \frac{1}{2} & \frac{1}{4} & \cdots & \cdots & \frac{1}{4} \\ \vdots & \frac{1}{4} & \ddots & \ddots & & \vdots \\ \vdots & \vdots & \ddots & \ddots & \ddots & \vdots \\ \vdots & \vdots & & \ddots & \ddots & \frac{1}{4} \\ \frac{1}{2} & \frac{1}{4} & \cdots & \cdots & \frac{1}{4} & \frac{1}{2} \end{pmatrix}$$

since the bits of Z are uniform and independent. The product of this matrix and the following matrix should give the identity:

$$\boldsymbol{S} = \frac{1}{N_a} \begin{pmatrix} n+1 & -2 & \cdots & \cdots & \cdots & -2 \\ -2 & 4 & 0 & \cdots & \cdots & 0 \\ \vdots & 0 & \ddots & \ddots & & \vdots \\ \vdots & \vdots & \ddots & \ddots & \ddots & \vdots \\ \vdots & \vdots & & \ddots & \ddots & 0 \\ -2 & 0 & \cdots & \cdots & 0 & 4 \end{pmatrix}$$

Let $A = \boldsymbol{S} \cdot \boldsymbol{M}_k^{\mathsf{T}} \cdot \boldsymbol{M}_k$. Except for the first line of A which is worth $(n+1-n, \frac{n+1}{2} - 1 - \frac{n-1}{2}, \dots, \frac{n+1}{2} - 1 - \frac{n-1}{2})$, the first column worth $(n+1-n, -2+2+0, \dots, -2+2+0)^{\mathsf{T}}$ and the diagonal which is $(n+1-n, -1+2+0, \dots, -1+2+0)$, the other elements of A are $-1+1+0$.

Thus:

$$A = \boldsymbol{S} \cdot \boldsymbol{M}_k^{\intercal} \cdot \boldsymbol{M}_k$$
$$= \begin{pmatrix} 1 & 0 & \dots & 0 \\ 0 & \ddots & \ddots & \vdots \\ \vdots & \ddots & \ddots & 0 \\ 0 & \dots & 0 & 1 \end{pmatrix}$$

Exercise 5.4. *Demonstrate that* $\mathcal{D}_{\mathcal{S}_\mathcal{T}}^{mi}[k] = \sum_{\mathbf{x}} \sum_z \Pr(\mathrm{Z} = z, \mathbf{X} = \mathbf{x}) \log_2 \frac{\Pr(\mathrm{Z}=z,\mathbf{X}=\mathbf{x})}{\Pr(\mathrm{Z}=z)\cdot\Pr(\mathbf{X}=\mathbf{x})}$.

$$\begin{aligned}
\mathcal{D}_{\mathcal{S}_\mathcal{T}}^{mi}[k] &= \mathsf{H}(\mathrm{Z}) + \mathsf{H}(\mathbf{X}) - \mathsf{H}(\mathrm{Z}, \mathbf{X}) \\
&= -\sum_z \Pr(\mathrm{Z} = z) \log_2 \Pr(\mathrm{Z} = z) - \sum_{\mathbf{x}} \Pr(\mathbf{X} = \mathbf{x}) \log_2 \Pr(\mathbf{X} = \mathbf{x}) \\
&\quad + \sum_{\mathbf{x}} \sum_z \Pr(\mathrm{Z} = z, \mathbf{X} = \mathbf{x}) \log_2 \Pr(\mathrm{Z} = z, \mathbf{X} = \mathbf{x}) \\
&= -\sum_z \sum_{\mathbf{x}} \Pr(\mathrm{Z} = z, \mathbf{X} = \mathbf{x}) \log_2 \Pr(\mathrm{Z} = z) \\
&\quad - \sum_{\mathbf{x}} \sum_z \Pr(\mathbf{X} = \mathbf{x}, \mathrm{Z} = z) \log_2 \Pr(\mathbf{X} = \mathbf{x}) \\
&\quad + \sum_{\mathbf{x}} \sum_z \Pr(\mathrm{Z} = z, \mathbf{X} = \mathbf{x}) \log_2 \Pr(\mathrm{Z} = z, \mathbf{X} = \mathbf{x})
\end{aligned}$$

$$\mathcal{D}_{\mathcal{S}_\mathcal{T}}^{mi}[k] = \sum_{\mathbf{x}} \sum_z \Pr(\mathrm{Z} = z, \mathbf{X} = \mathbf{x}) \log_2 \frac{\Pr(\mathrm{Z} = z, \mathbf{X} = \mathbf{x})}{\Pr(\mathrm{Z} = z) \cdot \Pr(\mathbf{X} = \mathbf{x})}$$

Exercise 5.5. *Let a set of traces* (x_i) *be acquired with a uniform plaintext* p_i *and a fixed key* $k^\star$, *both of a single bit, such that a trace at each instant can be modeled by* $x_i = p_i \oplus 1 \oplus k^\star + b_i$, *knowing that* P *follows a uniform distribution and* B *is independent of* Z. *Compare the distinguisher scores in the case where the attacker defines* $\varphi(\mathrm{Z}_k) = p \oplus k$.

The variance of X does not depend on k. The variance of $\varphi(\mathrm{Z}_k)$ is $\frac{1}{N_a}\sum_i (p_i \oplus k)^2$. Now $\frac{1}{N_a}\sum (p_i \oplus 1)^2 = \frac{1}{N_a}\sum p_i^2 = \frac{1}{2}$, so the variance of $\varphi(\mathrm{Z}_k)$ does not depend on k either.

We can now compare the product expectation of X and $\varphi(\mathrm{Z}_k)$ of the covariance in the numerator:

$$\begin{aligned}\mathbb{E}\left[\mathrm{X}\cdot\varphi(\mathrm{Z}_k)\right] &= \frac{1}{N_a}\sum_i (p_i \oplus 1 \oplus k^\star + b_i)(p_i \oplus k) \\ &= \frac{1}{N_a}\sum_i (p_i \oplus 1 \oplus k^\star)(p_i \oplus k) + \frac{1}{N_a}\sum_i b_i(p_i \oplus k)\end{aligned}$$

If P is uniform, $\mathbb{E}\left[\mathrm{X}\cdot\varphi(\mathrm{Z}_k)\right] = \frac{1}{N_a}\sum_i (p_i \oplus 1 \oplus k^\star)(p_i \oplus k)$.

As $\frac{1}{N_a}\sum(p_i \oplus 1)^2 = \frac{1}{N_a}\sum p_i^2 = \frac{1}{2}$ and $(p_i \oplus 1)(p_i) = 0$, we have the following two cases:

$$\begin{aligned}k^\star = 0 &\implies \mathbb{E}\left[\mathrm{X}\cdot\varphi(\mathrm{Z}_1)\right] = \frac{1}{2} \; > \; \mathbb{E}\left[\mathrm{X}\cdot\varphi(\mathrm{Z}_0)\right] = 0 \\ k^\star = 1 &\implies \mathbb{E}\left[\mathrm{X}\cdot\varphi(\mathrm{Z}_0)\right] = \frac{1}{2} \; > \; \mathbb{E}\left[\mathrm{X}\cdot\varphi(\mathrm{Z}_1)\right] = 0\end{aligned}$$

We can see that the key is never found.

Exercise 5.6. *Let* $\mathbf{x}$ *be a trace of dimension 3, such that* $\mathbf{x}[0] = z^\star$, $\mathbf{x}[1] = z^\star + k^\star$ *and* $\mathbf{x}[2] = p$. *We wish to model each instant by the univariate model defined by* $m_k = (\mathbf{C}(p, k)) + b = z + b$. *Under what conditions does this modeling follow Assumption 5.3 of noise independence?*

The error made by the attacker will be transferred to the noise component. Thus, for a fixed key hypothesis k, the noise is $b = \mathbf{x}[0] - z = 0$ at time $t = 0$ and $b = \mathbf{x}[1] - z = k$ at time $t = 1$. In both cases, the noise B is constant and independent of Z_k. For time $t = 2$, the noise is $b = \mathbf{x}[2] - z = p - z$, so the noise B is dependent on Z_k. In the multivariate case, it is not independent either.

Exercise 5.7. *Show that the Hamming weight function at the output of an AES S-box has the EDS property, although it is not bijective. Is this true for DES? Why is this?*

The Hamming weight function at the output of the AES S-box S is defined by: $p, k \in \{0, \ldots, 255\}^2 \mapsto \mathrm{HW}(S(p \oplus k)) \in \{0, \ldots, 8\}$ with HW as the Hamming weight function. Since $(p, k) \mapsto p \oplus k$ has the EDS property, so does its composite by the function $i \mapsto S(i)$. So the composite of $(p, k) \mapsto S(p \oplus k)$ by the function $z \mapsto HW(z)$ has the EDS property.

DES differs from AES in the non-bijectivity of the S-box, which takes six bits as input and returns four, and the addition of an expansion function before the exclusive or between the message and the key. We have seen that non-bijectivity is not a problem, but expansion makes the input distribution of the exclusive non-uniform, even if Pt is uniform.

Exercise 5.8. *Show that if* $\mathbf{C}$ *has the EDS property and* P *is uniform, then the variance of the random variable* $\delta(\mathrm{Z}_k)$ *is identical for all* $k \in \mathcal{K}$.

The random variable $\delta(\mathrm{Z}_k)$ is rewritten as $\delta(\mathbf{C}(\mathrm{P}, k))$. Since P is uniform and $\mathbf{C}$ has the EDS property, the function $(p, k) \mapsto \delta \circ \mathbf{C}$ has the EDS property. So the distributions of the variables $\delta(\mathbf{C}(\mathrm{P}, k))$ are identical for all values $k \in \mathcal{K}$ and so is their variance.

5.9. Notes and further references

Historical aspects: the DPA (*differential power analysis*) attack is the first attack mentioned in the literature by Kocher et al. (1999). The sensitive data are reduced to a single bit (or equivalently, only one bit of the sensitive data is leaked) and the distinguisher performs an absolute difference of the averages of two groups of traces, separated according to the value of the targeted bit.

The difference of means is a simple tool for comparing two distributions. The DoM (*Difference of Mean*) attack is a generalization of DPA. It corresponds to the attack published by Messerges et al. (2002) under the name *generalized DPA*. The idea is to define a criterion relating to the sensitive data that splits the set of traces into two groups and introduces an imbalance in their averages according to the key hypothesis. The criterion is defined on the basis of a leakage model. The difference in averages is then used to check the validity of the leakage model, that is, knowledge of the sensitive data, and then to recover the secret. The criterion can be made time dependent to consider univariate attacks. If the attacker has a very precise idea of the form of the leak, it is in the attacker's interest to use likelihood, or MIA if considering Gaussian noise is not realistic. Likewise, if the anticipated model is close to a linear relationship, CPA is the best choice.

While this single-bit model may make sense in asymmetric cryptography, where the secret exponent bits are processed one by one, it is very restrictive when the sensitive data have a higher entropy and all the bits contribute to the leakage. To compensate for this shortcoming, several distinguishers then appeared as extensions of the DPA, until the arrival of the CPA with the publication of the article by Brier et al. (2004). Bevan and Knudsen (2003) proposed adding DPA distinguishers for each bit of sensitive data. Messerges et al. (1999) used the DPA distinguisher with a partition into two groups on the sensitive data values. A few suggestions are made for the choice of partition. In particular, the authors suggested using the group of values with extreme Hamming weight and the group of zero values; the other values were not used, which amounts to assigning them zero weight in the distinguisher formula. Following on from this idea, Le et al. (2006) proposed to consider all the Hamming weight values of the sensitive data and to consider weighting the averages for each group according to the importance of the information they provide (values with maximum Hamming weight being more informative than those with average Hamming weight). The authors also showed that this distinguisher is in fact equivalent to that of CPA.

Generally speaking, Doget et al. (2011) have shown that DoM, along with all these historical distinguishers, are equivalent to CPA with a judicious choice of model.

– Section 5.3. The LRA is introduced by Lomné et al. (2013), where numerous computational optimizations are given.

– Section 5.4. For a more in-depth study of MIA, the interested reader can turn to the article by Cristiani et al. (2021).

The choice of the number of classes N_c is left to the attacker, but is not trivial. For example, Gierlichs et al. (2008) recommend choosing $N_c = |\varphi(\mathcal{Z})|$ classes, so that each class noted c_j contains an approximately equal number of values for any $j \in N_c$.

For example, Batina et al. (2011) advise choosing bandwidth $h = 1.06 \times \min\left(\sigma\left(\mathrm{X}\right), \frac{\mathrm{IQR(X)}}{1.34}\right) \times N_a^{\frac{1}{5}}$, where IQR is the interquartile range.

– Section 5.6. There are other assumptions about the nature of the noise studied in Heuser et al. (2014), such as uniform or Laplacian noise.

5.10. References

Batina, L., Gierlichs, B., Prouff, E., Rivain, M., Standaert, F.-X., Veyrat-Charvillon, N. (2011). Mutual information analysis: A comprehensive study. *Journal of Cryptology*, 24(2), 269–291.

Bevan, R. and Knudsen, E. (2003). Ways to enhance differential power analysis. In *ICISC 02*. Springer, Heidelberg.

Brier, E., Clavier, C., Olivier, F. (2004). Correlation power analysis with a leakage model. In *CHES 2004*. Springer, Heidelberg.

Cristiani, V., Lecomte, M., Maurine, P. (2021). Revisiting mutual information analysis: Multidimensionality, neural estimation and optimality proofs. Cryptology ePrint Archive, Report 2021/1518 [Online]. Available at: https://eprint.iacr.org/2021/1518.

Doget, J., Prouff, E., Rivain, M., Standaert, F.-X. (2011). Univariate side channel attacks and leakage modeling. *Journal of Cryptographic Engineering*, 1(2), 123–144.

Gierlichs, B., Batina, L., Tuyls, P., Preneel, B. (2008). Mutual information analysis. In *CHES 2008*. Springer, Heidelberg, 426–442.

Heuser, A., Rioul, O., Guilley, S. (2014). Good is not good enough – Deriving optimal distinguishers from communication theory. In *CHES 2014*. Springer, Heidelberg.

Kocher, P.C., Jaffe, J., Jun, B. (1999). Differential power analysis. In *CRYPTO'99*. Springer, Heidelberg.

Le, T.-H., Clédière, J., Canovas, C., Robisson, B., Servière, C., Lacoume, J.-L. (2006). A proposition for correlation power analysis enhancement. In *CHES 2006*. Springer, Heidelberg.

Lomné, V., Prouff, E., Roche, T. (2013). Behind the scene of side channel attacks. In *ASIACRYPT 2013*. Springer, Heidelberg.

Messerges, T., Dabbish, E., Sloan, R. (1999). Investigations of power analysis attacks on smartcards. In *USENIX Workshop on Smartcard Technology*. USENIX Association, Berkeley.

Messerges, T.S., Dabbish, E.A., Sloan, R.H. (2002). Examining smart-card security under the threat of power analysis attacks. *IEEE Transactions on Computer*, 51(5), 541–552.

6

Quantities to Judge Side Channel Resilience

Elisabeth OSWALD
University of Klagenfurt, Austria

6.1. Introduction

Evaluations in the context of side-channel attacks can take different forms, depending on the intended outcomes. For instance, a developer might want to evaluate their implementation with respect to some specific attack vectors, a tester might want to evaluate different configurations for a specific attack vector, or it might be desirable to determine how good the "best" attack might look for a given device in a formal evaluation scheme, etc. Depending then on the goal, an evaluation strategy has to be selected. In this chapter, we will review the most widely used metrics[1] which are used within informal and formal evaluation schemes.

We proceed by tackling increasingly more comprehensive metrics: this means that we will start by utilizing intuitive ways to judge the quality of concrete attack vectors, which will bring us naturally to the concept of the key rank (and thereby judging the remaining effort of an adversary). Thereafter, we will review how to compute (independently of an attack vector) how much an implementation leaks, and contrast

1 Formally speaking, we are reviewing quantities that enable us to compare distributions (or properties of distributions) meaningfully; none of the quantities that we will review actually satisfies the mathematical definition of a metric.

Embedded Cryptography 1,
coordinated by Emmanuel PROUFF, Guénaël RENAULT,
Matthieu RIVAIN and Colin O'FLYNN.

this with the concept of leakage detection, which is to decide whether there is leakage (or not) without performing attacks. Finally, we will investigate how these techniques are used in formal evaluation schemes.

6.1.1. *Assumptions and attack categories*

Most evaluations, tests, and attacks happen in the so-called "standard Differential Power Analysis (DPA) attack" scenario (Kocher et al. 1999) as defined in Mangard et al. (2011). We will briefly explain the underlying idea as well as review the necessary terminology here. We assume that the power consumption $\mathcal{L}$ of a cryptographic device depends on some internal value (or state) $F_{k^*}(X)$, which we call the *target*: a function $F_{k^*} : \mathcal{X} \rightarrow \mathcal{Z}$ of some part of the known plaintext – a random variable $X \overset{R}{\in} \mathcal{X}$ – which is dependent on some part of the secret key $k^* \in \mathcal{K}$ (also called subkey). Consequently, we have that $\mathcal{L} = L \circ F_{k^*}(X) + \varepsilon$, where $L : \mathcal{Z} \rightarrow \mathbb{R}$ describes the data-dependent component and ε comprises the remaining power consumption, which can be modeled as independent random noise (this simplifying assumption is common in the literature). In order to exploit the information contained in the measurements, we will use a so-called distinguisher $\mathcal{D}$, which computes a score value for each subkey guess $\mathcal{D} = \{\mathcal{D}(L \circ F_{k^*}(\mathbf{x}) + \mathbf{e}, M \circ F_k(\mathbf{x}))\}_{k \in \mathcal{K}}$, where $\mathbf{x}$ are the known inputs, M represents the (abstract) model that an adversary has about the internal workings of the device under attack and $\mathbf{e} = \{e_i\}_{i=1}$ is the observed noise.

While side-channel attacks can extract information about secret plaintexts or any secret data in general, we will now focus exclusively on attacks that aim to recover secret keys. We will next review the two "classical settings" for side-channel key recovery attacks, and then briefly comment on the worst-case adversary that may be able to mix both settings.

6.1.1.1. *Single trace attacks (i.e. Simple Power Analysis (SPA) style)*

The attacker may only gather measurements corresponding to a single known plaintext (or equivalent ciphertext). Consequently, information about the key is obtained by utilizing the information that is contained within the entire trace: such an attack strategy utilizes multiple points within the measurement trace corresponding to multiple intermediate values.

The leakage of a single intermediate value may be directly related to a portion of the secret key (subkey). For instance, this is often the case in the context of public key cryptography, where the secret key may be applied bit by bit. A side-channel attacker uses a distinguisher to estimate a likelihood (or score) for each key portion, given the leakage of an intermediate value as it is represented by a portion of a leakage trace.

It may also be that multiple intermediate values directly relate to a portion of the secret key. This is often the case in the context of symmetric cryptography, in byte-oriented ciphers like Advanced Encryption Standard (AES). A side-channel attacker might then try and combine the information from multiple portions of a trace (corresponding to multiple intermediate values) to derive some probabilistic information about a portion of the secret key. This may require knowledge about the location of leaks, which may have to be acquired in a step prior to the attack (profiling).

6.1.1.2. *Multiple trace attacks (i.e. DPA style)*

The attacker has N power measurements corresponding to encryptions of N known plaintexts (or equivalently ciphertexts) $x_i \in \mathcal{X}$, $i = 1, \ldots, N$ and wishes to recover a subkey k^*. The attacker can accurately compute the internal values as they would be under each key hypothesis $\{F_k(x_i)\}_{i=1}^N$, $k \in \mathcal{K}$ and uses whatever information they possess about the true leakage function L to construct a prediction model M.

DPA works because the model predictions under the correct subkey hypothesis explain the true trace measurements better than the model predictions under an incorrect subkey hypothesis. We measure how well the model predictions match the true data using a distinguisher. The exact value of the outcome of the application of a distinguisher is impossible to calculate in all but simulated scenarios. In practice, we can only ever estimate the distinguisher value based on the number of traces that we have available: $\hat{\mathcal{D}}_N = \{\hat{\mathcal{D}}_N(L \circ F_{k^*}(\mathbf{x}) + \mathbf{e}, M \circ F_k(\mathbf{x}))\}_{k \in \mathcal{K}}$ (where $\mathbf{x} = \{x_i\}_{i=1}^N$ are the known inputs and $\mathbf{e} = \{e_i\}_{i=1}^N$ is the observed noise).

A distinguisher may utilize different models, ranging from generic models to highly device-specific models. Furthermore, a distinguisher might work with univariate models or multivariate models. However, for this chapter, these specifics are not relevant.

6.1.1.3. *Worst-case attacks*

Clearly, the most powerful attacks will be those that combine multiple points from within each trace (SPA style) across multiple observations (DPA style). In the literature, such attacks are sometimes referred to as horizontal attacks, multi-target attacks, soft-analytical side-channel attacks, etc. (Veyrat-Charvillon et al. 2014). The key characteristics of worst-case adversaries is that they will aim to exploit all available leakage (i.e. they are assumed to be able to derive precise models for intermediate values, possibly including internal randomness for countermeasures), and they have full knowledge of an implementation so they can take advantage of multiple intermediate values.

6.1.2. *Attack success*

Any attack is characterized by:

– the nature and accuracy of the used leakage model(s);

– the type of distinguisher;

– the utilized leakage points and/or targets;

– the number of leakage traces;

– the way by which the information is combined.

Depending on these characteristics, we speak of either a single trace attack (i.e. SPA), a differential attack (i.e. standard DPA) or a multi-target attack (multiple traces and intermediates). When comparing different attack vectors, it is then clearly important to clearly state all these characteristics, such that at the end of the comparison, it is clear whether the comparison is like for like (i.e. attacks with similar characteristics are compared) or not.

All attack strategies deliver likelihoods, or scores, for subkeys. An adversary will, after an attack, either use the scores as input to some cryptanalytic method, or, enumerate keys in order of their likelihood. In the standard setting, we focus only on adversaries who try to work out the key directly from the subkey scores.

We call an attack *o-th order successful* if there are no more than o key values that have a score that is higher than the score of the secret key $\#\{k \in \mathcal{K} : \hat{\mathcal{D}}_N[k^*] \leq \hat{\mathcal{D}}_N[k]\} \leq o$. As we always work with estimations in real-world attack scenarios, attack outcomes vary: for different sets of observations (with N traces each), attacks using N traces will produce different distinguishing vectors. A single attack therefore only gives a snapshot, and to draw any meaningful conclusions about what a practical adversary can achieve, we must conduct repeat attacks in an evaluation.

If we then consider the evaluation scenario where we do repeat attacks with a known secret key, we can look at the percentage of attack outcomes in which the secret key is ranked highly. The (oth order) *success rate (SR)* of an attack is the percentage of attack outcomes in which the correct key is ranked among the top o most likely keys (according to their distinguishing scores). In many published works, the term *SR* refers to the *first-order* success rate. We can consider success rates for scores that relate to portions of the secret key, or for the joint scores that relate to the entire key.

6.2. Metrics for comparing the effectiveness of specific attack vectors

A question that is often encountered is that of "which attack vector" is most effective for some given implementation. Although side-channel theory has made some significant contributions here (Heuser et al. 2014; de Chérisey et al. 2019), real-world adversaries do not meet all assumptions of these works (i.e. have exact models) and therefore we have to deal with the perhaps more messy business of comparing concrete attack vectors.

Assuming now that we consider a concrete comparison, which metrics are suitable? In the literature, many metrics have been used over the years.

6.2.1. *Magnitude of scores*

When considering types of attack strategies that utilize a clean divide-and-conquer strategy (like typical DPA style attacks), attack vectors that recover subkeys have been judged directly by their ability to produce a high-score value for a (fixed) distinguisher. For instance, we might be interested if an attack using a weighted Hamming weight model with a correlation distinguisher performs better than using the same distinguisher with a standard Hamming weight model. A larger distinguishing value of the correct subkey would indicate a stronger distinguisher because a larger value implies that fewer traces are needed to distinguish it from the scores of incorrect subkeys (Whitnall and Oswald 2011).

A criticism of simply using the highest distinguisher score is that the score of incorrect subkeys could also be large. This is correct and the relationship between correct and incorrect subkeys strongly depends on the selected target function (Fei et al. 2012). Therefore, an alternative would be to consider the difference between the score of the correct subkey and its nearest rival (Whitnall and Oswald 2011).

6.2.2. *Number of needed leakage traces/success rate estimation*

The magnitude of the distinguishing scores are mathematically linked to the number of leakage traces during the estimation of the distinguishing scores. The magnitudes also impact the number of subkeys that have larger scores than the correct subkey. Consequently, a general way to judge attack strategies is to either fix a success order and ask how many traces are necessary to reach this success order with some probability, or to fix the number of traces and then look at the resulting success order probabilities.

Of course, the number of traces, and the success order link to the magnitude of the scores, and estimations based on precise assumptions about the distinguisher and target functions can be calculated (Fei et al. 2012; Rivain 2009). Such estimations are also called "shortcuts" in the literature.

While there is much literature which aims to improve the quality of the estimation of the number of needed traces, or equivalently the success rates, much less thinking has gone into the following questions:

- Should success at first order be considered only?
- Is success at lower orders also a relevant property?
- Should an average measure, such as the key guessing entropy, be preferred?

6.3. Metrics for evaluating the leakage (somewhat) independent of a specific attack vector

In the context of comparing implementations, or perhaps even devices, the salient question in practice is how much does an implementation or device leak? This means that we are interested in separating the leakage of the implementation from any specific attack vector as much as possible.

Naturally, a complete separation is infeasible; we have to make at least some assumptions, or equivalently, put some constraints on what we are estimating: are we aiming to capture the leakage in a single point (i.e. univariate leakage for one or several concurrent target function)? Are we aiming to capture the multivariate leakage of a single target function? Are we aiming to capture the (multivariate) leakage of multiple target functions jointly?

Within the existing literature, there are two very popular metrics in use: the signal-to-noise ratio (SNR) and the mutual information (MI) metric. Both metrics aim to capture and compare some of the characteristics of what we need to define as the "meaningful" part of the overall leakage and the "not meaningful" part of the overall leakage. Using our notation from before, that is, $\mathcal{L} = L \circ F_{k^*}(X) + \varepsilon$, it is clear that the meaningful part (i.e. signal) will relate to the data- and key-dependent component, which is a function of X, k^*, and the not meaningful component is the independent noise ε. The challenge in computing both the SNR and MI is to define the actual function of X, k^*.

In the side-channel literature, the most common approach is to define the function via choosing interesting intermediate values in algorithms of interest. In other words, we link the SNR or MI directly to a target function that we might want to choose in an attack. However, it is also possible to compute SNR and MI values with respect to device-specific functions. For instance, for a given assembly instruction, we vary its operands, or given a circuit, we can fix a component of it and vary its inputs to compute an SNR or an MI.

6.3.1. *Signal to noise ratio*

The concept of an SNR appears in many engineering contexts, leading to different definitions. The type of SNR that is commonly used in the side-channel area compares the signal variance and the noise variance:

$$\text{SNR} = \frac{Var(\mathcal{L}|f(X, k^{ast}))}{Var(\varepsilon)} \qquad [6.1]$$

The function f defines the signal that depends on X, k^*. Thus, f could be related to a cryptographic intermediate (e.g. an S-box output), or some other operation that occurs on the device (e.g. the exclusive or between two bytes of k^{ast})). Hence, the SNR captures the signal at just one point in time (or during just one intermediate step during the execution of an algorithm). It is a purely univariate metric that characterizes the leakage at one specific moment.

A device then cannot be said to have just one SNR, because in each computation step, potentially different components of the device are active. In order to assess a device, we have to compute multiple SNRs that correspond to different "configurations" of the device (e.g. we can compute SNRs for different low-level instructions). Similarly, an implementation of an algorithm cannot be said to have just one SNR, because an algorithm typically operates as a sequence of many (different) steps. Consequently, in order to assess the implementation of an algorithm, we have to compute multiple SNRs corresponding to the different steps that the algorithm takes.

The actual computation of the SNR in practice requires the estimation of the signal and the noise variance. This can be done easily by using the empirical variance as a plug-in estimator, and grouping the observed traces according to $f(X, k^*)$ (e.g. $f = S(X \oplus k)$, or $f = (x_1 \oplus x_2)$), etc.

6.3.2. *Mutual information*

The mutual information (MI) expresses how much knowing about one (set of) random variable(s) helps to explain another random variable. It is (in contrast to the correlation between two variables) a measure that takes the entire "shape" of the random variables into account. If two variables are statistically independent, then the MI equals zero.

The most common definition of the MI is via the Kullback–Leiber divergence, which measures the statistical distance between two probability distributions (i.e. the distributions associated with the random variables of interest). The exact mathematical expression of its definition depends on the nature of the random variables; either both variables are discrete, or both are continuous, or they are mixed variables.

In the context of side-channel research, we are ultimately interested in how much we learn about the secret key, or a function of the secret key, etc., given some leakage (potentially also depending on some other public information). Depending on the nature of the observed leakage, the random variable associated with the leakage can be either understood as continuous (e.g. traces after signal processing) or discrete. The other random variable of interest is often discrete (e.g. the key or a target function that depends on key and input), but it could be continuous (e.g. a model applied to a target function).

The actual computation of the MI in practice requires its estimation. Unlike the SNR, this is no longer a straightforward process if we must deal with a mixed variable setting (i.e. one variable is discrete and one is continuous). Even if we considered a purely discrete setting, the estimation process without distributional assumptions can lead to biased estimators (Paninski 2003). Various works have been proposed in the literature, which are based on replacing the estimation process by using a priori estimated profiles or a mix of both (Durvaux and Standaert 2015; Bronchain et al. 2019a). These approaches lead to quantities (Hypothetical Information (HI) and Perceived Information (PI)) which are related to the MI that is desired.

6.4. Metrics for evaluating the remaining effort of an adversary

Recall that an attack outputs an estimated distinguishing vector for each subkey $\hat{\mathcal{D}}_N$. We call an attack successful at order o if no more than $o - 1$ incorrect subkey distinguishing scores have a higher score than the score of the correct subkey value. An attack that is successful at order o implies that an adversary will only recover the actual key if they use *key enumeration* in addition to a side-channel attack.

6.4.1. *Key rank*

Another expression for the same idea is the term "key rank". The notion of *rank* or *key rank* is more frequently found in the literature today. It is important to be clear about whether the rank of a subkey is studied, or the rank of the full secret key. The full key rank evidently depends on the ranks of all its subkeys. If the subkeys can be regarded as independent random variables, then so can the random variables be, which represent the corresponding subkey ranks. Assuming independence, the rank of the distribution of the full secret key rank can be easily represented as a direct sum of the distribution of the subkey ranks.

Subkey rank: given the distinguishing vector $\hat{\mathbf{D}}_N^{\,j}$ for the jth subkey, and the distinguishing score $\hat{D}[k^*]_N^j$ for the correct subkey, we denote by $\text{rank}(\mathbf{D_N}^j)$, the number of subkey values with distinguishing score strictly larger than $\hat{D}[k^*]_N^j$.

Rank: given the distinguishing vectors $\mathbf{D}_N = (\hat{\mathbf{D}}_N^{\,0}, \ldots, \hat{\mathbf{D}}_N^{\,m} - 1$ for m subkeys, and the distinguishing score $W = \sum_j \hat{D}[k^*]_N^j$ for the secret key, we denote by $\text{rank}(\mathbf{D_N})$ the number of key values with distinguishing score strictly larger than W.

The practical computation of a subkey rank is typically trivial, because subkeys are typically "short". The computation of the full key rank is non-trivial, but efficient algorithms exist. The two most popular ones, because they enable a high degree of precision, whilst retaining good performance, are Glowacz et al. (2015); Martin et al. (2015). They are mathematically equivalent (Martin et al. 2018), and the latter comes with easy to derive performance figures and it can be used to produces scores in such a way to make it compatible with a structured version of Grover's algorithm (thus the side-channel advantage could be exploited with a quantum computer) (Martin et al. 2017).

A simple observation is that the variance of the rank of a full key is always considerably larger than the variance of the rank of a subkey: this follows immediately from the fact that the variance of the joint distribution of m random variables is the sum of the individual variances. This fact holds irrespective of the estimation process (for the distinguisher and/or the rank).

Evidently, the key rank (irrespective of whether it is for a subkey or for the full key) depends on the number of traces of the underlying side-channel attack, as well as the specific instance of the attack itself. In other words, for the same device, and the same number of attack traces, because the distinguishing scores will vary, the key rank will vary too. Consequently, a key rank that is derived from a single experiment does not enable strong conclusions; we must consider repeat experiments.

6.4.2. *Average key rank measures*

The guessing entropy (Massey 1994) gives the expected number of guesses (with an optimum strategy) to correctly guess the value of a random variable (in our scenario, the secret key). This concept clearly links with the key rank because the key rank is the number of guesses that an optimal adversary would take to guess the secret key.

Subkey guessing entropy: the subkey guessing entropy is defined as the expected value of the subkey rank, namely:

$$GE({D_N}^j) = \mathbb{E}(\text{rank}({D_N}^j)).$$

A key observation is that the guessing entropy is the *expected value* of the distribution of the subkey rank. Rivain found that the distribution of a *distinguishing vector* tends to a multivariate Gaussian (Rivain 2009), but the general distribution of the subkey rank itself has not been thoroughly explored.

Provided that subkeys are independent random variables, it is easy to define the key guessing entropy for a full key.

Key guessing entropy: the key guessing entropy is defined as:

$$GE(D_N) = \mathbb{E}(\text{rank}(D_N)).$$

Note that the guessing entropy $GE(D_N)$ is defined as the expectation of the rank. In practice, we need to estimate this expectation, which is typically done using the sample mean via the arithmetic average. When working with full keys in practice, the rank values that we consider can be very large, and the arithmetic mean is not suitable – consider a hypothetical scenario in which a DPA attack is evaluated 2^8 times (i.e. we use the average of 256 experiments). Suppose that in 255 of the experiments, the rank of the key is 1, and in just one attack, the rank of the key is 2^{32}. The arithmetic mean in this case is (just over) 2^{24}, which does not truly represent the strength of the attack (after all, the attack succeeded perfectly in all but one repetition). Thus in practice, the geometric mean of N samples $x_1, x_2, \ldots, x_N$ may be more appropriate to correctly estimate the average rank. It is defined as: $\tilde{x} = \left(\prod_{i=1}^{N} x_i\right)^{\frac{1}{N}}$.

Observe that the logarithm of the geometric mean of $\widetilde{rank}(D_N)$ is the arithmetic mean taken on $(\log rank(D_N))$. In our prior "extreme example", the geometric mean would deliver an average rank of (just over) 1 – a much better judgment on an adversary's strength.

It remains an open question if there are other efficient estimators for (average) key ranks available. Choudary and Popescu (2017) provide a biased estimator; recent works by Zhang et al. (2020) utilize a theoretical characterization of the rank distribution.

6.4.3. *Relationship with enumeration capabilities*

Some of the key ranking algorithms can be directly turned into key enumeration algorithms: they allow us to specify and return keys with certain constraints on their ranks. Thus, we can create a sorted list of keys (this happens on the fly) with which we can test these keys, given a known plaintext–ciphertext pair. Testing a key requires a fast and key-agile implementation of the considered crypto algorithm.

In the AES, such a side-channel enhanced enumeration effort has been described and attempted (Longo et al. 2016). This work took place in an academic setting: a state-of-the-art high-performance computing facility was available, but only a short amount of time could be booked. They enumerated 2^{48} keys in about 32 h, using 400 Sandy Bridge Intel Xeon E5-2670 CPUs, clocked at 2.6 GHz and with 4 GiB RAM available per core. The enumeration tool is open source and available at: https://github.com/sca-research/labynkyr.

6.5. Leakage detection as a radical alternative to attack driven evaluations

A radically different way of evaluating the security of an implementation is to ask if there is leakage at all and/or how many leaks there are. This question can be answered by a formal leakage detection test, where a test statistic is computed and evaluated. The test statistic is then our way of translating the informal notion of "finding leakage" into a mathematical concept. As with any statistical procedure, the results always depend on a number of factors (e.g. the number of traces, the nature of the traces, the effect size, the configuration of the test with regard to power as well as false positives).

To test for leakage, we set up a so-called hypothesis test, which compares two hypotheses, H_0 (also called the "null" hypothesis) and H_1 (also called the "alternative" hypothesis). As statistics can never prove a statement, but only ever refute it, we set up the null hypothesis in such a way that it gives the statement that we aim to refute by collecting evidence. In the context of leakage detection, this then leads to the following setup:

H_0: *no leakage*

H_1: *leakage*

Specific detection: one option to design concrete tests is to use "known key attacks": assuming that we can control the secret key, we could ask, "Is my distinguishing score for the correct key indistinguishable from the score of an incorrect key (or from 0) or not?". In terms of hypothesis, this would translate into H_0: *scores are equal*, H_1: *scores are different*. To test the hypotheses, we collect data, compute a suitable test statistic (i.e. one that corresponds to the distinguisher that is being used), and see if we have enough evidence to refute H_0. This idea is also referred to as *specific detection*, because the strategy is indeed specific to one target value. Clearly, if a detection strategy is specific to a single target function, then it is incapable of finding arbitrary leaks in an implementation.

Non-specific detection: a second option to design concrete tests is to use "fixed versus random" tests: assuming that we can control the key and the inputs, we record one set of measurements with a fixed choice of parameters, and we record a second set of measurements where we vary the parameters. The idea is then that if we cannot distinguish the two sets of measurements (H_0: *sets are indistinguishable*; H_1: *sets are distinguishable*), then there has been no impact of the varying parameters on the observable leakage. In principle, any statistical metric can be used in this setting. An extremely popular test statistic is based on comparing distribution means. The advantages of using distribution means is that the estimation of them can be very efficiently accomplished by the empirical means (i.e. averages). Thus, *if* the leakage indeed shows in the distribution means, then this is the most data efficient way to detect it. However, if the leakage is not located in the distribution means, then the test inevitably fails. We can use other test statistics, for example, the MI or its less demanding cousin, the χ^2 test, which will pick up complex leakage, or we shift the leakage into the first central moment (Goodwill et al. 2011; Mather et al. 2013; Schneider and Moradi 2015; Moradi et al. 2018).

Dealing with many points: most leakage traces consist of more than a single point. Thus, an obvious question is: what are the implications of using univariate test statistics? There is a complex relationship between the power of the test (i.e. the probability of not missing true leaks) and the rate of false positives (i.e. the probability of not incorrectly identifying leaks).

These two error probabilities need to be carefully balanced out already in the univariate case: keeping them both low requires us to use a very large number of traces, and determining this required number requires either knowledge or assumptions about the underlying "effect size" (i.e. the magnitude of the leakage that we wish to discover). It gets more complex when dealing with the outcomes of multiple tests (i.e. when we use a univariate test on many trace points), especially because points in leakage traces are typically statistically dependent.

There exist different statistical approaches to deal with this problem (these are called multiplicity corrections), which were discussed extensively in Mather et al. (2013) and Whitnall and Oswald (2019b). The former publication "fixes" problems with both the original TVLA specification and its first inclusion in ISO 17825 (a revised version of this standard is now available).

Another option of dealing with the multivariate nature of traces is to switch to multivariate tests, such as Hotellings (Bronchain et al. 2019b). On the surface, this should solve the problem; however, in practice, it does not necessarily do so. Multivariate tests have a much lower power than univariate tests (i.e. they are less likely to identify true leaks). Thus, only if a trace is very "leaky" will a multivariate test pick this up with a probability that is greater than the corresponding univariate test (with the same number of traces). Otherwise, a correctly configured univariate test with multiplicity corrections in place will outperform the multivariate test (Whitnall and Oswald 2019a) The same argument also applies if we switch out classical statistics with deep learning, such as suggested in Moos et al. (2021). Perhaps the biggest asset of using a multivariate learning approach is that it is more likely to capture complex leakage (i.e. leakage that is expressed in differences in higher order moments or non-central moments). This means that neither multiplicity corrections are necessary nor trace processing techniques to "shift" leakage into the first moment.

None of the published methods deliver "explainable" outcomes: in simple terms, if we find leakage indicated by a test, we are left with the challenge of how to explain it and how to exploit it.

6.6. Formal evaluation schemes

Two evaluation schemes dominate industrial practice for the development of cryptographic modules: common criteria (CC) and FIPS 140. CC evaluations are "attack driven". They systematically capture and categorize attack vectors. CC features a range of evaluation assurance levels (so-called EALs). To reach the higher levels requires more rigorous testing. Depending on the evaluation target, side-channel and fault attacks are considered. CC evaluations are typically required within Europe.

FIPS 140 evaluations are "conformance style" evaluations for cryptographic modules which rely on checking some minimum criteria relating to the security of a product. FIPS 140-3 is the current version, and is mandated in the United States. It is also used in Canada and some other countries (e.g. Japan) that have begun adopting it as well.

In both approaches, the manufacturer/developer acts as the financial sponsor for the evaluation. The product is tested by an accredited testing laboratory, and a government agency oversees this process, and eventually issues a certificate according to the scheme.

6.6.1. *CC evaluations*

CC evaluations are complex processes that are governed by several documents. The main methodology has been adopted as an international standard with the name ISO (2009). For any target of an evaluation, two documents are of particular relevance: the so-called protection profile (PP) and the security target (ST). A PP is a generic document that applies to a category of products, for instance, travel documents, Java Cards, IC, etc. A PP is typically created by a user community, but it could be put forward by the sponsor (i.e. manufacturer/developer). The idea of a PP is to specify implementation independently (as much as possible) of specific security requirements for a "class of devices": it lists threats, security objectives, assumptions, security functional requirements (SFRs), security assurance requirements (SARs), etc. The ST is specific to the product and details the secure implementation of the product. It may use (or not) a PP as reference. The ST uniquely identifies the product and describes the assets, the threats, the security objectives (both on the TOE and on the environment), the perimeter of the evaluation, the SFRs and the lifecycle. Vendors typically make the ST details available to their customers.

During the evaluation process, sponsors must state the envisioned security level (EAL). The EAL indicates a minimal level for requirements for each subclass (development process, guidance, conformity of security target, vulnerability assessment, etc.) that will be taken into account during the evaluation. The EAL is intended to reflect the rigor of the evaluation: EAL 1 is the most basic and level 7 is the most rigorous level. Higher EALs thus do not necessarily imply a higher level of security; they imply that the claimed security assurance of the TOE has been more rigorously verified. It is possible to "augment" a level with specific requirements from a higher level. Among all subclasses, the more relevant for practical side-channel resilience is AVA_VAN (vulnerability assessment), with levels going from 1 (resistance to basic attackers) to 5 (resistance to attackers with high attack potential). It describes the search for vulnerabilities and defines a rating scale for attacks, depending on the means of the adversary.

6.6.1.1. *Specifics for integrated circuit evaluations*

In the specific case of secure integrated circuits (and related software/firmware), the International Security Certification Initiative (ISCI) brings together all stakeholders: certification bodies, evaluation laboratories, hardware vendors, software vendors, card vendors and service providers. ISCI has two working groups. ISCI-WG1 defines the methodology and best practice for smart security device evaluation. ISCI-WG2 (also known as JHAS) defines and maintains the state of the art in potential attacks against smart security devices.

Two documents are maintained by JHAS. The "Application of Attack Potential to Smart Cards" (SOG-IS 2019) is a public document that provides a "rating system" for attacks. The "Attack Methods for Smart Cards and Similar Devices" (SOG-IS 2020) is a confidential document that describes attack vectors that are considered "relevant". The rating system aims to compare the "security strength" of different products objectively.

6.6.2. *FIPS 140-3*

FIPS 140 comes in several versions: FIPS 140-2 has just been replaced by FIPS 140-3 at the time of writing this chapter (FIPS 2020). Like CC, the methodology has been mapped to ISO international standards. These are the ISO standards (ISO/IEC 19790:2012(E) and ISO/IEC 24759:2017(E)). The main difference between FIPS 140-2 and FIPS 140-3 is the inclusion of testing against side-channel attacks. The methodology for testing is given in ISO/IEC 17825:2016. The minimum requirements for setups and calibration of setups are defined in ISO/IEC 20085-1 and 20085-2. NIST special publications SP800-140 A-F may modify these in the future.

FIPS 140 offers four evaluation levels: a higher level requires a more rigorous analysis. In the context of side-channel attacks, a higher level also implies that more observations (or more time) are allowed during the analysis.

ISO/IEC 17825:2016 distinguishes between power, timing and EM attacks, as well as attacks against symmetric and asymmetric cryptographic algorithms. For symmetric encryption, ISO/IEC 17825:2016 relies on using leakage detection procedures instead of attempting attacks. In all other cases, it requires us to test an implementation against standard DPA style attacks (the type of attacks/methodology are listed in the standard). At the time of writing this chapter, ISO/IEC 17825:2016 is undergoing a revision.

6.6.3. *Worst-case adversaries*

Intuitively, the goal of an evaluation should be to determine the true security level of a product. The FIPS approach for side-channel evaluations (via ISO/IEC 17825:2016) sets the bar rather low by mandating a testing regime that captures a reasonably well resourced and capable adversary but it does not mandate getting close to the "best practical adversary". The CC approach clearly aims to find the "best practical adversary" by its attack driven methodology. However, defining the "best practical adversary" is difficult because what is "practical" tends to change over time.

In contrast, in academia, the idea of aiming for the "worst-case attacks" has become more popular. An adversary striving for worst-case attacks will utilize multiple leaking intermediate variables, aim for a multivariate characterization of each leaking intermediate variable, choose either a divide-and-conquer or an analytical information extraction method and it will have enumeration capabilities. To achieve such an adversary, various types of capabilities, for example, in terms of knowledge of the target implementation, profiling, trigger points, etc., can be granted to the evaluator.

The argument has been made that such an adversary is "more stable" (i.e. the worst case assumptions listed before seem to be stable) and that giving enhanced capabilities to the evaluator does not increase evaluation cost. Furthermore, the worst-case adversary puts a long-term perspective on the outcomes of evaluations: if a product withstands a worst-case adversary, then it is more likely to be secure not just at the time of evaluation, but also for a longer period after the evaluation (Azouaoui et al. 2020).

6.7. References

Azouaoui, M., Bellizia, D., Buhan, I., Debande, N., Duval, S., Giraud, C., Jaulmes, É., Koeune, F., Oswald, E., Standaert, F. et al. (2020). A systematic appraisal of side channel evaluation strategies. In *Security Standardisation Research – 6th International Conference, SSR 2020*, van der Merwe, T., Mitchell, C.J., Mehrnezhad, M. (eds). Springer, Cham.

Bronchain, O., Hendrickx, J.M., Massart, C., Olshevsky, A., Standaert, F.-X. (2019a). Leakage certification revisited: Bounding model errors in side-channel security evaluations. In *Advances in Cryptology – CRYPTO 2019*, Boldyreva, A. and Micciancio, D. (eds). Springer, Heidelberg.

Bronchain, O., Schneider, T., Standaert, F.-X. (2019b). Multi-tuple leakage detection and the dependent signal issue. *IACR Transactions on Cryptographic Hardware and Embedded Systems*, 2019(2), 318–345.

de Chérisey, E., Guilley, S., Rioul, O., Piantanida, P. (2019). Best information is most successful. *IACR Transactions on Cryptographic Hardware and Embedded Systems*, 2019(2), 49–79.

Choudary, M.O. and Popescu, P.G. (2017). Back to Massey: Impressively fast, scalable and tight security evaluation tools. In *Cryptographic Hardware and Embedded Systems – CHES 2017*, Fischer, W. and Homma, N. (eds). Springer, Heidelberg.

Durvaux, F. and Standaert, F.-X. (2015). Towards easy leakage certification. Cryptology ePrint Archive, Report 2015/537 [Online]. Available at: https://eprint.iacr.org/2015/537.

Fei, Y., Luo, Q., Ding, A.A. (2012). A statistical model for DPA with novel algorithmic confusion analysis. In *Cryptographic Hardware and Embedded Systems – CHES 2012*, Prouff, E. and Schaumont, P. (eds). Springer, Heidelberg.

FIPS (2020). FIPS 140-3, Security requirements for cryptographic modules [Online]. Available at: http://csrc.nist.gov/groups/ST/FIPS1403/.

Glowacz, C., Grosso, V., Poussier, R., Schüth, J., Standaert, F.-X. (2015). Simpler and more efficient rank estimation for side-channel security assessment. In *Fast Software Encryption – FSE 2015*, Leander, G. (ed.). Springer, Heidelberg.

Goodwill, G., Jun, B., Jaffe, J., Rohatgi, P. (2011). A testing methodology for side-channel resistance validation. In *NIST Non-invasive Attack Testing Workshop*.

Heuser, A., Rioul, O., Guilley, S. (2014). Good is not good enough: Deriving optimal distinguishers from communication theory. In *Cryptographic Hardware and Embedded Systems – CHES 2014*, Batina, L. and Robshaw, M. (eds). Springer, Heidelberg.

ISO (2009). Information technology – Security techniques – Evaluation criteria for IT security. International Organization for Standardization, Geneva.

Kocher, P.C., Jaffe, J., Jun, B. (1999). Differential power analysis. In *Advances in Cryptology – CRYPTO'99*, Wiener, M.J. (ed.). Springer, Heidelberg.

Longo, J., Martin, D.P., Mather, L., Oswald, E., Sach, B., Stam, M. (2016). How low can you go? Using side-channel data to enhance brute-force key recovery. Cryptology ePrint Archive, Report 2016/609 [Online]. Available at: https://eprint.iacr.org/2016/609.

Mangard, S., Oswald, E., Standaert, F.-X. (2011). One for all – All for one: Unifying standard DPA attacks. *IET Information Security* 5(2), 100–110.

Martin, D.P., O'Connell, J.F., Oswald, E., Stam, M. (2015). Counting keys in parallel after a side channel attack. In *Advances in Cryptology – ASIACRYPT 2015*, Iwata, T. and Cheon, J.H. (eds). Springer, Heidelberg.

Martin, D.P., Montanaro, A., Oswald, E., Shepherd, D.J. (2017). Quantum key search with side channel advice. In *SAC 2017: 24th Annual International Workshop on Selected Areas in Cryptography*, Adams, C. and Camenisch, J. (eds). Springer, Heidelberg.

Martin, D.P., Mather, L., Oswald, E. (2018). Two sides of the same coin: Counting and enumerating keys post side-channel attacks revisited. In *Topics in Cryptology – CT-RSA 2018*, Smart, N.P. (ed.). Springer, Heidelberg.

Massey, J.L. (1994). Guessing and entropy. In *IEEE International Symposium on Information Theory*, Trondheim.

Mather, L., Oswald, E., Bandenburg, J., Wójcik, M. (2013). Does my device leak information? An a priori statistical power analysis of leakage detection tests. In *Advances in Cryptology – ASIACRYPT 2013*, Sako, K. and Sarkar, P. (eds). Springer, Heidelberg.

Moos, T., Wegener, F., Moradi, A. (2021). DL-LA: Deep learning leakage assessment. *IACR Transactions on Cryptographic Hardware and Embedded Systems*, 2021(3), 552–598.

Moradi, A., Richter, B., Schneider, T., Standaert, F.-X. (2018). Leakage detection with the χ^2-test. *IACR Transactions on Cryptographic Hardware and Embedded Systems*, 2018(1), 209–237.

Paninski, L. (2003). Estimation of entropy and mutual information. *Neural Computation*, 15, 1191–1253.

Rivain, M. (2009). On the exact success rate of side channel analysis in the Gaussian model. In *SAC 2008: 15th Annual International Workshop on Selected Areas in Cryptography*, Avanzi, R.M., Keliher, L., Sica, F. (eds). Springer, Heidelberg.

Schneider, T. and Moradi, A. (2015). Leakage assessment methodology – A clear roadmap for side-channel evaluations. In *Cryptographic Hardware and Embedded Systems – CHES 2015*, Güneysu, T. and Handschuh, H. (eds). Springer, Heidelberg.

SOG-IS (2019). Application of attack potential to smartcards and similar devices [Online]. Available at: https://www.sogis.eu/documents/cc/domains/sc/JIL-Application-of-Attack-Potential-to-Smartcards-v3-0.pdf.

SOG-IS (2020). Attack methods for smartcards and similar devices [Online]. Available at: https://www.sogis.eu/documents/cc/domains/sc/JIL-Application-of-Attack-Potential-to-Smartcards-v3-1.pdf.

Veyrat-Charvillon, N., Gérard, B., Standaert, F.-X. (2014). Soft analytical side-channel attacks. In *Advances in Cryptology – ASIACRYPT 2014*, Sarkar, P. and Iwata, T. (eds). Springer, Heidelberg.

Whitnall, C. and Oswald, E. (2011). A comprehensive evaluation of mutual information analysis using a fair evaluation framework. In *Advances in Cryptology – CRYPTO 2011*, Rogaway, P. (ed.). Springer, Heidelberg.

Whitnall, C. and Oswald, E. (2019a). A cautionary note regarding the usage of leakage detection tests in security evaluation. Cryptology ePrint Archive, Report 2019/703 [Online]. Available at: https://eprint.iacr.org/2019/703.

Whitnall, C. and Oswald, E. (2019b). A critical analysis of ISO 17825 ('testing methods for the mitigation of non-invasive attack classes against cryptographic modules'). In *Advances in Cryptology – ASIACRYPT 2019*, Galbraith, S.D. and Moriai, S. (eds). Springer, Heidelberg.

Zhang, Z., Ding, A.A., Fei, Y. (2020). A fast and accurate guessing entropy estimation algorithm for full-key recovery. *IACR Transactions on Cryptographic Hardware and Embedded Systems*, 2020(2), 26–48.

7

Countermeasures and Advanced Attacks

Brice COLOMBIER and Vincent GROSSO
Laboratoire Hubert Curien, UMR 5516, CNRS, Institut d'Optique Graduate School, Université Jean Monnet, Saint-Étienne, France

7.1. Introduction

In this chapter, we present the main algorithmic countermeasures for protecting software implementations of cryptographic algorithms against side-channel attacks. This chapter is based on notions already covered in previous chapters, in particular, Chapters 3 and 6 and some knowledge of symmetric cryptography. We do not cover lower level solutions such as adding noise with parallel computations, dual-rail logic aimed at balancing side-channel traces, or the use of asynchronous logic. Indeed, their impact is more difficult to quantify, and the exploitation of traces with these countermeasures generally requires signal processing techniques or the exploitation of different physical properties to foil the countermeasures.

To illustrate the various countermeasures presented in this chapter, we will take the AES (Daemen and Rijmen 2002) symmetric encryption algorithm as an example, and, more specifically, the first nonlinear transformation of the encryption: the SubBytes transformation of the first round. This operation can be represented in pseudo-code as in Algorithm 7.1. In this algorithm, `S-Box` is a mapping array storing the 256 possible output values of the AES S-box.

Embedded Cryptography 1,
coordinated by Emmanuel PROUFF, Guénaël RENAULT,
Matthieu RIVAIN and Colin O'FLYNN.

Algorithm 7.1. SubBytes Transformation

Input State (a 4×4 table, the current state of the AES).
Output State (a 4×4 table, the AES state after the SubBytes transformation).

```
for i = 0; i < 16; i++ do
    State[i/4][i%4] = S-Box[State[i/4][i%4]]
return State
```

In this implementation, we can see that the state entries are considered sequentially. They are therefore manipulated at a precise point in time, depending solely on the loop index i. As seen in previous chapters, the attacker will link one or more points of the trace obtained by observing side-channel leakages to a sensitive data. In our example, these sensitive data are a byte of the S-box output. For the sake of simplicity, we will not repeat the inputs/outputs in the following algorithms.

We will use modifications of Algorithm 7.1 to present the various countermeasures. We simulate the traces as corresponding to the Hammimg weight of the various state elements, to which Gaussian noise is added at several consecutive points corresponding to this information. The various elements are separated by points containing only noise. This simple model provides a good representation of microcontroller leakage. This simulation corresponds to the function `simulate_unprotected` in the attached notebook.

In Figure 7.1, we can see three examples of traces and the associated signal-to-noise ratio (SNR), at the bottom of the figure, computed on the basis of 50,000 simulated traces; the SNR has been introduced in Chapter 3. We have distinctively colored the different parts of the signal as a function of the byte, that is, the i index of the loop, manipulated at a given time. The sequential manipulation of 16 different values is clearly visible. We note that the SNR value associated with each byte is concentrated in a few points in the same identified zones corresponding to byte manipulation. These points therefore have information on the secret value manipulated, that is, depending on the secret key, hence they are called "point of interest". A time sample corresponds to a point on the trace without distinction as to its "interest". Informative points are used when manipulating the data analyzed during an execution. It is therefore a notion specific to simulations. Points of interest, on the other hand, are detected by statistical analysis, such as SNR.

As a reminder, the SNR is a tool for detecting points of interest in a side-channel trace. These points are those which vary according to the value of the manipulated data, and which can therefore be considered as *informative*. The SNR can also be used to quantify the *intensity* of information leakage. A high SNR value indicates a significant information leak, and therefore an attack which is easier to carry out, that is, requiring fewer traces. There are a number of criteria for comparing the effectiveness of a side-channel attack, such as the number of traces required, the average rank of the correct key hypothesis, time, a priori knowledge of the system, etc. In this chapter, we evaluate the effectiveness of an attack by the number of traces needed to achieve a success rate close to 1.

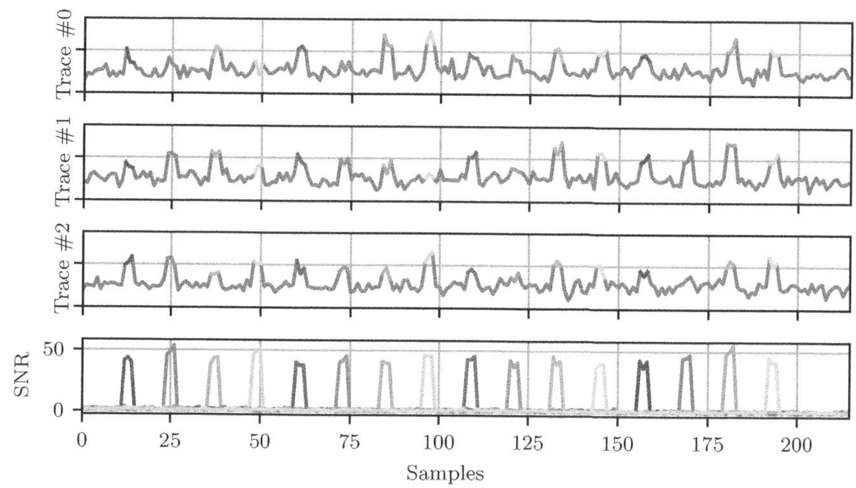

Figure 7.1. *Examples of side-channel traces and SNR for an unprotected SubBytes transformation implementation. For a color version of this figure, see www.iste.co.uk/prouff/cryptography1.zip*

In the rest of this chapter, we present some countermeasures against side-channel attacks. Algorithms 7.2, 7.3 and 7.4 will thus be modifications of Algorithm 7.1. We detail the impact of these countermeasures on the traces and the SNR value. We also briefly discuss the additional cost of these countermeasures in terms of execution time and computation overheads required. Finally, we will look at the attacks an attacker can mount when some of these countermeasures are implemented.

7.2. Misalignment of traces

One of the first steps in side-channel attacks is the selection of points of interest in the trace, so as to retain only those where there is information that depends on the secret to be recovered, as introduced in Chapter 3. One idea frequently employed to reduce the effectiveness of side-channel attacks is therefore to misalign the traces from one run to the next. The scattering of informative points over time affects trace analysis, which is carried out independently for each time sample, that is, vertically on the figures. As a result, since the information is now dispersed according to the traces considered, the information contained at a given time sample in the trace is reduced. The SNR value obtained at each point is therefore also reduced. It is well known that the success of a first-order attack depends on the SNR (as shown in Chapter 3), hence the interest in reducing it to make side-channel attacks more complex.

7.2.1. *Countermeasures*

In this section, we will introduce three countermeasures designed to de-synchronize sensitive operations, that is, to ensure that, considering several consecutive traces, the points of interest where sensitive data are manipulated are at different time samples.

7.2.1.1. *Random initial delay*

The aim of a countermeasure using a random initial delay is to break the alignment between time samples from consecutive traces. This alignment is required for the realization of attacks, which consider the leakage of information at a given time on a set of traces. In order to desynchronize the traces, the start of the algorithm execution is delayed. This is illustrated in Algorithm 7.2, where wait is a procedure that pauses the system for a time defined by its argument, and rand is a function generating a random number.

Algorithm 7.2. SubBytes transformation protected by adding a random initial delay

```
r = rand()
wait(r)
for i = 0; i < 16; i + + do
    State[i/4][i%4] = S-Box[State[i/4][i%4]]
return State
```

A random initial delay countermeasure has an effect comparable to poor trace slicing around the target operation, or poor sensitization of the acquisition trigger signal. In all cases, while the informative parts of the traces are within a fixed and restricted interval $[t_0, t_0 + \Delta_t]$, the start of this time interval t_0 is not the same for all traces.

The impact of the random initial delay can be seen on the simulated traces in Figure 7.2. We note a horizontal misalignment of the traces, whereas in the examples of the non-protagged case in Figure 7.1, we can see that the different traces were well aligned; in the case with a random initial delay, we notice that we have a temporal shift of the traces.

The introduction of this countermeasure has several consequences for SNR. On the one hand, the maximum value of the SNR is lower because the SNR is a univariate measure. Also, the countermeasure will mix informative and non-informative points in the same temporal position. On the other hand, the number of points that are considered informative is higher: the window of attack is wider.

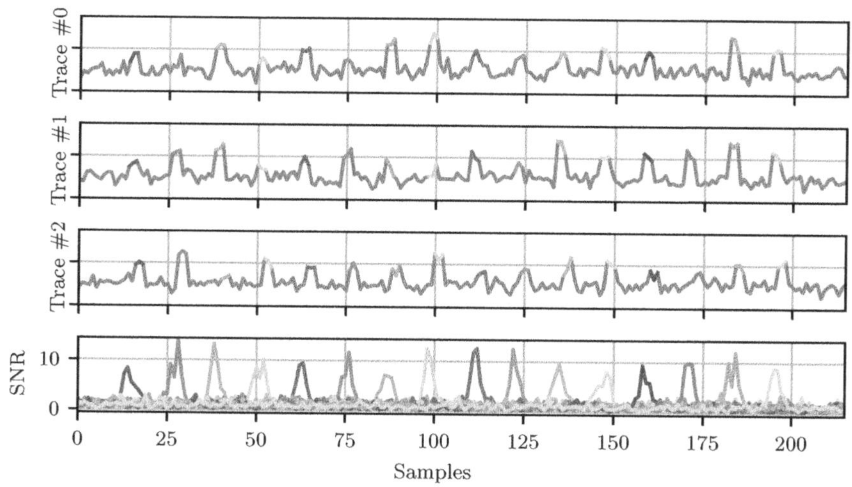

Figure 7.2. *Examples of side-channel traces and SNR for an implementation of the SubBytes transformation protected by the addition of a random initial delay. For a color version of this figure, see www.iste.co.uk/prouff/cryptography1.zip*

When an implementation is protected by a random initial delay, the additional cost is limited. The execution time is increased by the added delay. Concerning the required randomness, only one random number is required per execution.

The practical effectiveness of this countermeasure is limited by the pattern that characterizes the execution of the sensitive part of the encryption algorithm; in this case, the SubBytes transformation remains identical. It is easy to identify this recurring pattern in a set of traces and resynchronize them using methods such as the convolution product (i.e. in the frequency domain) or cross-correlation.

7.2.1.2. *Random delay interrupts*

This countermeasure consists of inserting random delay interrupts between sensitive operations. These additional instructions do not modify the internal state of the device: they are sometimes referred to as *dummy operations*. To illustrate these *dummy operations*, we will use some NOP instructions. The instruction NOP, for *no operation*, does nothing except increment in the instruction pointer.

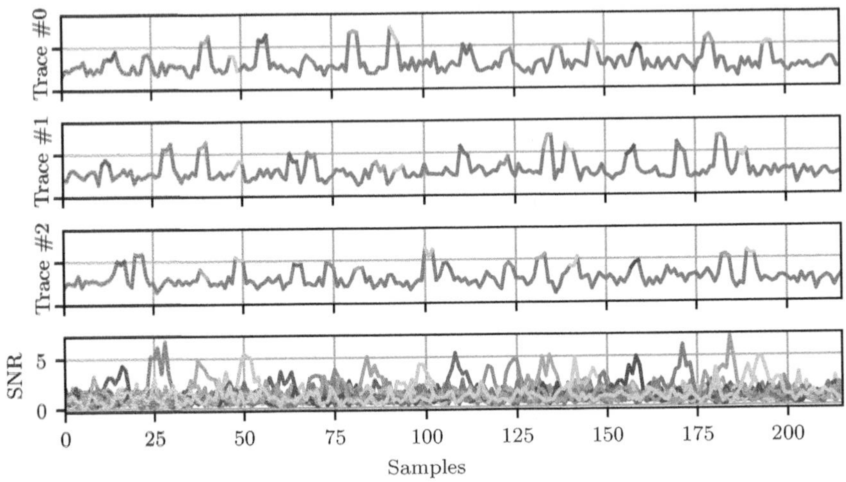

Figure 7.3. *Examples of consumption and SNR traces for an implementation of the SubBytes transformation protected by insertion of random delay interrupts. For a color version of this figure, see www.iste.co.uk/prouff/cryptography1.zip*

Algorithm 7.3. SubBytes transformation protected by insertion of random delay interrupts

for $i = 0; i < 16; i++$ **do**
    $r = rand()$
    for $j = 0; j < r; j++$ **do**
        NOP
    $State[i/4][i\%4] = \texttt{S-Box}[State[i/4][i\%4]]$
return State

By inserting these instructions, the traces will become increasingly desynchronized during execution.

Inserting several small desynchronizations throughout execution makes resynchronizing traces with signal processing techniques more complex.

In Figure 7.3, we can observe simulated side-channel traces where random interrupts have been inserted.

When an implementation is protected with random delay interrupts, the extra cost is higher than with a countermeasure with random delay only. As far as the required randomness is concerned, the countermeasure requires sixteen random values this time, instead of just one previously. However, this increase in the number of delays also makes trace resynchronization operations more complex. The execution time of the algorithm is not necessarily greatly increased.

These temporal countermeasures are particularly effective against attacks requiring temporal precision.

7.2.1.3. *Shuffling independent operations*

Another possible countermeasure, designed to disperse points of interest, is to *shuffle* independent operations. The principle is to execute certain operations of the algorithm, which have the property of being independent, in a random order. In the case of the AES SubBytes transformation, the same operation is repeated 16 times: reading a value from memory, substitution, writing a value to memory. The various iterations of this operation are independent of each other. Thus, they can be performed in any random order without altering the final result. A pseudo-code for the countermeasure is written in Algorithm 7.4, where shuffle is a function that randomly shuffles an array that is passed as input.

The main advantage of shuffled operations, as opposed to previous countermeasures based on delay insertion, is that the general pattern observable in successive traces remains *identical*. This makes it difficult for an attacker to use signal processing techniques to realign the points in successive traces corresponding to the manipulation of the same intermediate value.

Algorithm 7.4. Transformation SubBytes protected by shuffling independent operations

1: $S = \{0, 1, \ldots, 15\}$
2: $S = \mathsf{shuffle}(S)$
3: **for** $i = 0; i < 16; i++$ **do**
4: $\quad j = S[i]$
5: $\quad State[j/4][j\%4] = \texttt{S-Box}\,[State[j/4][j\%4]]$
return State

Figure 7.4 represents the traces associated with the countermeasure of shuffling independent operations. In this figure, we are only showing the operations that take place from line 3 of Algorithm 7.4. We therefore ignore the part where the array is permuted to define the random order in which operations will be performed.

Figure 7.4 shows the impact of shuffling independent operations on simulated traces. We can see that the traces are well aligned, unlike countermeasures using random initial delays or unnecessary operations. What is more, we can see that at a given point in time, it is impossible to know which index is being used. Thus, the leaks corresponding to the sixteen independent operations are effectively superimposed.

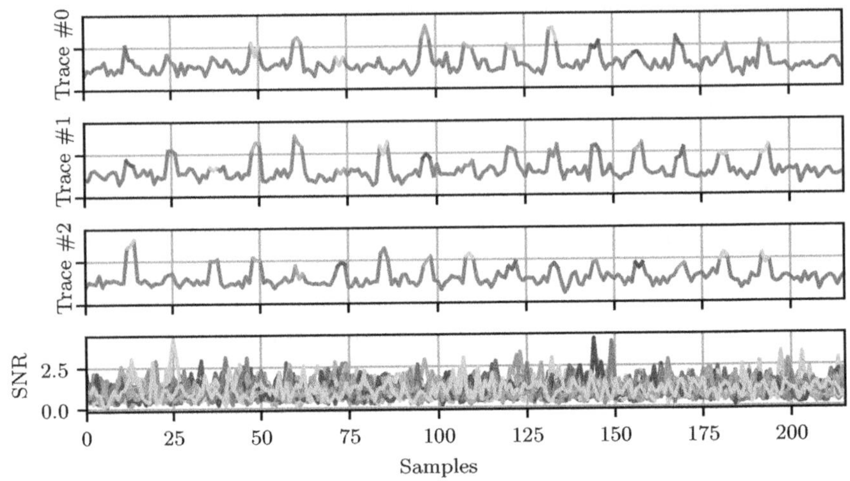

Figure 7.4. *Examples of side-channel traces and SNR for a shuffling-protected implementation of the SubBytes transformation. For a color version of this figure, see www.iste.co.uk/prouff/cryptography1.zip*

Due to its impact on the traces, where any byte (index j in the loop) can be used at any time, the shuffling of independent operations behaves in a similar way to parallel hardware implementations, where all operations are carried out simultaneously. When the attacker is unable to exploit any information about the permutations used in the various executions, the number of traces needed to carry out an attack is multiplied by the number of operations required, in the case of AES SubBytes by 16.

In order to increase the number of operations available to swap the order of execution, instructions that are unnecessary for the desired calculation can be added. These unnecessary operations will disperse the information into more positions. This is particularly useful when the number of similar operations is small. Following the example of AES, the MixColumns transformation operates on the columns of the internal state. As there are only four, the number of operations to be shuffled is too small and a brute-force attack is possible.

The overhead for a countermeasure using a shuffling of independent operations is mainly linked to the management of index permutation. There are several methods for managing a good permutation efficiently and with a negligible bias. We give a brief reference to this in section 7.5.

7.2.2. *Attacks*

An attacker is considered as someone wishing to carry out a univariate attack, such as a correlation power analysis (CPA) attack.

To attack implementations with countermeasures based on delay insertion, an attacker can proceed as if no countermeasure had been implemented. Here, the attacker will only consider the most informative point to find the correct sub-key. In this case, other informative points not aligned with the first will be ignored.

To measure the effectiveness of the countermeasure, we can consider that the traces necessary for the attack are divided into two groups. In the first, we find the traces for which the point of interest corresponds to an informative point. The second set includes traces where the point of interest does not correspond to an informative point. If we consider that the countermeasure distributes information uniformly over m different time samples, then the first set will be $m - 1$ times less populated than the second. Since it is this first set alone that contributes to the success of the attack, an attacker will therefore need at least $(m - 1) \times N$ traces to achieve first-order success equivalent to an attack achievable with N traces on an unprotected implementation. What is more, the points in the second set are noisy, so the previous reasoning underestimates the number of traces.

This can be observed by comparing the evolution of the correlation curves of the CPA attack without countermeasures with those of the CPA attacks with delays in the attached notebook.

In the case of countermeasures based on delay insertion, the dispersion of informative points can be significant. The attack may then require a number of traces greater than the number of informative points and the number of points on which they can be found. If we have one informative point and it can be dispersed over five time samples, then the attack on the implementation with protection will require five times as many traces. Let us imagine there is an oracle that can sort traces where the informative point is at time t_0. If the countermeasure evenly distributes the informative points, the oracle will only see one-fifth of the traces. On the other hand, the dispersion brought about by these countermeasures can be reduced by signal processing techniques. These techniques exploit the repetition of target instruction patterns in the trace to realign the traces.

In the case of countermeasures based on the shuffling of independent operations, the dispersion of the points of interest is limited by the number of independent operations, which is often smaller than the typical value of the delay or random interruption. On the other hand, the signal processing techniques described above are more difficult to apply in this case.

A second method of attacking protected implementations is to use the so-called *integration* technique. The idea this time is to no longer consider a single point as informative, but a set of points. For countermeasures based on delay insertion, we will consider a window of width w and create a new trace T_N from the initial trace T_R. Each index sample i of the new trace T_N corresponds to the sum of w index samples i to $i + w - 1$ of the raw trace T_R. In general, starting from a raw trace with n points, if the attacker wants to perform integration with a window of size w, then they must perform the following transformation:

$$\forall i \in \{0, n - w\}, T_N[i] = \sum_{j=0}^{w-1} T_R[i + j].$$

Using the new trace T_N, the attacker can then carry out a classic attack. The advantage of the integration method is that the information points, if close enough to be included in the width window w, are no longer out of sync. It has been shown that when integration is used, the number of traces required for a successful attack is multiplied by a factor w , where w is the size of the integration window. This is due to the fact that integration will add points with no information and only noise, if there is a single informative point in the window.

We consider only the impact for unprofiled attacks. However, the impact of shuffling can be reduced when an attacker also exploits permutation generation with profiled attacks.

In the end, we can see that these countermeasures are a compromise between their cost in terms of execution and time, and their impact on the temporal dispersion of informative samples. This temporal dispersion is the basis of the effectiveness of these countermeasures.

7.3. Masking

The noise inherent in the operation of electronic circuits makes attacks more difficult, since it masks (to some extent) the relationship between the secret data manipulated and the trace obtained by observation of side channels. The aim of masking is to force the attacker to combine several points on the trace in order to carry out the attack. As a result, the attacker will combine and amplify the noise at each point to retrieve the information they require.

These methods are discussed in more detail in the relevant chapters of the book, and we refer the reader to Part 1 of Volume 2 for further details.

7.3.1. *Countermeasures*

The first countermeasures we saw were designed to shift the time at which a sensitive operation is carried out. There are other countermeasures designed not to de-synchronize traces, but to make operations non-sensitive, that is, not directly manipulating sensitive data.

To achieve this, sensitive data are divided using a method known as secret sharing. The sharing outputs by the method is different for each trace and it is uniformly randomly chosen from the set of possible secret sharing. Secret sharing consists in dividing a secret x into d shares $\{x_i\}_{i=1}^{d}$, so that if an attacker observes $d-1$ shares, they obtain no information about the secret x. Only the possession of all d shares can reveal the original x secret.

The secret sharing used for the encryption algorithms we will be considering here is most often a *Boolean* sharing. This is the one we are going to describe. In this case, the secret x is shared in d independent shares. To do this, $d-1$ shares are chosen randomly and the last one is computed so that the relationship given in equation [7.1] is satisfied.

$$x = x_1 \oplus x_2 \oplus \cdots \oplus x_d \quad [7.1]$$

Thus, any set of $d-1$ shares is independent of the secret x: it is as if a *one-time pad* had been applied to the secret. Nevertheless, if a person knows the d shares, they can reconstruct x.

The next question is how to perform calculations on shared secrets. One solution is to recalculate the substitution table to take into account the masked data and refresh the mask as described in Algorithm 7.5.

Algorithm 7.5. Masked SubBytes transformation with table recalculation

Input State a table $4 \times 4 \times (d)$, the current state of the masked AES, d the number of shares (here $d = 2$).

Output State a table $4 \times 4 \times (d)$, AES status after SubBytes transformation.

for $i = 0; i < 16; i++$ **do**
  $r = rand()$
  $x_2 = \text{State}[i/4][i\%4]][1]$
  for $j = 0; j < 256; j++$ **do**
    $\texttt{MS[j]} = \texttt{S-Box}[j \oplus x_2] \oplus r$
  $\text{State}[i/4][i\%4][0] = \texttt{MS}[\text{State}[i/4][i\%4][0]]$
  $\text{State}[i/4][i\%4][1] = r$
return State

In Algorithm 7.5, a new table is computed to access the masked value. An input mask and an output mask are used to calculate all possible outputs according to the masked value. During this pre-computation, only one input mask and one output mask are used. In this way, there can be no leakage of information. Then the table is used with the second input mask to calculate the masked output of the S-box. As the pre-calculated table unmasks the input, calculates the output value and masks the output, when evaluating with the pre-computed table, no information can be obtained by observing the output mask. This ensures that both output masks form a partition of the S-box output.

The advantage of masking is that the secret is never manipulated directly at any time during the execution. Information leaks through side-channels are therefore independent of secret data.

The extra cost of masking is significant. On the one hand, it is linked to the generation of random numbers. So, $d - 1$ random bytes are needed per secret and per table to be recomputed. The extra cost in terms of execution time is also significant, particularly for table recomputation. There are other, more advanced methods for limiting this overhead. This can be achieved by exploiting sharing methods based on field operations on which computations are performed. However, masking remains much more costly than the desynchronization methods described in section 7.2.

7.3.2. *Attacks*

To attack an implementation protected by a masking countermeasure, the attacker will have to combine several points in the trace in order to recover the secret. As mentioned above, this will entail combining measurement errors. It is this combination of time samples, and therefore noise, that gives masking its security. It can be shown that masking has an exponential efficiency in the number of shares used in sharing over the number of traces needed to carry out an attack. If N traces were needed to carry out a side-channel attack on an unprotected implementation, it would take on the order of $N \times \sigma^{2d}$ to attack the protected implementation, where d is the number of shares in the sharing and σ is the standard deviation of the noise in the traces. In particular, we can perform a theoretical information analysis and show that information decreases exponentially. This means that the effectiveness of all attacks is impacted by masking.

To carry out an unprofiled CPA attack, the attacker must pre-process the traces in order to combine the points in the traces that are informative about each of the pieces of the share. There are several combination functions C available for this purpose. From the original trace T_R of size n and this combination function, the attacker will create a new trace of size n^d. For ease of reading, we give the formula for $d = 2$ in equation [7.2], its generalization to higher d values being trivial.

$$\forall (i, j) \in \{0, n-1\}^d, T_N[i \times n + j] = C(T_R[i], T_R[j]). \qquad [7.2]$$

The most frequently used combination functions are described below. Their effectiveness varies according to the level of noise in the traces.

– Centered product: for this combination function, it is necessary to compute the average of each point of the traces. For N attack traces $\{T_i\}_{i=1}^{N}$, the attacker calculates the average of the traces point by point $M_p = \frac{1}{N}\sum_{i=1}^{N} T_i[p]$, then constructs the new traces with the combination function $C(T[p_1], T[p_2]) = (T[p_1] - M_{p_1}) \times (T[p_2] - M_{p_2})$.

– Manhattan distance: this is the absolute value of the difference between the points: $C(T[p_1], T[p_2]) = |T[p_1] - T[p_2]|$.

The attacker can carry out the classic non-profiled attacks on this new trace.

For high noise levels, the centered product is the most efficient combination and leads to a smaller number of necessary traces for the attack to be successful. Conversely, for lower noise levels, the absolute value of the difference or the sum of the points are more effective.

7.4. Combination of countermeasures

As we have just seen, masking provides a high level of resistance against side-channel attacks. However, for masking to be effective, it needs sufficient noise. We have also seen a number of countermeasures that increase noise. The question then arises: how can these countermeasures be combined?

The most effective countermeasure for adding noise, and one that still stands up to signal processing techniques, is the shuffling of independent operations. So, it is natural to want to combine this countermeasure with masking. It can be shown that if shuffling of independent operations is applied to the pieces for each operation, masking amplifies the noise introduced by shuffling. This is described in Algorithm 7.6.

In Algorithm 7.6. two countermeasures are combined: masking with table recomputation and operation shuffling. For this, the 16 tables are recomputed at the same time and in a different order for each of the 256 outputs to make it difficult for an attacker to combine the different information on the same input mask. Second, these different tables are also used in random order. This eliminates the need for memory to store the recalculated tables.

If the shuffling of independent operations is applied to secret shares (i.e. only to loop indices), then masking does not amplify the noise introduced by shuffling, but this solution is far more efficient in terms of calculation and random numbers to manage.

Algorithm 7.6. SubBytes transformation protected by masking with table recalculation and shuffling

Input State a table $4 \times 4 \times (d)$, the current state of the AES being masked, d the number of pieces (here $d = 2$).

Output State a table$4 \times 4 \times (d)$, AES status after SubBytes transformation.

$S = \{0, 1, \ldots, 15\}$
$S = \mathsf{shuffle}(S)$
for $i = 0; i < 16; i++$ **do**
    $\mathtt{R}[S[i]] = rand()$
for $j = 0; j < 256; j++$ **do**
    $S = \mathsf{shuffle}(S)$
    for $i = 0; i < 16; i++$ **do**
        $x_2 = \text{State}[S[i]/4][S[i]\%4]][1]$
        $\mathtt{MS}[S[i]][j] = \mathtt{S\text{-}Box}[j \oplus x_2] \oplus \mathtt{R}[S[i]]$
$S = \mathsf{shuffle}(S)$
for $j = 0; j < 16; j++$ **do**
    $i = S[j]$
    $\text{State}[i/4][i\%4][0] = \mathtt{MS}[i][\text{State}[i/4][i\%4][0]]$
$S = \mathsf{shuffle}(S)$
for $j = 0; j < 16; j++$ **do**
    $i = S[j]$
    $\text{State}[i/4][i\%4][1] = \mathtt{R}[i]$
return State

This brings us back to the main discussion. When a developer wants to implement a countermeasure to protect an implementation, what security can be expected and at what extra cost?

7.5. To go further

In this chapter, we have tried to give an intuition of countermeasures against side-channel attacks. For the interested reader, we have provided a few references to further explore the various points made in this chapter.

– For countermeasures with random time interrupts, we recommend Coron and Kizhvatov (2010), and to explore countermeasures and attacks in more detail, we recommend Durvaux et al. (2012).

– For the countermeasure using the shuffling of independent operations, a detailed study is proposed in Veyrat-Charvillon et al. (2012).

– For table recalculation-based masking, we cite Coron (2014), and for demonstrations of the exponential advantage of countermeasure, we recommend Duc et al. (2014).

– For evaluation of countermeasures and demonstrations of the benefits of various countermeasures, we refer the reader to Rivain et al. (2009). For analysis of the combination of independent operations and masking, we refer the reader to Azouaoui et al. (2021).

– For combination functions, we refer the reader to Standaert et al. (2010) and Bruneau et al. (2014) for proofs of the optimality of combination functions.

7.6. References

Azouaoui, M., Bronchain, O., Grosso, V., Papagiannopoulos, K., Standaert, F. (2021). Bitslice masking and improved shuffling: How and when to mix them in software? *IACR Cryptol. ePrint Arch* [Online]. Available at: https://eprint.iacr.org/2021/951.

Bruneau, N., Guilley, S., Heuser, A., Rioul, O. (2014). Masks will fall off – Higher-order optimal distinguishers. In *Advances in Cryptology – ASIACRYPT 2014 – 20th International Conference on the Theory and Application of Cryptology and Information Security, Kaoshiung, Taiwan, R.O.C.*, Sarkar, P. and Iwata, T. (eds). Springer, Heidelberg. doi: 10.1007/978-3-662-45608-8_19.

Coron, J. (2014). Higher order masking of look-up tables. In *Advances in Cryptology – EUROCRYPT 2014*, Nguyen, P.Q. and Oswald, E. (eds). Springer, Heidelberg. doi: 10.1007/978-3-642-55220-5_25.

Coron, J. and Kizhvatov, I. (2010). Analysis and improvement of the random delay countermeasure of CHES 2009. In *Cryptographic Hardware and Embedded Systems, CHES 2010, 12th International Workshop, Santa Barbara, CA, USA, August 17-20, 2010. Proceedings*, Mangard, S. and Standaert, F. (eds). Springer, Heidelberg. doi: 10.1007/978-3-642-15031-9_7.

Daemen, J. and Rijmen, V. (2002). *The Design of Rijndael: AES – The Advanced Encryption Standard*. Springer, Heidelberg. doi: 10.1007/978-3-662-04722-4.

Duc, A., Dziembowski, S., Faust, S. (2014). Unifying leakage models: From probing attacks to noisy leakage. In *Advances in Cryptology – EUROCRYPT 2014*, Springer, Heidelberg. doi: 10.1007/978-3-642-55220-5_24.

Durvaux, F., Renauld, M., Standaert, F., van Oldeneel tot Oldenzeel, L., Veyrat-Charvillon, N. (2012). Efficient removal of random delays from embedded software implementations using hidden Markov models. In *Smart Card Research and Advanced Applications – 11th International Conference, CARDIS 2012*, Mangard, S. (ed.). Springer, Heidelberg. doi: 10.1007/978-3-642-37288-9_9.

Nguyen, P.Q. and Oswald, E. (eds). (2014). *Advances in Cryptology – EUROCRYPT 2014 – 33rd Annual International Conference on the Theory and Applications of Cryptographic Techniques, Copenhagen, Denmark, May 11–15, 2014. Proceedings*. Springer, Heidelberg. doi: 10.1007/978-3-642-55220-5.

Rivain, M., Prouff, E., Doget, J. (2009) Higher-order masking and shuffling for software implementations of block ciphers. In *Cryptographic Hardware and Embedded Systems – CHES 2009, 11th International Workshop*, Clavier, C. and Gaj, K. (eds). Springer, Heidelberg. doi: 10.1007/978-3-642-04138-9_13.

Standaert, F., Veyrat-Charvillon, N., Oswald, E., Gierlichs, B., Medwed, M., Kasper, M., Mangard, S. (2010). The world is not enough: Another look on second-order DPA. In *Advances in Cryptology – ASIACRYPT 2010 – 16th International Conference on the Theory and Application of Cryptology and Information Security*, Abe, M. (ed.). Springer, Heidelberg. doi: 10.1007/978-3-642-17373-8_7.

Veyrat-Charvillon, N., Medwed, M., Kerckhof, S., Standaert, F. (2012). Shuffling against side-channel attacks: A comprehensive study with cautionary note. In *Advances in Cryptology – ASIACRYPT 2012 – 18th International Conference on the Theory and Application of Cryptology and Information Security*, Wang, X. and Sako, K. (eds). Springer, Heidelberg. doi: 10.1007/978-3-642-34961-4_44.

8

Mode-Level Side-Channel Countermeasures

Olivier PEREIRA, Thomas PETERS and François-Xavier STANDAERT
Crypto Group, ICTEAM Institute, UCLouvain, Belgium

8.1. Introduction

Let $\mathsf{BC}_k(.)$ be an n-bit block cipher parameterized by an n-bit secret key k. Differential power analysis (DPA) attacks are powerful side-channel attacks that continuously leak information about the secret key. For this purpose, the adversary monitors multiple executions of the block cipher $\mathsf{BC}_k(.)$ on different inputs x_i $(1 \leq i \leq q)$, each of these executions giving rise to a noisy leakage l_i. Assuming for simplicity that each execution of the cipher can be modeled as an independent communication channel and that its leakage provides the adversary with λ bits of information, a DPA can reveal the full key after the observation of approximately $\lceil \frac{n}{\lambda} \rceil$ block cipher executions.

The direct approach to prevent DPA is to implement the block cipher with hardware-level countermeasures (e.g. noise addition) or algorithmic countermeasures (e.g. masking). However, such a direct approach suffers from two drawbacks. On the one hand, these countermeasures can be expensive as the target security level increases. On the other hand, their secure implementation can be challenging and require strong expertise to deal with the various physical defaults which can break their underlying assumptions. As a result, an important line of research has investigated options to improve cryptographic designs in order to make their secure

Embedded Cryptography 1,
coordinated by Emmanuel PROUFF, Guénaël RENAULT,
Matthieu RIVAIN and Colin O'FLYNN.

implementation cheaper and simpler. In this chapter, we survey the benefits of this approach. We denote it as mode-level countermeasures since (in the symmetric setting) it works by adapting cryptographic modes of operation to limit leakage, rather than by adapting the implementation of the primitives used in these modes.

For this purpose, we start with an intuitive introduction of some basic building blocks that offer improved security against leakage. More precisely, we show in section 8.2 that it is possible to design leakage-resilient pseudo-random generators (PRGs) and pseudo-random functions (PRFs) based on block ciphers that only require security against a weaker form of side-channel attacks, namely, simple power analysis (SPA). We then describe how these basic building blocks can be used to authenticate and encrypt with leakage. In section 8.3, we adapt standard cryptographic definitions for this purpose. In section 8.4, we discuss the models that are needed to analyze authentication and encryption in the presence of leakage, and their connection with concrete attacks such as SPA and DPA. Eventually, we analyze how these security definitions can be matched by actual authentication, encryption and authenticated encryption schemes in section 8.5. These results put forward that mode-level countermeasures provide an interesting path toward leveled implementations, where different parts of a cryptographic construction require different levels of security against leakage and therefore different (more or less expensive) hardware-level or algorithmic countermeasures.

8.2. Building blocks

A leakage-resilient PRG is depicted in Figure 8.1. From a random seed s_0, it works by iterating a length-doubling function that produces a fresh seed $s_{i+1} = \mathsf{BC}_{s_i}(\delta_0)$ and a pseudo-random output string $y_{i+1} = \mathsf{BC}_{s_i}(\delta_1)$, with δ_0 and δ_1 two distinct constant plaintexts. It is easy to see that in this case, a side-channel adversary can only exploit the execution of $q = 2$ plaintexts per key s_i.[1]

From an operational viewpoint, leakage-resilient PRGs are limited by the need to agree on the initial seed s_0. For this purpose, a standard solution is to use a leakage-resilient PRF $\mathsf{F}_k(.)$, as depicted in Figure 8.2. From the master key k, it generates n intermediate keys k_i $(1 \leq i \leq n)$ such that $k_{i+1} = \mathsf{BC}_{k_i}(\delta_0)$ if $x(i) = 0$ and $k_{i+1} = \mathsf{BC}_{k_i}(\delta_1)$ if $x(i) = 1$, with $x(i)$ the ith bit of the input x, δ_0 and δ_1 two distinct constant plaintexts, an initialization $k_0 = k$ and the output set as $\mathsf{F}_k(x) = k_n$. This construction can be seen as a tree of depth n with 2^n leaves. Here, a side-channel adversary can only exploit the execution of $q = 2$ plaintexts per intermediate key. The output of this leakage-resilient PRF can then be used as a seed of the PRG in Figure 8.1.

1 Assuming no key collisions, which are expected with birthday probability only if a block cipher is used.

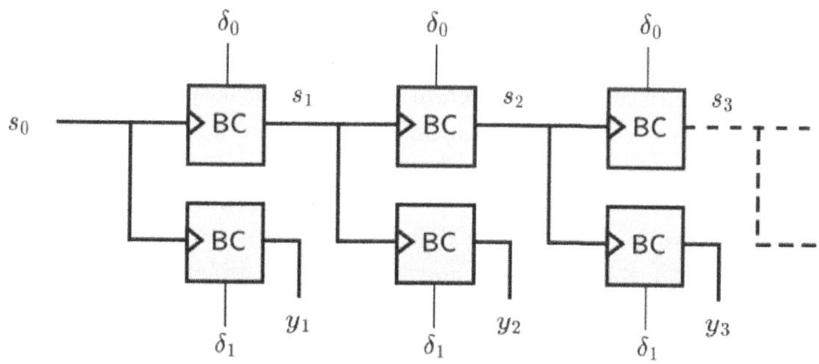

Figure 8.1. *Leakage-resilient PRG*

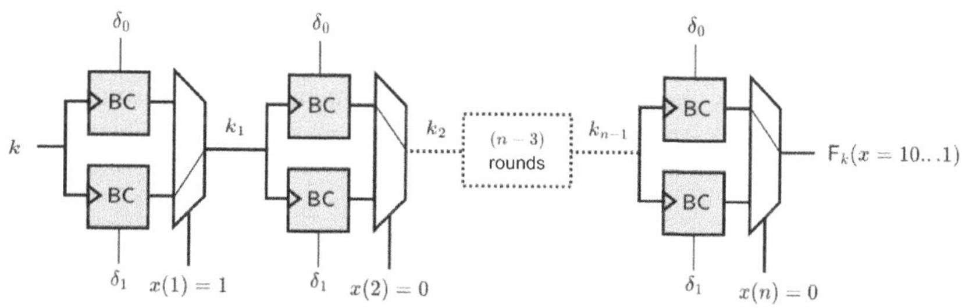

Figure 8.2. *Leakage-resilient PRF*

The main physical security parameter of the previous leakage-resilient constructions is the bound q on the number of different block cipher executions per key that can be observed by the adversary (with different plaintexts). The leakage-resilient PRG of Figure 8.1 and the leakage-resilient PRF of Figure 8.2 are similar in this respect. In their basic form, they bound the adversary to $q = 2$ block cipher executions per key. They both enable security versus efficiency tradeoffs by increasing q. Since leakage security decreases exponentially in q, such a tradeoff can only be exploited to a limited extent (an unbounded q corresponds to DPA). For simplicity, we next assume $q = 2$.

However, these constructions also differ by one fundamental aspect. In the leakage-resilient PRG case (and assuming the initial key is fresh), the adversary cannot ask for multiple measurements of the same (constant) plaintext δ_i. By contrast, in the leakage-resilient PRF case, they can repeat such measurements. The interest of these repeated queries is to get rid of the noise that possibly affects the leakage measurements. This difference leads us to the following definition.

DEFINITION 8.1 (Bounded side-channel attack).– A side-channel attack against a block cipher implementation is (q, r)-bounded if the adversary is only able to observe the leakage of at most q different plaintexts per key and the leakage of each plaintext can be observed at most r times. By extension, a scheme is (q, r)-bounding if it limits the adversary to (q, r)-bounded attacks.

Using this definition, we can see that a DPA is not (q, r)-bounded since both q and r are selected by the adversary and quantify the attack (data) complexity. The leakage-resilient PRG of Figure 8.1 limits the adversary to $(2, 1)$-bounded attacks, which are sometimes referred to as SPA. The leakage-resilient PRF of Figure 8.2 limits the adversary to $(2, .)$-bounded attacks (i.e. r is selected by the adversary), which we will refer to as an SPA with averaging (avgSPA for short). The SPA versus avgSPA requirements of the block cipher calls in Figures 8.1 and 8.2 are reflected by their different shade of gray (and an even darker shade will later be used for DPA security).

The rationale behind mode-level countermeasures, which is widely supported by the literature, is that it is cheaper and simpler to implement countermeasures against SPA than against avgSPA, and simpler to implement countermeasures against avgSPA than against DPA.

8.3. Security definitions

We now introduce the cryptographic primitive of authenticated encryption with the corresponding leaking algorithms (in section 8.3.1), before defining integrity and confidentiality in the presence of leakage (in sections 8.3.2 and 8.3.3, respectively). We consider a composite treatment of authenticated encryption with leakage, where integrity and confidentiality are defined and analyzed separately. While this is in contrast with the standard situation without leakage, where all-in-one definitions have become increasingly popular, this choice is motivated by the very different (physical) assumptions which can be used to ensure integrity and confidentiality with leakage. For example, integrity with leakage can be preserved with some intermediate computations leaked in full (which therefore removes the need of countermeasures), while such unbounded leakages cannot be used if confidentiality with leakage is required – we refer to sections 8.4 and 8.5 for the details. Besides, we note that our focus is on the strongest possible security notions that allow leveling the implementations. In other words, it is of course always possible to define security with leakage just as security without leakage by adding the appropriate leakage functions in the definitions. In the extreme case where a security definition can only be satisfied by requiring all the computations to be strongly protected against leakage, thanks to hardware-level and algorithmic countermeasures, we fall back into the situation where mode-level protections are hardly effective, which we aim to avoid.

8.3.1. *Authenticated encryption and leakage*

The purpose of authenticated encryption is to provide both confidentiality and integrity in a single cryptographic scheme. First, we provide the general description of such a scheme.

DEFINITION 8.2 (Nonce-Based Authenticated Encryption with Associated Data).– A *nonce-based authenticated encryption scheme with associated data* is a tuple $\mathsf{AE} = (\mathsf{Gen}, \mathsf{Enc}, \mathsf{Dec})$ of algorithms such that, for any security parameter n, and keys in $\mathcal{K}$ generated from $\mathsf{Gen}(1^n)$:

– Enc: $\mathcal{K} \times \mathcal{N} \times \mathcal{AD} \times \mathcal{M} \to \mathcal{C}$ deterministically maps a key from $\mathcal{K}$, a nonce from $\mathcal{N}$, some blocks of associated data from $\mathcal{AD}$ and a message from $\mathcal{M}$ to a ciphertext in $\mathcal{C}$.

– Dec: $\mathcal{K} \times \mathcal{N} \times \mathcal{AD} \times \mathcal{C} \to \mathcal{M} \cup \{\perp\}$ deterministically maps a key from $\mathcal{K}$, a nonce from $\mathcal{N}$, some blocks of associated data from $\mathcal{AD}$ and a ciphertext from $\mathcal{C}$ to a message in $\mathcal{M}$ if integrity checking succeeds or to a special symbol $\perp$ if integrity checking fails.

The sets $\mathcal{K}, \mathcal{N}, \mathcal{AD}, \mathcal{M}, \mathcal{C}$ are completely specified by the security parameter n. Given a key $k \leftarrow \mathsf{Gen}(1^n)$, $\mathsf{Enc}_k(N, A, M) := \mathsf{Enc}(k, N, A, M)$ and $\mathsf{Dec}_k(N, A, C) := \mathsf{Dec}(k, N, A, C)$ are both deterministic functions of which the implementations may be probabilistic.

Since we only focus on nonce-based authenticated encryption with associated data, we simply refer to it as *authenticated encryption*. Given a ciphertext $C \in \mathcal{C}$ of an encrypted message $M \in \mathcal{M}$, the decryption algorithm should always be able to recover M. This is captured by the *correctness* property: for any security parameter n, any key $k \in \mathcal{K}$, any nonce $N \in \mathcal{N}$, any associated data $A \in \mathcal{AD}$, and any message $M \in \mathcal{M}$, $\mathsf{Dec}_k(N, A, \mathsf{Enc}_k(N, A, M)) = M$. Whenever the algorithm Dec_k returns a message $M \neq \perp$ on input (N, A, C), we say that the ciphertext is *valid*.

Our definitions will additionally require the following algorithms:

Leaking algorithm: a leaking version of an algorithm Algo is denoted LAlgo. It runs both Algo and a *leakage function* $\mathsf{L}_{\mathsf{Algo}}$, which captures the additional information given by an implementation of Algo during its execution. LAlgo simply returns the outputs of both Algo and $\mathsf{L}_{\mathsf{Algo}}$, which all take the same input. We thus have $\mathsf{LEnc} = (\mathsf{Enc}, \mathsf{L}_{\mathsf{Enc}})$ and $\mathsf{LDec} = (\mathsf{Dec}, \mathsf{L}_{\mathsf{Dec}})$.

Adversary: by a $(q_1, \ldots, q_\omega, t)$-bounded adversary $\mathcal{A}$, we mean a probabilistic algorithm that has access to ω oracles, $O_1, \ldots, O_\omega$, making at most q_i queries to its ith oracle O_i, and performing computation bounded by running time t. We write $\mathcal{A}^{O_1,\ldots,O_\omega}$ to specify those oracles.

8.3.2. *Integrity with leakage*

Authenticity of authenticated encryption is defined as the infeasibility for any efficient adversary to produce a valid *fresh* ciphertext, known as a *forgery*. A ciphertext is fresh if it is not the output of any previous honest encryption that the adversary would have been able to eavesdrop.

More precisely, for a secret key $k \leftarrow \mathsf{Gen}(1^n)$, the goal of the adversary is to produce a forgery by providing (N, A, C) such that $\mathsf{Dec}_k(N, A, C) \neq \perp$. In order to capture the ability to observe ciphertexts and to strengthen the adversary, they are granted access to encryption and decryption oracles as detailed below. This security notion is called *ciphertext integrity* (CI).

Besides, in our definition, the adversary is actually deemed successful as long as the triple (N, A, C) is fresh in the sense that C has not been returned by the encryption oracle given (N, A, M) for some message M. We next highlight that the adversary may repeat nonces in encryption and decryption oracles, as well as in the forgery, by using the term *nonce-misuse* (M).

We further extend this notion to capture the ability of the adversary to observe the *leakage* (L) of the encryption and decryption algorithms *during* their computation. We thus extend the oracles so as to return the result of LEnc_k and LDec_k instead of Enc_k and Dec_k in the black box case.

DEFINITION 8.3 (CIML2).– An authenticated encryption $\mathsf{AE} = (\mathsf{Gen}, \mathsf{Enc}, \mathsf{Dec})$ with leakage function pair $\mathsf{L} = (\mathsf{LEnc}, \mathsf{LDec})$ satisfies (q, t, ϵ)*-ciphertext integrity with nonce misuse and leakage both in encryption and decryption*, denoted as CIML2, if for all (q, t)-bounded adversaries $\mathcal{A}$, we have:

$$\Pr\left[\mathsf{CIML2}_{\mathsf{AE},\mathsf{L},\mathcal{A}} \Rightarrow 1\right] \leq \epsilon,$$

where the security game $\mathsf{CIML2}^b_{\mathsf{AE},\mathsf{L},\mathcal{A}}$ is defined in Figure 8.1, and $q = (q_e, q_d)$ is an upper bound on the total number of queries made to the leaking encryption and decryption oracles, respectively.

We note that when the decryption device is not under the physical control of the adversary, it cannot measure the leakage when the decryption algorithm is running. For instance, this happens when a sender and a receiver use another secret key when their roles are permuted and the receiver wants to send encrypted plaintexts to the sender. We capture this scenario by only providing the adversary with the leakage during the encryption queries and refer to CIML1 security in that case. In the corresponding CIML1 experiment, the oracle LDec is replaced by the black box oracle Dec. The number 1 or 2 in the CIML1 or CIML2 notations indicates the number of *leaking* oracles.

<table>
<tr><th colspan="2">$\mathsf{CIML2}_{\mathsf{AE},\mathsf{L},\mathcal{A}}(1^\lambda)$ experiment</th></tr>
<tr><td>Initialization:
$k \leftarrow \mathsf{Gen}(1^\lambda)$ s.t. $|k| = n := n(\lambda)$
$\mathcal{S} \leftarrow \emptyset$
Finalization:
$(N, A, C) \leftarrow \mathcal{A}^{\mathsf{LEnc}(\cdot,\cdot,\cdot),\mathsf{LDec}(\cdot,\cdot,\cdot)}$
If $(N, A, C) \in \mathcal{S}$, return 0
If $\perp = \mathsf{Dec}_k(N, A, C)$, return 0
Return 1</td><td>Oracle $\mathsf{LEnc}(N, A, M)$:
$(C, \ell_e) = \mathsf{LEnc}_k(N, A, M)$
$\mathcal{S} \leftarrow \mathcal{S} \cup \{(N, A, C)\}$
return (C, ℓ_e)

Oracle $\mathsf{LDec}(N, A, C)$:
$(M', \ell_d) = \mathsf{LDec}_k(N, A, C)$
return (M', ℓ_d)</td></tr>
</table>

Table 8.1. CIML2 *game*

8.3.3. *Confidentiality with leakage*

Confidentiality of authenticated encryption follows the general blueprint of the indistinguishability of encrypted plaintexts against *chosen ciphertext attacks* (CCA). In this scenario, the goal of the adversary is to compute two messages for which they will get the encryption of only one of them, resulting in the so-called *challenge ciphertext*, with the task of detecting which message has been encrypted. To make this adversary more powerful, they can query the encryption of any message and the decryption of any ciphertext, except the challenge ciphertext. This is captured by the encryption and decryption oracles that return the outputs of Enc_k and Dec_k, respectively.

We make the leakage available to the adversary by turning these oracles into their leaking versions LEnc_k and LDec_k. Even the challenge ciphertext is computed from LEnc_k, which captures the ability of the adversary to observe the device encrypting one message among the two they choose. It means that no restriction is set on the algorithm execution with respect to leakage (L).

As far as nonce reuse is concerned, we allow the adversary to repeat nonces except the one used in the computation of the challenge ciphertext, which may not appear in any other leaking encryption query. However, it may be involved in any decryption query. Such a notion is usually referred to as nonce misuse-resilience (m), as opposed to nonce misuse-resistance (M), where no restriction is made on the reuse of nonces. Misuse-resilience captures concrete situations where, for instance, a counter providing the nonce has been unintentionally reset or shifted. It ensures that the security of the challenges is then restored as soon as the counter recovers increments and provides fresh nonce values. We elaborate on this definitional choice in section 8.3.4.

Finally, we go one step further by allowing the adversary to observe the leakage corresponding to the decryption of the challenge ciphertext without returning the underlying plaintext. This addition is valuable in applications where users are allowed to use some code or content (e.g. firmware updates, or on-demand games or movies) but not to access this content due to IP restrictions.

DEFINITION 8.4 (CCAmL2).– An authenticated encryption $\mathsf{AE} = (\mathsf{Gen}, \mathsf{Enc}, \mathsf{Dec})$ with leakage function pair $\mathsf{L} = (\mathsf{L}_{\mathsf{Enc}}, \mathsf{L}_{\mathsf{Dec}})$, is (q, t, ϵ)*-chosen-ciphertext secure with nonce misuse-resilience and leakage both in encryption and decryption*, denoted CCAmL2, if for all (q, t)-bounded adversary $\mathcal{A}$:

$$\left|\Pr\left[\mathsf{CCAmL2}^0_{\mathsf{AE},\mathsf{L},\mathcal{A}} \Rightarrow 1\right] - \Pr\left[\mathsf{CCAmL2}^1_{\mathsf{AE},\mathsf{L},\mathcal{A}} \Rightarrow 1\right]\right| \leq \epsilon,$$

where the security game $\mathsf{CCAmL2}^b_{\mathsf{AE},\mathsf{L},\mathcal{A}}$ is defined in Figure 8.2, and $q = (q_e, q_d)$ is an upper bound on the total number of queries made to the leaking encryption and decryption oracles, respectively.

$\mathsf{CCAmL2}^b_{\mathsf{AE},\mathsf{L},\mathcal{A}}$ is the output of the following experiment:
Initialization: generates a secret key $k \leftarrow \mathsf{Gen}(1^\lambda)$ s.t. $\lvert k\rvert = n := n(\lambda)$ and sets $\mathcal{E}_{ch}, \mathcal{E} \leftarrow \emptyset$ *Leaking encryption queries*: $\mathcal{A}^{\mathsf{L}}$ gets adaptive access to $\mathsf{LEnc}(\cdot,\cdot,\cdot)$, $\mathsf{LEnc}(N, A, M)$ outputs $\perp$ if $(N, *, *) \in \mathcal{E}_{ch}$, else computes $C \leftarrow \mathsf{Enc}_k(N, A, M)$ and $\ell_e \leftarrow \mathsf{L}_{\mathsf{Enc}}(k, N, A, M)$, updates $\mathcal{E} \leftarrow \mathcal{E} \cup \{N\}$ and finally returns (C, ℓ_e) *Leaking decryption queries*: $\mathcal{A}^{\mathsf{L}}$ gets adaptive access to $\mathsf{LDec}(\cdot,\cdot,\cdot)$, $\mathsf{LDec}(N, A, C)$ outputs $\perp$ if $(N, A, C) \in \mathcal{E}_{ch}$, else computes $M \leftarrow \mathsf{Dec}_k(N, A, C)$ and $\ell_d \leftarrow \mathsf{L}_{\mathsf{Dec}}(k, N, A, C)$ and returns (M, ℓ_d) *Challenge queries*: on a single occasion $\mathcal{A}^{\mathsf{L}}$ submits $(N_{ch}, A_{ch}, M^0, M^1)$, If M^0 and M^1 have different length or $N_{ch} \in \mathcal{E}$, returns $\perp$, else computes $(C^b, \ell_e^b) \leftarrow \mathsf{LEnc}_k(N_{ch}, A_{ch}, M^b)$, sets $\mathcal{E}_{ch} \leftarrow \{(N_{ch}, A_{ch}, C^b)\}$ and returns (C^b, ℓ_e^b) *Decryption challenge leakage queries*: $\mathcal{A}^{\mathsf{L}}$ gets adaptive access to $\mathsf{L}_{\mathsf{decch}}(\cdot,\cdot,\cdot)$, $\mathsf{L}_{\mathsf{Dec}}(N_{ch}, A_{ch}, C^b)$ computes and outputs $\ell_d^b \leftarrow \mathsf{L}_{\mathsf{Dec}}(k, N_{ch}, A_{ch}, C^b)$ if $(N_{ch}, A_{ch}, C^b) \in \mathcal{E}_{ch}$, else it outputs $\perp$; *Finalization*: $\mathcal{A}^{\mathsf{L}}$ outputs a guess bit b' which is defined as the output of the game

Table 8.2. *The* $\mathsf{CCAmL2}^b_{\mathsf{AE},\mathsf{L},\mathcal{A}}$ *game*

As for the relation between CIML2 and CIML1 for integrity, we capture the scenario where the decryption device is not under the physical control of the adversary by only providing them with the leakage during the encryption queries, and refer to CCAmL1 security in that case. In the corresponding CCAmL1 experiment, the oracle LDec is replaced by the black box oracle Dec.

8.3.4. *Discussion*

We next provide a more detailed discussion of the rationale behind our definitional choices.

On stronger security notions: as outlined by our notations, security definitions against leakage can consider leakage in encryption only (1) or in encryption and decryption (2), with nonce misuse-resilience (m) or misuse-resistance (M). As a result, it is explicit that the CIML2 guarantee is the strongest that can be achieved for integrity, while for confidentiality, we only focus on CCAmL2.

The reason why we do not focus on a combination of leakage-resistance and misuse-resistance (which would be coined CCAML2) is that it would require all the blocks of the corresponding modes to be strongly protected against leakage, hence canceling the interest of mode-level protections. A bit more precisely, we first observe that standard side-channel attacks usually aim at extracting secrets: long-term ones in the case of DPA, ephemeral ones in the case of SPA. However, CCAML2 security would further require that no adversary can detect nonce reuse for different messages. In this context, the following attack is possible: select two messages that are identical for some blocks and differ afterward, and detect when the messages start to differ thanks to leakage. As a result, the two passes that misuse-resistant modes of operations leverage are circumvented thanks to leakage. Also, the attack does not require us to extract secrets like standard DPAs and SPAs: it only requires us to compare the leakage of two states. Concretely, such a *state comparison attack* is therefore much harder to prevent than a key recovery attack because all the operations of an implementation can directly be exploited in the comparison (which is in contrast with key recovery attacks, which can only exploit the leakage of operations that can be guessed such as S-box computations in block ciphers). As a result, preventing state comparison attacks (which is necessary to reach CCAML2 security) essentially requires that all the block cipher calls in a mode are sufficiently protected to make the leakage of two different messages versus the leakage of two identical messages hard to identify, which eventually prevents any possibility of efficiently leveling the implementation. In other words, there is no theoretical impossibility to define CCAML2 security and it could be achieved by requiring all the block cipher calls of a mode to be leak free. However, as a result, such a definition leads to quite uninteresting designs from the model-level leakage-resistance point-of-view.

Given that we cannot combine leakage resistance, misuse resistance and efficient leveled implementations, we next observe that we could then consider CCAMl2 or CCAmL2. The first one reflects a setting where the leakage of the challenge plaintext is excluded from the adversary's view and is denoted as leakage resilience. The second one does not make restriction on the leakages obtained by the adversary, but considers that the nonce used to encrypt the challenge plaintext is fresh (i.e. a misuse-resilience setting). Following our rationale to focus on the strongest security notion that allows leveling the implementations, thanks to mode-level design techniques, our discussions only consider CCAmL2 security. The main reason of this choice is that by removing the leakage of the challenge ciphertext, CCAMl2 deems designs that leak their plaintext in full as secure. By contrast, CCAmL2 encourages the protection of the plaintext and, as discussed in section 8.5, is therefore calling for modes leveraging internal re-keying processes that would otherwise not be needed. We insist that there is no theoretical impossibility nor practical difficulty to define CCAMl2. There are even efficient constructions that match this security target. Overall, leakage-resilience (l) offers a different flavor of security than leakage-resistance (L), where confidentiality vanishes when leakage is available to the adversary, but is restored when this leakage is not available anymore.

We note that CCAmL2 security implies that so-called *message comparison attacks*, where the adversary aims to distinguish two messages thanks to leakage, are a concern for the implementers. Whether strong protections against these attacks (e.g. leading to negligible advantage for the adversaries) can be formalized remains an open problem. However, contrary to the aforementioned state comparison attacks, which can be mitigated by design (thanks to internal re-keying), message comparison attacks are an unavoidable issue, since the message at least has to be manipulated to be encrypted or decrypted. So, either as a security target to ensure thanks to hardware-level and algorithmic countermeasures, or as an inherent weakness that must be considered when dealing with the confidentiality of cryptographic implementations, such a leakage cannot be ignored.

Differences with black box definitions: while the definitions of integrity and confidentiality with leakage can be viewed as natural extensions of the definitions without leakage with some additional impossibilities, they also differ in some fundamental aspects, which we detail here.

Left-or-right versus real-or-random: our CCAmL2 (and CCAmL1) notions follow the so-called left-or-right paradigm to capture confidentiality. That is, the adversary has to distinguish the (say left) experiment $\mathsf{CCAmL2}^0_{\mathsf{AE},\mathsf{L},\mathcal{A}}$, where M_0 is encrypted in the challenge ciphertext, with the (say right) experiment $\mathsf{CCAmL2}^1_{\mathsf{AE},\mathsf{L},\mathcal{A}}$, where M_1 is encrypted in the challenge ciphertext. By contrast, in the real-or-random paradigm that can be used equivalently (and is usually considered more convenient) in the black box setting, the adversary has to distinguish a real encryption algorithm from an idealized function $\$$ returning random values in the ciphertext space. The reason why we use a left-or-right definition is that in order to adapt confidentiality with leakage in the real-or-random paradigm, we would have to define the leakage of an idealized function that (*i*) has by definition no implementation and (*ii*) creates a level of independence between the function's inputs and the outputs, which is precisely what side-channel attacks threaten. As a result, left-or-right definitions are conceptually more appealing in a leakage setting, especially if aiming to obtain standard proofs without idealized assumptions, which we deem as an important long-term research goal.

Separation results: when considering AE without leakage, the combination of CPA security with ciphertext integrity implies CCA security. It can be proven that such an implication does not hold with leakage. Furthermore, combining CIML1 and CCAmL2 (resp., CIML2 and CCAmL1) is not sufficient to get CIML2 (resp., CCAmL2) either. This is shown by modifying a leaking AE that achieves the premise notions into another leaking AE which still satisfies them but fails to satisfy the consequent notion. Therefore, the proposed combination of CIML2 and CCAmL2 is the strongest one (given the impossibility to ensure CCAML2 efficiently). Such separation results also lead to a strict hierarchy between the following model-level security grades:

– *Grade 1*: AE achieving either CCAL1 security (Grade 1a) or CIML2 security (Grade 1b);

– *Grade 2*: AE achieving both CIML2 security and CCAmL1 security;

– *Grade 3*: AE achieving both CIML2 security and CCAmL2 security and two-pass decryption.

We insist that a higher mode-level security grade does not imply a higher concrete side-channel security. These grades should rather be seen as different tradeoffs between model-level protections and hardware-level/algorithmic countermeasures. In general, modes for which the security can be proven in leakage models that allow leveled implementations (i.e. for which the proof can leverage weaker security requirements for some computations) gain interest over modes that require a uniform protection of all their computations, if the corresponding grade has to be reached. However, it is always possible to reach all the grades thanks to strong physical assumptions.

Extensions: All our notions are described in the single-user setting and the confidentiality notions are also only given in the single-challenge setting. There are natural extensions of them modeling (realistic) threats where an adversary can see the execution of the scheme for many users and several challenge ciphertexts in a single experiment. These notions are actually asymptotically equivalent to those presented here, and they are mainly useful to prove better security bounds.

8.4. Leakage models

An implementation leaking all its secrets in full cannot offer any security guarantee. Hence, satisfying the security definitions of section 8.3 requires limiting the leakage with some hardware-level or algorithmic countermeasures. The goal of mode-level protections is to limit the need of such lower-level countermeasures and to prove the leakage security of authentication or encryption schemes with weak and falsifiable assumptions. We next discuss assumptions that can be used for this purpose, link them to our attack taxonomy of section 8.2 and discuss the challenges they raise. We do this for integrity and confidentiality separately since, as already mentioned, it allows us to take advantage of the fundamentally different requirements to reach these security notions.

8.4.1. *Models for integrity*

Informally, it is possible to design a Message Authentication Codes (MAC) such that a majority of its internal computations can be leaked in full and only one block cipher execution is strongly protected against DPA. Formally, such MACs are proven in the unbounded leakage model.

DEFINITION 8.5 (Unbounded leakage model).– An implementation of a scheme is said to offer a security property in the unbounded leakage model if that property is satisfied, even if the leakage yields all the internal states produced during each execution of the scheme, including keys and random coins and excluding the internal state of strongly protected components (if there are any).

Informally, the strongly protected components capture the parts of the implementation that require security against DPA. Formally, there are different options to model such components. A first one is to assume them to be *leak-free*. That is, to assume that this component does not provide the adversary with any leakage. While conceptually simple, and frequently useful as a first step to identify schemes that have good properties against leakage, it suffers from the drawback of being a strong and idealized assumption. A weaker and more realistic (empirically falsifiable) alternative is to assume that the leaking block cipher implementation remains unpredictable with leakage.

DEFINITION 8.6 (Unpredictability with leakage).– A block cipher $\mathsf{BC} : \{0,1\}^n \times \{0,1\}^n \longmapsto \{0,1\}^n$ with leakage function pair $\mathsf{L} = (\mathsf{L}_{\mathsf{eval}}, \mathsf{L}_{\mathsf{inv}})$ is $(q_e, q_i, q_{\mathsf{L}}, t, \epsilon)$ strongly unpredictable with leakage in evaluation and inversion, or $(q_e, q_i, q_{\mathsf{L}}, t, \epsilon)$-SUL2, if for any $(q_e, q_i, q_{\mathsf{L}}, t)$-adversary A, we have:

$$\Pr[\mathsf{SUL2}^{\mathsf{BC},\mathsf{L}}_{\mathsf{exp}} \Rightarrow 1] \leq \epsilon,$$

with q_e evaluation queries, q_i inversion queries, q_{L} (offline) queries to the leakage function (for profiling), time complexity t and the $\mathsf{SUL2}^{\mathsf{BC},\mathsf{L}}_{\mathsf{exp},\mathsf{A}}$ experiment defined in Table 8.3.

Concretely, the parts of an implementation that can leak in an unbounded manner do not require any lower-level countermeasure. Besides, unpredictability is among the weakest possible requirements for a block cipher. For example, it is widely believed that without leakage, block ciphers become unpredictable with less rounds than needed to become pseudo-random permutations. Combined with the fact that unpredictability with leakage is easy to test for evaluation laboratories, as breaking it essentially requires performing a successful key-recovery (which is the focus of most published side-channel attacks), it puts the analysis of integrity with leakage in a comfortable situation where theoretical assumptions easily translate into requirements for implementers.

$\mathsf{SUL2}^{\mathsf{BC,L}}_{\mathsf{exp,A}}$ experiment	
Initialization:	Oracle $\mathsf{LEval}(x)$:
$k \xleftarrow{\$} \{0,1\}^n$	$y = \mathsf{BC}_k(x)$
$\mathcal{L} \leftarrow \emptyset$	$\ell_e = \mathsf{L}_{\mathsf{eval}}(k, x)$
	$\mathcal{L} \leftarrow \mathcal{L} \cup \{(x, y)\}$
Finalization:	Return (z, ℓ_e)
$(x, y) \leftarrow \mathsf{A}^{\mathsf{L}_{\mathsf{eval}}(\cdot,\cdot),\mathsf{L}_{\mathsf{inv}}(\cdot,\cdot),\mathsf{L}}$	
If $(x, z) \in \mathcal{L}$	Oracle $\mathcal{L}_{\mathsf{inv}}(y)$:
Return 0	$x = \mathsf{BC}_k^{-1}(y)$
If $y == \mathsf{BC}_k(x)$	$\ell_i = \mathcal{L}_{\mathsf{inv}}(k, y)$
Return 1	$\mathcal{L} \leftarrow \mathcal{L} \cup \{(x, y)\}$
Return 0	Return (x, ℓ_i)

Table 8.3. *Strong unpredictability with leakage in evaluation and inversion experiment*

8.4.2. *Models for confidentiality*

The situation of confidentiality with leakage is more delicate than the one of integrity with leakage. One reason is that, as explained in section 8.3.4, the very definition of confidentiality with leakage is harder to capture. Another reason is that, contrary to integrity, confidentiality requires bounding the leakage of most of (if not all) its computations in some sense. For example, the unbounded leakage of a message trivially breaks its confidentiality (not its integrity). So, on the one hand, confidentiality with leakage requires some strongly protected components that withstand DPA, and we can use the leak-free (or, ideally, unpredictability) assumption(s) of the previous section for this purpose. On the other hand, implementing all the components of an encryption scheme so that they offer these strong guarantees cancels the interest of mode-level countermeasures for confidentiality, since it implies that the implementation needs to be uniformly protected against DPA. As a result, and in order to enable leveled implementations, leakage-resistant encryption schemes aim to leverage the execution of a few strongly protected components, leaving the rest of their computations leaking in a more liberal, yet still bounded in some sense, manner.

Besides, one more difficulty is that formally, confidentiality with leakage not only requires bounding the leakage's informativeness but also its computational power. A notorious example is the one of so-called "future computation attacks" that are easily explained from Figure 8.1. Let us consider that the leakage function only leaks one bit per block cipher execution. If the leakage function is efficient (e.g. polytime) and adaptive, then it is possible to leak one bit of s_{128} when computing s_1 (letting the leakage function computing 128 block cipher executions), another bit of s_{128} when computing s_2, and so on, leading to a full key leakage after 128 iterations of the PRG round. The attack is admittedly unrealistic (i.e. it is unlikely that a leakage function leaks about future computations) but it shows that formalizing leakage with standard computational assumptions is challenging. In particular, it must deal with the paradox that solving Maxwell's equations for a complex circuit is a computationally intensive problem (which can take weeks with computer aided design software), but access to the physical circuit provides an instantaneous solution to it.

Overall, no physical assumption enables us to analyze confidentiality with leakage in a way that is at the same time theoretically sound and practically relevant in the current state-of-the-art. However, existing assumptions share some necessary practical conditions. For example, bounded leakage for some computation at least requires that it ensures security against SPA (as in the case of the PRG in Figure 8.1), or average SPA (as in the case of the PRF in Figure 8.2). In a bit more detail, the main solutions to bound the informativeness of the leakage for the analysis of confidentiality include:

1) *Hard-to-invert leakage*: which simply assumes that a value remains hard to guess even after the observation of its leakage. It is the weakest possible solution and, like the unpredictability with leakage, it is quantifiable/falsifiable by evaluation laboratories.

2) *Bounded range or information*: which rather assumes that the leakage function has a bounded range or that it preserves the (pseudo)entropy of the key. The first assumption is generally unrealistic for power or electromagnetic leakages, since a single power or electromagnetic trace can contain hundreds or even thousands of samples, and therefore directly exhausts the key entropy. The second one is more realistic but is hard to quantify/falsify in practice.

As for the main solutions to bound the computational power of the leakage, they include:

a) *Combining the only computation leaks assumption with design tweaks*: by doubling the key size of the PRF of Figure 8.1 and tweaking it in such a way that block cipher executions use one or the other half of the key (using a so-called alternating structure), we prevent the future computation attack as long as the leakage does not leak about the unused key part.

b) *Oracle-free leakage functions*: which rather assumes that the block ciphers of Figure 8.1 are random oracles that can be queried by the adversary but not by the leakage function.

The most theoretically-satisfying solution would be to mix hard-to-invert leakages (1) with the only computation leaks assumption and design tweaks (a). The best state-of-the-art solutions either mix leakage with bounded range or information (2) with the only computation leaks assumption and design tweaks (a), or hard-to-invert leakages (1) with the idealized oracle-free assumption (b).

Eventually, another solution is to consider a simulatable leakage assumption. Its general idea is to avoid modeling the (computational power of the) leakage function and to directly assume that it is possible to simulate the leakage trace of a block cipher using the same hardware as used to generate it, but without knowledge of its secret key. However, in the current state-of-the-art, no proposal of leakage simulator can ensure simulatability that guarantees negligible adversarial advantage.

8.4.3. *Practical guidelines*

The assumptions used in proofs of security with leakage can be used in order to specify which parts of an implementation must be protected and how much. In particular, the computations that can leak in an unbounded manner do not require any protection. Block cipher implementations modeled as leak-free or unpredictable with leakage must ensure security against DPA. Block cipher implementations that require bounded leakage for confidentiality must ensure security against SPA in case of $(q,1)$-bounding constructions, and security against avgSPA in case of $(q,.)$-bounding constructions. Concretely, protecting block cipher implementations against DPA is generally achieved thanks to the masking countermeasure. By contrast, security against SPA or avgSPA is best achieved thanks to parallel implementations (in hardware) of shuffling (in software). We finally note that the leakage-resilient PRF shown in Figure 8.2 can be used to instantiate a strongly protected component by reducing its DPA security requirement to an avgSPA security requirement.

8.5. Constructions

The most common generic approach to the design of an authenticated encryption scheme proceeds by encrypting messages with a CPA-secure encryption scheme, then authenticating the ciphertext with a MAC. This section explores the challenges associated to the design of these two key ingredients in the presence of leakages, starting with a MAC, then turning to encryption. We conclude by discussing the application of these results to the design of a leakage-resistant AE.

8.5.1. *A leakage-resilient MAC*

We consider the security of a MAC $(\mathsf{Gen}, \mathsf{Mac}, \mathsf{Vrfy})$ in the presence of a side-channel adversary. By analogy with the CIML2 game presented in Table 8.1, we assume an adversary who can repeatedly query the $\mathsf{LMac}(\cdot)$ and $\mathsf{LVrfy}(\cdot,\cdot)$ oracles that return the evaluation of Mac and Vrfy on a secret key, together with the corresponding leakages, when queried on message and message-tag pairs. The adversary wins if they can produce a forgery, that is, a valid message-tag pair for a fresh message, based on the information that they collected thanks to their queries to leaking algorithms.

8.5.1.1. *What can go wrong with a standard MAC?*

Let us consider, as a starting point, one of the most common block-cipher based MAC, namely CBC-MAC, which is illustrated in Figure 8.3 and is part of the CCM authenticated encryption mode (standing for Counter with cipher block Chaining Message authentication code), which is included in the TLS 1.3 cipher suite, for instance. We know that CBC-MAC is secure for fixed-length messages, so an adversary would need to rely on leakages in order to win the CIML2 security game. This could be done in at least two different ways:

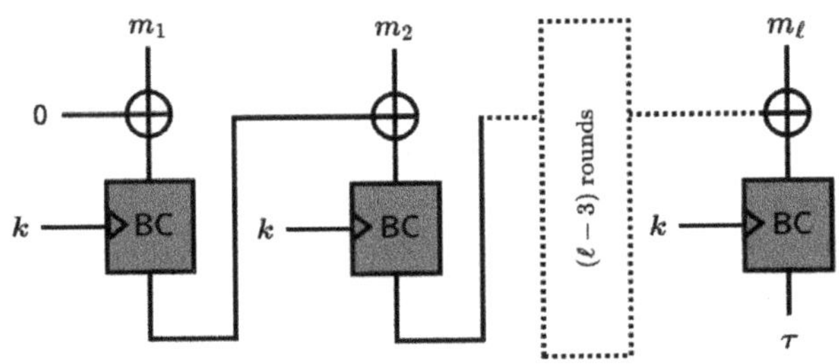

Figure 8.3. *CBC-MAC authenticates a message $M = m_1, m_2, \ldots, m_\ell$ with key k. The tag verification recomputes the correct tag and compares it to the given one*

1) The adversary can try to extract the secret key k from the leakages that they obtain from the LMac and LVrfy oracles. For an ℓ-block message, each query will give them ℓ leakages of the block cipher evaluation operating with key k. The first and last of these block-cipher evaluations would be particularly appealing as they proceed on a known plaintext or on a known ciphertext.

2) The adversary can try to extract the tag associated with a message M for which they did not issue a $\mathsf{LMac}(M)$ query, by performing multiple $\mathsf{LVrfy}(M, \tau^*)$ queries for random values of τ^*, and trying to recover the correct tag τ when it is computed by Vrfy and compared to τ^*.

8.5.1.2. *Designing a leakage-resilient MAC*

Let us try to gain protection against these two attack avenues, starting with the first one. As k is a static parameter of Mac and Vrfy, and in the absence of a simple option to update the value of k between calls to LMac and LVrfy, we will rather require that BC is only evaluated with k as part of a strongly protected implementation.

Of course, one straightforward option would be to entirely evaluate Mac using the strongly protected BC implementation (which is reflected by the dark gray block cipher calls in Figure 8.3). However, as already mentioned, this would be quite expensive in time and energy, and we therefore aim for better. Furthermore, it remains desirable to reduce the exposure of the strongly protected implementation (since strong protections may not be perfect), and to make use of it sparingly.

It is fortunately quite simple to make sure that the strongly protected block cipher is only used once per message, independently of the number blocks in the message. One option is to define $\mathsf{Mac}_k(M) = \mathsf{BC}_k(\mathsf{H}(M))$, where H is a collision-resistant hash function with an output of the length of a block (which can itself be implemented with an unprotected block cipher). If the strongly protected implementation of BC is modeled as leak-free, implying that it leaks nothing about the key k, then the LMac oracle will not provide any useful leakage information to the adversary, and the LMac is just as good as a Mac oracle that would not offer any leakage. The security of this construction can be proven (and gracefully degrades) with the weaker unpredictablity with leakage assumption. Of course, the black box security of this MAC is quite weak: if we use a block cipher of 128-bit block size, then the collision resistance of the hash function cannot go up the birthday bound, and an adversary who can evaluate around 2^{64} hashes may already be able to make a forgery. Improved solutions exist (e.g. from the use of tweakable block ciphers).

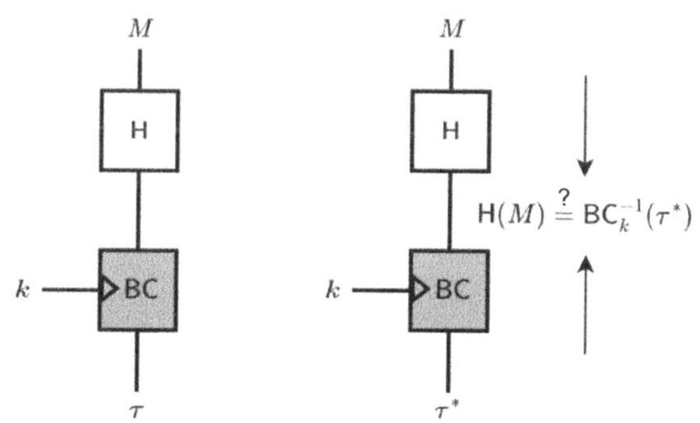

Figure 8.4. *The HBC MAC together with its tag verification operation*

Turning to the second attack avenue, we can observe that we do not have much improvement if we follow the obvious way of defining $\mathsf{Vrfy}_k(M, \tau^*)$ as testing if $\mathsf{Mac}_k(M) \stackrel{?}{=} \tau^*$. Indeed, even if we assume that BC does not leak anything about its output either, the implementation would still require a strongly protected equality testing component, since otherwise, the comparison may leak the value of $\mathsf{Mac}_k(M)$ thanks to a standard DPA leveraging the leakage of multiple τ^* values.

There is however another way of defining the Vrfy function, illustrated in the right part in Figure 8.4: we may also test whether $\mathsf{H}(M) \stackrel{?}{=} \mathsf{BC}^{-1}(\tau^*)$, taking advantage of the block cipher's invertibility. The advantage of this definition of Vrfy is that if the adversary provides an incorrect tag τ^*, and even if the comparison operation leaks its inputs in full, the adversary would only learn $\mathsf{BC}^{-1}(\tau^*) \neq \mathsf{H}(M)$ rather than learning the correct tag. The analysis of such a scheme is delicate though, as it requires considering the interaction between the hash function and the block cipher. Improved solutions can come from the use of tweakable block ciphers (e.g. by using $\mathsf{H}(M)$ as a tweak and encrypting a constant value with this tweak in order to produce the tag).

8.5.2. *A leakage-resistant encryption scheme*

We focus here on a simple CPAL security notion, which is considerably less demanding than the CCAmL2 security notion discussed above (see Definition 8.4), but already brings important ingredients that are used in the design of a complete authenticated encryption scheme.

The CPAL security game is identical to the traditional CPA security game, except that all the encryption operations performed by the challenger return a leakage together with a ciphertext. More precisely, we consider an adversary who can repeatedly query a $\mathsf{LEnc}(\cdot)$ oracle that returns the evaluation of Enc on an adversarially chosen message with a secret key, together with the corresponding leakage. The adversary can additionally send a challenge query with two messages (M_0, M_1) of identical lengths. The challenger will flip a coin b and return an encryption of M_b, together with the associated leakage. The adversary wins if they can guess the coin b.

8.5.2.1. *What can go wrong with a standard CPA encryption mode?*

Let us consider the counter (CTR) mode illustrated in Figure 8.5 as our starting point, as it is used to encrypt messages in both the CCM and GCM modes included in the TLS 1.3 cipher suite, for instance.

The CTR mode offers CPA security, so winning the CPAL game with non-negligible probability requires taking advantage of the leakages. Again, two main approaches can be considered:

1) The adversary can try to extract the secret key k from the leakages that they obtain from the LEnc oracle. Each message block of each LEnc query and of the challenge query gives them a leakage of the block cipher evaluation operating with the key k. If k is recovered, the challenge ciphertext can be decrypted to determine whether M_0 or M_1 was encrypted.

2) The adversary can try to exploit the leakage obtained during the encryption of M_b during the challenge query, in order to identify whether it is M_0 or M_1 that is encrypted.

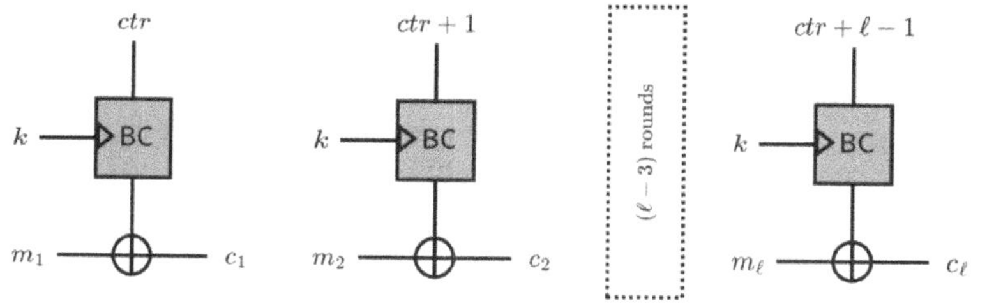

Figure 8.5. *The CTR mode used to encrypt a message $M = m_1, m_2, \ldots, m_\ell$ with key k*

From a practical point-of-view, the two strategies come with very different requirements. The first one is a standard key recovery attack. It requires recovering a full secret value, with the help of a potentially large number of leakages. The second one is a message comparison attack. It requires recognizing a message within a set of two chosen messages which, as discussed in section 8.3.4, is a considerably less demanding goal. However, that goal must be accomplished with a single leakage.

8.5.2.2. *Designing a* CPAL*-secure encryption scheme*

In order to mitigate attack strategies targeting the encryption key, we want, as we did for the MAC construction, to make sure that this key is used as little as possible, meaning in a few block cipher evaluations per message encryption, and have only these block cipher evaluations strongly protected. However, contrary to the MAC case, we cannot process the whole plaintext without any keying material: we need a key to hide it. One solution is to start the encryption process with a key derivation process: given a unique nonce N, we derive a per-message key $k^* := \mathsf{BC}_k(N)$, and use k^* in order to encrypt the message using the CTR mode (e.g. we could use the concatenation of the nonce and the message block number as a counter for the CTR mode). If the key derivation operation is sufficiently protected, then the only key that an adversary could recover using leakages would be the per-message key.

If we aimed for leakage-resilience (i.e. CPAl security) instead of leakage-resistance (i.e. CPAL security), then this would already be good enough: the challenge query would not offer any leakage, and the leakages obtained through the LEnc queries would, in the worst case, offer per-message keys that would be unrelated to the per-message key used in the challenge query. For CPAL security though, the per-message key derivation leaves us with the task of protecting the per-message key of the challenge query: that key is still used in every block in the

CTR mode, which may therefore be enough to mount a successful DPA attack if long messages are encrypted by the adversary.

We can address this challenge by switching to an encryption mode that additionally derives a fresh key per message block. We also observe that this mode may only offer a weaker form of security: since we already have per-message keys from our key derivation operation, the mode only needs to offer eavesdropper security instead of CPA security. In effect, we only need a leakage-resilient PRG, as proposed in Figure 8.1, which would use the per-message key as its seed, and to XOR the output of this PRG with the message. The resulting mode is depicted in Figure 8.6.

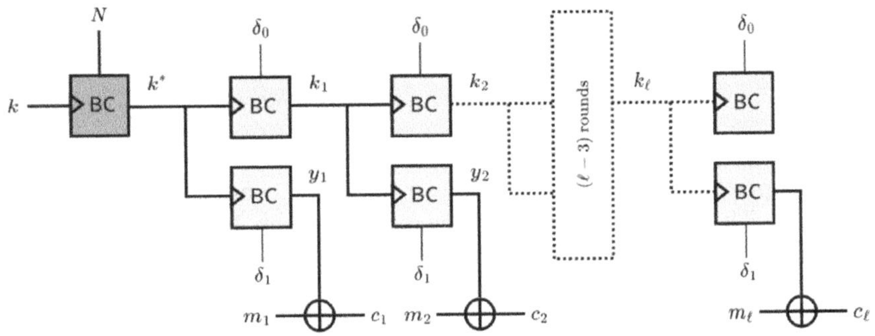

Figure 8.6. *A* CPAL *secure encryption mode*

More precisely, it is possible to demonstrate that this mode offers CPAL security when the initial key derivation block cipher is modeled as leak-free and when the leakages of all the other block cipher evaluations are simulatable (see discussion in section 8.4.2). The analysis shows that as long as two executions of a leaking block cipher with a single key do not leak too much information about that key, then winning the CPAL game will essentially be as hard as guessing which one of the two challenge messages is encrypted, given the leakages of the XOR operation on the plaintext message blocks (i.e. a message comparison attack). That target seems to be the minimal demand that we can make from a mode of operation, since the plaintext has to be processed at some point, and we must leave the protection of that minimum processing to lower level countermeasures.

We note that the encryption scheme of Figure 8.6 provides CPAmL security – we eluded a discussion of nonce misuse in this section to simplify the exposition of the scheme main design ideas.

8.5.3. *A leakage-resistant AE scheme*

Eventually, the MAC in section 8.5.1 and the encryption scheme in section 8.5.2 can be combined into the leakage-resistant AE illustrated in Figure 8.7. Informally, this scheme offers CIML2 security under the sole assumption that the two dark gray block cipher calls are strongly protected against DPA (all the other block cipher calls and the hash function can then leak in full), and CCAmL2 security under the additional requirement that the light gray block cipher calls used in the encryption scheme are secure against SPA. It uses two different long-term keys, but it is possible to halve the key material with a separation bit for the block ciphers used in the encryption and the MAC parts.

We note that the composite definitional framework presented in this chapter does not benefit from generic composition theorems. So, the analysis of leakage-resistant AE like the one shown in Figure 8.7 for now requires an ad hoc investigation. The literature contains many other modes that offer better bounds or target different mode-level security grades. We list some of them in the final section.

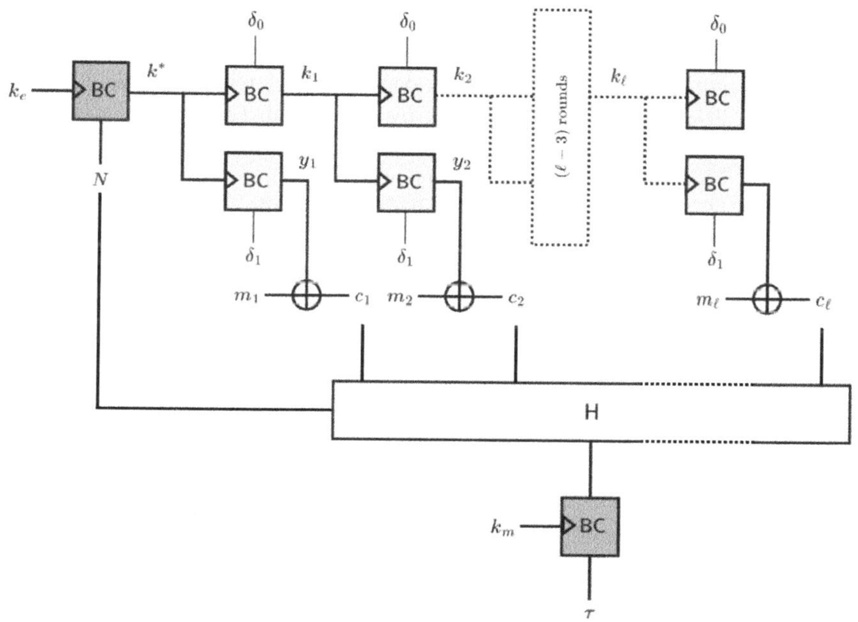

Figure 8.7. *Exemplary leakage-resistant AE*

8.6. Acknowledgments

Thomas Peters and François-Xavier Standaert are associate researcher and senior research associate of the Belgian Fund for Scientific Research (F.R.S.- FNRS). This work has been funded in part by the ERC consolidator grant SWORD (724725) and by the Walloon region CyberExcellence project number 2110186 (acronym Cyberwal).

8.7. Notes and further references

A longer discussion of definitions, models and designs for leakage-resistance was given in a Eurocrypt 2019 invited talk by Standaert (2019). A systematic investigation of some leakage-resistant AE according to their mode-level security grade (listed in section 8.3.4) is proposed by Bellizia et al. (2020), and is also the basis of the practical guidelines in section 8.4.3. It includes both constructions based on (tweakable) block ciphers, the formal analysis of which is based on the aforelisted references, and constructions based on permutations, the formal analysis of which is treated by Dobraunig and Mennink (2019), Degabriele et al. (2019) and Guo et al. (2020b). The additional challenges raised by the tag verification for permutation-based designs are discussed by Dobraunig and Mennink (2021). Examples of constructions based on (tweakable) block ciphers include TEDT by Berti et al. (2019b) for Grade 3, Triplex by Shen et al. (2022) for Grade 2 and AES-LR by Guo et al. (2020a) for Grade 1b. Examples of constructions based on permutations include ISAP by Dobraunig et al. (2020) for Grade 3, Ascon by Dobraunig et al. (2021) for Grade 2, and PHOTON-Beetle by Bao et al. (2019) for Grade 1a. For most of these schemes, the strongly protected primitive calls have to be implemented with state-of-the-art higher-order masking (see Goudarzi and Rivain (2017) for an example in software, and Cassiers et al. (2021) for an example in hardware). Alternatively, it is possible to use a leakage-resilient PRF for this purpose: ISAP achieves this with a permutation-based design, while LR-BC does it with block ciphers (see Bronchain et al. 2021). Yet another solution is to rely on a fresh re-keying scheme that generates a key with an easy-to-mask (e.g. key-homomorphic) primitive. Various models and proposals have been introduced for this purpose: for example, see Medwed et al. (2010), Dobraunig et al. (2015), Dziembowski et al. (2016), Mennink (2020) and Duval et al. (2021).

– Section 8.2. The leakage-resilient building blocks in section 8.2 are based on the seminal work of Dziembowski and Pietrzak (2008). Early examples of PRG constructions and analyzes can be found in Pietrzak (2009) and Yu et al. (2010). Early examples of PRF constructions and analyzes can be found in Faust et al. (2012) and Yu and Standaert (2013). These formal results follow more heuristic investigations highlighting the interest of re-keying against leakage by Kocher (2003) and Petit et al. (2008).

– Section 8.3. The definitional framework of section 8.3 is adopted from Guo et al. (2019). An alternative all-in-one definition can be found in Barwell et al. (2017). The first one is composite and considers a mix of leakage-resistance with nonce misuse-resilience. The second one is all-in-one and considers a mix of leakage-resilience with nonce misuse-resistance. The difficulty to define confidentiality in the presence of leakage, hinting toward the need to distinguish leakage-resistance and leakage-resilience, dates back to the seminal work of Micali and Reyzin (2004). It is worth noticing that the state comparison attack that is argued to be very expensive to prevent in section 8.3.4 is similar to the attacks against the FO transform which are known to raise fundamental challenges for the implementation security of post-quantum public-key encryption schemes (Azouaoui et al. 2022; Ueno et al. 2022). The equivalence between real or random and left or right definitions in the context of black box symmetric encryption is proven in Bellare et al. (1997). The fact that CPA security combined with ciphertext integrity implies CCA security is proven by Katz and Yung (2000).

– Section 8.4. The unbounded leakage model described in section 8.4 was introduced by Berti et al. (2018). Unpredictability with leakage was introduced by Berti et al. (2019a) and is used by Berti et al. (2021) to prove the security of a leakage-resilient MAC without idealized assumptions. Hard-to-invert leakages were introduced by Dodis et al. (2009) and used in Yu et al. (2010) to analyze a leakage-resilient PRG under an idealized assumption. Bounded leakage or information are already used in the first work of Dziembowski and Pietrzak (2008). Simulatable leakages were introduced by Standaert et al. (2013) and pitfalls regarding the instance of simulator proposed in this reference are discussed by Longo et al. (2014). Relations between these leakage assumptions are analyzed by Fuller and Hamlin (2015). The only computation leaks assumption dates back to Micali and Reyzin (2004) and is combined with an alternating structure to prevent future computation leakage in Dziembowski and Pietrzak (2008) and Pietrzak (2009). The assumption of oracle-free leakage function was introduced by Yu et al. (2010) to analyze a more efficient PRG.

– Section 8.5. A concrete application of the second attack path against CBC-MAC in section 8.5.1 can be found in Bronchain et al. (2021). The following leakage-resilient MAC corresponds to the HBC construction analyzed by Berti et al. (2019a). The leakage-resistant encryption scheme discussed in section 8.5.2 was proposed by Pereira et al. (2015). We note that generating an ephemeral key as in this section may not only help in the context of side-channel attacks, but can also improve the bounds of black box security analyzes (see Gueron and Lindell (2017) for instance). An alternative treatment of leakage-resilient symmetric encryption based on re-keying can be found in the work of Abdalla et al. (2013). The leakage-resistant AE of section 8.5.3 is a nonce-based variant of the EDT scheme proposed by Berti et al. (2017).

8.8. References

Abdalla, M., Belaïd, S., Fouque, P.-A. (2013). Leakage-resilient symmetric encryption via re-keying. In *CHES 2013*, Bertoni, G. and Coron, J.-S. (eds). Springer, Heidelberg.

Azouaoui, M., Bronchain, O., Hoffmann, C., Kuzovkova, Y., Schneider, T., Standaert, F. (2022). Systematic study of decryption and re-encryption leakage: The case of Kyber. In *COSADE*. Springer, Heidelberg.

Bao, Z., Chakraborti, A., Datta, N., Guo, J., Nandi, M., Peyrin, T., Yasuda, K. (2019). PHOTON-Beetle authenticated encryption and hash family. *NIST Lightweight Cryptography Standardization Effort.*

Barwell, G., Martin, D.P., Oswald, E., Stam, M. (2017). Authenticated encryption in the face of protocol and side channel leakage. In *ASIACRYPT 2017*, Takagi, T. and Peyrin, T. (eds). Springer, Heidelberg.

Bellare, M., Desai, A., Jokipii, E., Rogaway, P. (1997). A concrete security treatment of symmetric encryption. In *38th FOCS*. IEEE Computer Society Press, Washington, D.C.

Bellizia, D., Bronchain, O., Cassiers, G., Grosso, V., Guo, C., Momin, C., Pereira, O., Peters, T., Standaert, F.-X. (2020). Mode-level vs. implementation-level physical security in symmetric cryptography – A practical guide through the leakage-resistance jungle. In *CRYPTO 2020*, Micciancio, D. and Ristenpart, T. (eds). Springer, Heidelberg.

Berti, F., Pereira, O., Peters, T., Standaert, F.-X. (2017). On leakage-resilient authenticated encryption with decryption leakages. *IACR Trans. Symm. Cryptol.*, 2017(3), 271–293.

Berti, F., Koeune, F., Pereira, O., Peters, T., Standaert, F.-X. (2018). Ciphertext integrity with misuse and leakage: Definition and efficient constructions with symmetric primitives. In *ASIACCS 18*, Kim, J., Ahn, G.-J., Kim, S., Kim, Y., López, J., Kim, T. (eds). ACM Press, New York.

Berti, F., Guo, C., Pereira, O., Peters, T., Standaert, F. (2019a). Strong authenticity with leakage under weak and falsifiable physical assumptions. In *Inscrypt*. Springer, Heidelberg.

Berti, F., Guo, C., Pereira, O., Peters, T., Standaert, F.-X. (2019b). TEDT: A leakage-resistant AEAD mode. *IACR TCHES*, 2020(1), 256–320.

Berti, F., Guo, C., Peters, T., Standaert, F.-X. (2021). Efficient leakage-resilient MACs without idealized assumptions. In *ASIACRYPT 2021*, Tibouchi, M. and Wang, H. (eds). Springer, Heidelberg.

Bronchain, O., Momin, C., Peters, T., Standaert, F.-X. (2021). Improved leakage-resistant authenticated encryption based on hardware AES coprocessors. *IACR TCHES*, 2021(3), 641–676.

Cassiers, G., Grégoire, B., Levi, I., Standaert, F. (2021). Hardware private circuits: From trivial composition to full verification. *IEEE Trans. Computers*, 70(10), 1677–1690.

Degabriele, J.P., Janson, C., Struck, P. (2019). Sponges resist leakage: The case of authenticated encryption. In *ASIACRYPT 2019*, Galbraith, S.D. and Moriai, S. (eds). Springer, Heidelberg.

Dobraunig, C. and Mennink, B. (2019). Leakage resilience of the duplex construction. In *ASIACRYPT 2019*, Galbraith, S.D. and Moriai, S. (eds). Springer, Heidelberg.

Dobraunig, C. and Mennink, B. (2021). Leakage resilient value comparison with application to message authentication. In *EUROCRYPT 2021*, Canteaut, A. and Standaert, F.-X. (eds). Springer, Heidelberg.

Dobraunig, C., Koeune, F., Mangard, S., Mendel, F., Standaert, F. (2015). Towards fresh and hybrid re-keying schemes with beyond birthday security. In *CARDIS*. Springer, Heidelberg.

Dobraunig, C., Eichlseder, M., Mangard, S., Mendel, F., Mennink, B., Primas, R., Unterluggauer, T. (2020). *IACR Trans. Symm. Cryptol.*, 2020(S1), 390–416.

Dobraunig, C., Eichlseder, M., Mendel, F., Schläffer, M. (2021). Ascon v1.2: Lightweight authenticated encryption and hashing. *Journal of Cryptology*, 34(3), 33.

Dodis, Y., Kalai, Y.T., Lovett, S. (2009). On cryptography with auxiliary input. In *41st ACM STOC*, Mitzenmacher, M. (ed.). ACM Press, New York.

Duval, S., Méaux, P., Momin, C., Standaert, F.-X. (2021). Exploring crypto-physical dark matter and learning with physical rounding. *IACR TCHES*, 2021(1), 373–401.

Dziembowski, S. and Pietrzak, K. (2008). Leakage-resilient cryptography. In *49th FOCS*. IEEE Computer Society Press, Washington, D.C.

Dziembowski, S., Faust, S., Herold, G., Journault, A., Masny, D., Standaert, F.-X. (2016). Towards sound fresh re-keying with hard (physical) learning problems. In *CRYPTO 2016*, Robshaw, M. and Katz, J. (eds). Springer, Heidelberg.

Faust, S., Pietrzak, K., Schipper, J. (2012). Practical leakage-resilient symmetric cryptography. In *CHES 2012*, Prouff, E. and Schaumont, P. (eds). Springer, Heidelberg.

Fuller, B. and Hamlin, A. (2015). Unifying leakage classes: Simulatable leakage and pseudoentropy. In *ICITS 15*, Lehmann, A. and Wolf, S. (eds). Springer, Heidelberg.

Goudarzi, D. and Rivain, M. (2017). How fast can higher-order masking be in software? In *EUROCRYPT 2017*, Coron, J.-S. and Nielsen, J.B. (eds). Springer, Heidelberg.

Gueron, S. and Lindell, Y. (2017). Better bounds for block cipher modes of operation via nonce-based key derivation. In *ACM CCS 2017*, Thuraisingham, B.M., Evans, D., Malkin, T., Xu, D. (eds). ACM Press, New York.

Guo, C., Pereira, O., Peters, T., Standaert, F.-X. (2019). Authenticated encryption with nonce misuse and physical leakage: Definitions, separation results and first construction – (extended abstract). In *LATINCRYPT 2019*, Schwabe, P. and Thériault, N. (eds). Springer, Heidelberg.

Guo, C., Khairallah, M., Peyrin, T. (2020a). AET-LR: Rate-1 leakage-resilient AEAD based on the Romulus family. In *NIST LWC Workshop*, Shadong.

Guo, C., Pereira, O., Peters, T., Standaert, F.-X. (2020b). Towards low-energy leakage-resistant AE from the duplex sponge. *IACR Trans. Symm. Cryptol.*, 2020(1), 6–42.

Katz, J. and Yung, M. (2000). Unforgeable encryption and chosen ciphertext secure modes of operation. In *FSE*. Springer, Heidelberg.

Kocher, P.C. (2003). Leak-resistant cryptographic indexed key update. US Patent 6,539,092.

Longo, J., Martin, D.P., Oswald, E., Page, D., Stam, M., Tunstall, M. (2014). Simulatable leakage: Analysis, pitfalls, and new constructions. In *ASIACRYPT 2014*, Sarkar, P. and Iwata, T. (eds). Springer, Heidelberg.

Medwed, M., Standaert, F.-X., Großschädl, J., Regazzoni, F. (2010). Fresh re-keying: Security against side-channel and fault attacks for low-cost devices. In *AFRICACRYPT 10*, Bernstein, D.J. and Lange, T. (eds). Springer, Heidelberg.

Mennink, B. (2020). Beyond birthday bound secure fresh rekeying: Application to authenticated encryption. In *ASIACRYPT 2020*, Moriai, S. and Wang, H. (eds). Springer, Heidelberg.

Micali, S. and Reyzin, L. (2004). Physically observable cryptography (extended abstract). In *TCC 2004*, Naor, M. (ed.). Springer, Heidelberg.

Pereira, O., Standaert, F.-X., Vivek, S. (2015). Leakage-resilient authentication and encryption from symmetric cryptographic primitives. In *ACM CCS 2015*, Ray, I., Li, N., Kruegel, C. (eds). ACM Press, New York.

Petit, C., Standaert, F.-X., Pereira, O., Malkin, T., Yung, M. (2008). A block cipher based pseudo random number generator secure against side-channel key recovery. In *ASIACCS 08*, Abe, M. and Gligor, V. (eds). ACM Press, New Yok.

Pietrzak, K. (2009). A leakage-resilient mode of operation. In *EUROCRYPT 2009*, Joux, A. (ed.). Springer, Heidelberg.

Shen, Y., Peters, T., Standaert, F., Cassiers, G., Verhamme, C. (2022). Triplex: An efficient and one-pass leakage-resistant mode of operation. *IACR Trans. Cryptogr. Hardw. Embed. Syst.*, 2022(4), 135–162.

Standaert, F.-X. (2019). Towards and open approach to secure cryptographic implementations (invited talk). In *EUROCRYPT I* [Online]. Available at: https://www.youtube.com/watch?v=KdhrsuJT1sE.

Standaert, F.-X., Pereira, O., Yu, Y. (2013). Leakage-resilient symmetric cryptography under empirically verifiable assumptions. In *CRYPTO 2013*, Canetti, R. and Garay, J.A. (eds). Springer, Heidelberg.

Ueno, R., Xagawa, K., Tanaka, Y., Ito, A., Takahashi, J., Homma, N. (2022). Curse of re-encryption: A generic power/EM analysis on post-quantum KEMs. *IACR Trans. Cryptogr. Hardw. Embed. Syst.*, 2022(1), 296–322.

Yu, Y. and Standaert, F.-X. (2013). Practical leakage-resilient pseudorandom objects withminimum public randomness. In *CT-RSA 2013*, Dawson, E. (ed.). Springer, Heidelberg.

Yu, Y., Standaert, F.-X., Pereira, O., Yung, M. (2010). Practical leakage-resilient pseudorandom generators. In *ACM CCS 2010*, Al-Shaer, E., Keromytis, A.D., Shmatikov, V. (eds). ACM Press, New York.

PART 3

Fault Injection Attacks

9

An Introduction to Fault Injection Attacks

Jean-Max DUTERTRE[1] and Jessy CLÉDIÈRE[2]

[1]*École des Mines de Saint-Étienne, France*

[2]*CEA-Leti, Université Grenoble Alpes, France*

Fault injection attacks target the operations performed by integrated circuits. They consist of disrupting the operation by introducing calculation errors and erroneous behavior for attack purposes. They belong to the family of physical (or hardware) attacks, as they exploit the physical mechanisms of circuits (rather than the software and algorithmic aspects exploited in software attacks). They are active attacks that intentionally disrupt a circuit with the aim of introducing faults into its operation. Their purpose is manifold.

If we consider a microcontroller or a processor (CPU), the aim may be to modify the flow of code that will be executed by the integrated circuit (e.g. in order to access a password-protected function). The injected fault may corrupt the data to be manipulated, stored in volatile memory (RAM, registers) or non-volatile memory (OTP, ROM, EEPROM and FLASH). The fault may also affect the combinatorial logic implementing the processor core, in which case, the code remains intact but is executed incorrectly.

For a color version of all of the figures in this chapter, see www.iste.co.uk/prouff/cryptography1.zip.

Embedded Cryptography 1,
coordinated by Emmanuel PROUFF, Guénaël RENAULT, Matthieu RIVAIN and Colin O'FLYNN.

In the context of a crypto-processor, the aim may also be to inject faults into the target's cryptographic calculations in order to extract information on the encryption key used by observing the obtained faulty cipher texts, a so-called differential fault attack (DFA), as detailed in Chapters 10 and 11. Another approach is to modify the algorithm's behavior in order to weaken its security level (algorithm modification attacks), for example, by reducing the number of rounds of an iterative algorithm in order to diminish its security level.

9.1. Fault injection attacks, disturbance of electronic components

Integrated circuits are designed to operate correctly under nominal conditions (e.g. over given voltage, temperature or frequency ranges). Outside these ranges, or when subjected to an aggressive environment (exposure to radiation or electromagnetic (EM) disturbance), they cease to function correctly, and may even be destroyed if the stress level is too high. At an intermediate level of disturbance, they continue to function, but incorrectly.

The first intentional fault injections into integrated circuits were carried out to characterize these phenomena for failure analysis purposes in order to make their use more reliable. These injection techniques, such as laser illumination or circuit power manipulation, were subsequently among the first to be used for fault injection attacks. They are introduced in the first part of this section. The second part lists the most common fault injection techniques and describes the associated physical mechanisms as well as the properties of the injected faults. The hardware used to inject faults is described in the third section. Finally, a more general description of fault models and simulation tools is given in the fourth section.

9.1.1. *History of integrated circuit disturbance*

9.1.1.1. *Failure analysis*

The use of light, and more specifically laser beams, in the world of electronic safety owes much to the world of failure analysis. However, for a long time, these two worlds remained very separate.

In 1965, D. Habing published a proposal to use a neodymium laser (*Nd*) to simulate ionizing radiation and its transient effects. This intuition was confirmed in 1976 by Sawyer and Berning, who used a helium-neon laser (*He-Ne*) to obtain the internal state of MOS transistors and also to change their states.

A.H. Johnston is interested in the backplane for laser failure analysis in order to avoid the metallization levels that reflect light and screen when illuminated from the front of a circuit. In his 1993 publication, he refers to the work of E.E. King, who also studied the backplane for semiconductor laser testing back in 1982.

The 1980s and 1990s also saw the emergence of OBIC, LIVA, OBIRCH and TIVA techniques for laser imaging in failure analysis. Dean Lewis' Habilitation à Diriger les Recherches (or HDR, French acronym for "Habilitation to Supervise Research") manuscript from the University of Bordeaux in 1982 provides an overview of these techniques and their use.

Finally, in 1978, May and Woods introduced the notion of logical fault injection in RAM memories.

9.1.1.2. *The 1990s, voltage glitches and ITSEC evaluations at CNET*

The stage is set for the use of light systems to deliberately disrupt components. However, this aspect of failure analysis was not exploited in the field of electronic component safety until the 1990s. Unbeknownst to him, Raphaël Bauduin, at the Centre d'Evaluation de la Sécurité des Technologies de l'Information (CESTI, Information Technology Security Evaluation Center) of the Centre National d'Etudes des Télécommunications (CNET, National Center for Telecommunications Studies) in Caen, in 1996, as part of ITSEC (Information Technology Security Evaluation Criteria) evaluations, launched the trend toward the use of white light with camera flash, followed by focused laser light.

To compensate for the lack of light focus, the component to be attacked, previously opened at the front, was partially masked with black paint. Such masking was done with great care under binocular imaging, using model paint applied with a brush. Such masking on an old component is illustrated in Figure 9.1.

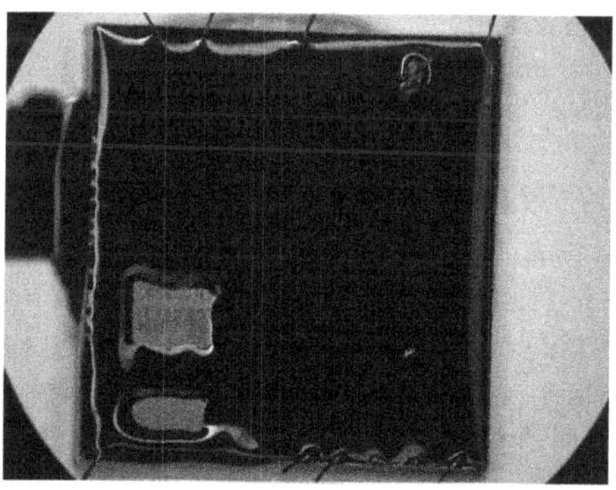

Figure 9.1. *Mask in black paint to reveal only the parts of the component to be illuminated for fault injection purposes*

The light was then emitted by a flash lamp from a camera. The photo in Figure 9.2 (left) illustrates the use of eight camera lamps capable of delivering eight flashes of light at eight different points in time. Temporal multi-faults, that is, the ability to inject faults successively in time, were already taken into account before the end of the 1990s.

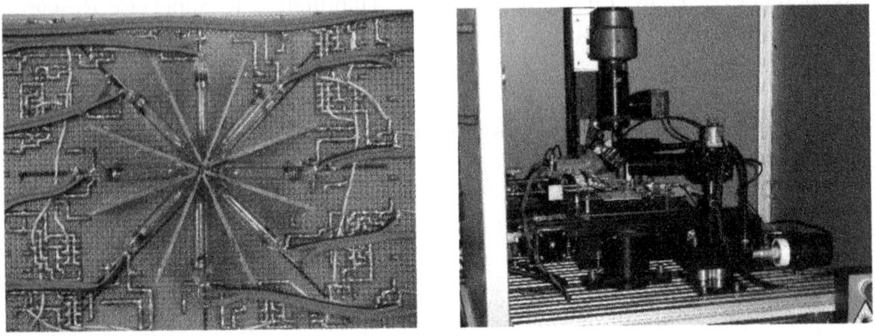

Figure 9.2. *Fault injection device using light disturbances: use of camera flashes to inject multiple faults over time (left, model with eight light flashes); first injection bench using laser illumination (right, CNET Caen, 1999)*

It is known that the duration of illumination could not be controlled with such a light source; Bauduin specified the first laser diode bench (built by Christian Hubert of the Errol company). This first bench can be seen in the photo on the right-hand side of Figure 9.2.

The 1990s in terms of electronic component security also resonates with the voltage glitch attacks (i.e. a transient disruption in the power level of integrated circuits) of pay-TV. The smart cards used to manage TV rights have always been a favorite target for hackers.

9.1.1.3. *From 2002 to the present day – who uses fault injection?*

The 2002 Cryptographic Hardware and Embedded Systems (CHES) conference, held that year in the San Francisco Bay Area, publicized the light attacks featured in the paper by Sergei Skorobogatov of Cambridge University in England. Although it is considered as well using a flash-lamp as a perturbation source, this publication was a landmark starting point for all academic activity on electronic component disturbances in the field of cybersecurity.

Who uses fault injection? There are four main categories of people practicing fault injection for different purposes: (1) attackers; (2) manufacturers designing secure systems; (3) system security assessment and certification centers; and (4) research teams interested in this field.

They may be hackers (*white hats*) or hobbyists whose aim is to experiment with fault injection out of curiosity, or to extract the embedded code of a circuit in order to understand it. Governments also use fault injection attacks, for example, to extract data from a cell phone as part of a criminal investigation (a field known as *forensics*). Hackers use it illegally to make a financial profit. Secure circuits used in pay-TV systems or game consoles are a regular target of their attacks.

Industrial designers of secure circuits use fault injection to test the resistance of their products before they go to market. They design countermeasures against fault injection, which must be experimentally validated against state-of-the-art attacks.

There are also entities (evaluation laboratories and certification bodies) specialized in evaluating and certifying the level of resistance of circuits to hardware attacks. They evaluate and certify the fault resistance of secure circuits by testing them on fault injection benches. They issue certificates according to a set of international standards dedicated to the fields of digital identity, bankcards, etc. (e.g. the *common criteria* standard). Evaluation laboratories also carry out private analyses for manufacturers who do not have fault injection equipment.

Finally, many research teams are studying fault injection mechanisms and attack techniques with the aim of understanding the underlying physical phenomena, the impact on hardware, the fault models obtained and even to improve these techniques. The aim of their work is to design and validate countermeasures to these attacks. This has led them to equip themselves with injection benches.

In the case of these last three players, we are more likely to talk about evaluation or characterization in the face of fault injection, rather than attacks. The injection target is sometimes referred to as a device under test (or DUT). Fault injection belongs to the field of hardware attacks (attacks targeting hardware implementation, as opposed to software attacks targeting program flaws). It is a field linked to confidential industrial know-how, characterized by minimal communication, with the exception of the work of researchers, which constitutes the main accessible source. The following section (mainly based on research work) describes the physical mechanisms associated with the various injection techniques. Understanding them is essential for assessing the level of threat these attacks pose to electronic components and for designing countermeasures.

9.1.2. *Fault injection mechanisms*

Historically, the first fault injection techniques used consisted of disrupting a target circuit by taking it outside its nominal operating conditions. There are three common approaches to this: by modifying its supply voltage, clock frequency or temperature. These disturbances can be permanent or temporary (referred to as transient disturbances, or *glitches*). Faults can also be induced when a circuit is exposed to an EM disturbance or an energetic light pulse produced by a camera flash or laser source.

The aim of this section is to describe the physical mechanisms associated with these techniques and to explain how they lead to the appearance of faults in integrated circuit operations. Knowledge of these mechanisms enables us to understand the properties of the faults injected and to anticipate the potential that these different techniques offer an attacker. It also enables the development of appropriate countermeasures.

The various fault injection techniques can be separated (in terms of their underlying mechanisms) into two families, based respectively on the violation of the timing constraints of synchronous digital circuits (section 9.1.2.1) or on exposure to a laser pulse (described in section 9.1.2.3). Finally, section 9.1.2.4 describes injection techniques (X-rays and radiation) that do not fall into the preceding families.

9.1.2.1. *Fault injection through time constraint violation*

Digital circuit timing constraints and fault injection

The vast majority of digital circuits operate synchronously, that is, their operation is cadenced by a periodic clock signal. The operations they perform using combinational logic blocks are synchronized and stored in registers on the rising edges of their clock. Their internal architecture can be symbolized by the diagram in Figure 9.3, representing a logic block (marked Σ) surrounded by two banks of registers (made up of D Flip-Flops or DFF).

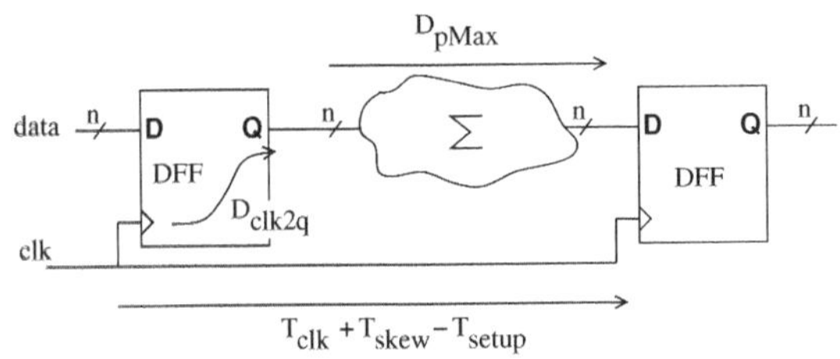

Figure 9.3. *Basic internal architecture of a digital integrated circuit*

This architecture imposes a time constraint, the setup time constraint, which can be exploited to inject faults. Schematically, this constraint means that the data propagation time through the Σ logic must be less than the clock signal period. The data presented at the input of Σ is in fact updated on a rising edge of the clock (corresponding to its storage by the upstream register bank) and must have been propagated through Σ to be stored in the downstream register bank on the next rising edge of the clock, that is, in less than one clock period. Equation [9.1] expresses this constraint rigorously for a worst-case scenario.

$$T_{\text{clk}} > D_{\text{clk2q}} + D_{\text{pMax}} + T_{\text{setup}} - T_{\text{skew}} \qquad [9.1]$$

The maximum propagation time through Σ is denoted D_{pMax} (also known as the critical time of the logic block), and the delay in updating the register flip-flop outputs after the rising edge of the clock signal is denoted D_{clk2q}. The clock period is denoted T_{clk}. T_{skew} expresses the phase difference between the clock edges of the leading and trailing registers. The setup time, expressed as T_{setup}, represents the minimum time interval between the stabilization of the input of a D flip-flop and the rising edge of its clock, otherwise a metastability phenomenon may occur, leading to the storage of erroneous data.

Figure 9.4 graphically illustrates the propagation of a signal Q_{upstream} through the logic Σ to the input of a downstream flip-flop, signal $D_{\text{downstream}}$ and its storage (signal $Q_{\text{downstream}}$ at output). In this example, $D_{\text{downstream}}$ undergoes several variations in its value (noted as *logical glitches*) before stabilizing at the end of time D_{pMax}. The chronogram (a) shows the case where the time constraint is respected: there is a time margin (the *slack* in jargon) between the instant of $D_{\text{downstream}}$ stabilization and the start of the *setup* interval preceding the clock edge. In this case, the data are stored correctly (transition to the high level of $Q_{\text{downstream}}$ on the second rising edge of the clock).

Violation of this timing constraint can have the effect of injecting a calculation error, which we will call a fault, into the circuit's operations. There are two usual ways of achieving a violation of the constraint expressed by equation [9.1]: reducing the clock period T_{clk} or increasing the propagation time through the logic D_{pMax}. This second alternative is illustrated by the chronograms (b) and (c) in Figure 9.4.

The chronogram (b) corresponds to a *setup* time violation, characterized by a logical transition of $D_{\text{downstream}}$ in the interval T_{setup} preceding the rising edge of the clock. The D flip-flop is then metastable, and the value it finally stores after a non-deterministic time is random. The $Q_{\text{downstream}}$ signal may sometimes stabilize at a correct value, and sometimes at its complement (the latter corresponds to the injection of a fault).

Chronogram (c) illustrates the case of a larger increase in D_{pMax}, for which the sampling window around the rising edge of the clock corresponds to a stable value of $D_{\text{downstream}}$ among those in the series of logic glitches. This value, although erroneous, is sampled correctly by the flip-flop. In this case, a fault is injected deterministically (no metastable phenomenon is created). It corresponds to what we call early data memorization (or early data sampling).

The chronograms (b) and (c) provide theoretical evidence of a characteristic (and sometimes puzzling) property of fault injection through *setup* time violation. Depending on the size of the disturbance causing a fault, its appearance can be either deterministic or random. Note also that D_{pMax}, as expressed in equation [9.1], represents the maximum propagation time through the logic. However, the propagation time, D_p, depends on the data being manipulated. Thus, depending on the data manipulated at the time of the disturbance (and therefore on the corresponding D_p value) and for identical experimental conditions, three different behaviors can be observed: the absence of a fault (case (a)), the non-deterministic injection of a fault (case (b)), or the deterministic injection of a fault (case (c)).

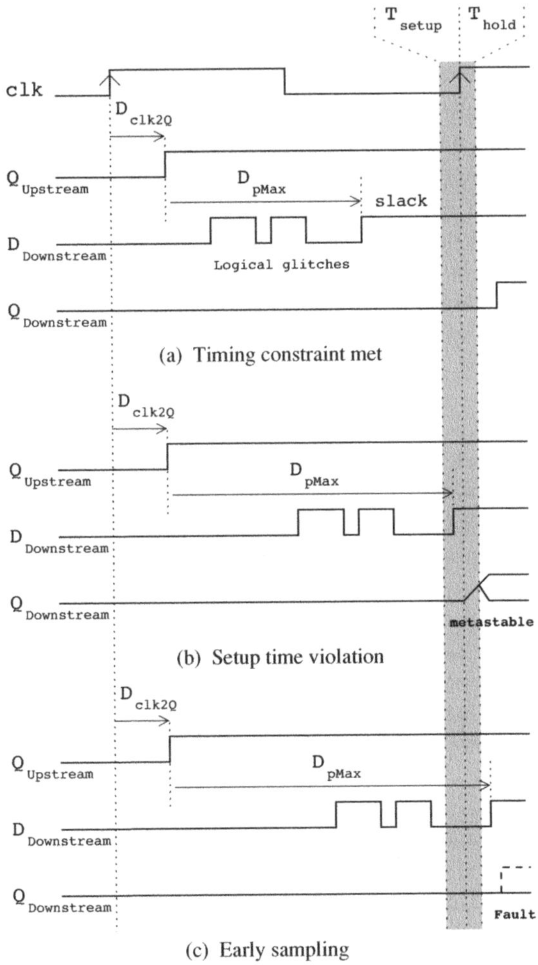

Figure 9.4. *Illustration of the fault injection mechanism by violation of setup time constraints*

Figure 9.4 illustrates fault injection by violating the timing constraints of a digital circuit, induced by an increase in the propagation time of logic gates. The disturbance causing this increase can be created by raising the temperature of a circuit, reducing its supply voltage or exposure to an EM disturbance. In a similar way, the same mechanism for injecting faults by violating the *setup* time constraint can be achieved by reducing the clock period.

Test circuit for characterizing fault injection mechanisms

The description of fault injection mechanisms by time constraint violation given in the following paragraphs is illustrated by experimental fault injection results performed on a test circuit. The target is a hardware encryption co-processor using the AES-128 symmetric cryptographic algorithm implemented in a programmable FPGA-type circuit. The AES-128 version of this algorithm uses a 128-bit secret key and encrypts a 128-bit plaintext in 11 rounds of iterative calculations. Figure 9.5 shows the architecture used in this implementation.

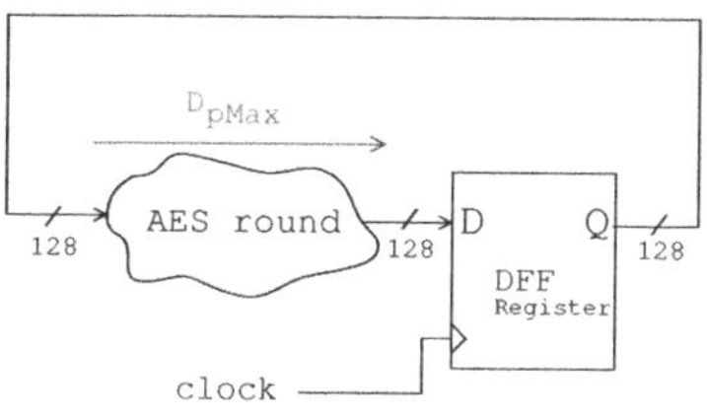

Figure 9.5. *Architecture of the AES encryption block*

All the algorithm's transformations are grouped together in a single combinatorial logic block (denoted `AES round`, critical time D_{pMax}) inserted in a loop closed on a memory register. Each clock cycle corresponds to the calculation of an AES round, and the intermediate state of the AES is then stored in the register. Full encryption is achieved in 11 clock cycles. The AES-128 co-processor is clocked at a frequency of 100 MHz (i.e. a period $T_{\text{clk}} = 10$ ns, greater than the logic propagation time measured at around 7 ns under nominal conditions, corresponding to the case illustrated in Figure 9.4(a)).

Fault injection through clock disruption

Overclocking: the corresponding decrease in the circuit's clock period leads to the appearance of faults in the AES-128 co-processor when T_{clk} becomes smaller than the maximum propagation time D_{pMax} in the logic. Figure 9.6 illustrates this mechanism using the example of Figure 9.4. As the clock period decreases, the flip-flop memorizes a 0 (lower part of the figure) instead of a 1 when the time constraints are respected (upper part): a fault is injected.

This decrease in T_{clk} below its nominal value can be interpreted as the application of stress, resulting in the appearance of faults. This stress is applied uniformly to each clock cycle: overclocking does not allow you to precisely choose when to inject faults. Faults are likely to appear at every clock cycle.

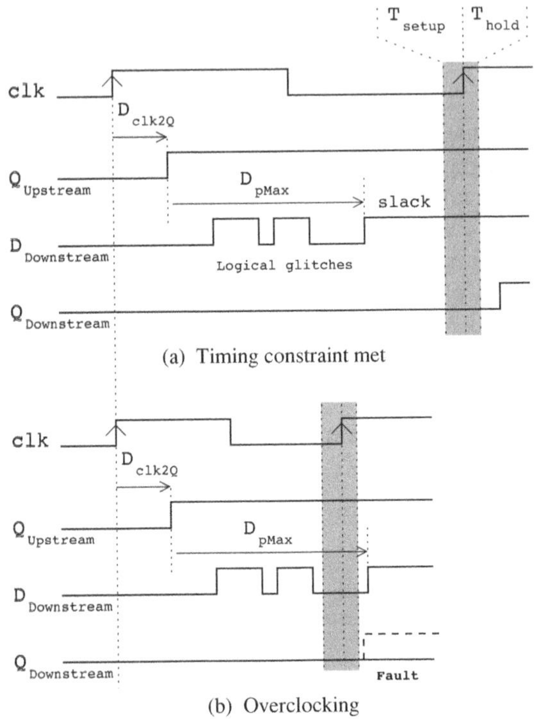

Figure 9.6. *Illustration of the overclocking fault injection mechanism*

Figure 9.7 illustrates two features of fault injection by time violation: (1) the dependence of propagation time on the data processed by the logic, and (2) the progressive nature of fault injection. It contains two graphs giving the maximum propagation times D_{pMax} through the AES-128 logic (on the ordinate) for each of the 10 main rounds (on the abscissa, the initial round is omitted), each graph being plotted for different data (different secret keys and plaintexts). The D_{pMax} are different for each round, as the data handled is different for each round.

Thus the value of the stress applied that leads to the injection of a first fault is different in the two cases ($T_{\text{clk, Injection}}$ shown in red), and the fault is injected at different rounds (R9 and R5, respectively). The progressive nature of fault injection as the stress applied is increased (i.e. as T_{clk} decreases) is characterized by the successive violation of the propagation times associated with each of the 128 bits of the AES-128 state at each round. Thus, for a variation step of $\sim$ 20 ps, the first faults injected were on a single bit in just over 90% of cases (referred to as single-bit faults). As the applied stress increased, the faults affected 2 bits, then 3 bits, up to a large number of bits and bytes. This dual character of data dependency and progressiveness is illustrated by the results reported in Figure 9.8 from practical injection tests carried out by progressively increasing the frequency until a first single-bit fault is obtained, considering 10,000 different key and plaintext pairs. The figure shows the percentage of faults obtained for each AES round.

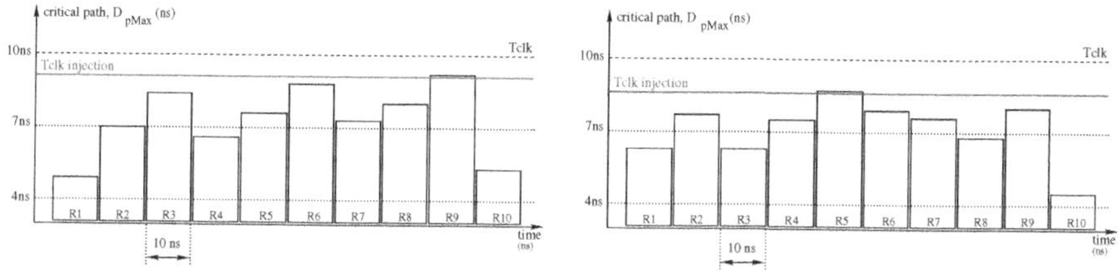

Figure 9.7. *AES-128: demonstrating the data dependency of fault injection by overclocking*

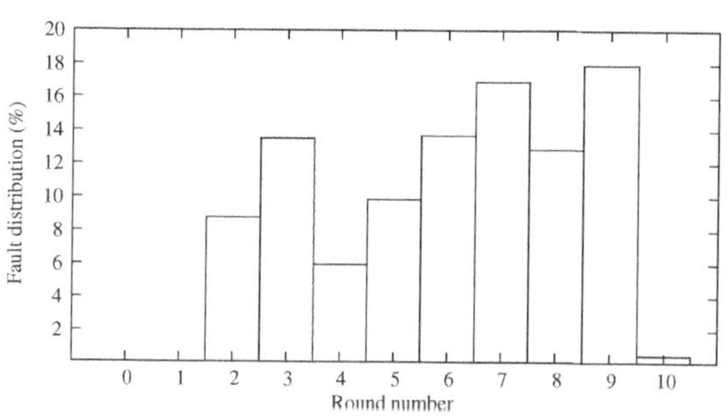

Figure 9.8. *Distribution of single-bit faults injected by increasing the clock frequency during AES-128 encryption*

Figure 9.8 clearly highlights the lack of temporal resolution offered by overclocking, whereas carrying out an attack often requires the choice of a precise injection time (in particular to implement the differential analysis techniques described in Chapter 10). However, this shortcoming is not irreversible, as shown by the work describing the CLK SCREW attack carried out by overclocking a phone processor based on ARM architecture. For this attack, the target's internal frequency was software altered while AES encryptions were performed. A large number of faulty results were accumulated, from which those allowing extraction of the secret key used were selected. This successful attack shows that the technique of fault injection by overclocking remains relevant and applicable to a modern circuit.

Clock glitch: the term clock glitch is used when a single clock period is reduced so as to inject a fault by violating the target's timing constraints. This corresponds to the best achievable temporal resolution, in which case, the stress is applied transiently to a single clock cycle. Figure 9.9 illustrates (lower part) the shape of a clock glitch enabling fault injection: its period is reduced below the time constraint expressed by equation [9.1] (whereas that of the nominal clock represented in the upper part is greater).

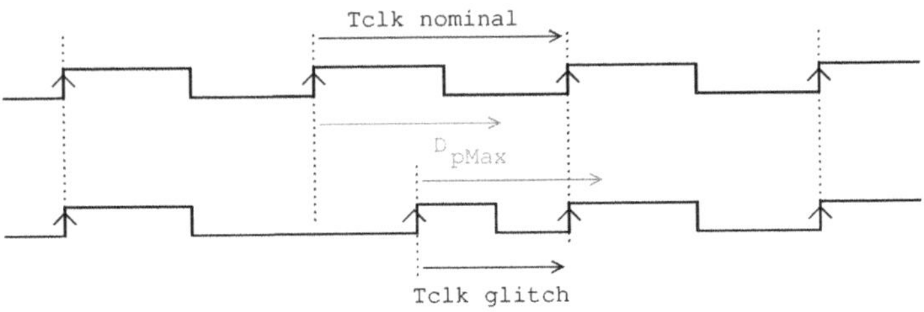

Figure 9.9. *Representation of a nominal clock signal (upper part) and a clock glitch (lower part)*

Applied to the case of AES-128 considered above, the use of a clock glitch makes it possible to choose the fault injection round. Considering the configuration represented in the graph on the left of Figure 9.7, it is not possible to inject a fault into the calculations of R6 by overclocking, without first faulting those of R9. A clock glitch makes this possible. Figure 9.10 illustrates this mechanism for the application of increasing stress creating up to three faults in the calculations of R6 without faults being injected into other rounds of AES-128.

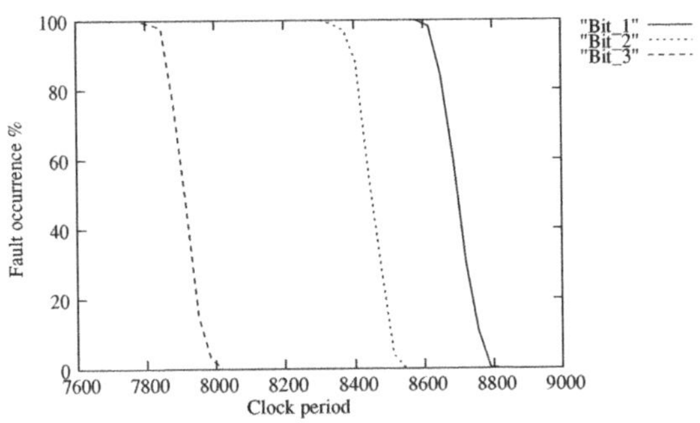

Figure 9.10. *Clock glitch fault injection*

This represents the evolution of the success rate of fault injection on 3 bits of the AES-128 state as $T_{\text{clk glitch}}$ decreases. It illustrates the progressive nature of clock glitch fault injection as the stress applied increases: the number of faults injected increases progressively, starting with the injection of a single-bit fault (in around 95 % of cases). All the faults injected are in the round R6 targeted by the clock glitch.

Clock glitch fault injection can also be used to fault a program during execution by a microcontroller. It targets a particular instruction and, depending on the stress applied and the instruction under consideration, modifies the data manipulated, the registers accessed, or even changes the type of instruction by corrupting its encoding bits (its opcode). In the case of high stress, the instruction may not even be executed (as if it had been erased, in which case, we speak of instruction skipping).

Fault injection through temperature increase

An increase in circuit temperature leads to an increase in data propagation times through the logic (due to a reduction in charge carrier mobility in the transistor channels). At a sufficiently high temperature, the increase in propagation times induces the appearance of faults through violation of timing constraints, as illustrated in Figure 9.4(c).

Figure 9.11 shows the evolution of the critical time of the AES-128 test circuit as a function of temperature for three different datasets (plain text and AES-128 key). Faults were injected when D_{pMax} exceeded 10 ns (i.e. T_{clk}).

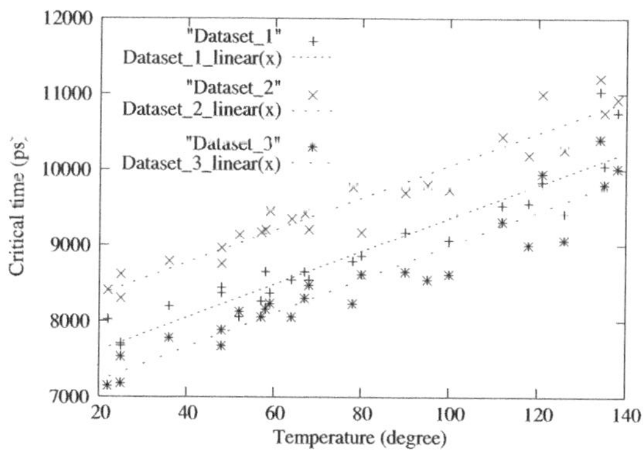

Figure 9.11. *Evolution of the critical time of the AES-128 co-processor data path as a function of temperature for three different datasets*

Faults injected by increasing temperature are characterized by (1) the progressivity of the number of faults injected as the applied stress increases (allowing single-bit faults to be injected when applying progressive stress), and by (2) the data dependency of the injected faults (as illustrated in Figure 9.11).

As a circuit's temperature variations suffer from significant inertia (on the scale of its clock period), this injection method shares the properties of overclocking. It does not allow us to target a particular cycle of the target's activity.

Fault injection through supply voltage disturbance

A drop in the supply voltage of an integrated circuit (and more precisely that of its core voltage, noted Vdd) leads to an increase in propagation times in the logic. This increase in D_{pMax} is likely to induce the appearance of faults by violation of time constraints, as illustrated in Figure 9.4(c). Conversely, an increase in Vdd leads to a decrease in D_{pMax} and should therefore not induce faults (the *slack*, or temporal margin, increases).

Underpowering: Figure 9.12 shows the evolution of the critical time of the AES-128 test circuit (for three different datasets) as the FPGA core voltage Vdd is lowered below its nominal voltage of 1.2 V (from right to left). Depending on the data manipulated by the AES, D_{pMax} gradually increases to exceed the clock period (10 ns) as Vdd decreases between 1.1 V and 1.0 V. Faults start to be injected during AES encryption at this stage, with a distribution similar to that observed during overclocking stress (as shown in Figure 9.8).

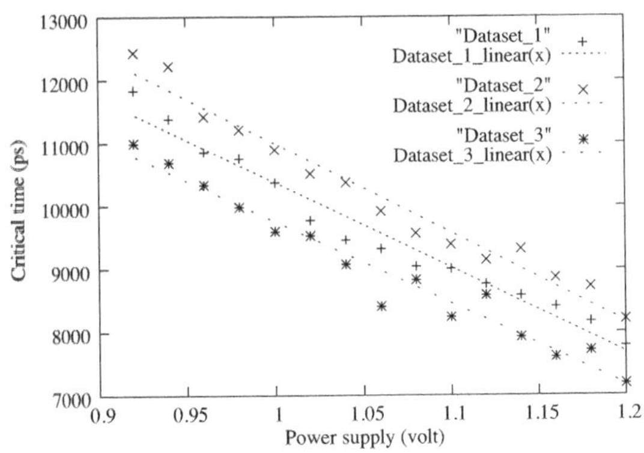

Figure 9.12. *Evolution of the critical time of three data paths as a function of the core voltage Vdd*

The characteristics of fault injection by underpowering are identical to those obtained by overclocking or temperature increase: (1) progressiveness of the injection mechanism, enabling single-bit faults to be obtained, and (2) dependence on the data manipulated. This is also a global injection method: stress is (globally) applied identically to the entire target circuit.

This injection method is sometimes difficult to implement, as many circuits have internal voltage sensors that trigger a reset when the voltage drops below a programmable value.

Despite these limitations, this fault injection technique is still very much in vogue, as demonstrated by its use in the Plundervolt attack, revealed in 2019, which enabled the SGX trusted execution environment of an Intel microprocessor to be defeated by a software takeover of its internal voltage setting device.

Negative voltage glitch: a voltage pulse generator is used to generate a transient drop in the supply voltage to a target circuit, so that faults are only injected over a reduced time range (this is known as a voltage glitch). The corresponding mechanism is illustrated in Figure 9.13. The negative voltage glitch shown is characterized by its duration (approximately three clock periods in the case illustrated), the rise and fall times of the glitch (in the drawing, their sum corresponds to the total duration of the glitch), and its amplitude (the maximum voltage subtracted from the nominal voltage). This has the effect of increasing the propagation times associated with three AES rounds (shown in gray in the figure). Maximum stress is applied to round R6, for which D_{pMax} exceeds the clock period T_{clk}: faults are injected by violating the time constraints associated with this round's calculations. The propagation times of adjacent rounds (R5 and R7) undergo a smaller increase, which is not associated with fault injection.

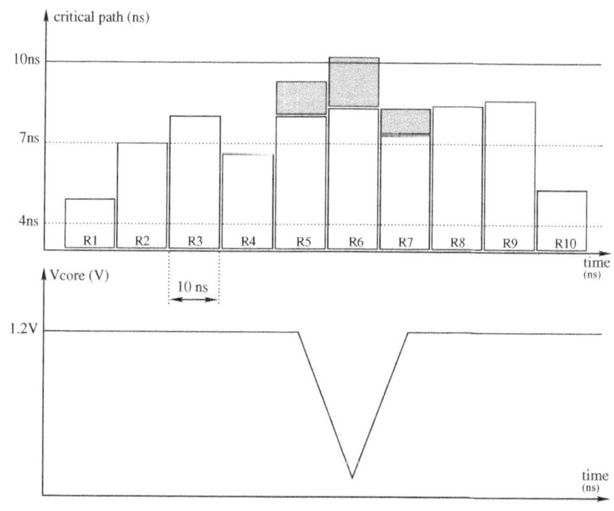

Figure 9.13. *Representation and effect of a negative voltage glitch on AES-128 calculations*

The results illustrated in Figure 9.13 were obtained in practice, illustrating the ability of a voltage glitch to achieve very good temporal resolution. In over 90% of cases, a progressive increase in applied stress (the amplitude of the voltage *glitch*) led to the injection of a single-bit fault. Of these single-bit faults, 77% were indeed injected into the targeted round, 7% were injected into adjacent rounds, and 6% corresponded to the violation of logical paths of immediately sub-critical ranks (i.e. whose propagation time is less than D_{pMax} but very close, mainly at the second or third rank).

Complex glitch shapes can be used, for example, voltage glitches of various shapes have been used to disable the read-back protection of microcontroller Flash memory, enabling an attacker to extract embedded code for reverse engineering purposes.

Positive voltage glitch: an increase in a circuit's core voltage has the effect of reducing propagation times in its logic and does not allow faults to be injected by violating timing constraints. The same should be true when our AES-128 test circuit is exposed to a positive voltage glitch, as illustrated on the left-hand side of Figure 9.14: the effect of a transient voltage pulse (extending over a time span of approximately three computation rounds) is to decrease the D_{pMax} of rounds R5 to R7 (decrease represented by stripes), making fault injection more difficult (slack is increased).

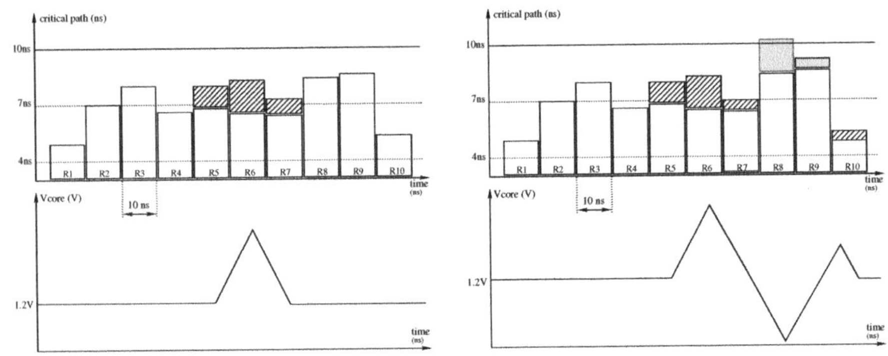

Figure 9.14. *Representation of the theoretical (left) and real (right) effects of a positive voltage glitch*

However, counter-intuitively, exposing our test circuit to positive voltage glitches enabled us to inject faults into the AES-128 calculations. The resulting faults have the characteristics of faults induced by time constraint violation (progressivity of the injection mechanism and data dependency). This is due to glitch bounce effects transmitted into the target circuit core. This phenomenon is illustrated on the right-hand side of Figure 9.14, where the positive glitch is followed by an attenuated negative glitch (and other glitches in the form of attenuated oscillations). It is the negative glitch that causes faults to appear, according to the mechanism described above (when calculating round R8 in the figure).

Uniqueness of the fault injection mechanism for time constraint violations

A series of experiments to inject faults into AES-128 operations were carried out by applying stress to the clock (overclocking or glitch), power supply (underpowering or negative and positive glitches) and temperature (increase) using the same dataset. In over 90% of cases, identical faults were injected. Furthermore, they share the same properties of data dependency and progressivity of fault appearance as applied stress increases. This identity of faults and their properties for these types of disturbances (frequency, supply voltage or temperature) constitutes experimental proof of the uniqueness of the associated mechanism for fault injection by violation of temporal constraints.

A practical consequence is that these three methods can be used together to inject faults. This is illustrated in Figure 9.15, which shows the evolution of D_{pMax} for variations in supply voltage and temperature. Integrated circuits have voltage and temperature sensors that trigger an alarm when a certain threshold is crossed. The simultaneous use of these two types of disturbance can enable an attacker to stay below the individual detection thresholds of these sensors, while applying sufficient stress to inject faults.

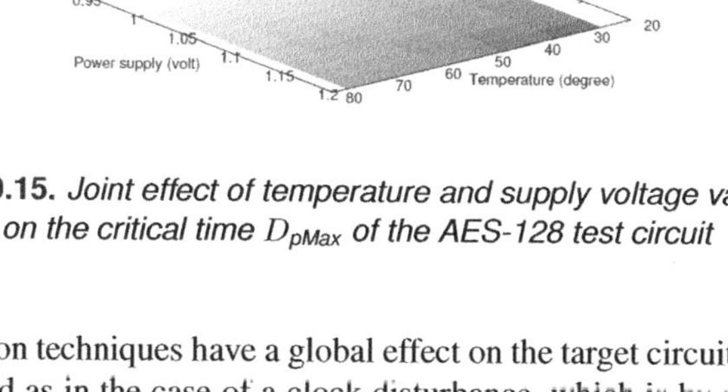

Figure 9.15. *Joint effect of temperature and supply voltage variations on the critical time D_{pMax} of the AES-128 test circuit*

These injection techniques have a global effect on the target circuit, since the same faults are injected as in the case of a clock disturbance, which is by definition global (this is probably a little less true for voltage glitch injection, for which this rate drops to 90%).

For a complex circuit comprising several functional blocks, the use of a global injection technique implies that faults will be injected mainly in the block with the longest propagation times (the one for which the time constraint is the strictest).

In the case of a microcontroller, it is generally the transfer of instructions from Flash memory to the processor core that has the highest critical time. This leads to the corruption or even skipping of executed instructions.

Injecting faults into sub-critical blocks then requires the application of higher stress, which can lead to a target reset (due to catastrophic faults injected into the most critical block). This makes it impossible for an attacker to exploit the injected faults. The use of other techniques such as EM fault injection or laser illumination, which have local effects, enables an attacker to bypass this limitation.

9.1.2.2. *Fault injection using electromagnetic interference*

The first results of fault injection by EM disturbance in a circuit were obtained using the electric arc of a gas-lighter device. Although effective, this approach does not allow precise control of the strength of the disturbance and the time of its appearance.

Today's commonly used devices use voltage pulse generators combined with injection probes in the form of small coils. These professional-grade generators enable precise control of the injection time and the strength of the stress applied to the target circuit.

One of the advantages of EM disturbance fault injection is that it does not require opening the target circuit package or modifying its electronic board.

Electromagnetic disturbance generation and fault injection

The EM disturbance that causes fault injection in a target circuit is created by a voltage pulse delivered to an injection probe. The probe is formed by winding an insulated conductive wire around a ferrite core (usually less than 1 mm in diameter). The voltage pulse is characterized by its amplitude, duration, and the slope of its rising and falling edges. At the time of its rising and falling edges, the voltage pulse causes a variation in the current in the injection probe (which is a solenoid) and therefore a variation in the magnetic field emitted by it. The resulting EM coupling with the target circuit's supply network (induction phenomenon with the loop-shaped patterns of the target circuit's Vdd and Gnd distribution networks) leads to the appearance of transient variations in the target's internal voltage in the area of effect of the applied EM disturbance. EM stress applied to a target circuit creates faults by inducing a variation in its internal voltage.

Typical characteristics of voltage generators used for EM injection are: adjustable amplitude over the $\pm 400\,\text{V}$ range, pulse duration between 10 and 100 ns, and rising and falling edges over the 2–5 ns range. The steepness of the fronts (i.e. their slope expressed in V/ns) and their duration are important EM injection parameters, as the induction phenomenon that creates the EM disturbance applied to the target directly depends on them. The steepness of the edges is generally a generator constant.

The stress applied to the target is then adjusted by adjusting the amplitude of the voltage pulse; an increase in the latter leads to an increase in the stress induced by the EM disturbance.

Figure 9.16 (left view) shows a view of an EM injection probe mounted on an SMA connector. It consists of a dozen or so contiguous conductive coils wound around a slightly tapered ferrite core. This is a hand-crafted probe. Figure 9.16 (center view) and 9.16 (right view) respectively show the positioning of an injection probe (of a different type) above a microcontroller and an FPGA. In the latter two cases, the probes are positioned as close as possible to the target (a few hundred micrometers) to maximize the level of stress applied. The intensity of the induced EM stress decreases with the square of the distance separating the injection probe from the target circuit (more precisely, from the silicon chip, which sometimes requires the package to be opened in order to inject faults). Beyond about ten millimeters, it is no longer possible to inject faults.

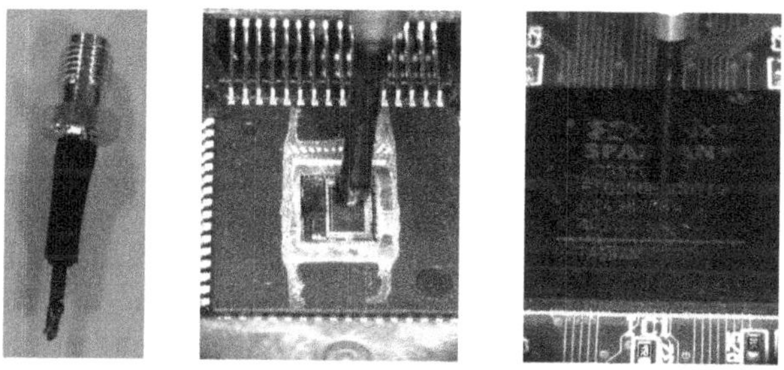

Figure 9.16. *Injection probes EM: (left) detail of the injection probe; (center) a microcontroller with an open housing to allow the probe to be approached as closely as possible; (right) injection probe above an FPGA*

The coupling between the injection probe and the target is local, and the stress can be applied to a limited part of the circuit, depending on the probe diameter (probes with diameters ranging from 200 μm to 2–3 mm are commonly used). Figure 9.17 illustrates this local character of EM fault injection for the case of an AES-128 implemented in an FPGA. The left-hand side shows the spatial distribution on the FPGA silicon of the main AES blocks: the control state machine (FSM), the encryption block (RoundExe) and the key calculation block (KeyExp). The right-hand side of the figure shows a map of the FPGA's spatial sensitivity to fault injection in the form of the number of bytes faulted during AES calculations as a result of an EM disturbance for different probe positions above the FPGA. Faults are mainly injected when the probe is positioned above the encryption and key calculation blocks, highlighting the locality of EM injection.

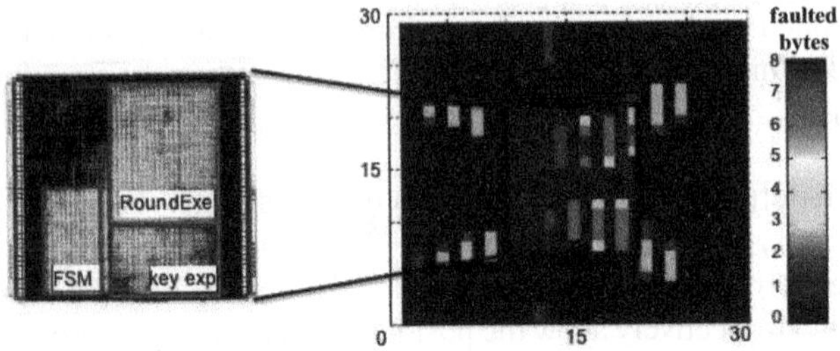

Figure 9.17. *Distribution of AES encryption block elements on the FPGA surface and sensitivity map to EM pulse fault injection*

The previous example demonstrated the ability to inject faults by EM disturbance into an AES-128 encryption hardware block (or co-processor).

The application of EM stress also makes it possible to fault instructions executed by a microcontroller or microprocessor. There is a wide variety of assembler instructions. They are coded in binary form and generally include an identifier (the opcode), operands (for example, the source and destination register references for an arithmetic instruction) and a possible hexadecimal value (immediate value) used for an operation or as an address. Depending on the target and experimental parameters, an EM disturbance can have the effect of corrupting the opcode (transforming one instruction into another), a register reference (erroneous data is used) or an immediate value. Depending on the level of stress applied, the target may interpret the corrupted instruction as a nop instruction (meaning "no operation"). The microcontroller then reacts as if the instruction had been erased, a faulty behavior referred to as instruction skipping in everyday language. Depending on the injection parameters, several successive instructions can be skipped.

Fault injection by violation of time constraints induced by an electromagnetic disturbance

The effect of an EM disturbance applied to a target circuit leads to a local disturbance of its internal supply voltage. One explanation for the occurrence of faults is that they are linked to a violation of the target's timing constraints. This is the first commonly accepted mechanism for EM stress fault injection.

Various tests on microcontroller or FPGA targets have shown that fault injection by EM disturbance is data dependent (the faults obtained change with the data processed). Data dependency being a characteristic property of fault injection by time constraint violation, this constitutes an argument in favor of this mechanism.

The progressive nature of EM stress injection has also been verified (another characteristic property of the temporal constraint violation mechanism). By progressively increasing the applied stress (via an increase in the amplitude of the voltage pulse generating the EM disturbance), the target gradually moves from non-faulty behavior to behavior marked by the injection of an increasing number of faults. It is possible to find experimental settings resulting in perfectly deterministic fault injection (as illustrated in Figure 9.4(c)). All this behavior is compatible with a fault injection mechanism based on violation of temporal constraints.

The injection of EM stress faults on the AES-128 algorithm implemented in an FPGA and with the same data as used for the injection of clock glitch faults (as described in section 9.1.2.1) shows that the injected faults are either identical (they affect bits whose propagation paths correspond to the critical times measured by clock glitch), or associated with propagation times immediately sub-critical to D_{pMax}. This provides experimental proof of the ability to inject EM stress faults into a target circuit using a setup time constraint violation mechanism. The fact that sub-critical paths are sometimes faulted is an illustration of the local nature of EM injection, with target logic gates affected differently, depending on their position in the target circuit.

This is one of the features of EM injection used to attack a complex circuit: it allows a sub-critical logic block to be faulted, while not faulting a block with higher propagation times but which could compromise the success of the attack (such as an attack sensor).

Other electromagnetic disturbance fault injection mechanisms

The EM disturbance that causes a fault is transmitted by EM coupling between the injection probe (similar to a transmitting antenna) and the target circuit (similar to a receiving antenna). Integrated circuits have three main internal networks which can act as receiving antennas:

– the supply network;

– the clock signal distribution network;

– the distribution network of the reset signal to zero (`reset`) or to one (`set`).

The mechanism for injecting EM faults by violating time constraints presented in the previous section is based on the assumption that coupling is carried out with the power supply network. This results in a decrease in the target's internal voltage and therefore an increase in propagation times in its fault-causing logic.

Other work has shown, based on experimental results, that EM coupling is also possible with a circuit's clock distribution network. The result is the appearance of clock glitches, which can cause faults.

The possibility of coupling with a circuit's `reset` and `set` signals was also suggested by practical tests carried out on an FPGA target whose clock was stopped (it is then impossible to create faults by violating timing constraints).

These different results highlight the possibility of fault injection by EM disturbance using several mechanisms. They are not contradictory insofar as they were obtained on different hardware targets with different injection parameters.

Other works describe a fourth EM fault injection mechanism, which is linked to the disruption of the data sampling operation (i.e. storage) in the flip-flops of a circuit. The resulting faults are called *sampling* faults. These faults occur when the EM disturbance is applied at the rising edge of the clock signal (corresponding to the moment when the data is stored in the flip-flops).

Figure 9.18 represents the faults injected into the rounds of an AES-128 implemented in an FPGA subjected to an EM disturbance. The number of bits and bytes faulted at the end of the AES encryption are plotted as a function of the time at which the EM disturbance was applied.

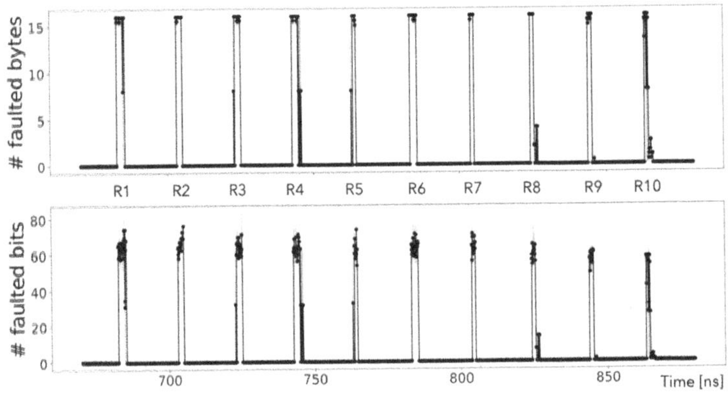

Figure 9.18. *Sampling faults injected by EM disturbance into AES-128 calculations*

In this test, the clock frequency was set to 50 MHz ($T_{\text{clock}} = 20\,\text{ns}$) and the maximum propagation time in the logic was measured as $D_{\text{pMax}} = 5\,\text{ns}$. In this configuration, the time margin was such (slack $\approx 15\,\text{ns}$) that the EM disturbance applied was unable to cause an increase in D_{pMax} sufficient to create a time constraint violation. The faults injected therefore seem to correspond to sampling faults. They are characterized by a window of vulnerability of a few nanoseconds (~ 2.4 ns in this case) corresponding to the rising edge of the clock signal: in Figure 9.18, the 10-fault injection time ranges correspond to the 10 main rounds of AES-128 (from R1 to R10).

Decreasing the frequency of a circuit's clock is a natural countermeasure to fault injection by violating its timing constraints (due to the increased timing margin). The existence of a mechanism for injecting sampling faults by EM disturbance, which is not linked to the clock signal period, would condemn this strategy.

In practice, integrated circuits are designed to operate with a minimum time margin (in order to maximize their performance). In this configuration, a synchronous digital circuit exposed to EM disturbance will be sensitive to both sampling fault injection and fault injection by violation of its timing constraints.

9.1.2.3. *Fault injection by laser illumination*

The exposure of an integrated circuit to laser pulses in order to create faults emulating singular radiative effects was evoked as early as 1965 by D. Habing. This fault injection technique was subsequently transposed to the injection of faults into secure circuits. Since then, it has been the subject of numerous works.

Fault injection by exposure to a laser pulse is characterized by a very marked local effect corresponding approximately to the size of the laser beam (its diameter can reach a minimum diameter of the order of 1 μm, due to the laws of optics). Pulse durations commonly used for fault injection are in the picosecond and nanosecond ranges. They provide excellent time resolution whatever the clock frequency of the target circuit. The ability to adjust the duration of a laser pulse makes it possible to apply a disturbance over a single clock period or over several successive periods.

Laser illumination fault injection mechanism

Laser fault injection in an integrated circuit requires direct illumination of the silicon, and more specifically of the sensitive areas of the transistors. The target circuit package must therefore be opened to expose the silicon chip, either from the front or the rear. Opening the package is illustrated in Figure 9.19. This can be done either chemically (using an acid) or mechanically. A mechanical opening for rear access must preserve the mirror-like polish of the silicon to allow laser beam penetration without reflection or diffraction.

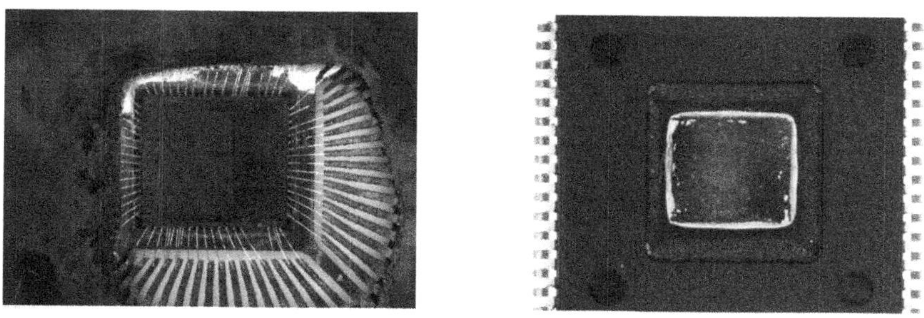

Figure 9.19. *Open microcontroller component for laser access: acid opening for front access (left) and mechanical opening for rear access (right)*

The mechanism for laser fault injection in an integrated circuit is based on the photoelectric effect. When a laser beam passes through the silicon of an integrated circuit, it creates electron-hole pairs along its path, provided the energy of its photons is greater than the gap energy of the silicon. The photoelectric effect is obtained at wavelengths ranging from the near infrared to the ultraviolet for sources used in safety characterization; for example, 1,064 nm for the near infrared (upper limit of the wavelength for creating a photoelectric effect), 532 nm (green), or 355 nm (UV). Only infrared can be used for both front- and back-side injection, as it can penetrate a few hundred micrometers into the silicon without being too strongly attenuated (the distance separating the back of the silicon from the sensitive areas of the transistors is of the order of 200 μm). The use of green or UV lasers is limited to front-side attacks, as their energy is fully absorbed in around 10 μm. Front-side injection, however, is made more difficult by the reflection of the laser beam off the circuit's metallizations (interconnect tracks, tiles added to meet flatness constraints, and any shields).

As a general rule, electron-hole pairs generated by laser illumination recombine without any noticeable effect on an integrated circuit's operation. However, if electron-hole pairs are generated in the vicinity of a reverse-polarized PN junction, the electric field will cause these charges to move in opposite directions, thereby creating an electric current. This current is a transient that ceases after all charges have either been swept away or recombined. Figure 9.20 illustrates this mechanism for the case of a CMOS logic inverter shown in cross-section. The inverter's input, denoted `in`, is 1 and its output, denoted `out`, is 0. In this logic configuration, the blocked PMOS drain forms a reverse-biased PN junction with the N-well (or NWell).

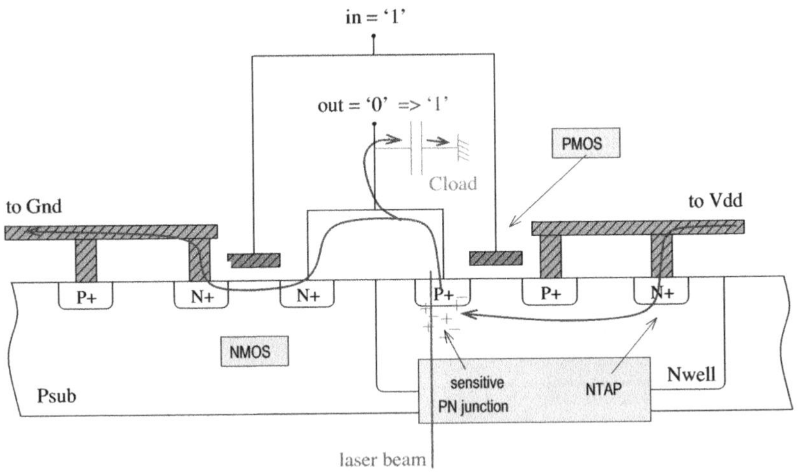

Figure 9.20. *Illustration of the fault injection mechanism using laser illumination on a cross-sectional view of a CMOS inverter*

If the drain is hit by a laser beam, the electron-hole pairs generated in the vicinity give rise to a transient current whose path from supply (Vdd) to ground (Gnd) is shown in red. Part of this current charges the inverter's output capacitance, denoted `Cload`. This causes the inverter output logic level to change from 0 to 1. When laser illumination ceases and all charges have been discharged, the current induced by laser illumination also ceases. The capacitor discharges again through the NMOS transistor in the ON state, and the output returns to its initial logic level of 0. It has undergone a voltage transient. This voltage transient will propagate into the logic downstream of the inverter, creating a possible fault if the transient is captured by a circuit register. Similar reasoning can be applied when the inverter input is set to 0, so the area sensitive to laser illumination is the NMOS drain (in the OFF state).

This leads to a general rule for finding areas sensitive to laser illumination: these are the drains of OFF transistors. Their location therefore varies with the input values of the logic gates.

The propagation of voltage transients in the logic of a circuit is a possible source of laser fault injection. When these transients are directly induced in a memory element such as a register or SRAM memory cell, they can cause it to toggle (i.e. flip), resulting in a fault. Registers and SRAM cells are based on the same type of structure, using two looped-back inverters to create a feedback effect for storing one bit of information (bistable structure). Figure 9.21 (left view) shows the schematic of a five-transistor SRAM cell (such as those used to store the configuration of an FPGA). Areas sensitive to laser illumination are indicated with a color code: red when the cell memorizes a logic 0, blue when it memorizes a logic 1 (the memorized value corresponds to the logic level of the output noted Data_out). When a sensitive area (whose location depends on the current state of the SRAM) is affected, a voltage transient is created at the output of the inverter to which the transistor in question belongs. This voltage transient then propagates through the second inverter, in turn inverting the input of the first. The bistable formed by the two inverters is now in a stable state, the opposite of its initial state. The data bit stored by the SRAM cell is inverted; a fault has been injected. The effect is not transient (as in the case of a voltage transient induced in a logic gate) but permanent, until a new value is written to the SRAM. This is known as a soft error, or SEU (*Single Event Upset*).

The term bit-set is used when the SEU switches the stored content to state 1. This phenomenon is likely to occur when a red zone, sensitive when the SRAM is in state 0, is illuminated by a laser pulse. In a similar way, a bit-reset corresponds to the switching of the SRAM to 0 when a blue zone, sensitive in state 1, is illuminated. The locations of the bit-set and bit-reset zones are separate, and their *activation* depends on the data stored by the SRAM cell. So, depending on the location of a laser spot directed at an SRAM cell and its state, it may or may not be sensitive to laser fault injection. This behavior corresponds to the bit-set/reset fault model.

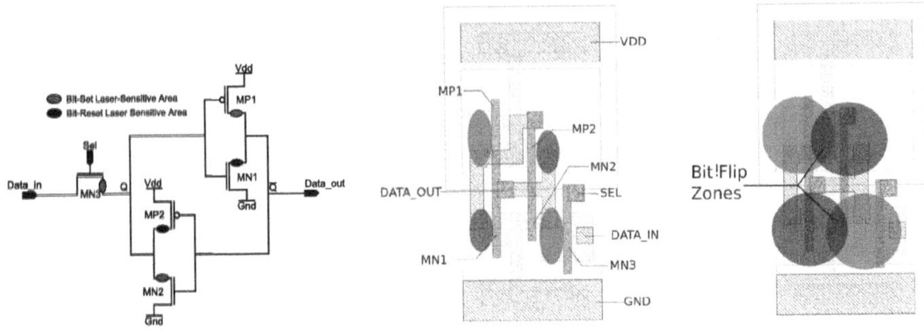

Figure 9.21. *Presentation of the areas of an SRAM cell sensitive to laser illumination: Schematic of the SRAM 5T (left), layout view of the SRAM according to the bit-set/reset hypothesis (center) and the bit-flip hypothesis (right)*

Figure 9.21 (middle section) shows the layout of the five-transistor SRAM cell under consideration. Bit-set and bit-reset areas are indicated with the same color code. In this drawing, an implicit assumption has been made about the validity of the bit-set/reset model: sensitive areas do not overlap. Figure 9.21 (right-hand side) illustrates an alternative: overlapping bit-set and bit-reset zones. It shows bit-flip zones for which a fault could be injected whatever the initial logic state of the cell (this hypothesis is dealt with in the next section).

Laser fault injection can be performed dynamically, that is, by corrupting data moving through the logic of a target circuit and transiting its registers and memories. Compared with other fault injection mechanisms, it also has the original feature of enabling data stored in registers or RAM-type memories (and cache memories too) to be corrupted, even though they reside there statically.

Fault models obtained by laser illumination, technological developments

Figure 9.21 raises the question of the influence of the zone of effect of a laser pulse on the fault model obtained in practice. This influence is linked to the size of the illuminated zone and to the technological node of the target circuit, which sets the dimensions of its logic gates. For older technologies used in the early 2000s (for example, CMOS 0.25 μm), it was possible to individually target the sensitive drain of a transistor and inject faults limited to a single bit of the data manipulated by the target. This precision is illustrated in Figure 9.22 for the case of a five-transistor SRAM cell integrated in a prototype circuit using CMOS 0.25 μm technology, and for the case of the RAM memory of a microcontroller manufactured using CMOS 0.35 μm technology (left and right, respectively).

These targets were initialized to memorize a given logic state (0 then 1), exposed to laser illumination, then re-read to determine whether a fault was injected. The exercise was repeated for several laser spot positions, enabling a laser fault injection sensitivity map to be drawn using a color code: red for bit-set faults, blue for bit-reset faults. In both cases, a laser pulse of 30 ps duration and a laser spot diameter of 1 μm were used. The laser pulse energy was 12 nJ for the SRAM cell and 3.2 nJ for the RAM memory. Injection was carried out through the rear face of the latter, and through the front face of the SRAM cell (a cutout of the sensitive areas corresponding to the cell metallizations is visible). In both cases, the four theoretical zones of sensitivity to laser injection of an SRAM cell are indeed present (the black frame delimits an elementary SRAM cell of the RAM in Figure 9.22). The fault model obtained in practice for these older technologies is indeed a bit-set/reset model characterized by separate sensitive zones, whose locations vary with the stored data (no bit-flip fault was obtained). When injecting faults into RAM memory, the laser parameters used only enabled one bit to be faulted at a time, a so-called single-bit fault.

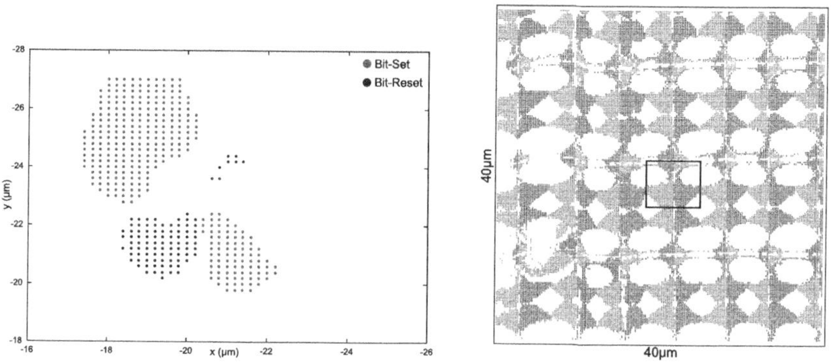

Figure 9.22. *Laser fault injection sensitivity maps of SRAM memories, bit-set and bit-reset areas: five-transistor SRAM cell – CMOS 0.25 μm (left), microcontroller RAM memory – CMOS 0.35 μm (right)*

This excellent precision is often called into question by technological developments: a laser spot of 1 μm (the minimum achievable size) covers several logic gates for advanced processes (the surface area of an SRAM cell at the 7 nm CMOS technology node is of the order of 0.027 μm^2). There are no experimental laser fault injection results in the bibliography for the most advanced technologies. However, accuracy is still very good at the 28 nm CMOS technology node. This is illustrated for fault injection by laser illumination in D flip-flops in Figure 9.23 (tests were carried out using a laser pulse of 30 ps duration performed via the rear face of the target).

Figure 9.23 (left view) shows the layout of a first test pattern in the form of a matrix of 64 D flip-flops forming a shift register (whose propagation path is shown in red). These flip-flops are assembled very compactly. Figure 9.23 (central view) shows the spatial map of laser injection sensitivity obtained for a laser pulse energy of 1 nJ. The third dimension gives the rank of the faulty flip-flop in the shift register (from 1 to 64). A color code indicates the number of bits faulted for 1 laser shot at the location in question. The majority of faults are 1 or 2-bit faults, with multiple faults mostly located toward the inside of the matrix (it is also possible to obtain single-bit faults in this zone). Figure 9.23 (right view) gives a more precise map of the sensitivity to laser illumination of the master latches of two successive flip-flops (the clock signal is then at logic level 1). We can see the four sensitive zones corresponding to the bit-set and bit-reset patterns characteristic of memory cells. Some points correspond to a bit-flip fault model.

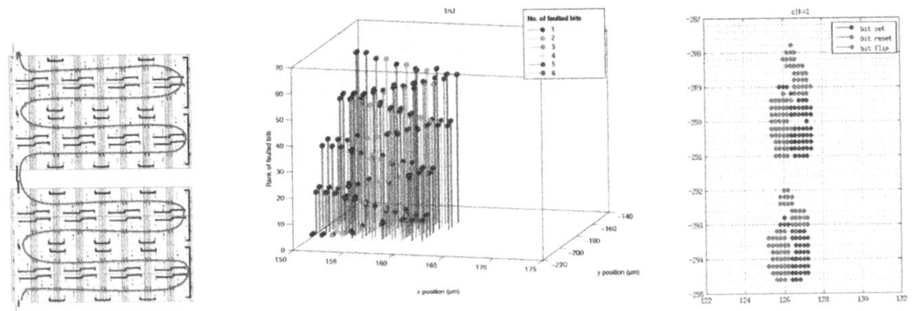

Figure 9.23. *Sensitivity maps for laser fault injection of D flip-flops in 28 nm CMOS technology, layout view of the associated D flip-flop matrix forming a shift register (left); map of the number of bits faulted for a laser shot (center); fault model obtained for the master latch of a D flip-flop (right)*

These results show that laser fault injection retains high accuracy at the 28 nm technology node. This may also be the case for 22 nm or 18 nm CMOS technologies. For higher levels of integration, however, this is not guaranteed.

Laser fault injection in microcontrollers

The ability to inject faults into a microcontroller by EM disturbance was discussed in section 9.1.2.2. Similarly, it is possible to inject faults by laser illumination of a running microcontroller, corrupting the instructions it executes. The description of injected faults requires the use of a high-level model, described in detail with practical examples of laser injection in section 9.1.4.1.

Evolution of laser fault injection techniques

Laser fault injection techniques continue to evolve. Two notable developments make these attacks ever more threatening: the simultaneous use of several laser spots and the appearance of so-called two-photon laser injection benches.

Multi-spot laser injection: laser fault injection is local, so the effect of the disturbance is essentially concentrated at the laser spot (and a few micrometers beyond). The minimum diameter achievable with a x100 lens is of the order of one micrometer. Higher diameters, up to several tens of micrometers, can be obtained with lower-resolution lenses, and possibly by de-focusing the laser beam in relation to the sensitive areas of the transistors (for larger surfaces, the laser power density supplied per unit area becomes too low for a significant effect to be obtained). The ability to disrupt only a few logic gates gives laser injection high spatial precision. This also makes it difficult to detect laser attacks using sensors (they require an attack to be carried out in their area of effect). However, this is also a limitation of laser attacks: they are unable to induce faults simultaneously in distant parts of a circuit.

However, it is possible to use several spots simultaneously to simultaneously fault several parts of a circuit. There are several examples of fault injection into a microcontroller's Flash memory using two and four laser spots. This enables them to simultaneously fault two or four bits when reading a 32-bit word from Flash memory (early laser tests on Flash were limited by their ability to fault only one bit, or also two immediately adjacent bits). This is made possible by the availability of laser benches with this functionality. The various laser beams are injected by means of mirrors into the optical axis and focused on the target through a single lens. The mirrors guiding the insertion of the beams are motorized, enabling them to be moved in the optical field of the lens by adjusting their orientation. This means they are no longer necessarily centered in the lens. The further they are from the optical axis, the greater their deformation, but this has no effect on their ability to inject faults.

Two photon absorption mechanism: laser fault injection relies on the photoelectric effect, which creates charge carriers that generate currents in the sensitive areas being illuminated. Usually, an electron–hole pair is created by the absorption of a single photon with an energy higher than the silicon bandgap. This is why the wavelength of the laser sources used is limited to around 1,064 nm (beyond this, photon energy is below the silicon bandgap and no charge carriers can be created).

However, it is possible to use a higher wavelength, at 1,300 nm, for example, to induce the appearance of fault-causing electron–hole pairs. This is possible provided the photon density is very high (i.e. for high laser power), thanks to a two-photon absorption effect in which the energy required to create an electron–hole pair is provided by absorbing two photons. This technique presents two interesting features for a potential attacker: (1) the laser pulses used are very short (a few tens or hundreds of femtoseconds); and (2) the charges are no longer generated along the entire laser beam but only where the photon density is highest, in a reduced volume at the focal point of the lens. Few studies describe laser fault injection using two-photon absorption, but this technique promises to increase the temporal and spatial precision of laser injection even further.

9.1.2.4. *Other fault injection techniques*

Fault injection techniques are not limited to those described above. Variations include the injection of voltage glitches directly onto the substrate of a target circuit, the use of radiative X-ray sources, or the exploitation of failure mechanisms in DRAM memory (so-called *RowHammer* attacks).

Fault injection using voltage glitches applied to the substrate, BBI

This technique is halfway between voltage glitch and EM disturbance fault injection. It involves applying a voltage glitch to the substrate of the target circuit, with the case of the latter open at the rear. Electrical contact is made with a metal needle, and the voltage glitch is delivered by a voltage pulse generator. These attacks are known as BBI (body biased injection). BBI attacks are characterized by a local effect linked to the position of the injection needle on the substrate in relation to the target's various logic blocks.

Another variant of the voltage glitch attack involves accessing an interconnect between logic gates on the target circuit (for example, using a FIB) and forcing its logic level to an arbitrary value. However, this method is particularly invasive.

Fault injection by X-ray exposure

Recent work has shown that it is possible to expose a circuit to focused X-rays for attack purposes. Semi-permanent stuck-at 1 or 0 faults in SRAM memories have been obtained using a focused X-ray beam (the injected faults are reversible after annealing the target circuit at 150°). The synchrotron beam used has a diameter of the order of a few tens of nanometers (well below the minimum micrometer size achievable with a laser spot). Forcing a Flash memory cell to 0, which causes instruction corruption during the start-up phase of a circuit, enabled the authors of this work to demonstrate the feasibility of attacks using focused X-rays.

Generally speaking, exposing a circuit to radiation can induce faults in its operations. This is the case, for example, with exposure to radiative particles, which can cause logical hazards (or faults). This phenomenon has been exploited using the alpha radiation-emitting radioactive source found in smoke detectors. The radioactivity level of these sources is low, but by placing them on an integrated circuit, it is possible to induce faults. The faults injected into the target are rare, not synchronized with its activity, and randomly affect one or another of its logic blocks. However, certain attacks are still possible, such as the injection of faults into the calculations of the RSA cryptographic algorithm, which are characterized by their long calculation time.

RowHammer fault injection attack

The RowHammer attack is an original attack targeting DRAM memories used as RAM memory by complex circuits (SoCs (*Systems on Chip*)). These memories are characterized by their high writing and reading speed, which explains their adoption in all systems using SoCs or modern micro-processors. They take the form of independent circuits interfaced to SoCs via ultra-fast communication buses. A DRAM memory cell stores information in a capacitor accessible via an access transistor. Their content must be periodically refreshed (every 64 ms for the DDR3 standard), as the capacitors are progressively discharged by leakage currents. DRAM memory cells are organized in the form of lines that can be read and written. When a given line is written repeatedly, adjacent lines are disturbed, causing a slight discharge of their capacitances. This phenomenon can be exploited repeatedly until certain capacities are completely discharged, at which point the logic level of the stored information is corrupted and a fault is injected. This phenomenon of hammering a line (which gives the attack its name) to inject faults into an adjacent line enables complex attacks (such as elevation of privilege) to be mounted remotely via a network connection. This attack exploits a failure mechanism linked to the close proximity of DRAM lines (manufacturers favor maximum memory density to reduce memory costs).

The preceding sections illustrate the wide variety of fault injection techniques and mechanisms. They also illustrate the inventiveness of attackers. New fault injection techniques will probably continue to be proposed in the years to come. Exploiting failure mechanisms (inspired by the RowHammer attack) is one possibility.

9.1.3. *Fault injection benches*

Fault injection attacks are based on disrupting the nominal operating conditions of a target circuit (e.g. its clock frequency, supply voltage or temperature). Faults can also be induced by exposing a circuit to an EM disturbance, or to an energetic light pulse produced by a camera flash or laser source.

Whatever the injection technique used, tests are generally carried out using fault injection benches dedicated to a particular technique. Fault injection can be carried out for attack purposes, but as these are criminal activities, the characteristics of the benches used by the attackers are not public. The practice of fault injection is not confined to attackers, and understanding the associated mechanisms is essential for threat assessment and the design of appropriate countermeasures. Manufacturers of secure circuits, as well as researchers studying injection mechanisms, are called upon to implement these techniques for evaluation purposes. The benches they use are better documented. Their architecture is described in the following sections.

There are also entities specializing in the evaluation and certification of circuit resistance to hardware attacks. They evaluate and certify the fault resistance of secure circuits by testing them on fault injection benches.

9.1.3.1. *General architecture of fault injection benches*

Conducting fault injection experiments requires (1) communicating with the target circuit so that it performs the operations targeted by the attack scenario; and (2) having a disturbance device at its disposal. Thus, a fault injection bench generally comprises the following elements:

– An electronic interface board which provides a communication link with the component under test and enables it to be solicited in relation to the function to be disturbed and to recover the response to fault injection.

– The injector which is the source of the disturbances causing the faults.

– For injection techniques of a local nature, the use of a two-axis translation table enables the effect of the disturbance to be focused on a particular zone of the circuit under test. A third translation axis can be used to move the source of disturbance away from the surface of the component. A visible optical camera shows the precise positioning of the injection means in relation to the component surface. If the injection is made from the rear of the component, a near-infrared optical camera can be used to visualize the positioning of the injection means in relation to the target through the thickness of the silicon.

– A digital oscilloscope to visualize compromising signals from the component under test. These signals, typically the power consumption signal and/or an EM radiation signal, are used for time tracking and to visualize the effect of the applied disturbance. These signals are also used by the synchronization tool described later in this section.

– A PC controlling all the equipment that implements an attack scenario.

Figure 9.24 shows the usual architecture of a fault injection bench made up of these different elements. A wide variety of benches are available using professional equipment or developed by their users at variable cost.

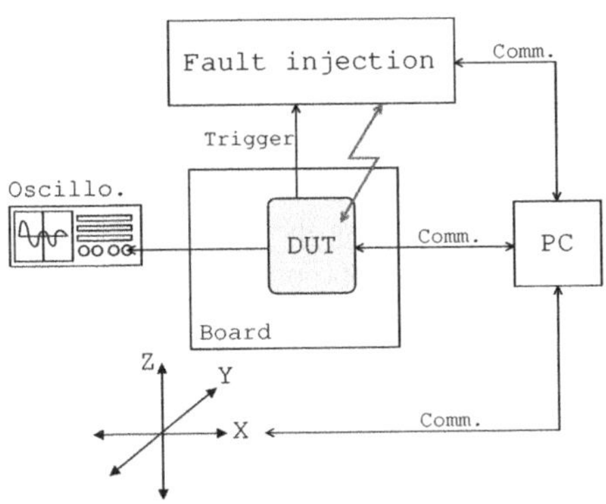

Figure 9.24. *General architecture of a fault injection bench*

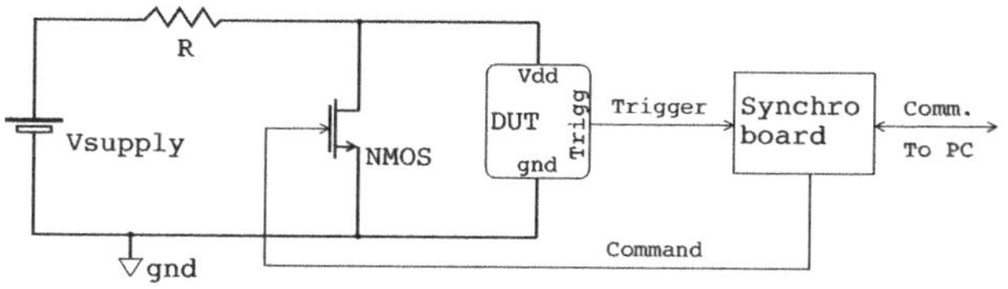

Figure 9.25. *Traditional power glitch generator using a transistor*

9.1.3.2. *Fault injection benches using clock or power supply glitches*

Fault injection by disturbing a circuit's clock or power supply is characterized by a global effect (the disturbance affects the entire target in a similar way). Glitch injection benches therefore do not require the use of XYZ translation tables. With this difference, a voltage or clock glitch fault injection bench uses the architecture shown in Figure 9.24.

For fault injection by clock disturbance, the injection device is responsible for delivering a clock to the circuit under test, including the glitch in the form described in Figure 9.9. Inserting a glitch into a clock's waveform can be done using delay-locked loops, which produce time-shifted images of the nominal clock. These images are then combined by logic gates to create the corrupted clock. All useful logic blocks can be found in FPGA-type programmable circuits.

Fault injection by disrupting the supply voltage of a target circuit can be done with traditional devices costing a few dozen euros (or $), like the one shown in Figure 9.25. An NMOS transistor is placed in parallel with the target supply voltage (marked DUT). When controlled in ON mode by a control and synchronization board (marked `Synchro board`), the supply voltage to the circuit is reduced to zero (a low-value resistor is added in series to prevent a short-circuit of the supply). The command to activate the NMOS is sent by the control board on receipt of a synchronization signal (or trigger) from the circuit under test. The duration of the resulting voltage glitch (from V_{dd} to 0 V) is set by the board. Although it may appear basic, this voltage glitch injection device is effective and can be used, for example, to defeat program memory readback protections on many microcontroller circuits.

More professional fault injection benches use commercially available voltage pulse generators. They offer greater parameter variety and resolution:

– fast reaction times (i.e. minimum delay between trigger reception and glitch emission) in the tens of nanoseconds range;

– very short pulse durations down to the picosecond range;

– ability to deliver positive or negative glitches of configurable amplitude (up to several hundred volts).

Purchase costs vary from several hundred euros to tens of thousands.

9.1.3.3. *Electromagnetic disturbance fault injection bench*

The principles of fault injection by EM disturbance have been described in section 9.1.2.2. Injection units using this mechanism follow the architecture described in Figure 9.24.

Figure 9.26 (right) gives a general view of an EM injection bench consisting of a voltage pulse generator (marked Pulse generator) connected to an EM injection probe. The injection probe is mounted on micrometer-resolution XYZ displacement stages so that its position relative to the target can be precisely adjusted. A synchronization signal (trigger from the target circuit) is used to synchronize the application of the EM disturbance with the activity of the target. An oscilloscope is used to check correct synchronization. A PC is used to control the various bench components.

Figure 9.26. *EM pulse fault injection devices in integrated circuits: principle architecture of EM injection bench (left); injection probe and target circuit (right)*

A close-up view of the target and the EM injection probe is shown in Figure 9.26 (on the right). In this picture, the circuit under test is an FPGA, with the polished rear-side of the silicon die visible below the probe.

The most expensive component of the test bench is the voltage pulse generator, costing just over 20,000 euros. This type of generator can generate positive or negative voltage pulses with an amplitude of several hundred volts. The range of pulse duration settings extends from tens to hundreds of nanoseconds. Pulse edges last a few nanoseconds.

9.1.3.4. *Laser illumination fault injection benches*

The physical effect (photoelectric effect) behind fault injection by laser illumination is described in section 9.1.2.3. The architecture of laser injection benches usually follows the schematic diagram shown in Figure 9.24. An example is shown in Figure 9.27.

Figure 9.27. *Laser fault injection bench*

A target circuit can be seen beneath the lenses used to focus the laser beam. The optical column on which the lenses are mounted is also visible. It contains an infrared camera and the entry points for the laser beams from the laser sources (this bench is capable of illuminating the target circuit with two laser spots from two independent laser sources). The use of a camera is essential for positioning the laser spots on a particular part of the circuit under test (the choice of an infrared wavelength means that this positioning can also be carried out from the rear of the circuit). Two laser sources are visible on the sides of the image (gray and apple green boxes), topped by synchronization cards. Laser pulses are transmitted from the sources to the optical column via fibers. The optical column and objectives are mounted on XYZ translation stages with a resolution of 0.1 μm. All this equipment is mounted on an optical table whose role is to filter vibrations. The whole is contained in a hermetically sealed enclosure to protect users from the risk associated with any reflected laser beam.

The effect of laser illumination is local. Using XYZ stages and the camera, you can carefully select the part of the circuit to be targeted. The use of lenses with variable magnifications enables laser spot sizes to be chosen to suit the desired effect. When characterizing a circuit, initial tests can be carried out by scanning the surface of the target with a wider spot to reduce the exploration time required. Once an area of interest has been identified, smaller spots can be used to make the most of the spatial precision offered by laser injection. Table 9.1 gives the spot sizes at the focus of common objectives, as well as the power transmission coefficient of a laser pulse passing through them.

Objective	Spot size	Transmission coeff.
5x	20 μm	~67%
20x	5 μm	~57%
100x	1 μm	~26%

Table 9.1. *Features of laser focusing lenses*

The minimum achievable diameter for a laser spot is 1 μm due to the laws of optics. At this size, the power from laser sources reaching the target is reduced by almost three-quarters (additional power is dissipated as it passes through the substrate when illuminated from the rear).

Several laser source technologies are commonly used for fault injection. The first benches designed in the early 2000s used YaG laser sources initially intended for cutting semiconductor materials (set at a fraction of their power). Their wavelengths (UV, green and IR) were compatible with the creation of a photoelectric effect, and their high power guaranteed the production of faults. However, they suffered from time limitations: fixed pulse duration (e.g. 5 ns) and reaction times of the order of a few hundred microseconds. Most sources on the market today are built around a laser diode driven by control electronics. They use two principles based either (1) on the creation of a laser pulse by switching the diode ON and OFF to define an adjustable pulse duration; or (2) on the use of a diode emitting a continuous beam into which a pulse is cut by means of an optical switch. The latter approach is illustrated in Figure 9.28.

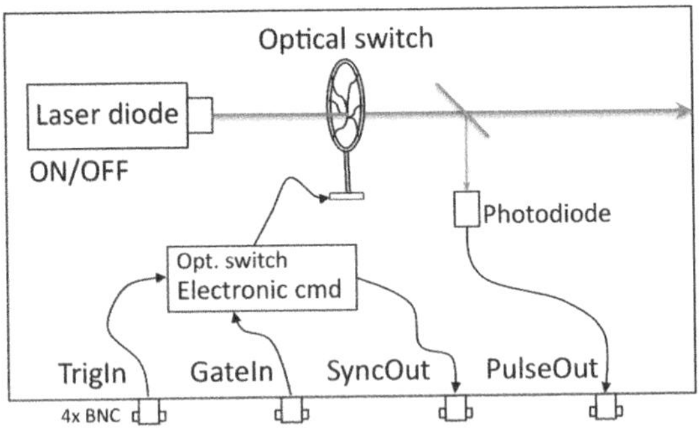

Figure 9.28. *Architecture of a laser source based on diode technology*

The *optical switch* cuts a laser pulse from the continuous beam emitted by a switched-ON laser diode. Control electronics operate the opening and closing of the optical switch. It is this electronics that triggers the opening of the switch on receipt of a control signal (*TrigIn* signal) after a configurable delay. The duration of the laser pulse is defined by the time elapsed before the switch is closed (the minimum pulse duration is defined by its opening and closing times). These laser sources can generate pulses lasting from a few nanoseconds to a second, with a reaction time of less than 200 ns. Their power is generally between 2 W and 3 W.

In the example shown in Figure 9.28, a photodiode captures a fraction of the laser pulse power by means of a semi-reflective plate. The resulting electrical signal, observed on an oscilloscope, provides an image of the laser pulse generated at the source's output, as shown in Figure 9.29.

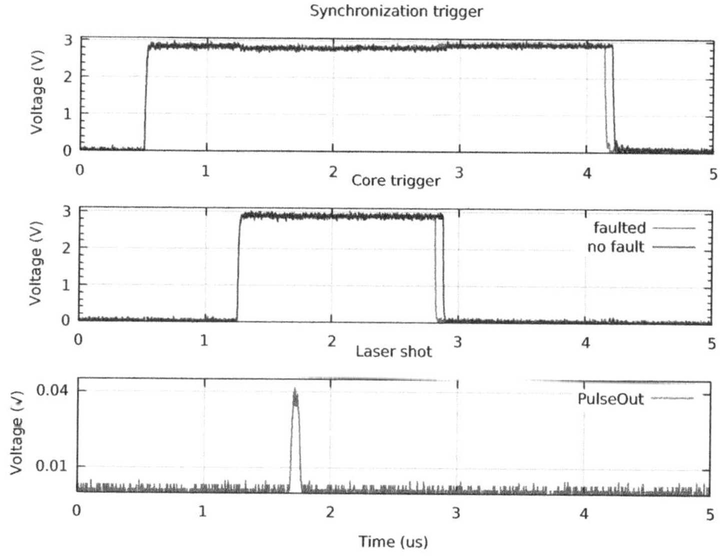

Figure 9.29. *Laser-induced instruction skip in a microcontroller test program, synchronization signals in the presence (red) and absence (blue) of faults, and image signal of the laser pulse*

This example corresponds to the injection of an instruction skip into the test code of a microcontroller (see section 9.1.4.1). The first two signals are triggers (triggered by specific instructions in the test code) used to trigger the laser shot, and to time it. The third signal *PulseOut* gives the image of the laser pulse striking the target. This type of test is typical of circuit characterization, where the operator has control over the program embedded in the target. This makes it easy to synchronize the effects of the laser with the running code.

The cost of commercial laser sources has come a long way in recent years. A diode-technology source capable of generating pulses in the nanosecond range costs around 10,000 euros. A complete bench like the one shown in Figure 9.27 can cost upwards of 150,000 euros.

Optical disturbances are not limited to the use of laser sources. Faults can also be injected by exposing a circuit to camera flashes, as shown in Figure 9.2, or by focusing them through a lens.

9.1.3.5. *Synchronization tools*

In the previous sections, we presented examples of characterization tests in which the synchronization of a disturbance with the activity of the circuit under test was achieved by means of synchronization signals (or triggers) emitted by the target. In the case of an attack, it is unlikely that the attacker will be able to insert the instructions needed to create a trigger into the target's embedded code. An attacker would therefore have to use other synchronization tools to achieve their ends.

This can be achieved by analyzing *compromizing* signals from the target, such as the evolution of its power consumption over time, or its EM emanations. These signals are strongly correlated with the target's electrical activity. They provide a temporal image of the target's electrical activity, which can be used to synchronize an attack (the emission of the disturbance) with a vulnerable part of the code executed by the target. This type of analysis can be likened to a simple power profile analysis technique (also known as SPA (simple power analysis)). This analysis typically uses the consumption signal of the component in question (or an EM radiation signal). It is captured on the oscilloscope by adding a resistor in the component's power supply circuit, across which the potential difference is measured, thus providing a good picture of its power consumption. This is then correlated with its logic activity. Figure 9.30 illustrates this technique by showing the power consumption trace at startup of a microcontroller.

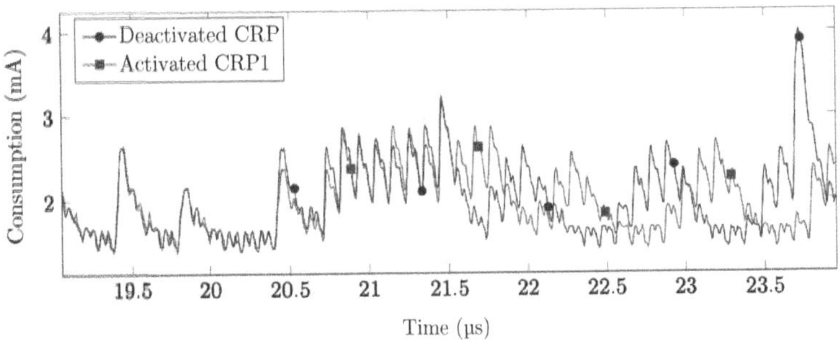

Figure 9.30. *Trace of a microcontroller's power consumption during start-up when the program memory read-back protection (abbreviated CRP) is activated (red) and deactivated (blue) (Courtesy of G. Assael, and C. Gernigon)*

This comprises two traces characterized by patterns linked to the instruction sequences executed by the microcontroller. It is difficult to associate a particular pattern with a given section of code. However, the comparison of traces corresponding to different configurations has enabled the time synchronization of an attack whose aim was to deactivate a protection blocking the readback of the program memory. The blue trace corresponds to the case where the protection (CRP) is deactivated and the red trace to the case where the protection is activated. By superimposing the two curves, we can identify the instant at which they differ, corresponding to the activation of memory protection. By synchronizing voltage glitches around this instant, we can easily deactivate it.

Previous synchronization was relatively easy to set up (time jitter was reduced), as it was performed on a target start-up sequence initiated by a synchronization point common to both traces being compared (the deactivation of a reset signal). Apart from this particular case, an attacker would have to be able to synchronize by analyzing the patterns of the target's consumption trace during code execution (on the fly). This can be achieved with a synchronization tool that captures the consumption trace and analyzes it to identify a particular pattern characteristic of its activity. From this time reference, the synchronization tool's role is to emit a synchronization signal triggering fault injection. This type of tool can be implemented by digitizing the consumption trace and implementing real-time pattern detection in an FPGA circuit, thus minimizing reaction time. In particular, this approach makes it possible to synchronize an attack, even for a target using de-synchronization techniques to randomize the execution of its program code.

A historical example of the use of a synchronization card to detect 12 computing loops in the processing of secret data is shown in Figure 9.34. From these 12 detections, seven light pulses are generated to corrupt access to the secret data.

Synchronization tools therefore play a vital role in fault injection attacks. Without these tools, it is difficult to imagine carrying out relevant attacks on products that are intended to be secure.

9.1.4. *Fault models and fault injection simulation*

9.1.4.1. *The main fault models*

Fault models are used to describe the properties of faults and their effects on a target. Different models are needed to best describe the complexity of the target (e.g. sub-part of a circuit or executed code). They are generally divided into two classes according to their level of abstraction. Low-level models are close to hardware and are well suited to describing fault injection mechanisms at logic gate level (see the modeling of laser fault injection in a SRAM memory described in section 9.1.2.3). The high-level models are close to the software and adapted to describing the effect of faults on the code executed by a microcontroller.

Fault model, definition

The term fault is used when a data item or variable manipulated by an integrated circuit is modified and takes on an erroneous value under the effect of a disturbance. The term error is also used, without any clear distinction.

A *fault model* describes the main characteristics of the fault under consideration. This expression is mainly used to describe:

– the properties of faults injected using a given fault injection technique (e.g. the fault model of laser injection into memory SRAM);

– the conditions to be met for a fault injection attack to succeed. This notion is often used to describe the conditions for successful key extraction attacks on cryptographic algorithms, such as the differential fault attacks discussed in Chapters 10 and 11.

The characteristics of a fault are many and varied; we generally consider:

– The type of fault in the sense of mathematical modeling (discussed in the next paragraph). There is often confusion over the use of the expressions "fault model" and "mathematical modeling" of a fault.

– The location of the fault, such as a given memory address.

– The time of fault injection. Most attacks require precise synchronization of the fault with the target's activity.

– The extent of the fault, for example, the number of bits or bytes faulted in a 32-bit word.

– The duration of the fault. Three categories are distinguished: (1) destructive faults, in the definitive sense, which can no longer be corrected (e.g. the sticking to 1 of a logic gate output created by its damage); (2) permanent faults which are corrected after a reset or shutdown of the affected circuit (this term is often a source of confusion); and (3) transient faults. The effect of the latter is limited in time. Their effect may last for several clock periods, or for a single period (corresponding to the optimum time resolution achievable).

– The probability of occurrence. Not all fault injection attempts are successful. Fault injection success rates of 100% can be achieved by carefully adjusting the injection parameters when good synchronization is ensured. When this is not the case, in the presence of timing jitter, for example, the fault injection rate can drop significantly.

Mathematical fault modeling, logical level

This model allows us to describe faults at the logical level. Consider a variable x (a binary variable consisting of one or more bits) which is subject to a fault according to equation [9.2]. Under the effect of a disturbance (symbolized by $\downarrow$), we obtain a faulty variable $\tilde{x}$.

$$x \xrightarrow{\downarrow} \tilde{x} = x \oplus e(x) \qquad [9.2]$$

$e(x)$ is the error term associated with the fault, such that $e(x) = x \oplus \tilde{x}$. Thus, the faulted variable can be expressed as the result of an exclusive or operation ($\oplus$) between the error term and the non-faulted variable (see equation [9.2]).

Three types of faults are commonly defined at bit level (x now represents one bit) and are presented below.

Bit-flip: this model corresponds to the inversion of the bit value as shown in equation [9.3].

$$x \xrightarrow{\downarrow} \tilde{x} = \bar{x} \qquad [9.3]$$

For a bit-flip, the error term is 1: $e(x) = 1$.

Bit-set: this model corresponds to setting the bit considered to 1, as shown in equation [9.4].

$$x \xrightarrow{\downarrow} \tilde{x} = 1 \qquad [9.4]$$

Its error term is: $e(x) = x \oplus 1 = \bar{x}$. When $x = 1$, the error term of a bit-set is zero. In this case, despite the presence of a disturbance, a fault is not *actually* injected; x remains unchanged.

The bit-set model is said to be data dependent: if the bit is initially set to 1, it is not modified (the target circuit's operations are not modified); if the bit is initially set to 0, it is set to 1 (an error is inserted into the target's calculations).

A data-dependent model makes it possible to extract information from the circuit under attack. If the attacker is certain of respecting this fault model and observes no change in the target's behavior, then the target bit was originally at 1. Conversely, if they observe a change in the target's behavior, they can deduce that the bit was originally at 0. The bit-flip model does not allow this type of direct information extraction.

Bit-reset: this model corresponds to setting the bit considered to 0, as indicated by equation [9.5]:

$$x \xrightarrow{\downarrow} \tilde{x} = 0 \qquad [9.5]$$

Its error term is: $e(x) = x \oplus 0 = x$. The error term of a bi-reset is zero for $x = 0$. In this case, despite the presence of a disturbance, a fault is not *actually* injected; x remains unchanged.

The bit-reset model is also data dependent: if the bit is initially set to 0, it is not modified; if the bit is initially set to 1, it changes to 0.

This model allows an attacker to set up a similar information extraction model to the bit-set model. If the attacker is certain of respecting a bit-reset model and observes no change in the target's behavior, this means that the bit in question was originally at 0. Conversely, if the attacker observes a change in the target's behavior, the attacker can deduce that the bit was originally at 1.

These mathematical fault models can be extended and combined to describe complex fault mechanisms. They are well-suited to describing what we call low-level phenomena, close to the hardware level (for example, logic gates). While they may still be relevant for describing the effect of faults on the scale of circuits, and especially on the execution of embedded code, higher level models are also used.

High abstraction fault model, instruction set architecture

The use of a high-level fault model is useful for studying the effect of faults on the execution of a circuit's embedded code. These models can be used to describe injection mechanisms at the Instruction Set Architecture level (ISA). Three models – instruction corruption, skipping and replay – apply to the assembly code executed by a microcontroller or processor core. They are well suited to describing the effects of injected faults on the binary code of instructions. They are described in the following for the particular case of laser fault injection, which is well suited to their application:

Instruction corruption: this targets the binary code of an instruction, consisting of its identifier (called opcode), its operands (for example, source and destination register numbers for an arithmetic instruction) and any hexadecimal values (called immediate values) representing, for example, an address. Corrupting the code of an instruction can result in the execution of another instruction (when the opcode is faulty), writing to a different register (if the destination register address is faulty), or a jump to an unexpected address (fault injected into an immediate address value). If an attacker has the ability to inject such faults precisely and intentionally, they can carry out highly effective attacks.

It is relatively easy to inject this type of fault into the instructions executed by a microcontroller by aiming a laser at its Flash memory. This is its embedded non-volatile memory, whose role is to store the microcontroller program. By exposing the Flash memory to a laser pulse when the program instructions are read before being executed by the microcontroller core, it is possible to force a bit of the read instruction to 1 (this is a bit-set fault). Note that these are transient faults:

the value stored in memory is not modified. A new execution of the program, in the absence of laser illumination, will not be faulty. In the same way, it is possible to fault data stored in Flash memory when it is read. Figure 9.31 shows an example of this for a 32-bit Cortex M3 microcontroller manufactured in 90 nm CMOS technology. An IR camera view of the circuit is shown on the left (taken from the back of the silicon, the large size of the Flash memory is highlighted by a dotted frame). The right-hand side shows a map of the Flash's laser sensitivity.

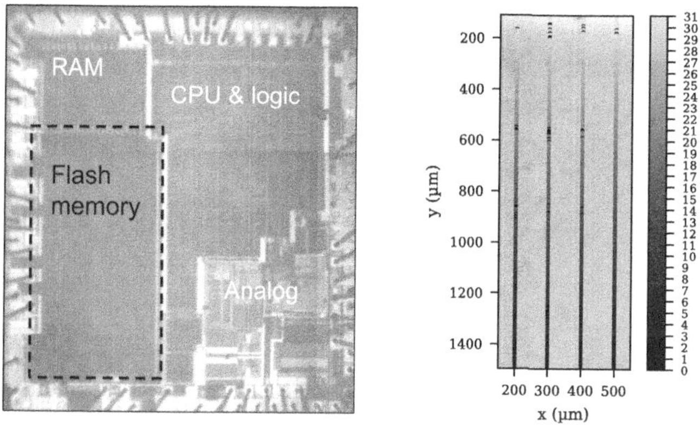

Figure 9.31. *Laser fault injection in instructions and data read from Flash memory by a microcontroller*

Experiments were carried out with a laser source generating IR laser pulses (wavelength 1,064 nm), duration 135 ns and power 1.1 W, via the back of the target. The Flash was scanned from bottom to top in four separate columns. These can be visualized by the color code indicating the index of the bit faulted in a 32-bit word when read. The faults obtained were of the bit-set type. Whatever the column considered, an attacker could choose to fault the bit of their choice by adjusting the position of the laser spot (from index 0 to 31, from bottom to top) with a success rate measured at 100%.

Instruction skip: it is also possible to induce instruction skips in a microcontroller exposed to a laser shot. The execution of its code then proceeds as if one or more instructions had been deleted. There are several mechanisms that can explain this type of fault. It can be obtained by setting all the bits of an instruction to zero, transforming it into an instruction with no effect (or nop instruction, from *no operation*). Another explanation is the corruption of an instruction, transforming it into another instruction with no effect on the program flow (this could also result in a program crash), in which case, everything happens as if the target instruction had not been executed. Finally, it is a fault that can be obtained by corrupting the target program counter (or PC) so that the execution of an instruction is skipped. The term instruction skipping has come into common parlance to describe the various faults that have the effect of blocking the execution of one or more instructions. Depending on the injection parameters, it is possible to skip a single instruction or several successive instructions.

Laser fault injection is well suited to obtaining instruction skips precisely. Figure 9.32 illustrates instruction skipping by laser injection in an 8-bit microcontroller target. The tests were carried out on part of a test code consisting of 10 successive instructions for writing to the target's `r16` to `r25` registers (marked on the ordinate of the graphs to indicate that the corresponding instruction has been skipped), each executing in 125 ns.

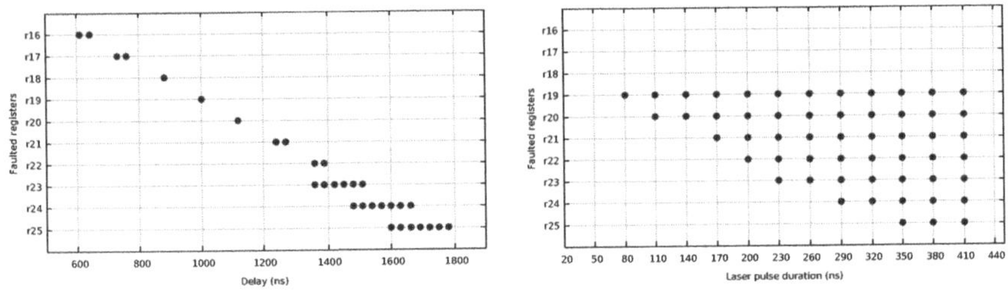

Figure 9.32. *Laser-induced single and multiple instruction skips during microcontroller program execution (rear injection, 1,064 nm, laser power 0.4 W, duration 75 ns and beyond): accurate injection of a single instruction skip (left); control of the number of consecutive instruction skips by controlling the laser pulse duration (right)*

The graph on the left (Figure 9.32) illustrates an attacker's ability to choose to skip a single instruction by precisely controlling the parameters of the laser shot, and in particular, the injection time (marked delay and expressed in ns on the x-axis).

The graph on the right (Figure 9.32) highlights the ability to skip several successive instructions when the laser shot duration (given in ns on the x axis) is progressively increased from 75 to 410 ns: from 1 to 7 instruction skips are obtained.

These results are reproducible, with a success rate of 100%.

Instruction replay: this fault model consists of replaying one or more previously executed instructions in place of a group of instructions of the same size. The latter instructions are then overwritten (not executed). The replay fault model is illustrated in Table 9.2, which gives an example of a section of assembler code made up of eight instructions (unexplained) in unfaulted versions and in the presence of a replay fault affecting instructions 3 and 4. The block made up of these two instructions is then executed twice, their second execution (or replay) overwriting the following instructions 5 and 6, which are not executed.

Unfaulty code	Faulty code
instruction 1	instruction 1
instruction 2	instruction 2
instruction 3	instruction 3
instruction 4	instruction 4
instruction 5	instruction 3
instruction 6	instruction 4
instruction 7	instruction 7
instruction 8	instruction 8

Table 9.2. *Two instruction replay fault model. For a color version of this table, please see www.iste.co.uk/prouff/cryptography1.zip*

The instruction replay fault model is achievable in practice, and Figure 9.33 shows the hotspots on a 32-bit microcontroller, allowing them to be obtained by laser fault injection. The points marked 1–6 extend from the instruction buffer at the output of the Flash memory containing the target's embedded code to the first stages of the core. The locations marked 1 and 3 are used to replay a block of two or four instructions, depending on the cache configuration, whether enabled or disabled (the other points are used to obtain jumps of one, two or four instructions). The number of instructions replayed is linked to the size of the instruction buffers and cache memory.

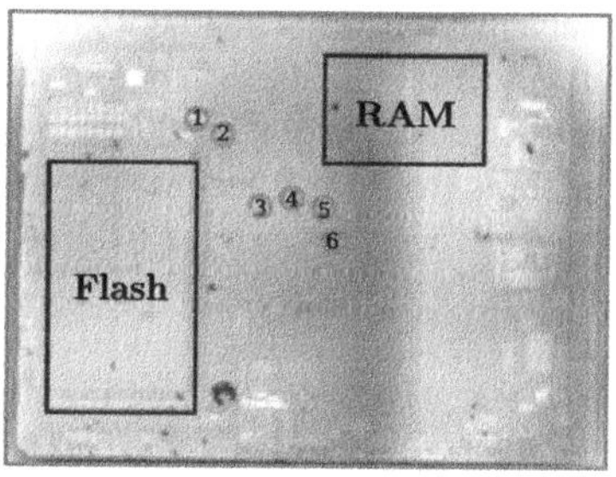

Figure 9.33. *Replay and instruction skips obtained by laser illumination of a microcontroller (infrared view from the rear-side)*

Test inversion: it is also possible to use higher level models that can be used when considering the C code of a program, such as test inversion. As its name suggests, test inversion models the fact that, under the effect of fault injection, the result of a logical test can be inverted (e.g. the execution of `ELSE` instead of `THEN` in a `IF...THEN...ELSE...` structure).

From the above models, it is possible to derive more or less targeted and/or abstract fault models. These fault models can then guide code analysis and the search for vulnerabilities in a sub-tested circuit. However, it should be noted that this fault model approach can sometimes be restrictive, representing only a subset of possible faults.

9.1.4.2. *Fault injection simulation tools*

The use of fault injection simulation tools enables injection mechanisms and attack scenarios to be explored in greater depth. These tools can be used as early as the circuit design phase to search for potential vulnerabilities. They save precious time when designing secure circuits, enabling weaknesses to be corrected before they are even manufactured (and vulnerabilities to be discovered during experimental testing). Fault injection simulation also enables hardware and software countermeasures to be validated at the design stage.

Fault injection can be simulated at different levels of abstraction: from a set of logic gates (hardware level) to the software level.

Simulation-based fault injection at hardware level

Fault injection simulation at hardware level may involve a reduced set of logic gates, in the case of electrical simulation, for example, or a complex logic block (part or all of a circuit), in the case of logic simulation.

Electrical simulation: the use of electrical simulation (such as *Spice*) enables us to explore fault injection mechanisms in transistors and logic gates. Electrical simulation is used to model laser fault injection in SRAM memory cells by inserting current sources representing the photoelectric currents induced by laser illumination of the transistors. This approach benefits from high accuracy in modeling effects, which are considered at the analog level. However, it is limited to circuit parts made up of a small number of logic gates, as it requires significant computing power.

Logic simulation (at RTL level): logic simulation tools using digital circuit modeling based on hardware description languages (such as VHDL or Verilog) enable fault injection via simulation. Unlike electrical simulation, logic simulation is ideally suited to large-scale digital circuits. Faults can be injected during simulation by using the simulation tool's commands (e.g. by forcing the value of a signal to a faulty value) and by following the fault models defined in section 9.1.4.1. The architecture of the circuit's logic gates can also be modified to model the occurrence of a fault when a dedicated signal is activated during simulation (two approaches, developed to study the operational reliability of circuits in the face of errors induced by exposure to radiative phenomena, based on the use of so-called saboteurs or mutants coexist). When the hardware descriptions used can be synthesized, it is possible to implement them in FPGA-programmable circuits, and thus carry out hardware fault injection on the design considered in operation. This approach, known as emulation, makes it possible to multiply tests by varying fault injection parameters in a shorter time than with simulations.

It is possible to combine the electrical and logic simulation approaches using tools from the integrated circuit design flow. One example is to combine the electrical simulation of the effect of a laser shot on a small number of logic gates located in the laser's area of effect with a global logic simulation of all the gates in a processor core. In this way, the effect of laser illumination is modeled with all the precision of electrical simulation on the area of interest, and propagated to the logic operations of a complex circuit through logic simulation.

Simulation-based fault injection at software level

The injection of faults into a microcontroller or processor core can be carried out at software level to analyze their impact on program execution. This approach is also well suited to the evaluation of software countermeasures. Software simulation can be carried out at the level of the assembly code obtained after compilation of the source code, or at the level of the source code itself. Injected faults generally follow the models presented in section 9.1.4.1: instruction skipping, instruction corruption (register content errors, substitution of one instruction by another, etc.), jump address corruption, test inversion, etc.

Assembly code simulation: fault injection by assembly code simulation is sometimes carried out directly on sections of source code written in assembler, for example, by replacing an instruction with a nop instruction (*no operation*) to model an instruction skip. The modified code is then simulated or executed by a microcontroller (emulation) to analyze the effects of the fault. The emulation approach can also be carried out by executing compiled code on a microcontroller using a debugging tool. This enables dynamic analysis of the code under runtime conditions. Various fault injection models can be tested using the tool's commands (insertion of breakpoints, modification of register contents, etc.). Fault emulation at the assembler level is the closest approach to the hardware target that can be used. The CELTIC tool is an example of a tool that enables dynamic analysis of the effect of fault injection at the micro-architecture level of a circuit.

If we consider the simulation of the corruption of a register's contents, the previous approaches require us to run a different simulation for each value of the fault injected. It is therefore impossible to test all the faulty values that a 32-bit register can take on. There are, however, more abstract approaches, such as symbolic execution, where faults can be represented symbolically and propagated as symbols (the propagated fault has no precise value). Coupled with formal analysis tools, this enables safety properties to be verified against the symbolized fault model (this approach enables all possible fault values to be processed in a single simulation). The formal proofs provided then relate to a particular property (e.g. compliance with a maximum number of attempts when entering an identification code) and to the fault model under consideration. Symbolic execution tools include SymPLFIED, which uses a program's assembly code.

Source code level simulation: there are also a number of tools available for analyzing the effects of fault injection at source code level (before the program is compiled) or on an intermediate representation obtained during the compilation phase. Examples include Frama-C and Lazart.

Ensuring the fidelity and representativeness of simulation results

Fault injection simulation can be used to characterize a circuit's vulnerabilities and validate countermeasures, without recourse to time-consuming and costly practical testing. It can also be used in the design phase of a circuit, even before it is manufactured.

However, there is still the question of the fidelity and representativeness of the simulation results. These tools use the fault models defined in 9.1.4.1. However, these models are not exhaustive, and the injection mechanisms on which they are based are still being researched. Other mechanisms may come to light, giving rise to original models not yet taken into account. There are two possible pitfalls in using these tools: (1) not taking into account fault models obtained in practice but not yet identified; and (2) taking into account models that are too complex, or erroneous, highlighting vulnerabilities impossible to obtain in practice (this would result in the addition of useless countermeasures). However, the use of fault simulation tools is an essential step in protecting integrated circuits from attack. They enable designers to correct most vulnerabilities at the earliest possible stage and at the lowest possible cost.

9.2. Practical examples of fault injection attacks

9.2.1. *Introduction*

In this section, we present two concrete examples of fault injection attacks on electronic components. A specific chapter is dedicated to DFA attacks on cryptographic algorithms, and the two attacks chosen here do not fall within this framework.

The first attack is aimed at manipulating a secret key in the DES encryption algorithm. This is a real, long-standing attack on a secure component. It illustrates the anteriority of fault injection attacks.

The second series of attacks presented targets an identification routine using a four-digit secret code (or PIN (*personal identification number*)). This is an example of an attack taken from the FISSC code examples of the SERTIF project. It illustrates the principles of microcontroller attacks using the instruction-skipping model described in section 9.1.4.1. The results can be reproduced on the ChipSHOUTER educational platform.

9.2.2. *1997 light attack on a secure product when loading a DES key*

This section illustrates an attack on a secure smartcard product in the 1990s. This product was evaluated according to the Information Technology Security Evaluation Criteria (ITSEC, the European ancestor of the Common Criteria) at the CNET in Caen in 1997. The tests were carried out by Raphaël Bauduin.

The component reference and application name are not quoted here, as this information would be meaningless. Note that this component and the application it runs have not been in the field for a number of years. The aim here is to show the level of the French certification scheme of the 1990s and to detail a concrete result on a secure product. The modus operandi and results obtained are presented to illustrate the technical level of the first hardware CESTI in the French certification scheme. This scheme was steered by the Service Central de la Sécurité des Systèmes d'Information (SCSSI, of which ANSSI is the successor). The hardware CESTIs of ANSSI have inherited this know-how, which was established at CNET.

Back in 1997, light attacks were already commonplace. In the test presented here, the aim is to discover the key to the DES algorithm used in a certificate calculation function for the application being tested.

The certificate calculation function reads the DES key stored in the smartcard's EEPROM memory in 12 successive 8-bit readings. The special formatting of this key includes four extra bytes in addition to the eight bytes of the DES key used.

A light disturbance applied to the EEPROM can be used to force a byte stored in this memory to be read at a fixed value, usually $0x00$ or $0xFF$. The first step in this test is to check that it is possible to force a byte to be read at a known value. This first step is carried out with a command that allows the application data to be read. The disturbance is performed with a flash lamp such as those shown in Figure 9.2. For this test, it is important that the program flow is not disturbed by the flash of light. As the CPU and RAM are also sensitive to light, it is necessary to mask the entire chip, with the exception of the EEPROM. This masking is done with black paint under binoculars using a fine brush, as shown in Figure 9.1.

The command for reading application data shows that the byte being read takes on the value $0x00$ when light is applied to the EEPROM block, regardless of the initial value. This phenomenon is not destructive: the byte being read resumes its normal value in the absence of the light flash (the value stored in non-volatile EEPROM memory has not been altered).

The next step is to analyze the processing corresponding to key manipulation during certificate calculation. The chip's power consumption signal is used to temporally identify DES key manipulation. The processing that follows the reception of the last byte of the command includes a desynchronized processing zone where 12 processing loops can be observed. These 12 loops are clearly out of sync from one execution to the next. A specific synchronization card is then used to generate 12 peaks corresponding to the 12 processing loops for reading a byte from EEPROM. Figure 9.34 shows the 12 pulses generated by the synchronization card (lower part) by analyzing the power consumption signal of the smartcard component. The variable spacing between these 12 pulses illustrates the desynchronization implemented by this secure code.

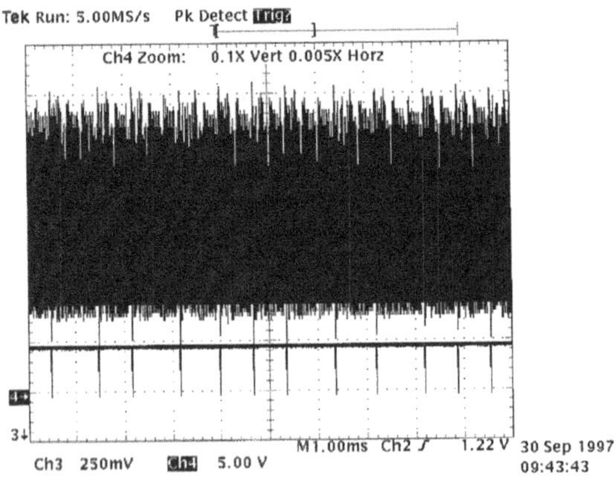

Figure 9.34. *Resynchronization of 12 DES key loading processes*

The next step is to sort out the eight pulses corresponding to the reading of the eight DES key bytes and discard the four application-specific formatting bytes.

The use of light flashes during processing enables the DES key bytes to be distinguished from the formatting bytes. The result of the certificate calculation is output at the end of the command. If a DES key byte is illuminated, the result issued by the command is modified with respect to the normal result issued without the use of the light flash. If a formatting byte is illuminated, the certificate calculation command emits an error code. This makes it possible to find the position of the 8-byte DES key read processing. These DES key reading loops are in positions 2, 3, 4, 6, 7, 8, 10 and 11.

The next step is to synchronize, for example, the first seven flashes with the first seven DES key reading loops. When the certificate calculation command is executed, the key read from EEPROM takes the value $0x00\ 00\ 00\ 00\ 00\ 00\ 00\ XX$. The entire key is set to zero, except for the last byte, which is set to the original but unknown value (noted as XX). The result of the certificate calculation command can then be used to discover this unknown value byte. An exhaustive search of the 128 possible values of this unknown byte is all that is required. As a reminder, a DES key is represented by the 8-byte word, but each byte has a parity bit. One byte therefore stores seven bits of the 56-bit DES key. Figure 9.35 illustrates the seven light pulses applied to the EEPROM memory.

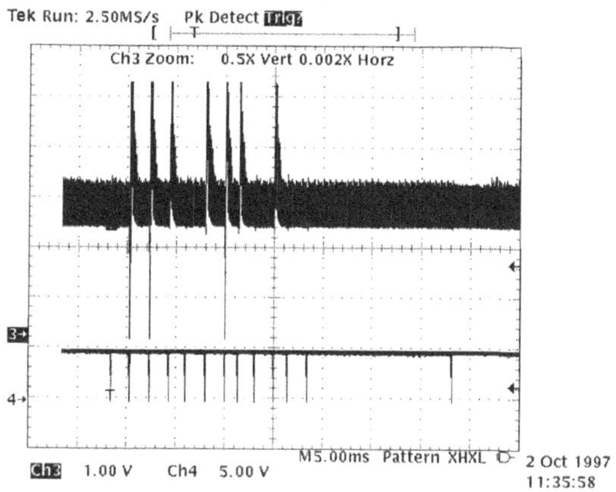

Figure 9.35. *Generation of seven flashes on the 12 DES key loading loops*

This exhaustive search uncovers one byte of the DES key. Then, when the certificate calculation command is run, only the first six flashes are required, and the result is analyzed. The key read in EEPROM lashes are required, and the result is analyzed. The key read in EEPROM $0x00\ 00\ 00\ 00\ 00\ 00\ YY\ XX$. The byte $0xXX$ is now known. An exhaustive search of 128 possible values reveals the byte $0xYY$.

In this way, all the bytes of the key can be obtained by an exhaustive search of 128 possible values.

This attack, carried out in 1997 at the CNET in Caen by Raphaël Bauduin, shows that it is possible to discover the 56 bits of the DES key used by the certificate calculation command of the application being evaluated. Once the experiment has been set up, an experienced person and suitable evaluation laboratory equipment (synchronization card, flash light) can obtain the DES key in less than a quarter of an hour.

9.2.3. *Experimental examples of an attack on a PIN identification routine*

This section describes three practical examples of fault injection attacks on an identification routine using a four-digit secret code (or PIN). These experiments were carried out using laser illumination or EM disturbance following an instruction-skipping model (described in 9.1.4.1). The microcontroller on which the routine was embedded and attacked is an 8-bit ATmega328 microcontroller mounted on an Arduino Uno board. The source code for the identification routine comes from an open source database of examples: the FISCC database (for *Fault Injection and Simulation Secure Collection*). This database offers code examples with different levels of protection against fault attacks for teaching and research purposes. We have chosen a moderately protected version to highlight the potential for instruction skipping attacks.

```
1  // verify PIN function
2  // set g_authenticated to BOOL_TRUE if g_userPIN = g_cardPIN
3  #define BOOL_TRUE 0xAA
4  #define BOOL_FALSE 0x55
5  UBYTE g_userPIN[4];          // user PIN code
6  UBYTE g_cardPIN[4];          // device's PIN code
7  UBYTE g_PINSIZE = 4;         // PIN code size, ie nb of caracters
8  UBYTE g_authenticated;       // TRUE if a valid user PIN is entered; otherwise FALSE
9  volatile int g_ptc = 3;      // max. nb. of tries to enter a correct PIN code
10 ...
11 void verifyPIN()
12 {
13   g_authenticated = BOOL_FALSE;
14
15   if(g_ptc > 0)
16   {
17     if(byteArrayCompare(g_userPIN, g_cardPIN) == BOOL_TRUE)
18     {
19       g_ptc = 3;
20       g_authenticated = BOOL_TRUE; // Authentication
21     }
22     else
23     {
24       g_ptc--;
25     }
26   }
27 }
```

Figure 9.36. *verifyPIN() PIN code verification*

The identification routine is called by the function `verifyPIN()` (shown in Figure 9.36), which in turn calls the function `byteArrayCompare()` in charge of comparing PIN codes (shown in Figure 9.37). Lines 3–9 of `verifyPIN()` list the main variables used (these are global variables with the prefix g_). The Boolean values TRUE and FALSE are encoded on one byte, and are `0xAA` and `0x55`, respectively; so as to require the inversion of all their bits in order to invert them, which constitutes an improbable fault model (a non-secure encoding would consist in encoding the false Boolean value by `0` and the true value by `1` or any other value; it then suffices to fault one bit of the false value to obtain a true Boolean value). The PIN code has a size of four digits set by `g_PINSIZE`. The character string entered for identification is stored in `g_userPIN` and compared with the reference PIN g_cardPIN. If the comparison is successful, superuser rights are activated. This last mode is encoded by the Boolean g_authenticated which changes to the TRUE value when identification is successful. Finally, the variable g_ptc contains the maximum number of consecutive identification errors allowed. It is initialized to 3 to protect the identification routine against brute-force attacks (or exhaustive attacks consisting of testing all PIN values until g_cardPIN is found). When a wrong PIN code is tested, g_ptc is decremented (line 24). If this number reaches 0, it is no longer possible to test a new PIN code, and identification is blocked (see the test on line 15 prior to invoking byteArrayCompare()). After successful identification, g_ptc is reset to 3 (line 19). The variable g_authenticated is initialized to the Boolean value FALSE as soon as verifyPIN() is called (line 13); it changes to TRUE on success. The function verifyPIN() does not compare the PIN codes g_userPIN and g_cardPIN; it delegates this role to the function byteArrayCompare() (see Figure 9.37).

```
// byteArrayCompare function
// compare two UBYTE arrays
// return BOOL_TRUE if identicals

BOOL byteArrayCompare(UBYTE* a1, UBYTE* a2)
{
  int i;

  BOOL auth_status = BOOL_FALSE;
  BOOL diff = BOOL_FALSE;

  for(i = 0; i < g_PINSIZE; i++) {
    if(a1[i] != a2[i]) {
      diff = BOOL_TRUE;
    }
  }

  if(i != g_PINSIZE) {
    countermeasure();
    return BOOL_FALSE;
  }

  if (diff == BOOL_FALSE) {
    auth_status = BOOL_TRUE;
  }
  else {
    auth_status = BOOL_FALSE;
  }

  return auth_status;
}
```

Figure 9.37. *byteArrayCompare() function for comparing user and super-user PIN code strings*

The function byteArrayCompare() uses two Boolean variables to secure the comparison of PIN codes: (1) auth_status the return value of the function indicating the success (or failure) of the identification and (2) diff a variable indicating whether the PIN codes are different (a TRUE value indicates that at least one difference was found during the comparison). auth_status is initialized to FALSE (line 9), changes to TRUE only if PIN codes are identical, then returned (line 30). diff is set to FALSE (line 10), indicating that at this stage no difference has been found between the PIN codes. These are compared one digit after the other in a for loop comprising g_PINSIZE iterations (lines 12–14); each time a difference is detected, a TRUE value is assigned to diff (line 14). The comparison is written in constant-time form, as all four digits are tested to completion even when a difference is found for the first few characters.

In this way, observation of the execution time of the identification routine is constant even in the event of failure, and the attacker obtains no information on the position of the differences. The conditional test on lines 23–28 assigns the value of auth_status according to that of diff: if no difference was found (diff is then FALSE), auth_status takes the Boolean value true (line 24) before being returned (line 30) to the calling function verifyPIN() (respectively, auth_status takes a FALSE value when diff is TRUE, indicating that the PIN codes are different).

These codes feature vulnerabilities studied in the FISCC database. Three fault injection attack scenarios based on the instruction skipping model are illustrated in the following sections.

Attack on the byteArrayCompare() function by electromagnetic interference

The attack presented in this section is based on obtaining a single instruction skip by means of an EM disturbance. It targets the portion of the code responsible for assigning the Boolean value of the variable auth_status within the function byteArrayCompare() located between lines 23 and 28 of the C code shown in Figure 9.37. It consists of forcing auth_status to the Boolean value TRUE, despite the entry of a false PIN code, resulting in the variable diff being set to TRUE (i.e. a difference has been found between the PIN code entered and the reference code g_cardPIN).

As the instruction skipping model applies at assembly level, the vulnerability exploited must be analyzed at the level of the corresponding assembly code shown in Figure 9.38. In this code, the r24 register represents, in turn, the diff variable on line 1, and the auth_status variable on lines 3 and 5 (the instructions corresponding to the return are not shown, as they follow line 5).

If diff is TRUE, the comparison on line 1 (comparing r24 with the Boolean false) is negative, and the branch instruction on line 2 (breq, or *branch if equal*) is not executed. Line 3 is then executed, assigning a FALSE value (0x55) to auth_status (r24). The next instruction on line 4 skips the instruction on line 5 (assigning auth_status to TRUE), which is not executed. The function byteArrayCompare() returns a FALSE value.

```
1 cpi r24, 0x55;
2 breq .+4;
3 ldi r24, 0x55;
4 rjmp .+2;
5 ldi r24, 0xAA
```

Figure 9.38. *Assembly instructions for assigning the Boolean value* `auth_status` *returned by the function* `byteArrayCompare()` *(lines 23–28 of the code given in Figure 9.37)*

This instruction sequence presents a vulnerability: the jump instruction rjmp .+2 on line 4 is replaced by an instruction nop under the effect of an EM disturbance, illustrated in Figure 9.39. This forces execution of the instruction on line 5. The variable auth_status takes the value TRUE (despite the fact that diff is TRUE), so the function byteArrayCompare() returns a Boolean TRUE, which allows switching to super-user mode.

```
1 cpi r24, 0x55;
2 breq .+4;
3 ldi r24, 0x55;
4 nop;
5 ldi r24, 0xAA
```

Figure 9.39. *Instruction skip, corresponding to the replacement of the instruction on line 4 by a* `nop` *instruction, enabling the vulnerability to be activated*

In practice, this is achieved by means of a 200 V pulse with a duration of 100 ns. An attack success rate of 100% is achieved when the time synchronization is fine-tuned.

Attack of the byteArrayCompare() function by multiple laser injection

It is also possible to attack the comparison loop of the byteArrayCompare() function (lines 12–16, Figure 9.37). An attack scenario consists of preventing the variable diff from changing to TRUE by replacing the corresponding instructions (line 14) with a nop instruction (instruction skip). The difficulty of this attack scenario lies in the need to inject four instruction skips consecutively in the four iterations of the comparison loop, with a delay of a few hundred nanoseconds between each injection. Laser fault injection is well suited to these constraints. Figure 9.40 illustrates the realization of this attack. The first signal shown (called *Core trigger*) is a synchronization signal indicating the entry and exit points of the `byteArrayCompare()` function. It illustrates the synchronization of laser shots with code execution (another synchronization signal, not shown, precedes the call to the `verifyPIN()` function and is used to synchronize laser shots). The second waveform (noted as *Laser shot*) gives the temporal position and shape of the four laser pulses (it comes from a photodetector built into the laser source, giving an image of the laser shots according to the principle illustrated by the *PulseOut* signal in Figure 9.28). It was captured during a successful attack. The four laser pulses are spaced 875 ns (the duration of a comparison loop), last 60 ns and have a power of 0.5 W. Once the parameters have been properly adjusted, this attack is reproducible, with a success rate of 100%.

The main difficulty in carrying out this attack lies in obtaining good synchronization. Assuming that the attacker has a fixed synchronization point with which to synchronize the emission of a laser pulse, it is relatively easy to synchronize the four laser pulses, assuming that the attacker has a reference circuit on which to train (i.e. a circuit implementing the same identification functions and for which the PIN code is known). We will start from this assumption. Knowing the PIN code, the attacker can carry out a series of test phases, during which they set the attack parameters (time synchronization and laser source parameters) and periodically reset the number of tests to 3 (by entering the correct PIN code). Synchronization can then be performed in four steps. In the first stage, the attacker selects a PIN code, only the first digit of which is incorrect. They then make a series of attack attempts at different injection times (taking care to reset the trial counter to 3 every two attempts, so as not to block their circuit). When their attack is successful, this means that the time setting corresponds to a jump from the first of the four assignments of `diff` to the TRUE Boolean value. For the second step, they test a code whose first two digits are false and now generates two laser pulses, the first with the synchronization found in step 1. Next, the attacker scans the injection time of the second pulse until it is successfully synchronized with the second loop's assignment of `diff` to TRUE. Then, to synchronize the four pulses with the comparison loops, stages 3 and 4 are iterated in the same way. The parameters obtained can then be used to reproduce the attack on an identical circuit whose PIN code is unknown.

Brute-force attack on the `verifyPIN()` function

The two attacks described above require the attacker to have a non-zero number of trials (`g_ptc` $>$ 0) in order to inject faults into the `byteArrayCompare()` function. This means that the attack will have to succeed in, at most, three attempts. This may seem an unlikely assumption.

When the attacker has exhausted the number of authorized attempts (`g_ptc` $=$ 0), it is no longer possible to test a new PIN code. Access to the `byteArrayCompare()` function is denied by testing code line 15 (`if (g_ ptc > 0)`) of the `verifyPIN()` function (see Figure 9.36). One attack scenario, known as a brute-force attack, consists of forcing the execution of lines 17–25 of `verifyPIN()` using a fault injection attack. This attack can be carried out by EM disturbance, targeting the conditional test of code line 15. In the event of repeated success, the attacker is able to force entry into the `byteArrayCompare()` function, enabling them to test a new PIN each time. An exhaustive test of all possible PIN codes until the correct one is found can then be carried out. This attack also makes it possible to find the code used by the victim, which was not possible with the other attacks.

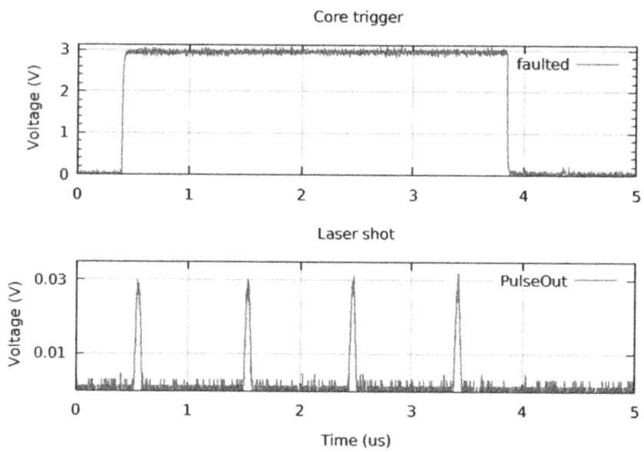

Figure 9.40. *PIN code bypass obtained by four consecutive laser shots (4× 60 ns, 0.5 W, 875 ns interval)*

Figure 9.41 illustrates the success of this attack for an EM injection following the instruction skipping model described above. The left-hand side (Figure 9.41) shows two signals indicating the entry into (change to high level) and exit from (return to low level) the `verifyPIN()` and `byteArrayCompare()` functions (in red and blue, respectively). In this example, the number of trials is exhausted (g_ptc= 0), so the `byteArrayCompare()` function is not called.

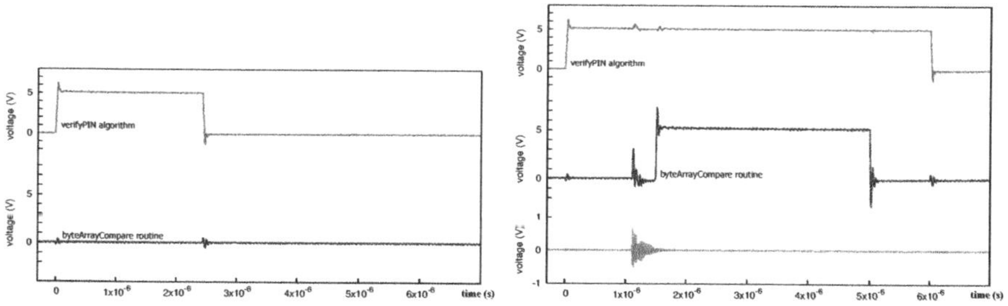

Figure 9.41. *Illustration of a brute-force attack on the PIN verification routine: synchronization signals when the number of attempts is exhausted for* g_ptc= 0 *(left); and when forcing input into the* `byteArrayCompare` *function (right)*

The right-hand side shows an additional signal: an image of the EM disturbance applied to the target (in purple). Under the effect of the induced instruction skip, the function `byteArrayCompare()` is executed, enabling comparison of an additional PIN code with the reference code. A voltage pulse of 200 V for a duration of 100 ns enables the experimental device used to achieve an attack success rate of 100% and to carry out a successful brute-force attack.

9.3. Notes and further references

References to the results and fault injection techniques presented in this chapter are given below.

– Section 9.1. Fault injection attacks: the following references relate to the failure analysis techniques mentioned at the beginning of this section: Habing (1965); Sawyer and Berning (1976); May and Woods (1978); King et al. (1982); Wilson (1984); Johnston (1993); Cole et al. (1994, 1998, 1999). These are the starting point for laser fault injection techniques.

The mechanisms underlying the various fault injection techniques presented are described in the following works: Horstmann et al. (1989); Rabaey et al. (2002); Schmidt and Hutter (2007); Agoyan et al. (2010); Balasch et al. (2011); Dehbaoui et al. (2012); Ordas et al. (2014); Zussa et al. (2014); Tang et al. (2017); Ghodrati et al. (2018); Bozzato et al. (2019); Dumont et al. (2019); Murdock et al. (2020); Dutertre et al. (2021).

Publications Mirbaha (2011); Buchner et al. (2013); Lacruche et al. (2015); Dutertre et al. (2018); Colombier et al. (2019); Dumont et al. (2021); Colombier et al. (2022) more specifically describe fault injection by laser illumination. Meanwhile, some previous studies (Maurine et al. 2012; Kim et al. 2014; Anceau et al. 2017) address less common injection techniques.

Explanations and details of the various fault models reported and their simulation are given in Balasch et al. (2011); Sarafianos et al. (2013); Colombier et al. (2019); Dutertre et al. (2019); Viera et al. (2019); Menu et al. (2020b); Khuat et al. (2021). Simulation tools are described in Pattabiraman et al. (2008); Proy et al. (2017); Laurent et al. (2019); Werner et al. (2020); Lacombe et al. (2021).

– Section 9.2. Practical examples of fault injection attacks: Dureuil et al. (2016); Menu et al. (2020a); Dutertre et al. (2019, 2021) will give the reader a more detailed understanding of the attacks described in this section.

9.4. References

Agoyan, M., Dutertre, J.-M., Naccache, D., Robisson, B., Tria, A. (2010). When clocks fail: On critical paths and clock faults. In *Smart Card Research and Advanced Application, 9th IFIP WG 8.8/11.2 International Conference, CARDIS 2010*. Springer, Heidelberg.

Anceau, S., Bleuet, P., Clédière, J., Maingault, L., luc Rainard, J., Tucoulou, R. (2017). Nanofocused x-ray beam to reprogram secure circuits. In *Cryptographic Hardware and Embedded Systems – CHES 2017*. Springer, Cham.

Balasch, J., Gierlichs, B., Verbauwhede, I. (2011). An in-depth and black-box characterization of the effects of clock glitches on 8-bit MCUs. In *2011 Workshop on Fault Diagnosis and Tolerance in Cryptography (FDTC)*. IEEE, Nara.

Bozzato, C., Focardi, R., Palmarini, F. (2019). Shaping the glitch: Optimizing voltage fault injection attacks. *IACR Transactions on Cryptographic Hardware and Embedded Systems*, 2, 199–224.

Buchner, S., Miller, F., Pouget, V., McMorrow, D. (2013). Pulsed-laser testing for single-event effects investigations. *IEEE Transactions on Nuclear Science*, 60(3), 1852–1875.

Cole, E.I., Soden, J., Rife, J., Barton, D., Henderson, C. (1994). Novel failure analysis techniques using photon probing with a scanning optical microscope. In *1994 IEEE International Reliability Physics Symposium. 32nd Annual Proceedings*. IEEE, New York.

Cole, E.J., Tangyunyong, P., Barton, D. (1998). Backside localization of open and shorted IC interconnections. In *1998 IEEE International Reliability Physics Symposium. 36th Annual Proceedings*. New York.

Cole, E.I., Tangyunyong, P., Benson, D., Barton, D. (1999). TIVA and SEI developments for enhanced front and backside interconnection failure analysis. In *Microelectronics Reliability*. Elsevier Science, Amsterdam.

Colombier, B., Menu, A., Dutertre, J., Moëllic, P., Rigaud, J., Danger, J. (2019). Laser-induced single-bit faults in flash memory: Instructions corruption on a 32-bit microcontroller. In *2019 IEEE International Symposium on Hardware Oriented Security and Trust (HOST)*. McLean.

Colombier, B., Grandamme, P., Vernay, J., Chanavat, É., Bossuet, L., de Laulanié, L., Chassagne, B. (2022). Multi-spot laser fault injection setup: New possibilities for fault injection attacks. In *Smart Card Research and Advanced Applications*, Grosso, V. and Pöppelmann, T. (eds). Springer, Cham.

Dehbaoui, A., Dutertre, J.-M., Robisson, B., Tria, A. (2012). Electromagnetic transient faults injection on a hardware and a software implementations of AES. In *2012 Workshop on Fault Diagnosis and Tolerance in Cryptography*. IEEE, Leuven.

Dumont, M., Maurine, P., Lisart, M. (2019). Electromagnetic fault injection: How faults occur. In *2019 Workshop on Fault Diagnosis and Tolerance in Cryptography (FDTC)*. IEEE, Atlanta.

Dumont, M., Moëllic, P.-A., Viera, R., Dutertre, J.-M., Bernhard, R. (2021). An overview of laser injection against embedded neural network models. In *2021 IEEE 7th World Forum on Internet of Things (WF-IoT)*. New Orleans.

Dureuil, L., Petiot, G., Potet, M.-L., Le, T.-H., Crohen, A., de Choudens, P. (2016). FISSC: A fault injection and simulation secure collection. In *International Conference on Computer Safety, Reliability, and Security*, Skavhaug, A., Guiochet, J., Bitsch, F. (eds). Springer, Trondheim.

Dutertre, J.-M., Mirbaha, A.-P., Naccache, D., Ribotta, A.-L., Tria, A., Vaschalde, T. (2012). Fault round modification analysis of the advanced encryption standard. In *2012 IEEE International Symposium on Hardware-Oriented Security and Trust, HOST 2012*, June 3–4, San Francisco.

Dutertre, J.-M., Beroulle, V., Candelier, P., De Castro, S., Faber, L.-B., Flottes, M.-L., Gendrier, P., Hély, D., Leveugle, R., Maistri, P. et al. (2018). Laser fault injection at the CMOS 28 nm technology node: An analysis of the fault model. In *2018 Workshop on Fault Diagnosis and Tolerance in Cryptography (FDTC)*. IEEE, Amsterdam.

Dutertre, J.-M., Riom, T., Potin, O., Rigaud, J.-B. (2019). Experimental analysis of the laser-induced instruction skip fault model. In *The 24th Nordic Conference on Secure IT Systems, Nordsec 2019*, Askarov, A., Hansen, R.R., Rafnsson, W. (eds). Springer, Cham.

Dutertre, J.-M., Menu, A., Potin, O., Rigaud, J.-B., Danger, J.-L. (2021). Experimental analysis of the electromagnetic instruction skip fault model and consequences for software countermeasures. *Microelectronics Reliability*, 121, 114133.

Endo, S., Sugawara, T., Homma, N., Aoki, T., Satoh, A. (2011). An on-chip glitchy-clock generator for testing fault injection attacks. *Journal of Cryptographic Engineering*, 1(4), 265–270.

Ghodrati, M., Yuce, B., Gujar, S., Deshpande, C., Nazhandali, L., Schaumont, P. (2018). Inducing local timing fault through EM injection. In *2018 55th ACM/ESDA/IEEE Design Automation Conference (DAC)*. IEEE, San Francisco.

Habing, D. (1965). The use of lasers to simulate radiation-induced transients in semiconductor devices and circuits, *IEEE Transactions on Nuclear Science*, 12(5), 91–100.

Horstmann, J.U., Eichel, H.W., Coates, R.L. (1989). Metastability behavior of CMOS ASIC flip-flops in theory and test. *IEEE Journal of Solid-State Circuits*, 24(1), 146–157.

Johnston, A. (1993). Charge generation and collection in p-n junctions excited with pulsed infrared lasers. *IEEE Transactions on Nuclear Science*, 40(6), 1694–1702.

Khuat, V., Danger, J., Dutertre, J.-M. (2021). Laser fault injection in a 32-bit microcontroller: From the flash interface to the execution pipeline. In *2021 Workshop on Fault Detection and Tolerance in Cryptography (FDTC)*. IEEE, Milan.

Kim, Y., Daly, R., Kim, J., Fallin, C., Lee, J.H., Lee, D., Wilkerson, C., Lai, K., Mutlu, O. (2014). Flipping bits in memory without accessing them: An experimental study of DRAM disturbance errors. *SIGARCH Comput. Archit. News*, 42(3), 361–372.

King, E.E., Ahlport, B., Tettemer, G., Mulker, K., Linderman, P. (1982). Transient radiation screening of silicon devices using backside laser irradiation. *IEEE Transactions on Nuclear Science*, 29(6), 1809–1815.

Kocher, P., Jaffe, J., Jun, B. (1999). Differential power analysis. In *Advances in Cryptology – CRYPTO'99*. Springer, Heidelberg.

Lacombe, G., Feliot, D., Boespflug, E., Potet, M.-L. (2021). Combining static analysis and dynamic symbolic execution in a toolchain to detect fault injection vulnerabilities. In *Proofs Workshop (Security Proofs for Embedded Systems)*. ArXiv, Beijing [Online]. Available at: https://hal-cea.archives-ouvertes.fr/cea-03499614.

Lacruche, M., Borrel, N., Champeix, C., Roscian, C., Sarafianos, A., Rigaud, J.-B., Dutertre, J.-M., Kussener, E. (2015). Laser fault injection into sram cells: Picosecond versus nanosecond pulses. In *2015 IEEE 21st International On-Line Testing Symposium (IOLTS)*. Halkidiki.

Laurent, J., Deleuze, C., Beroulle, V., Pebay-Peyroula, F. (2019). Analyzing software security against complex fault models with frama-c value analysis. In *2019 Workshop on Fault Diagnosis and Tolerance in Cryptography (FDTC)*. IEEE, Atlanta.

Maurine, P., Tobich, K., Ordas, T., Liardet, P.Y. (2012). Yet another fault injection technique: By forward body biasing injection. In *YACC'2012: Yet Another Conference on Cryptography*. HAL, Porquerolles Island.

May, T.C. and Woods, M.H. (1978). A new physical mechanism for soft errors in dynamic memories. In *16th International Reliability Physics Symposium*. IEEE, San Diego.

Menu, A., Dutertre, J.-M., Potin, O., Rigaud, J.-B., Danger, J.-L. (2020a). Experimental analysis of the electromagnetic instruction skip fault model. In *2020 15th IEEE International Conference on Design Technology of Integrated Systems In Nanoscale Era (DTIS)*, Marrakech.

Menu, A., Dutertre, J.-M., Rigaud, J.-B., Colombier, B., Moellic, P.-A., Danger, J.-L. (2020b). Single-bit laser fault model in nor flash memories: Analysis and exploitation. In *2020 Workshop on Fault Detection and Tolerance in Cryptography (FDTC)*. IEEE, Milan.

Mirbaha, A.-P. (2011). Study of the vulnerability of cryptographic circuits by laser fault injection. Thesis, Ecole Nationale Supérieure des Mines de Saint-Etienne.

Murdock, K., Oswald, D., Garcia, F.D., Van Bulck, J., Gruss, D., Piessens, F. (2020). Plundervolt: Software-based fault injection attacks against Intel SGX. In *Proceedings of the 41st IEEE Symposium on Security and Privacy (S&P'20)*, San Francisco.

Ordas, S., Guillaume-Sage, L., Tobich, K., Dutertre, J.-M., Maurine, P. (2014). Evidence of a larger em-induced fault model. In *13th Smart Card Research and Advanced Application Conference*. Springer, Cham.

Pattabiraman, K., Nakka, N., Kalbarczyk, Z., Iyer, R. (2008). SymPLFIED: Symbolic program-level fault injection and error detection framework. In *2008 IEEE International Conference on Dependable Systems and Networks With FTCS and DCC (DSN)*. Anchorage.

Proy, J., Heydemann, K., Berzati, A., Cohen, A. (2017). Compiler-assisted loop hardening against fault attacks. *ACM Trans. Archit. Code Optim.*, 14(4), 1–25.

Rabaey, J., Chandrakasan, A., Nikolic, B. (2002). *Digital Integrated Circuits*, 2nd edition. Prentice Hall, Hoboken.

Sarafianos, A., Roscian, C., Dutertre, J.-M., Lisart, M., Tria, A. (2013). Electrical modeling of the photoelectric effect induced by a pulsed laser applied to an SRAM cell. *Microelectronics Reliability*, 53(9–11), 1300–1305.

Sawyer, D. and Berning, D. (1976). Laser scanning of MOS IC's reveals internal logic states nondestructively. *Proc. IEEE (Lett.)*, 64, 393–394.

Schmidt, J.-M. and Hutter, M. (2007). Optical and EM fault-attacks on CRT-based RSA: Concrete results. In *Proceedings of the 15th Austrian Workhop on Microelectronics*. Verlag der Technischen Universität Graz, Graz.

Tang, A., Sethumadhavan, S., Stolfo, S. (2017). CLKSCREW: Exposing the perils of security-oblivious energy management. In *26th USENIX Security Symposium (USENIX Security 17)*. USENIX Association, Vancouver.

Viera, R.A.C., Maurine, P., Dutertre, J.-M., Bastos, R.P. (2019). Simulation and experimental demonstration of the importance of IR-drops during laser fault-injection. *IEEE Transactions on Computer-Aided Design of Integrated Circuits and Systems*, 39(6), 1231–1244.

Werner, V., Maingault, L., Potet, M. (2020). An end-to-end approach for multi-fault attack vulnerability assessment. In *2020 Workshop on Fault Detection and Tolerance in Cryptography (FDTC)*. IEEE, Milan.

Wilson, T. (1984). *Theory and Practice of Scanning Optical Microscopy*. Academic Press, London.

Zussa, L., Dutertre, J.-M., Clédiere, J., Robisson, B. (2014). Analysis of the fault injection mechanism related to negative and positive power supply glitches using an on-chip voltmeter. In *2014 IEEE International Symposium on Hardware-Oriented Security and Trust (HOST)*, Arlington.

10

Fault Attacks on Symmetric Cryptography

Debdeep MUKHOPADHYAY and Sayandeep SAHA
Indian Institute of Technology, Kharagpur, India

10.1. Introduction

Over the years, fault attacks (FA) have established themselves as one of the most potent classes of physical attacks. While their applicability is not limited to any specific class of security system,[1] FAs are especially popular in the context of block ciphers – the most widespread symmetric-key primitive. In this chapter, we shed light on the state-of-the-art block cipher FA. The aim will be to introduce the existing tools and techniques in this regard with the help of some notable examples.

Generally speaking, FAs exploit the fact that a faulty response of a cipher violates certain underlying security assumptions and properties, eventually resulting in key recovery. While this is indeed true in a block cipher context, what makes the block cipher FAs distinct from public key FAs is that in the former case, we try to create certain observable mathematical or statistical patterns (typically non-uniform/statistically biased) within the internal cipher states with faults. Block cipher states are otherwise random-looking, but such patterns eventually reduce the entropy of the faulty states and, thereby, of the key. The generation of the aforementioned patterns

1 In fact, they are not limited to cryptography only and can be applied as a general denial-of-service tool, for example, for deep neural networks.

Embedded Cryptography 1,
coordinated by Emmanuel PROUFF, Guénaël RENAULT,
Matthieu RIVAIN and Colin O'FLYNN.

can be realized in several different ways, giving rise to a diverse class of FA methodologies. In this chapter, we shall cover these methodologies according to the chronology. Another major component of FA research is countermeasure design, which we shall briefly touch on here, mainly for the sake of explaining some attacks on protected implementations. We shall also document some very recent advancements in automation and information leakage assessment tests for FAs.

10.2. Differential fault analysis

The seminal work of Biham and Shamir introduced the FAs in the symmetric-key context. The attack resembles differential cryptanalysis (DC) and, therefore, is named differential fault analysis (DFA). The main idea is to introduce a difference in the penultimate round of the data encryption standard (DES) block cipher, with the help of a fault. The XOR differential between the correct and the faulty state creates the differential pattern, which is propagated and exploited in a similar manner as DC. However, there are several fundamental differences between these two paradigms. First, differentials in DFA are created by faults and usually have short trails compared to differential cryptanalysis. Also, because of the randomness in the fault, the introduced differential is not chosen by the attacker. Finally, the differential propagation is deterministic in the sense that mostly the patterns occurring with probability 1 are used for FAs.

The nature of the faults, often called *fault models*, plays the most crucial role in any fault attack. Therefore, before presenting any of the attacks, in the next section, we will briefly introduce the fault models utilized in a DFA context. We should note that many of these fault models (with few extra properties) are also relevant for advanced FA, which will be described later in this chapter. Even before describing the fault models, we present a short overview of block cipher structures, which will put our further discussions in proper context.

10.2.1. *Block ciphers and fault models*

10.2.1.1. *Block ciphers*

Mathematically, block ciphers are tuples of two functions $\langle \mathcal{E}_k, \mathcal{D}_k \rangle$. $\mathcal{E}_k : \mathcal{P} \times \mathcal{K} \rightarrow \mathcal{C}$ is the encryption algorithm, which maps elements from the plaintext space $\mathcal{P} = \{0,1\}^n$ to the ciphertext space $\mathcal{C} = \{0,1\}^n$ with the help of keys from $\mathcal{K} = \{0,1\}^{k_s}$. $\mathcal{D}_k$ is the decryption algorithm that performs the inverse of the encryption operation. For a fixed key k, both $\mathcal{E}_k$ and $\mathcal{D}_k$ realize permutations over the input space. Also, without the knowledge of the key, it is hard to decrypt (respectively, encrypt) correctly.

Like most other attacks on primitives, the goal of FA is also to recover the secret key of the block cipher. The adversary model varies depending on the target application. For example, an adversary may have access to both plaintext and ciphertexts in many scenarios. The capability of repeatedly encrypting the same plaintext is also assumed in certain cases. On the other hand, certain attacks assume zero access to plaintexts/ciphertexts. Being a physical attack, however, the adversarial capability also depends upon the type of physical channel, which is the fault model in this case. We shall further discuss the fault model in the subsequent paragraphs of this section. Before that, we would like to provide a general description of the state-of-the-art block cipher structures. Modern block ciphers are iterative, which repeat the same (128/64-bit) bijective Boolean mapping several times (called *rounds* of a block cipher). Each round consists of linear and nonlinear Boolean mappings, where the nonlinear mappings are realized by the parallel composition of small (typically 3×3 to 8×8), specially crafted functions called *S-Boxes*. Linear layers can be realized in several ways. The most popular option is the multiplication of the cipher state with a maximum distance separable code (MDS) matrix or a bit/byte-wise permutation. Each round also involves a (128/64-bit) round-key addition step. The round keys are generated from a master secret key through a *key-schedule*.

A variety of round structures have been proposed over the years to realize block ciphers. The most popular among them are the Feistel and SPN structures. While both of them are equally popular (as well as equally susceptible to FAs), in this chapter, we shall mainly use SPN ciphers, mainly due to the fact that the AES algorithm belongs to this class.

10.2.1.2. *Fault models*

A standard practice in any engineering discipline is to capture physical events through mathematical models. Being an interdisciplinary topic between mathematics and semiconductor engineering, FAs are no exception. The only physical factor here is the fault, and it is captured in the mathematical framework of FAs via fault models. However, cryptographic faults are somewhat distinct from other fault models considered in semiconductor and very large scale integration (VLSI) engineering. Below, we briefly discuss the properties of cryptographic faults.

10.2.1.2.1. Fault timing

Classically, the faults utilized in FA are transient in nature. They occur at some specific clock cycle and then disappear, leaving traces in the subsequent cipher computation. We may wonder how we can practically realize such faults. Fortunately, such transient faults are practically easy to realize. The best means of performing timely fault injections is to synchronize the injection with the clock running in the encryption device. Typically, hardware implementations perform one to two rounds in a single clock cycle, so targeting a specific round is not difficult with proper synchronization. For software implementations, it becomes easier as computing a round takes several clock cycles, allowing more targeted injections at intermediate points.

10.2.1.2.2. Fault width

Apart from the fault timing, another major property of a fault model is the width of the fault. In general, FAs exploit those faults which affect only a part of some intermediate state of a block cipher. Traditionally, single-byte faults have gained the most attention from the community. This is because they are easy to generate, even with low-cost fault injection setups. However, other models are also practical. Bit-faults are extremely effective in some recently proposed FAs. Targeted bit-flips are practical to realize with modern laser/electromagnetic (EM) pulse-based FA setups, both for hardware and software targets. With precise profiling, we may also realize certain other variations of these fault models, such as nibble/multi-byte faults. They have been found effective against several constructions. Finally, there are certain platform-specific fault models, such as instruction-skip/modify, where some instruction in a microprocessor gets skipped or modified during execution under the influence of a fault. Such instruction-level faults are very general in the sense that they can be utilized to realize faults of different widths and types for software targets.

10.2.1.2.3. Fault distributions

The probability distribution of an injected fault (or the corrupted state after fault injection) is another crucial factor in FAs. Classically, for DFA attacks, we assume the fault to be uniformly random. While this assumption is sufficient for DFAs, it is not the only practical fault distribution that we see in practice. Rather, most of the fault distributions (i.e. probability distributions of faults/corrupted states) are statistically non-uniform (usually called *biased*). In this section, however, we shall focus on DFAs and continue with fault models having uniformly random fault distributions. The biased fault models will be considered for advanced attacks[2].

IMPORTANT. As already pointed out, fault models are logical abstractions of physical events that happen within a device under some external stimulus. For FAs in a cryptographic context, such external stimuli are realized by means of clock/voltage glitches, EM pulses or laser emission. A detailed discussion on such injection mechanisms is out of scope for this chapter, but we may gain some idea from the previous chapters describing the practical aspects. However, it is important to understand that the fault model and the accuracy vary with the injection mechanism. Low-precision mechanisms, such as voltage/clock glitching, usually result in random byte/bit faults with relatively low repeatability and controllability. The laser/EM-induced faults sit at the other end of the spectrum; these are precise enough to flip targeted bits with almost 100% repeatability. While the aforementioned techniques are mostly aimed toward embedded systems, there

2 We note that bias in a fault distribution is independent of the fault width/timing and can be considered as an extra property that becomes useful for certain attacks.

are also techniques enabling remote fault injection for high-end server machines. Most of these techniques exploit the software-controlled voltage/ frequency scaling mechanisms present in modern high-end processors and GPUs. Finally, there is the RowHammer DRAM bug, which has been utilized to generate bit-flip memory faults in several attacks. It is worth mentioning that injection techniques are improving continuously, and several injection setups are commercially available. Interested readers may refer to the further references section at the end of this chapter to find the respective references in this regard.

10.2.2. *DFA on AES: single-byte fault*

10.2.2.1. *AES: an overview*

With a general understanding of the fault models, we are now ready to describe the DFA attacks on block ciphers. Without loss of generality, we choose AES as our target cipher. More precisely, we shall only concentrate on the 128-bit version of this cipher. AES-128 is an SPN construction with a 128-bit state and 128-bit round keys. The byte-wise organizations of the AES state and round key are presented in equation [10.1]. Each of the bytes represents an element in the finite field $GF(2^8)$ with the irreducible polynomial $x^8 + x^4 + x^3 + x + 1$ ($+$ denote XOR operation).

$$S = \begin{bmatrix} a_{0,0} & a_{0,1} & a_{0,2} & a_{0,3} \\ a_{1,0} & a_{1,1} & a_{1,2} & a_{1,3} \\ a_{2,0} & a_{2,1} & a_{2,2} & a_{2,3} \\ a_{3,0} & a_{3,1} & a_{3,2} & a_{3,3} \end{bmatrix} \qquad k = \begin{bmatrix} k_{0,0} & k_{0,1} & k_{0,2} & k_{0,3} \\ k_{1,0} & k_{1,1} & k_{1,2} & k_{1,3} \\ k_{2,0} & k_{2,1} & k_{2,2} & k_{2,3} \\ k_{3,0} & k_{3,1} & k_{3,2} & k_{3,3} \end{bmatrix} \qquad [10.1]$$

The cipher has 10 iterative rounds, with the last round differing slightly from the first nine rounds. Each round consists of four Boolean mappings, also called *sub-operations*. The first one is the `SubBytes` sub-operation, which is the only nonlinear mapping in the AES round structure. A total of 16 (one for each byte) S-Box operations are performed in this step. Each S-Box operation consists of a finite field inverse followed by a bit-wise affine transform. The next sub-operation is called `ShiftRows`, which performs a byte-wise left circular shift for each row of the state. The third sub-operation is called `MixColumns`, which multiplies the entire state with a maximum-distance separable (MDS) code matrix. Finally, a round key is XOR-ed with the state in the final sub-operation, called `AddRoundKey`. The final round does not perform the `MixColumns`.

10.2.2.2. *The attack*

Let us now consider a scenario where the adversary injects a byte-fault at the beginning of the eighth-round computation of AES. Without loss of generality, we assume the fault to be injected at the 0th byte (see Figure 10.1). However, injection at other bytes also yields similar results. Furthermore, it is considered that the adversary can encrypt the same plaintext at least twice with the fault injected at one of the encryptions. Next, the propagation path of the fault through the cipher computation is considered. The fault propagation is manifested by considering the XOR differential between the correct and faulty computation states (also called *state differential*). The XOR difference at the injection point is denoted as f, as shown in Figure 10.1.

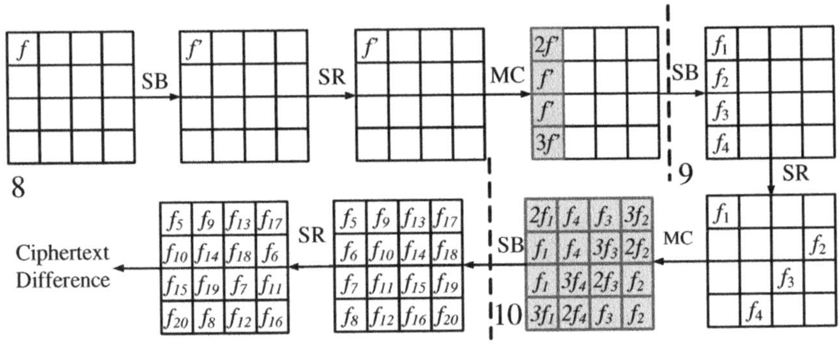

Figure 10.1. *Fault propagation path in AES for a byte fault injection in eighth-round input*[3]*. For a color version of this figure, see www.iste.co.uk/prouff/cryptography1.zip*

As it can be observed from Figure 10.1, the MixColumns matrix creates a 4-byte output state differential (i.e. a fault pattern) $(2f^{'}, f^{'}, f^{'}, 3f^{'})$ at the output of eighth-round MixColumns (state number 4 from the beginning in the figure) sub-operation, where $f^{'}$ is the output state differential after the S-Box sub-operation. Further diffusion results in similar linear patterns at the output of the MixColumns at ninth round. With such fault propagation, we can construct the following equations involving the ciphertext and last round key variables:

$$\begin{aligned} 2f_1 &= SBOX^{-1}(C_{0,0} + k_{0,0}^{10}) + SBOX^{-1}(C_{0,0}^{*} + k_{0,0}^{10}) \\ f_1 &= SBOX^{-1}(C_{1,3} + k_{1,3}^{10}) + SBOX^{-1}(C_{1,3}^{*} + k_{1,3}^{10}) \\ f_1 &= SBOX^{-1}(C_{2,2} + k_{2,2}^{10}) + SBOX^{-1}(C_{2,2}^{*} + k_{2,2}^{10}) \\ 3f_1 &= SBOX^{-1}(C_{3,1} + k_{3,1}^{10}) + SBOX^{-1}(C_{3,1}^{*} + k_{3,1}^{10}) \end{aligned} \qquad [10.2]$$

3 Recreated from the paper: Saha, S. et al. (2018).

Here, $(2f_1, f_1, f_1, 3f_1)$ is the first column of the state differential (third state from the end in the figure) at the output of the MixColumns at ninth round, $k_{i,j}^{10}$ denote bytes of the last round key, and $C_{i,j}$ and $C_{i,j}^*$ denote the correct and faulty ciphertext bytes, respectively. Similar equations can be written for other columns of this state differential as well. The equation system corresponding to a column involves four bytes (32 bits) of the last round key. The next step is to solve these systems, which will obviously have several solutions. However, the interesting fact is that the total number of solutions for the secret key is significantly lower than the total number of key possibilities (which is 2^{128}). Let us count the number of solutions for this equation system. If we consider the equations corresponding to a single column (i.e. equation [10.2]), we may observe that total 5-bytes are unknown in this equation system – namely, $(k_{0,0}^{10}, k_{1,3}^{10}, k_{2,2}^{10}, k_{3,1}^{10})$ and f_1. Furthermore, each equation in equation [10.2] has one solution for a given f_1, on average. Therefore, this system with five unknowns and four equations will have total $(2^8)^{5-4} = 2^8$ solutions. In other words, the total possible choices for $(k_{0,0}^{10}, k_{1,3}^{10}, k_{2,2}^{10}, k_{3,1}^{10})$ reduces from 2^{32} to 2^8 after solving this system of equations. Similarly, we can solve three other systems of equations corresponding to the rest of columns of the state differential and reduce the corresponding keyspaces. Overall, this step reduces the keyspace from 2^{128} to $(2^8)^4 = 2^{32}$. In a nutshell, one fault reduces the candidate keyspace from 2^{128} to 2^{32}, which makes key recovery a simple task with exhaustive enumeration.

In the next step, the number of key choices can be reduced further by utilizing the state differential at the end of the eighth-round MixColumns. One key feature utilized in this second step of the attack is that the key schedule of AES is invertible, and the ninth-round keys can be represented using the 10th round keys. Hence, we can utilize the 2^{32} key choices from the first step of the attack and eventually reduce the keyspace to 2^8 by constructing equations similar to the previous step. Overall, this attack requires a single fault injection to reduce the keyspace of AES from 2^{128} to 2^8, which can be searched exhaustively in a few seconds, we even with a standard desktop computer. While this attack is the most efficient one for AES to date, several other variants of this attack are feasible. One observation in this attack is that at least 2^8 key candidates remain, even after the completion of the attack. The correct key always belongs to this set. However, the keyspace cannot be reduced further. To uniquely identify the correct key, the adversary needs at least another fault injection at the same place but for a different plaintext. The rationale behind a further reduction in keyspace can be explained as follows. Let us, once again, consider equation [10.2]. The probability of this system having a solution is given by $\frac{2^8}{2^{32}} = 2^{-24}$. For the first fault injection, this reduces the 4-byte partial keyspace from 2^{32} to 2^8 (expected size). For another injection resulting in a new correct–faulty ciphertext pair, this probability remains constant. However, the expected size of keyspace (given that we have already exploited one correct–faulty ciphertext pair) now becomes $2^8 \times 2^{-24} = 2^{-16}$. This value is less than one. In practice, this uniquely identifies the correct partial key for the 4-key bytes. Repeating this for other key bytes extracts the entire correct key uniquely.

The next obvious question is what happens if the exact location of the fault at the eighth-round input remains unknown to the adversary. It is a practically important situation, as sometimes it becomes difficult to determine the exact corrupted byte. However, this situation is not difficult to overcome. The adversary can exhaustively formulate 16 different equation systems corresponding to each byte. One of these systems will match the actual fault scenario. The total number of key possibilities after a single fault injection then becomes $2^8 \times 16 = 2^{12}$. Therefore, even if the exact location of the fault is unknown, the attack still remains efficient.

10.2.3. *DFA on AES: multiple-byte fault*

Single-byte faults are fairly easy to generate with modern fault injection setups. However, there are situations where faults are not always single-byte. Rather, it can corrupt multiple-byte locations of the state. One interesting question is, whether these faults result in practical attacks. In this section, we shall investigate this point.

The answer lies in the fault propagation patterns of AES. To elaborate, let us first refer to the AES state in equation [10.1]. We can define four *diagonals* $Diag_i$ $(0 \leq i < 4)$ of the state matrix as follows:

$$Diag_i = \{a_{j,(j+i)mod4} : 0 \leq j < 4; 0 \leq i < 4\} \qquad [10.3]$$

One interesting observation here is that each single-byte fault within a diagonal is equivalent in terms of its propagation path after the first `MixColumns` sub-operation in the path. We might easily verify this by tracing the path for two different bytes in a diagonal. We leave this for the reader to verify. Rather, we investigate the situation where more than one byte in a diagonal becomes corrupted. Figure 10.2 illustrates one such situation for diagonal $Diag_0$. It is clearly established that the fault propagation path remains the same as the single-byte attack after the S-Box operation of the ninth round (for fault injection at the beginning of eighth round). We may verify that this observation holds even for other diagonals $Diag_1$, $Diag_2$ and $Diag_3$. As a result, any of these attacks result in a keyspace size of 2^{32}. The analysis is very similar to the single-byte case.

Next, we consider a more general scenario where the fault is not limited to a single diagonal. It was found that for most such cases, the attack remains feasible. While bytes belonging to two diagonals get corrupted, the complexity of the keyspace after the attack becomes 2^{64} with a single fault. If corruption happens in three diagonals, the complexity becomes 2^{96}. However, multiple correct–faulty ciphertext pairs can still recover the keys. However, no key recovery is feasible if all the diagonals get corrupted simultaneously. We refer the reader to the further references section at the end of this chapter for further details on these attacks. In a nutshell, the attacks on AES are found to be highly flexible and can work with minimum requirements regarding the fault models.

10.2.4. *DFA on AES: other rounds*

The reader may wonder what happens if the fault is injected in any other round. We may verify that the attacks are still feasible if the faults are injected at the ninth round. However, in this case, one injection can only recover 4-key bytes due to an incomplete diffusion of the fault. While the ninth-round attacks are fairly similar to the attack discussed in this section, attacks in a deeper round take a different form. If the fault is injected in the seventh round, we need to use a different property called *impossible-differentials* to perform the attack. Some other variants, such as *meet-in-the-middle*, are also feasible.

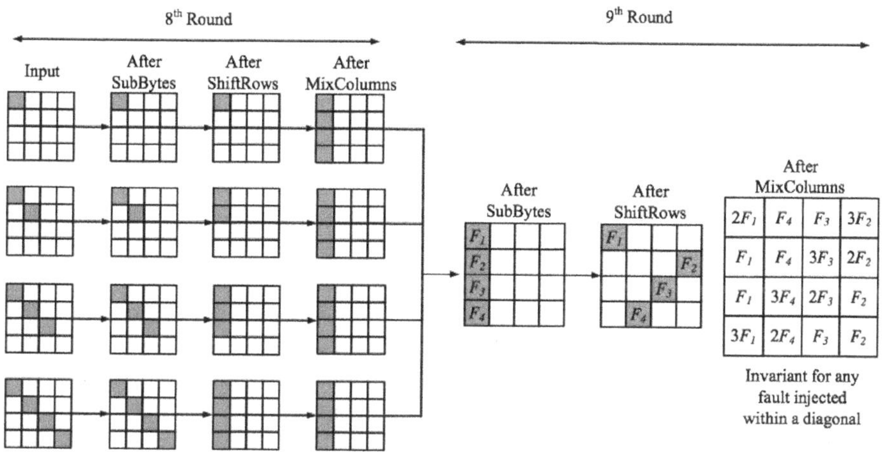

Figure 10.2. *Diagonal fault attack with the faults injected at the diagonal* $Diag_0$[4]

10.2.5. *DFA on AES: key schedule*

Another distinct attack possibility arises for the situations when the round keys are also computed during the cipher computation. The fault, in this case, propagates through both the key schedule and the cipher computation. The attack equations are similar but take more complex forms for key-schedule attacks. However, an attack is still feasible with a single fault with comparable complexity figures. An interested reader may refer to the further reference section for details of such attacks.

4 Recreated from the paper: Saha et al. (2009).

10.2.6. *DFA on other ciphers: general idea*

While DFA is applicable to any block cipher, the analysis technique varies significantly depending on the structure of the target. In general, every attack forms a system of equations involving the last round key, the fault differential before the last round S-Box operation, and the (correct/faulty) ciphertexts. The main difference arises due to the nature of the linear layer, which is the one responsible for creating the fault propagation patterns. On the other hand, S-Boxes also play a crucial role by determining the number of key candidates. In many cases, a single fault is not sufficient to extract the entire secret and multiple injections (even at different locations) might be needed. However, the total number of injections remains typically low for DFA, in general. In the later part of this chapter, we shall describe statistical attacks which would require a much higher number of fault injections to recover the secret. In terms of fault complexity, therefore, DFA remains the most efficient attack to date.

IMPORTANT. So far in this chapter, we have described DFA attacks by means of case studies. However, several theoretical questions are associated with DFA. The most obvious one in this regard is "what is the best attack possible for a given cipher, and how to determine that?" A handful of work has addressed this issue. One approach to analyze this is to take an information-theoretic approach. The main idea behind this technique is to first quantify the information leakage for fault injection in terms of Shannon entropy. Next, it relates the amount of information leaked with the remaining key complexity (i.e. the number of key candidates remaining after the attack). An attack is called *optimal* if the entropy-loss for the key due to fault injection (i.e. information leaked) matches with the remaining key complexity. Another approach in this respect is to reduce a differential attack to an FA and establish that if a better FA is feasible, this indicates a differential attack is also feasible with complexity less than the brute-force key search complexity. Surprisingly, both of these approaches reach the same conclusion for AES – the single-byte FA is an optimal attack strategy. Further details can be found in the respective papers mentioned at the end of this chapter.

10.3. Automation of DFA

Since its introduction, DFA remains one of the most efficient albeit complex FA strategies. In principle, every unprotected block cipher is vulnerable to this attack. However, the complexities and the attack strategies vary significantly among ciphers. It is, therefore, important to understand the attack space for each cipher thoroughly. This understanding helps us to perform a sound risk analysis, taking the deployment platform and available injection tools into account. The countermeasures can be decided accordingly. Now, the problem is that the fault space in a block cipher is of a formidable size. Furthermore, analyzing even a single fault instance is complex with manual efforts. If we consider the AES, it took nearly eight years to come up with the optimal attack, and new DFA instances or their variations are still arising. Also, there already exist hundreds of block ciphers today, and their number is continuously increasing due to the recent trend of designing application-specific customized designs. The only solution for analyzing attack space is, therefore, an automatic tool in this regard. In the rest of this section, we present one such tool, named ExpFault.

10.3.1. *ExpFault*

ExpFault is an automated framework for identifying *exploitable faults* in an unprotected block cipher algorithm. The tool takes the algorithmic description of a block cipher (in a specific input language) as input, along with fault simulation data corresponding to a specific fault (according to some fault model), and determines the exploitability of that fault for FA in seconds. Along with the exploitability, ExpFault also determines the attack complexity and provides a sketch of the attack algorithm through graphs. The main crux for characterizing the diverse fault space of a block cipher is to characterize the faults without explicitly performing the attacks (which can be computationally intense in some cases).

In order to automatically identify and characterize DFA attacks, the ExpFault framework formalizes the notion of DFA and the fault models. The fault models are characterized by the state, sub-operation, and round of injection (s_r^i), the total size of the target state (λ), the width of the fault wd (e.g. byte/bit/nibble/multi-byte) and the location t of fault in the state (e.g. byte index). The key component of a DFA attack is a *distinguisher*. Informally, distinguishers are certain mathematical constraints over the values assumed by an intermediate state (or more specifically, constraints over the XOR difference between the correct and faulty computation of an intermediate state called as *state-differentials*) of a cipher, resulting from the injection of a fault. They typically work as filters for eliminating wrong key candidates reducing the entropy of the secret key. The propagation of a fault creates distinguishers that are utilized for key recovery. The next step of a DFA is to devise a divide-and-conquer strategy for partially guessing the key bits and filtering the correct key candidates by evaluating the distinguishers. The final step is to estimate the complexity of distinguisher evaluation as well as the size of the remaining key-space, which has to be searched exhaustively to identify the correct key. If the size of this remaining key space is significantly large, we may choose to inject more faults to reduce the size of this space.

The present version of the ExpFault framework takes a block cipher algorithm as input in two forms – a graphical description and an executable. The executable is used for simulating faults at specific locations inside the cipher. The fault simulation data are analyzed using state-of-the-art association-rule mining algorithms to discover the distinguishers. In general, a state-differential having a Shannon entropy less than its maximum possible Shannon entropy can be marked as a distinguisher. Once the distinguishers have been found, the tool uses the graphical description of the cipher to construct a data-flow graph, called a cipher dependency graph (CDG). The distinguishers are linked with the CDG, and the divide-and-conquer strategy for key recovery is figured out using breadth-first-search (BFS) on this graph. The final stage is to identify the aforementioned complexity figures for the attack, which can be performed easily by utilizing the BFS trees found in the previous stage. A conceptual view of the framework is presented in Figure 10.3. Figure 10.4 presents an example of a CDG for the last round of AES.

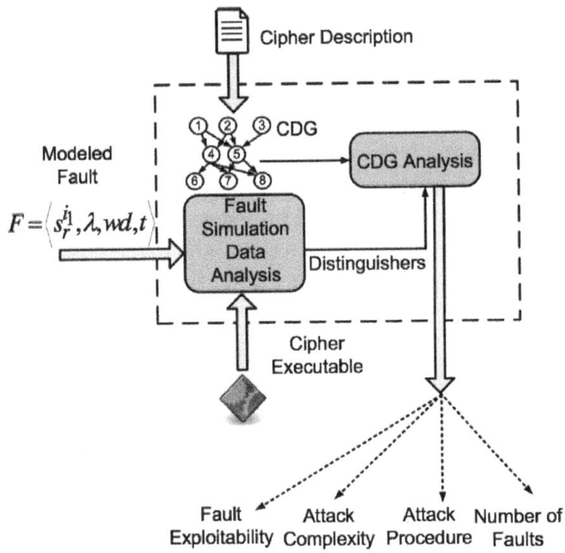

Figure 10.3. *ExpFault: conceptual view*[5]

To illustrate how ExpFault works, let us once again consider the single-byte FA on AES (see section 10.2.2). At the very first step, a fault simulation is performed considering every possible value of the byte fault (total 255 values) for different plaintext and keys. The intermediate state values are also stored. ExpFault consumes this fault simulation data, and, using data-mining strategies, figures out the linear patterns in the fault simulation path (e.g. the patterns at the outputs of the `MixColumns` steps; see Figure 10.1). It can also figure out other hidden patterns such as impossible differentials. These patterns work as the distinguishers in the attack. Next, the tool constructs the CDG and figures out the attack path and attack complexity. One important feature of ExpFault is that it can automatically find out

5 Recreated from the book chapter: Saha et al. (2018).

the most suitable distinguisher at any stage of an attack. For the AES case study, we have two distinguishers – one at the beginning of 10th round, and the other one at the beginning of ninth round. The tool is capable of using them whenever required.

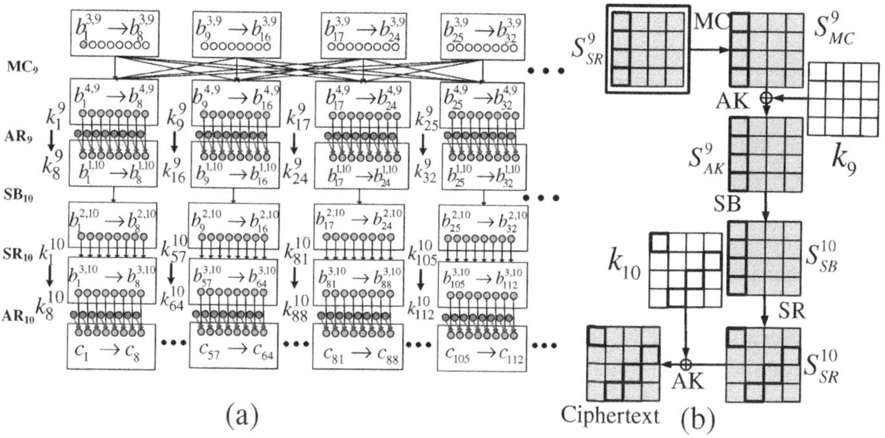

Figure 10.4. *Partial CDG of AES from ninth-round `MixColumns` till the ciphertexts. The gray circles in the graph represents the fault propagation path and the colored (red/blue) nodes represents the associated key bits*[6]*. For a color version of this figure, see www.iste.co.uk/prouff/cryptography1.zip*

The ExpFault framework has been utilized to recreate known attacks on both SPN and Feistel ciphers, such as AES, PRESENT and CLEFIA. It has also been applied on a recently proposed block cipher GIFT, for which no attack was previously known. The framework figures out attacks on GIFT within seconds. Interestingly, the attacks found by this tool for GIFT and AES are found to be information-theoretically optimal. There also exists another framework of a similar kind called XFC, which uses static analysis to trace out the fault propagation paths. However, the data-based approach of ExpFault is found to be more generic in the sense that it can even figure out complex attacks such as impossible differential.

10.4. DFA countermeasures: general idea and taxonomy

Fault tolerance is crucial for most safety-critical infrastructures and is a well-developed subject on its own. However, the interaction of faults with cryptographic systems is quite different from other state-of-the-art systems. As a

6 Recreated from the paper: Saha et al. (2018).

result, preventing FAs with fault tolerance principles needs special care, and applying the principles as it is may not always work. Nevertheless, most of the existing FA countermeasures begin with one intuitive and basic fault tolerance principle, that is, *redundancy*.

10.4.1. *Detection countermeasures*

In the simplest form, an FA countermeasure may repeat the encryption of a plaintext n times (at least twice) and only output the ciphertext if the results of all computations match. Computing multiple times with the same hardware/software in this manner is called *temporal redundancy*. On the other hand, we may put several parallel hardware units to perform the redundant computations, which are known as *spatial redundancy*. We may observe that implementing both of these is costly – either in terms of time or in terms of computational resources (100% overhead even for one redundant computation). However, the fault coverage obtained is also 100%. An efficient way of reducing the overheads is to apply error correction codes (ECCs). Countermeasures based on ECCs are called *information redundancy*, and efficient ECCs can achieve a fault coverage of 99% while incurring an overhead of 35–40% only.

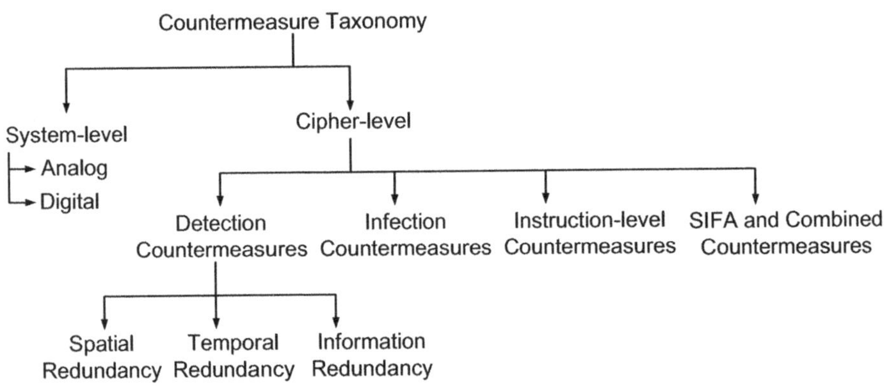

Figure 10.5. *Taxonomy of notable FA countermeasures*

Spatial, temporal and information redundancy countermeasures are often denoted as *detection countermeasures* given the fact that they detect the presence of a fault and stop the computation or outputs a random string, accordingly. While the fault coverage figures of such countermeasures are quite attractive, they can still be bypassed by an adversary. Taking the spatial and temporal redundancy into consideration, the simplest trick is to do a second fault on the error-check operation, which results in a faulty ciphertext getting outputted. In some cases, the redundancy can be applied in a per-round manner. However, the attack still remains feasible as faulting two different locations at a time is feasible. Another possibility is to perform equal faults in all of the computation branches so that the checks pass, even with faulty computations. This, too, is practical for low redundancy orders. Finally, for information redundancy, even a single injection may suffice. This is because the detection capability of an ECC depends on the number of faulted bits in a computation. If the ECC only corrects 1-bit faults and the adversary is able to make a 2-bit one, the countermeasure is evaded. Furthermore, no ECC provides 100% coverage, even for the designated number of bits it is used for. The issue in cryptographic FA is that an adversary can exploit this small coverage gap and perform an attack bypassing the check. Note that all these detection countermeasures look good from a fault tolerance perspective where the faults are considered randomly occurring. However, in cryptography, the adversary can perform targeted bit/byte faults, which renders these countermeasures useless.

10.4.2. *Infective countermeasures*

Several efforts have been made to address the shortcomings of detection countermeasures. We may observe that the error-check operation is one of the weakest points. One way of removing this weakness is to avoid an explicit check operation. Countermeasures that perform this are called *infective countermeasures*. The main idea is to embed the checking within the algorithm. If there is a fault, an infective countermeasure automatically randomizes the state of the block cipher and eventually outputs a randomized ciphertext that cannot be utilized for an attack. One crucial inclusion here is randomization, which is deemed essential to stop the adversary from utilizing the ciphertexts. Here, we first describe one prominent example of infective countermeasures, which was proposed for AES. Internally, this countermeasure maintains one actual and one redundant state to perform actual and redundant AES rounds. Additionally, it maintains a dummy state to perform dummy rounds. Dummy rounds are randomly performed between actual and redundant round computations with the aim of making the fault timing difficult. The countermeasure performs an XOR operation between the actual and the redundant state at the end of each round. If this XOR is found to be non-zero, a random 128-bit string is XOR-ed with the states and the computation continues. The checking here is not explicit and performed by means of an expression and, therefore, cannot be skipped or bypassed without affecting further computation. The expectation is that with the inclusion of the aforementioned random string, the faulty ciphertext becomes completely randomized.

While this countermeasure successfully prevents the attacks on the error check, it is still not secure. In fact, we can perform the single-byte fault-based DFA on this.

To see why, let us consider a randomized ciphertext coming out of the construction as (for single-byte fault injection at eighth-round input):

$$C = \begin{bmatrix} m_0 \oplus 2r_1 \oplus 1r_2 & 1r_3 & 3r_4 \oplus 1r_5 \oplus 1r_6 & 3r_7 \\ 1r_1 \oplus 3r_2 & 1r_3 & 2r_4 \oplus 3r_5 \oplus 1r_6 & m_1 \oplus 2r_7 \\ 1r_1 \oplus 2r_2 & 3r_3 & m_2 \oplus 1r_4 \oplus 2r_5 \oplus 3r_6 & 1r_7 \\ 3r_1 \oplus 1r_2 & m_3 \oplus 2r_3 & 1r_4 \oplus 1r_5 \oplus 2r_6 & 1r_7 \end{bmatrix} \quad [10.4]$$

Here, each r_i is a random byte and the m_is are related to the fault differentials. We may observe that by solving a few linear equations, we can recover all the m_is. In other words, the ciphertexts can be de-randomized and used for launching DFA attacks. Fortunately, a fix was proposed to address this. We refer an interested reader to the further references section for the respective papers for these countermeasures.

10.4.3. *Instruction-level countermeasures*

There exist several other variants of redundancy-based countermeasures. Another notable class is the instruction-level countermeasure, which repeats an instruction multiple times to make the job of the adversary difficult. It has been found that state-of-the-art instruction set architectures contain some instructions, which can be repeated any number of times without changing the semantics of the code (called *idempotent instructions*; e.g., `mov` instruction). Moreover, several arithmetic instructions can be implemented using one or multiple idempotent instructions. The instruction-level countermeasures mostly exploit this fact and come up with robust implementations without any check operation. However, these too can be bypassed with advanced injection setups, which can skip multiple contiguous instructions.

In the next section, we are going to describe advanced FA, some of which bypass almost every countermeasure described so far. Research on preventing such advanced attacks (such as SIFA, FTA, or combined side-channel and FAs) is fairly new and involved, and we do not discuss them here. An interested reader may refer to the further references section to find the relevant publications in this aspect.

10.5. Advanced FA

DFAs are indeed the most popular and widely explored class of FAs. However, over the years, several techniques have been devised to prevent this class of attacks. The countermeasures described in the previous section indeed make the job of an attacker difficult, even though they sometimes fall prey to the adversary. Consider the detection countermeasures as an example. Bypassing them requires at least two fault injections. For properly crafted infection countermeasures, DFAs are quite difficult to perform. Finally, DFAs always require the same plaintext to be encrypted two times and access to the faulty ciphertexts. These conditions might not work for certain applications. For example, direct access to the ciphertext is not available for certain authenticated encryptions (AE) and Secure Boot protocols. Therefore, even after being extremely efficient, DFA is not the ultimate tool in the attacker's arsenal.

The question is, can there be attacks that complement DFAs? The answer is affirmative, as we show in this section. Before describing the attacks, we will introduce the biased fault model, which is the main ingredient for most of the advanced FAs.

10.5.1. *Biased fault model*

In section 10.2.1, we mentioned that the probability distributions of faults are a crucial part of FAs. However, DFA typically does not exploit this property. In most devices, faults are not uniformly random. It is observed that a fault injection changes the value of an affected region only to a certain fixed set of values. In other words, the probability distribution of faulty values (or the XOR difference between the correct and faulty values at the injection point) is non-uniform, and in many cases, the faults only assume a specific set of values with high repeatability. All such scenarios are collectively called *biased faults*. One prominent example of a biased fault is a bit stuck-at-0 fault, which, while injected on an n-bit state, makes only 2^{n-1} values occurring repeatedly. The rest of the values (2^{n-1} of them) occur with probability 0. A stuck-at fault is, however, only an instance of such biased faults, and several other scenarios are feasible. It is worth mentioning that the value of an affected region may also get biased with a uniformly random bit-flip or some other kind of fault, such as an instruction skip. Some examples will be presented in the following sections.

10.5.2. *Statistical fault attack*

SFA was first proposed in Fuhr et al. (2013). A similar variant called (DFIA) was proposed independently at the same time in Ghalaty et al. (2014). SFA (and DFIA) requires multiple faulty ciphertexts for key recovery due to its statistical nature. However, unlike DFA, SFA and DFIA do not require the corresponding correct ciphertexts. The fault is injected at the same point (somewhere in the last few rounds) while encrypting several randomly chosen plaintexts, and the faulty ciphertexts are collected. The only requirement is that the faults have to be biased, which also makes the probability distribution of the corrupted state values (most often a byte/bit) biased. In the analysis step, the attacker guesses a key-value and partially decrypts the faulty ciphertexts up to the fault injection point. If the key guess is correct, the distribution of the faulty states at the fault injection point will display a non-uniform distribution. On the contrary, for each wrong key guess, the distribution will be uniformly random. This property, therefore, helps to distinguish the correct key value from the wrong key values. The statistical test, known as SEI, often used to distinguish the correct key is given as follows:

$$SEI(\hat{k}) = \sum_{i=0}^{255} \left(\frac{\#\{t|\hat{S}_j = i\}}{num} - \frac{1}{256} \right)^2 \quad [10.5]$$

In this expression, $\hat{k}$ denote a key guess, and $\hat{S}_j$ denotes the hypothetical value of the byte where the fault has been injected, calculated based on key guess $\hat{k}$. Furthermore, num denotes the count of faulty ciphertexts used for calculating the SEI, and $\#\{t|\hat{S}_j = i\}$ denotes the number of occurrences of each distinct value i of a byte. The key guess having the highest SEI is the correct key. In most cases, a unique key is returned after this attack. However, the number of faulty ciphertexts varies with the statistical bias in the fault distribution.

SFAs are found to be effective in scenarios that do not allow performing the same encryption multiple times. Additionally, the biased fault model makes it feasible to inject the same fault in multiple redundant branches with a high probability. As a result, SFA and their variants are used as the primary tools for bypassing detection and certain infection countermeasures. However, SFA, too, requires faulty ciphertexts to be available in most cases. In the next section, we show that this condition can be relaxed, which provides enormous power to the adversary.

10.5.3. *Statistical ineffective fault attack*

Statistical ineffective fault attack (SIFA) is one of the most recent inclusions in the arsenal of FAs, first proposed in TCHES 2018 and further extended in ASIACRYPT 2018. The main crux behind this attack is that a fault may or may not corrupt the ciphertext depending on the state value at the fault injection point. Such faults are called *ineffective faults*, and the distribution of intermediate state values for which a fault remains ineffective is statistically biased[7]. This feature of ineffective faults allows key recovery by utilizing correct ciphertexts (obtained from a fault injection campaign). The attack technique is similar to SFA. Since correct ciphertexts are utilized for key recovery, SIFA inherently bypasses most of the existing FA countermeasures based on fault detection (this also includes infective countermeasures). In other words, most of the existing countermeasure design principles fall prey to SIFA. It also works in scenarios when FA countermeasures are present along with masking countermeasures, the most prevalent side-channel countermeasure to date.

7 So, we may consider ineffective faults as a special case of the biased fault model.

The attack technique in SIFA is exactly the same as SFA. The only difference is that the faulty ciphertexts of SFA are replaced by the correct ciphertexts in SIFA. Let us briefly explain why SIFA attacks work. Without loss of generality, we consider a bit stuck-at-0 fault model, which corrupts the internal state of a cipher somewhere in the last few rounds. In general, the distribution of the state-bytes/nibbles/bits at these rounds are not distinguishable from uniform distribution, if randomly selected plaintexts are being encrypted. Therefore, if we specifically focus on the distribution of a byte or nibble (without any fault), all possible values will be equally likely. Now consider the same nibble with a stuck-at-0 fault is injected at the most significant bit (MSB). For eight of the values (where the MSB is already 0), there is no impact of this fault and a correct ciphertext can be obtained (see Figures 10.6(a) and (b)). For the rest of the nibble values, the nibble gets corrupted, and the faulty ciphertext is muted or randomized by the countermeasure. Now, if we consider the correct ciphertexts only, the corresponding internal nibble, where the fault has been injected can only assume eight possible values, whatever be the plaintexts were. This is indeed a biased distribution, where some of the values have zero probability of occurrence (see Figure 10.6(c)). Naturally, the SEI metric can distinguish the correct key using this biased distribution. It is worth mentioning that stuck-at-0 fault is only a special case of SIFA, and, in general, any fault that makes some internal state distribution biased would work. Even uniformly random bit-flips work for certain cases, if the fault location is chosen carefully. More precisely, if the S-Box mappings can be corrupted in a way so that it results in a biased state distribution for the correct ciphertexts, SIFA can be launched. Often corrupting the S-Box mapping can be performed with a random bit-flip, if the internal computation of the S-Box can be faulted. A typical use-case for that is masked implementations. An interested reader may refer to the papers referred to in the further references section.

IMPORTANT. Advanced FA, such as SIFA, SFA are mostly relevant for bypassing countermeasures. The most prominent side-channel countermeasure masking naturally comes in this context as it prevents certain classes of FAs, such as (SEA) or (BFA). Masking is a general strategy for randomizing the computation of a circuit based on the principles of secret sharing. In the context of block ciphers, masking splits each intermediate bit x into $(d+1)$ random bits called *shares*, which are statistically independent by their own, and also while considered in subsets of size up to d. Some linear (mostly XOR) combinations of the shares return x. Each underlying function of the cipher is also split into $(d+1)$ component functions respecting the correctness of the actual processing to compute on the shares. The order of protection d here intuitively means that an adversary has to simultaneously consider leakages for $(d+1)$ points, in order to gain some useful information about the intermediate computation. The trace requirements for the side-channel attack increase exponentially with d. There exist several strategies for masking, all of which ensure that the shares never combine (even accidentally due to some physical defaults like glitches or coupling) during the computation. Special care is taken for the non-linear functions to ensure this. An interested reader may refer to Chapter 7 of this volume and to Chapter 2 of Volume 2 for details on the state-of-the-art masking schemes.

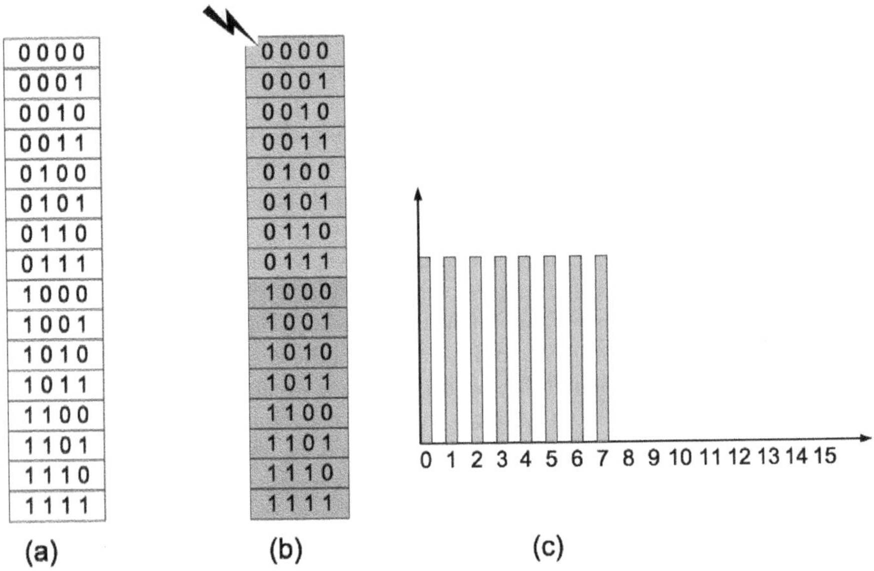

Figure 10.6. *Illustrating the root cause of SIFA: (a) the possible valuations of a 4-bit state; (b) with a stick-at-0 fault at MSB, half of the state values get affected (colored red). The rest remains unchanged (colored blue); (c) the biased state distribution for the correct key guess considering the correct ciphertexts only. For a color version of this figure, see www.iste.co.uk/prouff/cryptography1.zip*

10.5.4. *Fault template attacks*

The fact that a fault may remain ineffective, conditioned on the values of the corrupted state is an extremely powerful tool for the attackers. While SIFA exploits this for generating bias in the faulty state distributions, other exploitation is also feasible. In this section, we present one such exploitation technique, named fault template attacks (FTA). FTA belongs to a class of attacks where the adversary cannot explicitly access the correct/faulty ciphertexts. Also, the plaintext may remain fixed. Examples of such scenarios include certain AE schemes and Message Authentication Codes (MACs) where the secret is generated from a KeyGen module from a fixed secret state. Protocols, such as different secure-boot processes, are potential examples where sometimes such restricted scenarios may occur[8,9]. Such restricted access limits the adversary from launching DFA/SFA or SIFA attacks. The only option is to use stuck-at faults on the key/state in a bit-by-bit manner and recover the bits using the knowledge if the outcome is correct or faulty. Such an attack is known as SEA. A variant of this (with a slightly relaxed fault model), called BFA, is also an option.

Unfortunately, both SEA and BFA can be prevented using masking, which, although a side-channel countermeasure, is also effective against biased faults. That effectively makes implementations quite resilient if both masking and FA countermeasures are applied simultaneously (at least for a single injection per encryption). However, FTA proves that this is indeed not an ideal protection technique, and implementations remain equally vulnerable despite masking being present, even if the access to the ciphertexts is restricted. Another fact about FTA is that it can recover keys even if the faults are injected at the middle rounds of a cipher. Note that DFA/SIFA requires an injection in the last few rounds in order to make the attack complexity practical. Finally, FTA is the first template-based FA technique. Template attacks remain the strongest variant of side-channel attacks. From a theoretical viewpoint, a counterpart for faults is likely to exist, which is first established in FTA.

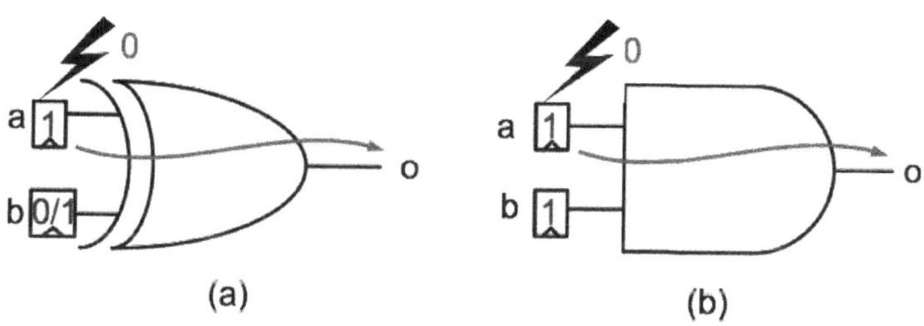

Figure 10.7. *Fault propagation: (a) XOR gate; (b) AND gate. The gate inputs are in blue and the value of the stuck-at fault is in red[10]. For a color version of this figure, see www.iste.co.uk/prouff/cryptography1.zip*

Let us now see how FTA attacks take place. The crux is to utilize some fundamental properties of logic gates. At this point, it is important to recall that most of the block ciphers consist of Boolean operations. While, for hardware

8 Available at: https://www.microsemi.com/document-portal/doc_download/133604-microsemi-secure-boot-reference-design-white-paper.

9 Available at: https://www.intel.com/content/www/us/en/programmable/documentation/cru1452898171006.html.

10 Recreated from the paper: Saha et al. (2020b).

implementations, any digital circuit is mapped to a network of gates, block ciphers, sometimes, are represented as a network of gates even in software to enable parallelization. Such implementations are called bitsliced implementations. Therefore, we exploit some fundamental gate properties to attack block ciphers in FTA. Let us consider the gates depicted in Figure 10.7 and stuck-at faults injected in one of their inputs. It can be observed that for an XOR gate, a stuck-at-(0/1) fault at one of the inputs (input a, in this case) leaks information about that specific input. For example, if the fault is a stuck-at-0, then a fault propagation at the output of the XOR indicates that the input value at the fault injection point (a) is 1. If the input is 0, then the fault does not propagate to the output. However, no information is leaked for the other input of the XOR due to this fault propagation. In contrast, for an AND gate, a stuck-at-0 fault at one of the inputs leaks information about all other inputs of the gate. For a two-input AND, a stuck-at-0 fault propagates to the gate output only if the injection point has a value 1, and the other input (input b in this case) has a value 1. Therefore, information regarding both the inputs leak in this case using a single fault. Such fault injection also leaks for AND gates if the injected fault is a uniformly random bit-flip fault. However, in this case, no information regarding the fault injection point is leaked, but the other input still gets leaked.

Such data dependency of fault propagation remains valid for any combinational logic. Based on this fault propagation property, FTA constructs its *fault templates*. It is assumed that the adversary is able to inject bit faults at different locations within the cipher, but it is restricted to a single injection at a specific location in each encryption. It is also assumed that the adversary can extensively profile a device which is similar to the target device, and construct the fault template which compiles information from different fault injections. The template is constructed assuming the key to be known, and utilized to attack a device where the key is unknown. The construction of templates allows key extraction merely based on the information on whether a ciphertext is faulty or not.

To illustrate further, let us consider the 3-bit χ_3 S-Box[11] described as follows:

$$
\begin{aligned}
y_0 &= x_0 + x_1\overline{x_2} \\
y_1 &= x_1 + x_2\overline{x_0} \\
y_2 &= x_2 + x_0\overline{x_1}
\end{aligned}
\qquad [10.6]
$$

In these equations, x_0, x_1, x_2 denote the input bits of the S-Box and y_0, y_1, y_2 represent the output bits. x_0 and y_0 denote the most significant bits (MSB) of the input

11 FTA and SIFA attacks mostly target the nonlinear components of a cipher.

and output, respectively. Considering a bit-flip fault at $\overline{x_1}$ [12], the outputs of this S-Box are correct for inputs $\{0, 1, 2, 3\}$ and faulty for $\{4, 5, 6, 7\}$. A closer view reveals that the outputs are correct when $x_0 = 0$ and faulty, otherwise (i.e. when $x_0 = 1$). This is because the computation of $x_0\overline{x_1}$ propagates the fault to the AND output only when $x_0 = 1$. The XOR computation following the AND operation unconditionally propagates the fault to the output. Therefore, the S-Box output becomes faulted only when $x_0 = 1$ in this case. The observation can also be extended for the stuck-at cases.

It is clear from the above discussion that the bit x_0 is revealed by this fault injection. In order to recover other bits, two other fault locations are required here. A fault injection in $x_2\overline{x_0}$ (at the x_0 input) reveals the value of x_2, and an injection in $x_1\overline{x_2}$ reveals x_1. It is worth mentioning that these injections happen at independent fault campaigns, and FTA does not need to inject more than one fault per encryption in this case. Combining the outcomes of all fault campaigns, we can construct templates that map the faulty or correct observables to the intermediate values. An example fault template for this S-Box is presented in Table 10.1, where the black cells represent faulty outcomes and the gray cells represent correct outcomes. For example, if none of the outcomes for the three chosen fault locations are faulty, then the associated intermediate value is 0.

Let us now illustrate how this attack extends for situations where masking is present. Note that in the presence of masking, every bit inside the cipher computation is randomized. To explain the attacks on masking, we consider the 4-bit S-Box of PRESENT block cipher. PRESENT is an SPN cipher having an S-Box layer followed by a bit-permutation-based linear diffusion layer. The first-order masked implementation of this S-Box (without loss of generality, we consider a masking scheme called threshold implementation (TI) which is usually implemented in hardware) shares each bit into three random shares. The S-Box is first represented as a composition of two quadratic Boolean functions, $F()$ and $G()$. Each of these functions is masked, and a register stage is put at the interface of these two functions to prevent physical defaults such as glitches.

To illustrate our attack, we just need to consider the masked version of the $F()$ function (see equation [10.7]), although the attack applies to $G()$ as well. We refer to the masked equations for $F()$ in equation [10.8]:

$$
\begin{aligned}
&F(x_3, x_2, x_1, x_0) = (f_3, f_2, f_1, f_0) \\
&f_3 = x_2 + x_1 + x_0 + x_3x_0; f_2 = x_3 + x_1x_0; f_1 = x_2 + x_1 + x_3x_0; \\
&f_0 = x_1 + x_2x_0.
\end{aligned} \quad [10.7]
$$

12 This fault can be practically generated for a bitsliced software by faulting the execution of the complement instruction. A stuck-at fault would also work here.

$$
\begin{aligned}
f_{10} &= x_1^2 + x_2^2\mathbf{x_0^2} + x_2^2x_0^3 + x_2^3\mathbf{x_0^2} & f_{11} &= x_2^2 + x_1^2 + x_3^2x_0^2 + x_3^2x_0^3 + x_3^3x_0^2\\
f_{20} &= x_1^3 + x_2^3x_0^3 + x_2^1x_0^3 + x_2^3x_0^1 & f_{21} &= x_2^3 + x_1^3 + x_3^3x_0^3 + x_3^1x_0^3 + x_3^3x_0^1\\
f_{30} &= x_1^1 + x_2^1x_0^1 + x_2^1\mathbf{x_0^2} + x_2^2x_0^1 & f_{31} &= x_2^1 + x_1^1 + x_3^1x_0^1 + x_3^1x_0^2 + x_3^2x_0^1
\end{aligned}
\qquad [10.8]
$$

$$
\begin{aligned}
f_{12} &= x_3^2 + x_1^2x_0^2 + x_1^2x_0^3 + x_1^3x_0^2 & f_{13} &= x_2^2 + x_1^2 + x_0^2 + x_3^2x_0^2 + x_3^2x_0^3 + x_3^3x_0^2\\
f_{22} &= x_3^3 + x_1^3x_0^3 + x_1^1x_0^3 + x_1^3x_0^1 & f_{23} &= x_2^3 + x_1^3 + x_0^3 + x_3^3x_0^3 + x_3^1x_0^3 + x_3^3x_0^1\\
f_{32} &= x_3^1 + x_1^1x_0^1 + x_1^1x_0^2 + x_1^2x_0^1 & f_{33} &= x_2^1 + x_1^1 + x_0^1 + x_3^1x_0^1 + x_3^1x_0^2 + x_3^2x_0^1
\end{aligned}
$$

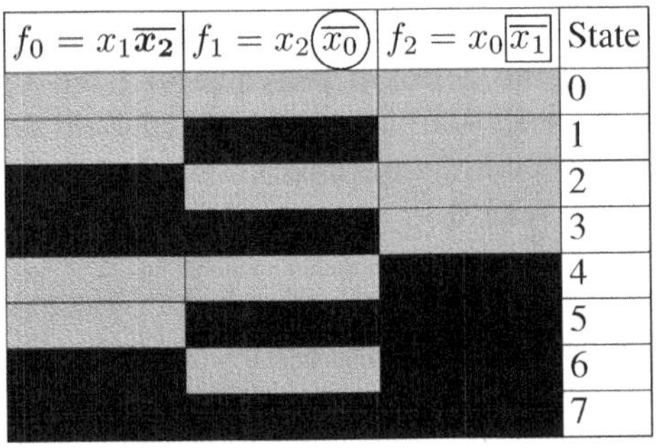

Table 10.1. *Fault template for the χ_3 S-Box*[13]

Let us consider the input share x_0^2 (represented in bold in equation [10.8]) for bit-flip fault injection during the computation of the shares (f_{10}, f_{20}, f_{30}). One may observe that this fault leaks about the expression $(x_2^2 + x_2^3 + x_2^1) = x_2$. This is because x_0^2 is AND-ed with all three shares of x_2 in this case, and the fault will only corrupt the actual outcome if the outcome of the aforementioned XOR of shares is corrupted. Note that the XOR of shares is never performed before the ciphertext, but the correctness property of the operations ensures that the leakage of x_2 takes place. In other words, masking only randomizes the computation and cannot change the correctness properties which are actually exploited in this attack. In a similar manner, other fault locations lead to the recovery of the rest of the bits. The template is illustrated in Table 10.2, which exposes the input of the S-Box. One should note that exposing two consecutive intermediate states of a cipher reveals the key. This attack was practically validated on a hardware implementation with EM fault injection.

13 Recreated from the paper: Saha et al. (2021).

$fl_0 = x_0^2$ (f_{10}, f_{20}, f_{30})	$fl_1 = x_0^2$ (f_{11}, f_{21}, f_{31})	$fl_2 = x_0^2$ (f_{12}, f_{22}, f_{32})	$fl_3 = x_3^2$ (f_{13}, f_{23}, f_{33})	State	$fl_0 = x_0^2$ (f_{10}, f_{20}, f_{30})	$fl_1 = x_0^2$ (f_{11}, f_{21}, f_{31})	$fl_2 = x_0^2$ (f_{12}, f_{22}, f_{32})	$fl_3 = x_3^2$ (f_{13}, f_{23}, f_{33})	State
				0					8
				1					9
				2					a
				3					b
				4					c
				5					d
				6					e
				7					f

Table 10.2. *Template for attacking TI PRESENT (middle round). The black cells indicate a faulty outcome and the grey cells represent correct outcome. The table header at each column indicates the fault injection location (x_j^i) in TI PRESENT and the output shares (f_{lm}) affected due to fault propagation*[14]

One interesting question in this regard is the prevention of FTA and SIFA attacks. It was generally observed that masking is essential for preventing these attacks, at least partially. More precisely, masking can prevent SIFA in case it uses biased faults. Unless the S-Box intermediates are corrupted, masking remains a good countermeasure. To prevent the attacks on the masked variants (and also some resulting combined attacks), the error-check operations are required to be carefully placed.

10.5.5. *Persistent fault attacks*

Every fault model discussed so far in this chapter is transient in nature. An interesting question is whether FAs are only limited to this class of faults. The answer is, however, negative. Although no potential FA exists for permanent faults, a semi-permanent fault model can be constructed, which is known as a *persistent fault model*. In a persistent fault model, the lifetime of the fault spans multiple encryption/decryption operations. Typically, the fault model corrupts the tables and constants, which are parts of an implementation (if it is a table-based implementation). In general, such faults are injected while the tables and constants are being loaded in the memory before beginning the encryption/decryption operation. Reloading removes the fault from the system and that is why it is called a persistent fault and not a permanent one. Potential targets for these fault models are the fast table-based software implementations of block ciphers present in encryption libraries such as OpenSSL. Certain table-based masking schemes can also be

14 Recreated from the paper: Saha et al. (2020b).

targeted. In fact, persistent fault models remain the only known attack instance for which a RowHammer vulnerability has been exploited in a symmetric-key context. Attacking hardware implementations is also feasible, given some parts are based on table lookup.

Let us now describe how persistent faults result in key recovery for block cipher implementations. Without loss of generality, let us consider a scenario where the nonlinear and some parts of the linear operations are implemented using table lookup (e.g. T-tables of OpenSSL). Persistent fault injection may flip one or multiple bits in such a table. For simplicity, if we restrict our attention to the S-Boxes only, we may find that such faults affect the S-Box mapping. In other words, it may happen that the input y to the S-Box maps to some v^*, while the correct output is v and $v \neq v^*$. Now, the fault being persistent, such corruption happens multiple times throughout the encryption operation. However, PFA only needs to consider corruption in the final round. For simplicity, let us consider AES in which the last round does not perform the `MixColumns` step. If several encryptions are considered, the probability of a ciphertext byte taking some value u becomes zero for PFA, where $u = S[y] + k = v + k$. This is indeed a statistical bias which can be observed in the ciphertext bytes. An adversary who knows the pattern of fault can easily recover y from here and, thereby, can recover the k in a per-byte manner.

Several variants of PFA exist, which can also perform the analysis to the deeper rounds. Surprisingly, in the case of deeper round analysis, the SEI distinguisher works well for key recovery. This is due to the fact that PFA also induces bias in the intermediate states of the cipher. We refer an interested reader to the further reading section for references on this attack.

10.6. Leakage assessment in fault attacks

This chapter so far presents several variants of FAs and their interactions with the countermeasures. The only exception is section 10.3, which presents automation for finding DFA attacks on unprotected implementations of block ciphers. An equally important problem is to evaluate the security of protected implementations, as there are several failure stories already pointed out in section 10.4. In this final section, we address the problem of identifying information leakage from protected implementations of block ciphers. The rationale behind focusing on information leakage is that it is the key cause behind any attack and does not typically depend on the attack strategy. While evaluating protected implementations, our goal is not to find attacks, but to establish that no attack can happen. Finding information leakage is, therefore, a judicious decision.

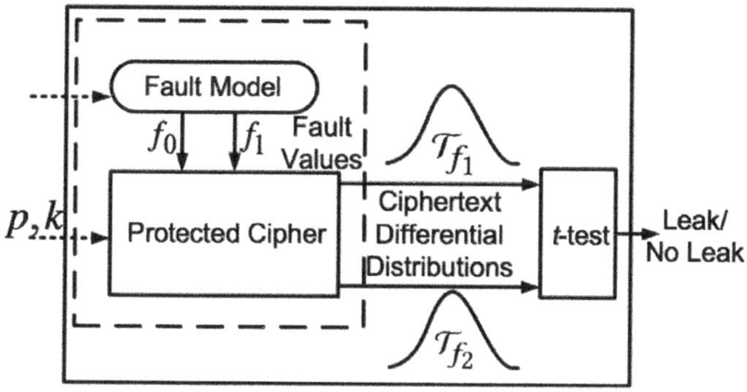

Figure 10.8. *ALAFA leakage assessment test*[15]

The only work addressing this problem is ALAFA. ALAFA begins with a formalization of the information leakage in the context of FAs. In general, the manifestation of leakage in FA happens through ciphertexts or some variables associated with ciphertexts. Therefore, the leakage is defined as:

$$\mathcal{L}_{FA} = C = \mathcal{F}(f, \mathcal{P}, \mathcal{K}), \qquad [10.9]$$

with f denoting the value of the intermediate state differential at the point of fault injection (also denoted as the *value of the fault mask* or simply *fault value*), $\mathcal{P}$ denoting the plaintext variable and $\mathcal{K}$ denoting the secret key variable. The parameter f takes value according to some fault model F. Furthermore, the function $\mathcal{F}$ represents the fault propagation path through the cipher computation. The *observable* for the adversary in FAs is the *ciphertext under the influence of faults* (C) (respectively, the differential between the correct and the faulty ciphertext denoted as ΔC). Next, we define the condition for no leakage as follows:

$$\mathcal{I}(C, \mathcal{K}|\mathcal{P}) = 0 \quad \text{and} \quad \mathcal{I}(C, f|\mathcal{P}) = 0 \qquad [10.10]$$

$\mathcal{I}(X, Y|Z)$ is the conditional mutual information between random variables X and Y given Z. Notably, the definition for no-leakage considers the fault f as an equally important quantity as the key. The reason behind this consideration is that in many cases, the knowledge of the fault mask f, exposes the value of the secret intermediate at the fault injection point. An inquisitive reader may refer to the paper of ALAFA for a proof of this fact.

15 Recreated from the paper: Saha et al. (2019).

Based on the conditions presented in equation [10.10], ALAFA eventually comes up with a statistical yes/no test for leakage assessment. Instead of estimating mutual information (which is difficult to estimate for multivariate cases), it exploits the equivalence between the definitions in equation [10.10] and the theory of *non-interference*. Eventually, it comes up with a leakage assessment test that decides the absence (respectively, presence) of leakage by comparing two distributions of ciphertexts arising due to two different fault values, according to some fault model. There is no leakage if the distributions are found to be equal. On the other hand, any statistically observable difference among the distributions indicates a potential leakage. Figure 10.8 illustrates one variant of the leakage assessment test.

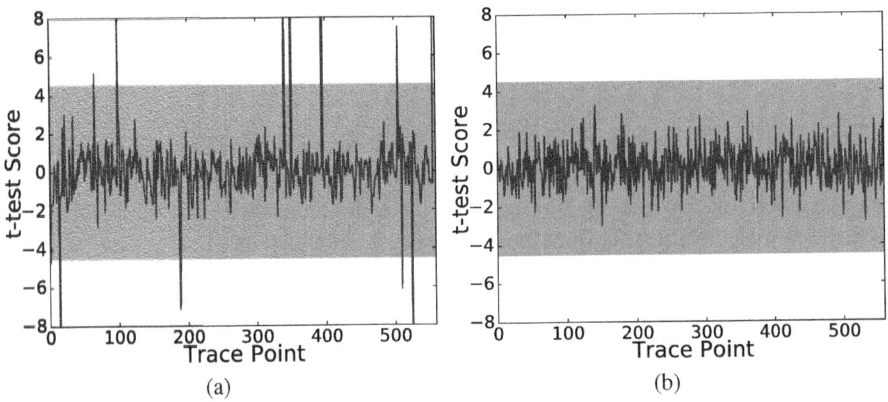

Figure 10.9. *t-test scores: (a) infection countermeasure, Gierlichs et al. (2012) (for third-order t-test); (b) leakage assessment for the corrected infective countermeasure for byte fault model. The points crossing the red region indicates leakage*[16]. *For a color version of this figure, see www.iste.co.uk/prouff/cryptography1.zip*

The next crucial question is how to reason about the equality of two ciphertext distributions. ALAFA utilizes Welch's t-test for this purpose. An interesting fact here is that if the leakage depends upon multiple ciphertext bytes, ALAFA can automatically detect that by performing a t-test for higher order statistical moments. For example, we might consider the derandomization attack on the infective countermeasure proposed in Tupsamudre et al. (2014) at CHES 2014, briefly mentioned in section 10.4. ALAFA detects this attack with the higher order statistical tests given only the ciphertexts as an input (see Figure 10.9(a)). The corrected version of this countermeasure is also proven to be leakage-free (see Figure 10.9(b))

16 Recreated from the paper: Saha et al. (2019).

by ALAFA, at least for byte fault models affecting the intermediate states. Most importantly, ALAFA does not require any other details of the countermeasure to be given as inputs. In that sense, it is oblivious to the structures of the cipher and the countermeasure under test and only needs to simulate the faults on the implementations according to some fault model. With some minor preprocessing, the test also works for any detection countermeasure (see Table 10.3). It is also worth mentioning that the test also extends to all advanced FA described in this chapter. Nevertheless, this research area is still in its infancy and a lot of theoretical and practical advances are yet to be made.

Countermeasure		1-Byte Fault	2-Equal Fault	Comment
Detection	Simple time/space Redundancy	Secure	Insecure (Univariate Leakage)	Insecure against combined attack
Detection	1-bit Parity (Information Redundancy)	Insecure (Univariate Leakage)	–	–
Infection	Infection Countermeasure (Gierlichs et al. 2012)	Insecure (Multivariate Leakage)	Insecure (Univariate Leakage)	–
Infection	Infection Countermeasure (Ghosh et al. 2015)	Insecure (Multivariate Leakage)	Insecure (Univariate Leakage)	–
Infection	Infection Countermeasure (Tupsamudre et al. 2014)	Secure	Insecure (Univariate Leakage)	Insecure against instruction skip

Table 10.3. *Summary of results*[17]

10.7. Chapter summary

The lion's share of research in FAs is attributed to the symmetric key cryptosystems. In this chapter, we tried to cover most of the important aspects in this regard. However, the topic is still an active area of research. Designing FA countermeasures is a really hard task, and the state-of-the-art only focuses on cases with single fault injections so far. Moreover, the countermeasures often incur significant overheads. Finally, we are yet to devise sound strategies against advanced attacks such as SIFA or FTA. The interactions of FA and side-channel countermeasures with combined FA and side-channel attacks are also not well

17 Recreated from the paper: Saha et al. (2019).

understood yet. Given such facts, it is evident that FAs in a symmetric key context will remain a crucial problem for quite some time in the future.

10.8. Notes and further references

FAs on block ciphers were first introduced in Biham and Shamir (1997) in the context of DES block cipher. Later, it was extended to AES. FAs also work for public key implementations and recently proposed post-quantum cryptosystems. Attacks on public-key implementations can be found in Chapter 11 of this volume. We also refer the readers to Liu et al. (2017), where FA has been utilized to attack artificial neural networks.

– Section 10.2. Fault models play a critical role in FAs. Attacks using transient faults are the most common (Biham and Shamir 1997; Tunstall et al. 2011). Discussions on fault models, fault width and different injection instruments can be found in Saha et al. (2009); Canivet et al. (2011); Bhattacharya and Mukhopadhyay (2016); Zhang et al. (2018); Murdock et al. (2020); Sabbagh et al. (2020); Saha et al. (2020b, 2021); Chen et al. (2021). The seminal work of Tunstall and Mukhopadhyay presented a single-byte fault attack on AES, which can extract the key within seconds (Tunstall et al. 2011). The attack also scales to multi-byte random faults (Saha et al. 2009) and key schedules (Ali and Mukhopadhyay 2011). Attacks on deeper rounds can be found in Derbez et al. (2011). Information-theoretic analysis on the optimality of FAs can be found in Ali et al. (2012); Sakiyama et al. (2012).

– Section 10.3. Details on automated tools such as ExpFault and XFC can be found in the respective papers (Khanna et al. 2017; Saha et al. 2018). Also, an open-source demonstration version of the ExpFault tool is available online with the supplementary material of the book.

– Section 10.4. Details of different detection countermeasures can be found in Bertoni et al. (2003); Di Natale et al. (2007); Guo et al. (2015). Some attacks on detection countermeasures have been reported in Patranabis et al. (2015); Selmke et al. (2016); Wang et al. (2016). For the infective described in this chapter, we refer to Gierlichs et al. (2012); Tupsamudre et al. (2014). Instruction level countermeasures are reported in Moro et al. (2014); Patranabis et al. (2017). Interested readers can also check the recently proposed SIFA countermeasures in Daemen et al. (2020); Saha et al. (2020c).

– Section 10.5. Detailed description on SFA can be found in Fuhr et al. (2013); Ghalaty et al. (2014). For SIFA, we refer to Dobraunig et al. (2018a, 2018b). The FTA attack can be found in Saha et al. (2020b). Interested readers may also refer to a combined attack strategy derived from FTA in Saha et al. (2021). The PFA attack and the persistent fault model are presented in Zhang et al. (2018); Pan et al. (2019); Chakraborty et al. (2020).

– Section 10.6. Leakage assessment in FAs is a relatively new topic. For the concepts described in this chapter, readers may refer to Saha et al. (2019, 2020a).

10.9. References

Ali, S.S. and Mukhopadhyay, D. (2011). A differential fault analysis on aes key schedule using single fault. In *2011 Workshop on Fault Diagnosis and Tolerance in Cryptography*. IEEE, Nara.

Ali, S.S., Mukhopadhyay, D., Tunstall, M. (2012). Differential fault analysis of AES: Towards reaching its limits. Cryptology ePrint Archive, Report 2012/446 [Online]. Available at: https://eprint.iacr.org/2012/446.

Bertoni, G., Breveglieri, L., Koren, I., Maistri, P., Piuri, V. (2003). Error analysis and detection procedures for a hardware implementation of the advanced encryption standard. *IEEE Transactions on Computers*, 52(4), 492–505.

Bhattacharya, S. and Mukhopadhyay, D. (2016) Curious case of rowhammer: Flipping secret exponent bits using timing analysis. In *CHES 2016*, Gierlichs, B. and Poschmann, A.Y. (eds). Springer, Heidelberg.

Biham, E. and Shamir, A. (1997). Differential fault analysis of secret key cryptosystems. In *CRYPTO'97*, Kaliski Jr., B.S. (ed.). Springer, Heidelberg.

Canivet, G., Maistri, P., Leveugle, R., Clédière, J., Valette, F., Renaudin, M. (2011). Glitch and laser fault attacks onto a secure AES implementation on a SRAM-based FPGA. *Journal of Cryptology*, 24(2), 247–268.

Chakraborty, A., Bhattacharya, S., Saha, S., Mukhopadhyay, D. (2020). ExplFrame: Exploiting page frame cache for fault analysis of block ciphers. In *Proceedings of 23rd Design, Automation & Test in Europe Conference & Exhibition, (DATE)*. IEEE, Grenoble.

Chen, Z., Vasilakis, G., Murdock, K., Dean, E., Oswald, D., Garcia, F.D. (2021). VoltPillager: Hardware-based fault injection attacks against Intel SGX enclaves using the SVID voltage scaling interface. In *USENIX Security 2021*, Bailey, M. and Greenstadt, R. (eds). USENIX Association.

Daemen, J., Dobraunig, C., Eichlseder, M., Gross, H., Mendel, F., Primas, R. (2020). Protecting against statistical ineffective fault attacks. *IACR Transactions on Cryptographic Hardware and Embedded Systems*, 3, 508–543.

Derbez, P., Fouque, P.-A., Leresteux, D. (2011). Meet-in-the-middle and impossible differential fault analysis on AES. In *Proceedings of 13th International Workshop on Cryptographic Hardware and Embedded Systems (CHES)*. Springer, Nara.

Di Natale, G., Flottes, M.-L., Rouzeyre, B. (2007). A novel parity bit scheme for SBox in AES circuits. In *Proceedings of 10th IEEE Design and Diagnostics of Electronic Circuits and Systems (DDECS)*, Kraków.

Dobraunig, C., Eichlseder, M., Gross, H., Mangard, S., Mendel, F., Primas, R. (2018a). Statistical ineffective fault attacks on masked AES with fault countermeasures In *Proceedings of 24th International Conference on the Theory and Application of Cryptology and Information Security (ASIACRYPT)*. Springer, Brisbane.

Dobraunig, C., Eichlseder, M., Korak, T., Mangard, S., Mendel, F., Primas, R. (2018b). SIFA: Exploiting ineffective fault inductions on symmetric cryptography. *IACR TCHES*, 3, 547–572.

Fuhr, T., Jaulmes, E., Lomné, V., Thillard, A. (2013). Fault attacks on AES with faulty ciphertexts only. In *Proceedings of 10th IEEE Workshop on Fault Diagnosis and Tolerance in Cryptography (FDTC)*, Santa Barbara.

Ghalaty, N.F., Yuce, B., Taha, M., Schaumont, P. (2014). Differential fault intensity analysis. In *Proceedings of 11th IEEE Workshop on Fault Diagnosis and Tolerance in Cryptography (FDTC)*. Busan.

Ghosh, S., Saha, D., Sengupta, A., Chowdhury, D.R. (2015). Preventing fault attacks using fault randomization with a case study on AES. In *Proceedings of 20th Australasian Conference on Information Security and Privacy (ACISP)*. Springer, Brisbane.

Gierlichs, B., Schmidt, J., Tunstall, M. (2012). Infective computation and dummy rounds: Fault protection for block ciphers without check-before-output. In *Proceedings of 2nd International Conference on Cryptology and Information Security in Latin America (LatinCrypt)*. Springer, Santiago.

Guo, X., Mukhopadhyay, D., Jin, C., Karri, R. (2015). Security analysis of concurrent error detection against differential fault analysis. *Journal of Cryptographic Engineering*, 5(3), 153–169.

Khanna, P., Rebeiro, C., Hazra, A. (2017). XFC: A framework for eXploitable Fault Characterization in block ciphers. In *Proceedings of 55th ACM/IEEE Design Automation Conference (DAC)*. IEEE, Austin.

Liu, Y., Wei, L., Luo, B., Xu, Q. (2017). Fault injection attack on deep neural network. In *2017 IEEE/ACM International Conference on Computer-Aided Design (ICCAD)*. IEEE, Irvine.

Moro, N., Heydemann, K., Encrenaz, E., Robisson, B. (2014). Formal verification of a software countermeasure against instruction skip attacks. *Journal of Cryptographic Engineering*, 4(3), 145–156.

Murdock, K., Oswald, D., Garcia, F.D., Van Bulck, J., Gruss, D., Piessens, F. (2020). Plundervolt: Software-based fault injection attacks against intel SGX. In *2020 IEEE Symposium on Security and Privacy*. San Francisco.

Pan, J., Zhang, F., Ren, K., Bhasin, S. (2019). One fault is all it needs: Breaking higher-order masking with persistent fault analysis. In *Proceedings of 22nd Design, Automation & Test in Europe Conference & Exhibition (DATE)*. IEEE, Florence.

Patranabis, S., Chakraborty, A., Nguyen, P.H., Mukhopadhyay, D. (2015). A biased fault attack on the time redundancy countermeasure for AES. In *Proceedings of 6th International Workshop on Constructive Side-Channel Analysis and Secure Design (COSADE)*. Springer, Berlin.

Patranabis, S., Chakraborty, A., Mukhopadhyay, D. (2017). Fault tolerant infective countermeasure for AES. *Journal of Hardware and Systems Security*, 1(1), 3–17.

Sabbagh, M., Fei, Y., Kaeli, D. (2020). A novel GPU overdrive fault attack. In *Proceedings 57th ACM/IEEE Design Automation Conference (DAC)*. IEEE, San Francisco.

Saha, S. and Mukhopadhyay, D. (2021). Transform without encode is not sufficient for SIFA and FTA security: A case study. In *COSADE 2021*, Lugano, 85–104.

Saha, D., Mukhopadhyay, D., Chowdhury, D.R. (2009). A diagonal fault attack on the advanced encryption standard. IACR Cryptology ePrint Archive.

Saha, S., Mukhopadhyay, D., Dasgupta, P. (2018). ExpFault: An automated framework for exploitable fault characterization in block ciphers. *IACR Transactions on Cryptographic Hardware and Embedded Systems*, 2, 242–276.

Saha, S., Kumar, S.N., Patranabis, S., Mukhopadhyay, D., Dasgupta, P. (2019). ALAFA: Automatic leakage assessment for fault attack countermeasures. In *Proceedings of the 56th ACM/IEEE Design Automation Conference (DAC)*. ACM, Las Vegas.

Saha, S., Alam, M., Bag, A., Mukhopadhyay, D., Dasgupta, P. (2020a). Leakage assessment in fault attacks: A deep learning perspective. IACR Cryptology ePrint Archive.

Saha, S., Bag, A., Roy, D.B., Patranabis, S., Mukhopadhyay, D. (2020b). Fault template attacks on block ciphers exploiting fault propagation. In *EUROCRYPT 2020*, Canteaut, A. and Ishai, Y. (eds). Springer, Heidelberg.

Saha, S., Jap, D., Roy, D.B., Chakraborty, A., Bhasin, S., Mukhopadhyay, D. (2020c). A framework to counter statistical ineffective fault analysis of block ciphers using domain transformation and error correction. *IEEE Transactions on Information Forensics and Security*, 15, 1905–1919.

Saha, S., Bag, A., Jap, D., Mukhopadhyay, D., Bhasin, S. (2021). Divided we stand, united we fall: Security analysis of some SCA+SIFA countermeasures against SCA-enhanced fault template attacks. In *ASIACRYPT 2021*, Tibouchi, M. and Wang, H. (eds). Springer, Heidelberg.

Sakiyama, K., Li, Y., Iwamoto, M., Ohta, K. (2012). Information-theoretic approach to optimal differential fault analysis. *IEEE Transactions on Information Forensics and Security*, 7(1), 109–120.

Selmke, B., Heyszl, J., Sigl, G. (2016). Attack on a DFA protected AES by simultaneous laser fault injections. In *2016 Workshop on Fault Diagnosis and Tolerance in Cryptography (FDTC)*. IEEE, Santa Barbara.

Tunstall, M., Mukhopadhyay, D., Ali, S. (2011). Differential fault analysis of the advanced encryption standard using a single fault. In *Proceedings of 5th Information Security Theory and Practice. Security and Privacy of Mobile Devices in Wireless Communication (WISTP)*. Springer, Crete.

Tupsamudre, H., Bisht, S., Mukhopadhyay, D. (2014). Destroying fault invariant with randomization. In *Proceedings of 16th International Workshop on Cryptographic Hardware and Embedded Systems (CHES)*. Springer, Busan.

Wang, B., Liu, L., Deng, C., Zhu, M., Yin, S., Wei, S. (2016). Against double fault attacks: Injection effort model, space and time randomization based countermeasures for reconfigurable array architecture. *IEEE Transactions on Information Forensics and Security*, 11(6), 1151–1164.

Zhang, F., Lou, X., Zhao, X., Bhasin, S., He, W., Ding, R., Qureshi, S., Ren, K. (2018). Persistent fault analysis on block ciphers. *IACR TCHES*, 3, 150–172.

11

Fault Attacks on Public-key Cryptographic Algorithms

Michael TUNSTALL[1] and Guillaume BARBU[2]

[1] *Google, Mountain View, United States*

[2] *IDEMIA, Courbevoie, France*

11.1. Introduction

The security of public-key cryptographic algorithms relies on the complexity of well-established mathematical problems. For example, the security of the RSA algorithm is based on the difficulty of factoring large numbers, while algorithms using elliptic curve cryptography (ECC) rely on the intractability of solving elliptic curve discrete logarithm problems. However, despite the theoretical strength of public-key cryptography, certain attacks can still exploit weaknesses arising from incorrect parameter usage or algorithm implementation.

Among the threats faced by public-key cryptography, fault attacks pose a significant challenge. The first fault attack on public-key cryptography was described in the literature in 1996. The authors presented an attack that could reveal an RSA-CRT key by a simple greatest common denominator (GCD) computation if a fault occurred during the signature generation. This work remained theoretical until descriptions of implementations were published a few years later. Prior to this, countermeasures against fault attacks were not considered necessary in devices such as smartcards. However, this seminal work triggered extensive research and led to the development of numerous attacks and countermeasures aimed at protecting public-key cryptography in embedded devices. This chapter explores the realm

Embedded Cryptography 1,
coordinated by Emmanuel PROUFF, Guénaël RENAULT,
Matthieu RIVAIN and Colin O'FLYNN.

of fault attacks on public-key cryptography. Fault attacks are often specific to individual algorithms, varying with the underlying mathematical problem and the implementation details. We present case studies of some well-known and illustrative attacks, while also introducing general fault attack strategies proposed in the literature.

11.2. Preliminaries

In this section, we will describe the algorithms that are of interest in this chapter and define the notations used.

11.2.1. *RSA*

RSA was the first public key cryptographic algorithm to appear in the literature, and is still widely used. An RSA keypair consists of a public key (n, e) and a private key (n, d) such that $n = pq$ is the product of two primes, and:

$$e\,d \equiv 1 \mod \phi(n)\,,$$

where ϕ is typically Euler's totient function, and in this case $\phi(n) = (p-1)(q-1)$. There is no requirement regarding the bit length of the individual primes. However, for an RSA modulus of bit length k, it is convenient to generate two primes in the interval $\left(2^{(k-1)/2}, 2^{k/2}\right)$. This ensures that the product of the two primes will have bit length k and that they require the same number of computer words in memory.

The value e must be chosen first, and is typically a constant such as $2^{16}+1$; then d must be computed as its inverse mod $\phi(n)$. The keypair can be used to create an encryption or signature scheme.

11.2.1.1. *The RSA signature scheme*

In a signature scheme, one user $\mathcal{A}$ can sign a message and any user can then verify that the message was signed by $\mathcal{A}$. For example, a message m can be signed using the private key belonging to user $\mathcal{A}$ to generate a signature s, that is:

$$s \leftarrow m^d \bmod n\,,$$

and can then be verified by any user who ascertains that:

$$m \stackrel{?}{=} s^e \bmod n.$$

11.2.1.2. *The RSA encryption scheme*

The RSA encryption scheme works the other way around. Any user can encrypt a message using the public key belonging to user $\mathcal{A}$, but one user can decrypt these messages.

For example, a message m can be encrypted using user $\mathcal{A}$'s public key to produce ciphertext c, that is:

$$c \leftarrow m^e \bmod n\,,$$

and user $\mathcal{A}$ can decipher the ciphertext by computing:

$$m \leftarrow c^d \bmod n.$$

11.2.1.3. *RSA using the Chinese remainder theorem*

Given the bit length of the elements of the private key pair, it can be quite time consuming to generate a signature by computing:

$$s \leftarrow m^d \bmod n.$$

The exponentiation can be replaced with two smaller exponentiations using the Chinese remainder theorem. That is, let $s_p = m^{d \bmod p-1} \bmod p$ and $s_q = m^{d \bmod q-1} \bmod q$, then we can compute:

$$s \leftarrow \left(s_p\, q^{-1} \bmod p\right) q + \left(s_q\, p^{-1} \bmod q\right) p. \qquad [11.1]$$

In practice, we would use an alternate form of [11.1], referred to as Garner's algorithm, as follows:

$$s \leftarrow \left(\left(s_p - s_q\right) q^{-1} \bmod p\right) q + s_q. \qquad [11.2]$$

The form in [11.2] is more commonly used as only one inversion is required and RSA-CRT private key is (p, q, d_p, d_q, i_q), where:

$$d_p \equiv d \pmod{p-1}\,, \quad d_q \equiv d \pmod{q-1} \quad \text{and} \quad i_q \equiv q^{-1} \pmod{p}.$$

11.2.2. *Elliptic curve cryptography*

In this section, we introduce the algorithms in the context of a group formed from the points on an elliptic curve. We define the elliptic curve $\mathcal{E}$ over a finite field $\mathbb{F}_p$, for a large prime p. $\mathcal{E}$ consists of points (x, y), with x, y in $\mathbb{F}_p$, that satisfy, for example, the short Weierstraß equation:

$$\mathcal{E} : y^2 = x^3 + a\,x + b$$

with $a, b \in \mathbb{F}_p$, and the point at infinity denoted $\boldsymbol{O}$. The set $\mathcal{E}(\mathbb{F}_p)$ is defined as $\mathcal{E}(\mathbb{F}_p) = \{(x, y) \in \mathcal{E} \,|\, x, y \in \mathbb{F}_p\} \cup \{\boldsymbol{O}\}$, where $\mathcal{E}(\mathbb{F}_p)$ forms an Abelian group under the chord-and-tangent rule and $\boldsymbol{O}$ is the identity element. There are two commonly used algorithms that use ECC.

11.2.2.1. *ECDH*

Elliptic curve Diffie–Hellman (ECDH) is used as a means of determining a common key without revealing any information to someone observing the communication. If we consider two users that generate two integers a and b, where $0 < a, b < p$, respectively, the users can take a system wide point $\mathbf{G}$ and compute the scalar multiplications:

$$\boldsymbol{P} = [a]\,\boldsymbol{G} \quad \text{and} \quad \boldsymbol{Q} = [b]\,\boldsymbol{G}.$$

The users can exchange $\boldsymbol{P}$ and $\boldsymbol{Q}$ and compute:

$$\boldsymbol{S} = [a]\,\boldsymbol{Q} \quad \text{and} \quad \boldsymbol{R} = [b]\,\boldsymbol{P},$$

respectively. Then the users can use the generated point to derive a cryptographic key since $\boldsymbol{S} = \boldsymbol{R}$. While a and b are typically ephemeral, it is important to consider the security of the case where long-term keys are used. That is, we consider the case where an attacker can increase their knowledge of a or b through repeated use of the ECDH.

11.2.2.2. *ECDSA*

Given a system wide base point $\boldsymbol{G} = (x, y)$ for an elliptic curve $\mathcal{E}$ over $\mathbb{F}_p$ with order $q = |\mathcal{E}|$, with private key d and hash function h, the signer that wants to sign a message hash h picks a random $\kappa < q$ and computes:

$$r \overset{x}{\leftarrow} [\kappa]\boldsymbol{G} \text{ and } s \leftarrow \kappa^{-1}\,(h + d\,r) \bmod q\,.$$

We denote the extraction of the x-coordinate of a point and its assignment to a variable by $\overset{x}{\leftarrow}$ and h is some hash function. The signature of m is the pair: $\{r, s\}$. We note that the security of this signature scheme relies on the fact that the random value κ is actually uniformly distributed and remains unknown to an attacker.

A signature can then be verified by any user who ascertains that:

$$r \stackrel{?x}{=} \left[h\, s^{-1} \bmod q\right] \boldsymbol{G} + \left[r\, s^{-1} \bmod q\right] \boldsymbol{P}_d,$$

where we are checking the x-coordinate of the result of the right-hand side and $\boldsymbol{P}_d$ is the public key corresponding the private key d.

11.3. Attacking the RSA using the Chinese remainder theorem

The discussion of fault attacks in the academic literature proposed a variety of methods for attacking public key cryptographic algorithms. The first fault attack targeting public-key cryptography, sometimes referred to as the "Bellcore" attack, targets an RSA implementation using the Chinese remainder theorem. The attack is very effective as it only requires one fault during the computation of a signature to factor an RSA modulus.

This attack requires a fault to be introduced in the computation of s_p or s_q before they are combined, as shown in [11.1] and [11.2]. If we assume that s_q is not computed correctly and results in s'_q, then the resulting signature will be:

$$s' \leftarrow \left(s_p\, q^{-1} \bmod p\right) q + \left(s'_q\, p^{-1} \bmod q\right) p. \qquad [11.3]$$

Then, we can evaluate the difference between s from [11.1] and s':

$$\begin{aligned} \delta &\equiv s - s' \\ &\equiv \left(s_q\, p^{-1} \bmod q\right) p - \left(s'_q\, p^{-1} \bmod q\right) p \\ &\equiv \left(\left(s_q - s'_q\right) p^{-1} \bmod q\right) p \pmod{n} \end{aligned} \qquad [11.4]$$

Hence, δ is a multiple of p and not of q. We can then extract p by computing a greatest common divisor (GCD) and we can determine the integer factors of n as follows:

$$p = \mathrm{GCD}\left(\delta \bmod n, n\right) \quad \text{and} \quad q = \frac{n}{p}.$$

The same process can be applied if s_p is changed to s'_p and will return q from the GCD. An attacker does not need to know which variable has been affected as the GCD will return either p or q, which is sufficient to factorize n.

Hence, all that is required to break RSA is one correct signature and one faulty one. Likewise, we could apply this to RSA decryption if the resulting messages can be analyzed.

This attack is particularly hard to prevent since many fault effects could be successful. It would also be tempting to assume that some blinding on the input would prevent the attack. However, that is not the case.

11.4. Attacking a modular exponentiation

In this section, we describe attacks on the modular exponentiation used to compute RSA, but the attacks are equally applicable to exponentiation in other groups, such as the scalar multiplication used in groups formed from the points on an elliptic curve used in ECDH.

The attack compares the result of generating signatures from the same message with and without faults. While a signature is being computed, an attacker generates a fault causing one bit of the private exponent to be changed, resulting in a faulty signature s'. If we assume that the ith bit of d is complemented to change it to d', then we have:

$$s'\, s^{-1} \equiv m^{d'-d} \equiv \begin{cases} m^{2^i} \pmod{n} & \text{if the } i\text{th bit of } d = 0, \\ m^{-2^i} \pmod{n} & \text{if the } i\text{th bit of } d = 1. \end{cases} \qquad [11.5]$$

This attack can be improved by raising the formula to the power of the public exponent e, much like the RSA-CRT analysis above, giving:

$$s'^{e}\, m^{-1} \equiv m^{e(d'-d)} \equiv \begin{cases} m^{2^i\, e} \pmod{n} & \text{if the } i\text{th bit of } d = 0, \\ m^{-2^i\, e} \pmod{n} & \text{if the } i\text{th bit of } d = 1. \end{cases} \qquad [11.6]$$

In this case, it is not necessary to know the correct signature s.

An attacker can compute $s'^{e}\, m^{-1} \bmod N$ for all the possible one-bit fault errors in d. This requires a total of $\log_2 d$ trials to completely derive d if an attacker is able to dictate which bit of d is complemented. It would seem reasonable that this should apply for faults that affect multiple bits. However, there would be some ambiguity on the effect of the fault, that is, if we consider a fault that affects two consecutive bits we cannot be sure which bits since:

$$2^i\, 2^{-(i+1)} = 2$$

for all possible i. The more bits that could be affected the larger this problem becomes, particularly if the number of bits that are effected is not known.

The attack can still be extended to consider faults that affect a byte of an exponent. To avoid any ambiguity, the fault is treated as an integer difference between a correct exponent byte and a faulted exponent byte. As above, we define the private key as d and d' as the corresponding corrupt private key. We define d_i and d'_i as the i-th byte of d and d' respectively. A fault on one byte will therefore produce:

$$d_i + \gamma = d'_i \qquad [11.7]$$

with $d_i, d'_i \in \{0, \ldots, 255\}$ and $\gamma \in \{-255, \ldots, 255\}$, where $\gamma = 0$ corresponds to no error. Given the set to which d_i and d'_i belong, the possible values for γ will be:

$$\gamma \in \{-d_i, \ldots, 255 - d_i\}. \qquad [11.8]$$

If two faults are observed, γ and γ', the possible values of d_i can be restricted to n values where:

$$\gamma < \gamma' : \gamma' - \gamma = 256 - n\,, \qquad [11.9]$$

which means that:

$$-\gamma < d_i \leq -\gamma + (n - 1). \qquad [11.10]$$

This attack is expected to identify a byte with 384 faults affecting a particular byte, as we need to observe the maximum positive and negative fault effect. If exponent bits are read in larger word sizes, the number of required faults is likely to be prohibitive.

If a fault can be produced that will only change bits in one direction, then it would be possible to directly determine the effect of a fault by determining the power of two in the difference between a correct and a faulted ciphertext. This effect can be produced by preventing exponent words from being read by a microprocessor. That is, attempt to skip a read instruction in a microprocessor so that the content of the target register is likely to be zero.

An alternative approach is to determine what operations affect the output of an algorithm. If we consider the binary exponentiation algorithm, as shown in Algorithm 11.1, an exponent is read bit-by-bit. If a bit is equal to zero then R_0 is squared, and if a bit is equal to one the R_0 is squared and multiplied by the input. It

Algorithm 11.1. The Binary Exponentiation Algorithm

Input: $x \in \mathbb{G}$, n-bit integers $\kappa = \sum_{i=0}^{n-1} k_i \, 2^i$
Output: x^{κ}

$R_0 \leftarrow 1_{\mathbb{G}}$
for $i = n - 1$ **down to** 0 **do**
  $R_0 \leftarrow {R_0}^2$
  if $k_i = 1$ **then** $R_0 \leftarrow R_0 \cdot x$
end for
return R_0

was noted that if we can observe some side channel and distinguish a squaring operation from a multiplication, the individual bit of the exponent could be determined.

A possible countermeasure to this type of attack consists of adding unnecessary (usually called *dummy*) operations to remove the side channel information. This is shown in Algorithm 11.2 where we can see a fixed pattern of squaring operations and multiplications as an exponent is read bit-by-bit. If a bit is equal to zero, then the output is written to R_0, but then this is not used in subsequent operations.

Algorithm 11.2. The Multiply and Square Always Algorithm

Input: $x \in \mathbb{G}$, n-bit integers $\kappa = \sum_{i=0}^{n-1} k_i \, 2^i$
Output: x^{κ}

$R_0 \leftarrow 1_{\mathbb{G}}$
$R_1 \leftarrow 1_{\mathbb{G}}$
for $i = n - 1$ **down to** 0 **do**
  $R_1 \leftarrow {R_1}^2$
  $R_{k_i} \leftarrow R_1 \cdot x$
end for
return R_1

11.5. Attacking the ECDSA

In section 11.2.2.2, we note that the nonce used in ECDSA is required to be uniformly distributed over the interval $[1, q)$ and what can happen if a nonce is the same for two signatures. This situation would be hard to produce using a fault. However, a fault injection can lead the loop copying the nonce into a co-processor to be terminated early. This would leave some memory untouched that would have a high chance of being zero. Moreover, if we can observe some side channel, it is possible to see that the attack has been successful as the time required to copy the nonce will be reduced.

If we assume that the nonce is copied into a co-processor from least significant word to most-significant word, then terminating this copy early can result in a certain number of the most-significant bits of the nonce being set to zero. In this case, attacks similar to those presented in Chapter 8 of Volume 3 can be applied to derive the private key by solving an instance of the hidden number problem using lattice reduction.

This technique can be applied when the most significant bits, the least significant bits, or even when some middle bits κ_i are set to a known value (typically zero).

11.6. Other attack strategies

Depending on the fault model that can be practically considered on the targeted device, we may devise other attack techniques. We describe some of them in the following.

11.6.1. *Safe errors*

A safe error is a fault that does not alter the output of the targeted algorithm. An explicit example of such attacks emerges from Algorithm 11.2, presented above. Indeed, if we could inject a fault into the multiplication in line 5 of Algorithm 11.2, it would reveal the value of k_i. That is, if we inject a fault and the bit equals zero, then the correct result would be produced and if the bit equals one then an incorrect result would be returned.

Safe errors have been proposed against various implementations in the literature. Their typical targets are operations that may or may not be dummy depending on a sensitive value. Beyond the square-and-multiply-always algorithm, it also concerns many SCA protections, such as the use of atomicity in the ECC context, as exposed in Chapter 10 of Volume 2.

11.6.2. *Statistical ineffective fault attacks*

Statistical fault attacks (SFA) are a kind of attacks where the adversary exploits the fact that the faulted output values are not uniformly distributed to recover the key with a divide and conquer approach.

Statistical ineffective fault attacks (SIFA) extend this type of attack and can also be seen as an evolution of safe errors. They share with SFA the assumption that the faulty values are not uniformly distributed, and like safe errors, they exploit the fact that the fault may or may not modify the result of the targeted operation, depending on the value of the targeted variable. The information gathered from this observation can then be accumulated for several faulted executions, like for a side channel attack.

The idea of SIFA applied to asymmetric cryptography is that, taking guesses $\hat{d}_i$ on a part d_i (a byte typically) of the targeted sensitive value d, the attacker can compute backward from the faulty output s' to the value $x'_{\hat{d}_i}$, which is the result of the fault on the genuine value x. Knowing the expected distribution f for x (or a function of x), the attacker can compute the distance between f and the observed distributions of $x'_{\hat{d}_i}$ (or a function of $x'_{\hat{d}_i}$) for all guesses $\hat{d}_i$. If the guess is incorrect, the observed distribution should be close to f. If the guess is correct, the observed distribution should reflect the bias induced by the fault injection, which allows us to discriminate the value d_i.

Figure 11.1 illustrates the results obtained when the most significant byte of the secret exponent d is faulted, following a random-AND fault model, that is:

$$x' = x \text{ AND } \textbf{rand}().$$

Here, the distribution of the Hamming weight of x' is observed. Intuitively, it is quite straightforward to realize that a fault model that sets some bits at zero like the random-AND fault model will always decrease the Hamming weight of the targeted value, and the squared Euclidean imbalance (SEI) is used to estimate the distance between the observed distribution and the expected one.

11.6.3. *Lattice-based fault attacks*

Following the first attack taking advantage of the lattice reduction technique, other approaches have been proposed to take into account faults impacting a large part of the manipulated variable. Instead of assuming known bits of a sensitive variable, here, the attacker assumes some known bits of the induced error ε. Typically the fault model considered in such attacks is called the bounded error fault model and defines the faulty value as:

$$x' = x + \varepsilon 2^l, \varepsilon < 2^w.$$

In other words, w bits of x are faulted, starting at the l-th bit. Such attacks, called lattice-based fault attacks or FA-LLL, have been applied to different signature and encryption schemes, such as the RSA plain encryption, EdDSA and the deterministic version of the ECDSA (dECDSA).

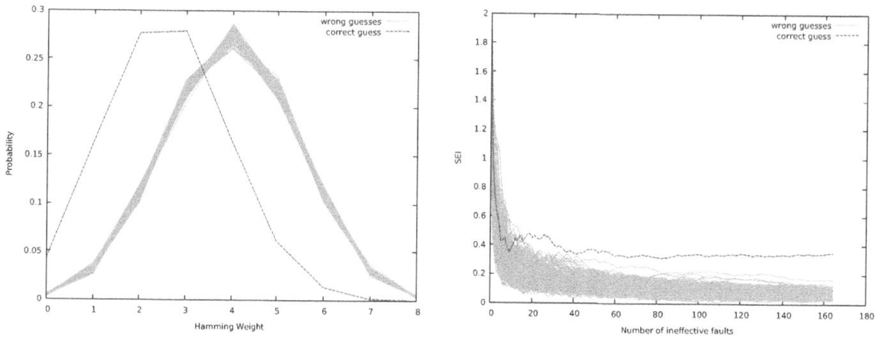

(a) Distribution of the Hamming weight of the intermediate result for all key hypotheses (correct one in dashed red)

(b) Convergence of the SEI for the different key hypotheses (correct one in dashed red)

Figure 11.1. *Result of the SIFA targeting the most significant byte of the secret exponent, from Barbu et al. (2021). For a color version of this figure, see www.iste.co.uk/prouff/cryptography1.zip*

For dECDSA, the ephemeral key is not obtained from a random source, but is rather derived from the private key and the input: $\kappa = F(e, d)$. So assuming that we inject a fault during the computation of the signature (say when computing $h + dr$), we get s':

$$s' \leftarrow \kappa^{-1} \left(h + dr + \varepsilon\, 2^l\right) \bmod q.$$

And thus ε can be expressed as:

$$\varepsilon = 2^{-l} \left(s' - s\right) \bmod q.$$

Obtaining several faulty for random faults ε_i and recalling that $\varepsilon_i < 2^w$, we can apply the hidden number problem approach described in Chapter 8 of Volume 3 to recover the deterministic κ and then the private key d.

11.7. Countermeasures

We have seen in the previous section that the discovery of a fault attack path leads to the necessity of defining countermeasures to this attack. Creating robust and efficient countermeasures is always a challenge and is detailed in Chapter 12. In the following. we discuss some topics more specifically related to public-key cryptography and emphasize the need to assess all possible attack paths on these countermeasures.

11.7.1. *Padding schemes*

A good portion of fault attacks on asymmetric cryptography schemes require the attacker to have knowledge of the message and the faulty output, or of the legitimate and faulty outputs for the same message. In legacy protocols, these assumptions are met, and thus many fault attacks are practical in a real-world setting. However, in most recent cryptographic protocols, the message is encoded before being processed by the considered crypto primitive, and some random quantities are introduced in the formatting, hindering the requirement for a fault attack defined above.

As an illustration, we can follow-up on the *Bellcore attack* case, considering now that a PKCS#1 v2.2 encoding scheme is applied to the message, following the probabilistic signature scheme (PSS) method. When computing the signature of a message M with the PSS encoding, we compute $s = \mathrm{EM}^d \mod n$. For two different signatures s_0 and s_1, two different values EM_0 and EM_1 are raised to the power of d modulo n. As a result, an attacker cannot exploit a faulty signature, as described in equation [11.4].

11.7.2. *Verification, detection and infection*

In parallel to the publication of new and inventive fault attacks, designers try to propose new methods to counteract such a major threat. Among the various ideas that have been proposed so far, we can split these proposals into three groups: the signature *verification*, the *detective* and the *infective* methods.

The first one is very specific to signature schemes and it is often very costly. For instance, verifying an ECDSA signature is as lengthy as the signature process itself.

The second method is based on redundancy checking. It avoids outputting the result when a check is wrong. But it also implies that the check may be the target of a second fault injection, which is the limit of this method.

The third and last method involves modifying and amplifying the injected error in such a way that the attacker cannot retrieve any information from the corresponding faulty output. This approach is definitely the most challenging way to counteract a fault attack. It is indeed very tricky to conceive such a countermeasure, in particular in the case of public-key cryptography. Indeed, the algebraic structure of the different elements turns out to be an advantage for the attackers and lets them identify and/or remove the amplified error. As far as we know, all published infective countermeasures for public-key cryptography have been broken.

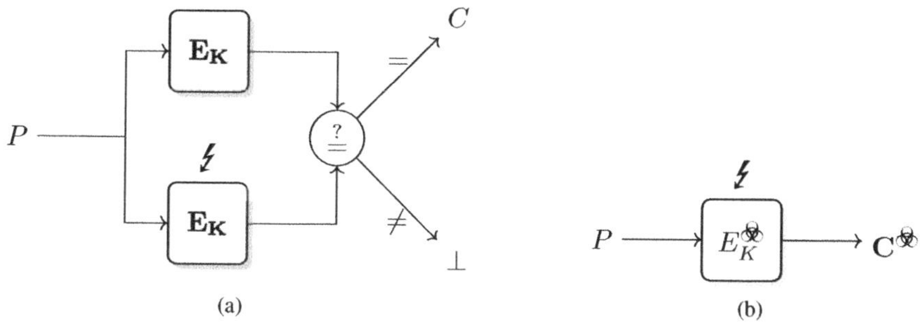

Figure 11.2. *Detective (left) and infective (right) countermeasures*

11.7.3. *Attacks on countermeasures*

When designing countermeasures, we should also make sure that the countermeasure does not introduce additional weaknesses. Obviously, a countermeasure against fault attacks should not introduce a new fault attack path. But it should also avoid the manipulation of sensitive variables that could be used in a side-channel attack. For instance, using a redundant check to counteract the Bellcore attack described in section 11.3, as illustrated in Figure 11.3, seems to be an efficient security mechanism. The verification step protects the algorithm from returning a faulty signature that can jeopardize the confidentiality of the secret key. However, assuming a fault has been induced during the execution, we should also ensure that the comparison does not introduce a side-channel vulnerability.

Indeed, if the input message m is faulted into $m+\varepsilon$ in one of the branch (say in the mod p branch for instance) at the very beginning of the blinding step of the scheme, then it holds that the faulty signature s' satisfies:

$$s'^e = m + \varepsilon q\,(q^{-1} \mod p) \mod n \qquad [11.11]$$

If the attacker can inject a constant fault ε, it is then possible for them to recover the value of $\varepsilon q\,(q^{-1} \mod p) \mod n$ by a side-channel attack targeting the selection function $m + \hat{k} \mod n$. Following this approach allows the secret value to be recovered byte by byte, and eventually leads to the recovery of q since it is the greatest common divisor of $\varepsilon q\,(q^{-1} \mod p) \mod n$ and n. In addition, using lattice reduction techniques allows the reduction of the number of side-channel attacks to be performed. Indeed, the full secret value can be recovered directly with the knowledge of about the half of its bytes with that approach.

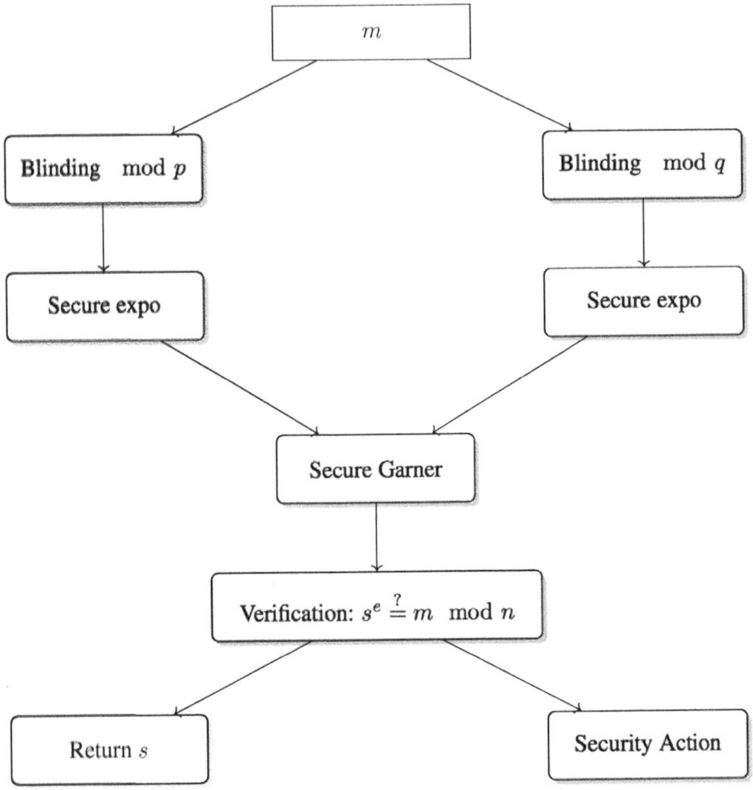

Figure 11.3. *CRT-RSA with a final verification*

11.8. Conclusion

In this chapter we described some case studies of attacks that can be applied to public-key cryptographic algorithms, and in most cases, practical instances of these attacks have been described. Each attack is very different, as the attacks typically use an injected fault to gain an advantage in solving the underlying problem used to construct the cryptosystem. While there are various approaches to fault attacks, there is no general strategy for constructing new fault attacks for public-key cryptographic algorithms, and each attack must be tailored to the specific targeted algorithm.

An illustrative example of this is the ongoing work of the community to assess the resistance of the algorithms highlighted by the recent effort to standardize public-key cryptosystems capable of withstanding the emergence of quantum computer.

While these algorithms are designed to resist the quantum computer threat, they are not inherently immune to fault attacks. As a result, several publications have proposed some fault attack paths against both signature and key encapsulation mechanisms. In particular, some mechanisms that are common to several candidates have been targeted:

– The Number-Theoretic Transform (NTT).

– The Fujisaki–Okamoto transform (FO).

Considering the extensive literature available on fault attacks on *classical* public-key cryptography, we can expect that a lot of work is still needed to implement post-quantum public-key cryptography that is secure against fault injection.

11.9. Notes and further references

– Section 11.1. The seminal fault attack on CRT RSA is described by Boneh et al. (2001). Some practical implementations can be found in Aumüller et al. (2003) and Bar-El et al. (2006).

– Section 11.2.1. The security of the RSA schemes relies on it being hard to factorize n, as, otherwise, any user would be able to compute $\phi(n)$. Hence, at the time of writing, the minimal recommended bit length of n is 3,000 bits as per SOG-IS Crypto Working Group (2023).

– Section 11.2.2.2. It is important that the random value κ is not reused and is uniformly distributed in the interval $[1, q)$. Several high-profile attacks have been published where ECDSA was implemented using the same value for κ, and an example is given by Brengel and Rossow (2018). If we take two message hashes h_1, h_2 to produce signatures $\{r, s_1\}$ and $\{r, s_2\}$, respectively, then the private key can be computed.

$$
\begin{aligned}
\frac{s_2\, h_1 - s_1\, h_2}{r\,(s_1 - s_2)} &= \frac{h_1\, h_2 + r\, h_1\, d - h_1\, h_2 - r\, h_2\, d}{r\, h_1 + r^2\, d - r\, h_2 - r^2\, d} \\
&= \frac{d\,(r\, h_1 - r\, h_2)}{r\, h_1 - r\, h_2} \\
&\equiv d \pmod{q}
\end{aligned}
$$

– Section 11.3. It was noted by Joye et al. (1999) that only one faulty signature is required as we could use the known message. That is, using the example above, the attacker would compute:

$$p = \mathrm{GCD}\left(s'^{e} - m \bmod n, n\right) \quad \text{and} \quad q = \frac{n}{p}.$$

The simplest blinding method would be to compute a signature where the input is multiplied by some random integer r, where $0 < r < n$, and the result is corrected at the end. That is, we compute a signature s:

$$s \leftarrow (r\,m)^d r^{-d} \bmod n$$

If the exponentiation with d is computed with the CRT, then we have:

$$s_p = (r\,m)^{d \bmod p-1} \bmod p \quad \text{and} \quad s_q = (r\,m)^{d \bmod q-1} \bmod q\,,$$

and:

$$s \leftarrow \left(\left(s_p\,q^{-1} \bmod p\right) q + \left(s_q\,p^{-1} \bmod q\right) p\right) r^{-d} \bmod n.$$

If, as above, we assume that s_q is changed to s'_q, then:

$$\begin{aligned}\delta \equiv s - s' &\equiv \left(\left(s_q\,p^{-1} \bmod q\right) p - \left(s'_q\,p^{-1} \bmod q\right) p\right) r^{-d} \pmod n\\ &\equiv \left(\left(s_q - s'_q\right) p^{-1} \bmod q\right) p r^{-d} \bmod n \pmod n\end{aligned}$$

We assume that r is the same in both cases without loss of generality, since r will not affect the value of s. We can see that δ is a multiple of p and the attack is largely unchanged.

Likewise, Ebeid and Lambert (2010) also propose using a random integer r, where $0 < r < n$, and computing a signature s as:

$$s \leftarrow (r^e\,m)^{d-1} r^{e-1} m \bmod n$$

which results in $s = r^{d\,e-1} m^d \bmod n$ where $r^{d\,e-1} \equiv 1 \pmod n$. If the exponentiation with $d - 1$ is computed with the CRT, then we have:

$$s_p = (r^e\,m)^{d-1 \bmod p-1} \bmod p \quad \text{and} \quad s_q = (r^e\,m)^{d-1 \bmod q-1} \bmod q\,,$$

and:

$$s \leftarrow \left(\left(s_p q^{-1} \bmod p\right) q + \left(s_q p^{-1} \bmod q\right) p\right) r^{e-1} m \bmod n.$$

If, as above, we assume that s_q is changed to s'_q, then:

$$\begin{aligned}\delta \equiv s - s' &\equiv \left(\left(s_q p^{-1} \bmod q\right) p - \left(s'_q p^{-1} \bmod q\right) p\right) r^{e-1} m \pmod{n} \\ &\equiv \left(\left(s_q - s'_q\right) p^{-1} \bmod q\right) p r^{e-1} m \bmod n \pmod{n}\end{aligned}$$

Again we assume that r is the same in both cases without loss of generality, since r will not affect the value of s, and we have a factor of p. A more complex version of this is described by Hamburg et al. (2021), but still does not prevent the attack.

– Section 11.4. The attack on the straightforward implementation of the RSA is defined by Bao et al. (1997). The improvement allowing us to perform the attack without the knowledge of the correct signature is demonstrated by Joye et al. (1997). The attack assuming a random byte fault model is described by Giraud et al. (2010). The use of dummy operations in the exponentiation loop was first proposed by Coron (1999). It was noted by Yen and Joye (2000) that if we could inject a fault into the multiplication in line 5 of Algorithm 11.2, it would reveal the value of k_i. That is, if we inject a fault and the bit equals zero, then the correct result would be produced, and if the bit equals one, then an incorrect result would be returned. This type of attack is typically referred to as a safe-error attack since the aim of an attacker is to inject a fault that does not affect the result.

– Section 11.5. Lattice attacks in such contexts are described by Howgrave-Graham and Smart (2001) and Nguyen and Shparlinski (2003). The first combination of lattice reduction techniques with fault attacks can be found in Naccache et al. (2005). When only a few bits of the extreme parts of the nonce are unknown, we should follow the approach presented by De Micheli and Heninger (2020).

– Section 11.6.1. This attack was first noted by Yen and Joye (2000).

– Section 11.6.2. SIFA were first applied to implementations of the AES, first on an unsecure version (Dobraunig et al. 2018b) and shortly after on a masked version (Dobraunig et al. 2018a). The reader can find a more detailed description of this kind of attack in Chapter 10. The approach mentioned in this section can be applied to other public-key algorithms, as detailed in Barbu et al. (2021).

– Section 11.6.3. Lattice-based fault attacks were introduced by Cao et al. (2022), where the authors showed that several implementations of deterministic signatures, namely, dECDSA and EdDSA, were vulnerable to such attacks. The bounded random error fault model considered in this work may seem far-fetched at first.

However, it is coherent with a fault affecting the source or destination pointers in a copy loop, for instance.

– Section 11.7.2. As far as we know, all infective countermeasures for public-key algorithms have been broken (Yen et al. 2002; Blömer et al. 2003; Ciet and Joye 2005; Schmidt et al. 2010; Lomné et al. 2012; Gierlichs et al. 2012; Tupsamudre et al. 2014; Rauzy and Guilley 2014; Cao et al. 2022; Bauer et al. 2022) (see Wagner 2004; Yen et al. 2006; Berzati et al. 2008; Feix and Venelli 2013; Battistello and Giraud 2015, 2016; Feng et al. 2020; Battistello and Giraud 2013; Barbu and Giraud 2023 for instance).

– Section 11.7.3. The proof for relation [11.11] can be found in Barbu et al. (2013), as well as the construction of the hidden number problem that helps to improve the attack.

– Section 11.8. Details of fault-attacks on post-quantum schemes can be found in Castelnovi et al. (2018); Xagawa et al. (2021); Karabulut and Aysu (2021); Ravi et al. (2022); Bettale et al. (2021); Ravi et al. (2023).

11.10. References

Aumüller, C., Bier, P., Fischer, W., Hofreiter, P., Seifert, J.-P. (2003). Fault attacks on RSA with CRT: Concrete results and practical countermeasures. In *Cryptographic Hardware and Embedded Systems – CHES 2002*, Kaliski Jr., B.S., Çetin Kaya, K., Paar, C. (eds). Springer, Heidelberg.

Bao, F., Deng, R.H., Han, Y., Jeng, A., Narasimhalu, A.D., Ngair, T. (1997). Breaking public key cryptosystems on tamper resistant devices in the presence of transient faults. In *Security Protocols*, Christianson, B., Crispo, B., Lomas, T.M.A., Roe, M. (eds). Springer, Berlin, Heidelberg.

Bar-El, H., Choukri, H., Naccache, D., Tunstall, M., Whelan, C. (2006). The sorcerer's apprentice guide to fault attacks. *Proceedings of the IEEE*, 94(2), 370–382.

Barbu, G. and Giraud, C. (2023). All shall FA-LLL: Breaking CT-RSA 2022 and CHES 2022 infective countermeasures with lattice-based fault attacks. In *Topics in Cryptology – CT-RSA 2023*, Rosulek, M. (ed.). Springer, Cham.

Barbu, G., Battistello, A., Dabosville, G., Giraud, C., Renault, G., Renner, S., Zeitoun, R. (2013). Combined attack on CRT-RSA – Why public verification must not be public? In *Public-Key Cryptography – PKC 2013 – 16th International Conference on Practice and Theory in Public-Key Cryptography*, Kurosawa, K. and Hanaoka, G. (eds). Springer, Berlin, Heidelberg. doi: 10.1007/978-3-642-36362-7_13.

Barbu, G., Castelnovi, L., Chabrier, T. (2021). Generalizing statistical ineffective fault attacks in the spirit of side-channel attacks. In *Constructive Side-Channel Analysis and Secure Design*, Bhasin, S. and De Santis, F. (eds). Springer, Cham.

Battistello, A. and Giraud, C. (2013). Fault analysis of infective AES computations. In *FDTC 2013*, Fischer, W. and Schmidt, J.-M. (eds). IEEE, Los Alamitos.

Battistello, A. and Giraud, C. (2015). Lost in translation: Fault analysis of infective security proofs. In *FDTC 2015*, Homma, N. and Lomné, V. (eds). IEEE, Saint-Malo.

Battistello, A. and Giraud, C. (2016). A note on the security of CHES 2014 symmetric infective countermeasure. In *COSADE 2016: 7th International Workshop on Constructive Side-Channel Analysis and Secure Design*, Standaert, F.-X. and Oswald, E. (eds). Springer, Heidelberg.

Bauer, S., Drexler, H., Gebhardt, M., Klein, D., Laus, F., Mittmann, J. (2022). Attacks against white-box ECDSA and discussion of countermeasures: A report on the WhibOx contest 2021. *IACR Transactions on Cryptographic Hardware and Embedded Systems,* 4, 25–55.

Berzati, A., Canovas, C., Goubin, L. (2008). (In)security against fault injection attacks for CRT-RSA implementations. In *FDTC 2008*, Breveglieri, L., Gueron, S., Koren, I., Naccache, D., Seifert, J.-P. (eds). IEEE, Washington, D.C.

Bettale, L., Montoya, S., Renault, G. (2021). Safe-error analysis of post-quantum cryptography mechanisms. In *FDTC 2021 – Fault Diagnosis and Tolerance in Cryptographie.* Virtual Event [Online]. Available at: https://inria.hal.science/hal-03330189.

Blömer, J., Otto, M., Seifert, J.-P. (2003). A new CRT-RSA algorithm secure against Bellcore attacks. In *ACM CCS 2003: 10th Conference on Computer and Communications Security*, Jajodia, S., Atluri, V., Jaeger, T. (eds). ACM Press, New York.

Boneh, D., DeMillo, R.A., Lipton, R.J. (2001). On the importance of eliminating errors in cryptographic computations. *Journal of Cryptology*, 14(2), 101–119.

Brengel, M. and Rossow, C. (2018). Identifying key leakage of bitcoin users. In *Research in Attacks, Intrusions, and Defenses*, Bailey, M., Holz, T., Stamatogiannakis, M., Ioannidis, S. (eds). Springer, Cham.

Cao, W., Shi, H., Chen, H., Chen, J., Fan, L., Wu, W. (2022). Lattice-based fault attacks on deterministic signature schemes of ECDSA and EdDSA. In *Topics in Cryptology – CT-RSA 2022*, Galbraith, S.D. (ed.). Springer, Cham.

Castelnovi, L., Martinelli, A., Prest, T. (2018). Grafting trees: A fault attack against the sphincs framework. Cryptology ePrint Archive, Paper 2018/102 [Online]. Available at: https://eprint.iacr.org/2018/102.

Ciet, M. and Joye, M. (2005). Elliptic curve cryptosystems in the presence of permanent and transient faults. *Designs, Codes and Cryptography*, 36(1), 33–43.

Coron, J.-S. (1999). Resistance against differential power analysis for elliptic curve cryptosystems. In *Cryptographic Hardware and Embedded Systems – CHES'99*, Çetin Kaya, K. and Paar, C. (eds). Springer, Heidelberg.

De Micheli, G. and Heninger, N. (2020). Recovering cryptographic keys from partial information, by example. Cryptology ePrint Archive, Paper 2020/1506 [Online]. Available at: https://eprint.iacr.org/2020/1506.

Dobraunig, C., Eichlseder, M., Gross, H., Mangard, S., Mendel, F., Primas, R. (2018a). Statistical ineffective fault attacks on masked AES with fault countermeasures. In *Advances in Cryptology – ASIACRYPT 2018*, Peyrin, T. and Galbraith, S. (eds). Springer, Cham.

Dobraunig, C., Eichlseder, M., Korak, T., Mangard, S., Mendel, F., Primas, R. (2018b). Sifa: Exploiting ineffective fault inductions on symmetric cryptography. *IACR Transactions on Cryptographic Hardware and Embedded Systems*, 3, 547–572.

Ebeid, N.M. and Lambert, R. (2010). A new CRT-RSA algorithm resistant to powerful fault attacks. In *Workshop on Embedded Systems Security – WESS 2010*. ACM Press, New York.

Feix, B. and Venelli, A. (2013). Defeating with fault injection a combined attack resistant exponentiation. In *COSADE 2013: 4th International Workshop on Constructive Side-Channel Analysis and Secure Design*, Prouff, E. (ed.). Springer, Heidelberg.

Feng, J., Chen, H., Li, Y., Jiao, Z., Xi, W. (2020). A framework for evaluation and analysis on infection countermeasures against fault attacks. *IEEE Trans. Inf. Forensics Secur.*, 15, 391–406.

Gierlichs, B., Schmidt, J.-M., Tunstall, M. (2012). Infective computation and dummy rounds: Fault protection for block ciphers without check-before-output. In *Progress in Cryptology – LATINCRYPT 2012: 2nd International Conference on Cryptology and Information Security in Latin America*, Hevia, A. and Neven, G. (eds). Springer, Heidelberg.

Giraud, C., Knudsen, E.W., Tunstall, M. (2010). Improved fault analysis of signature schemes. In *International Conference on Smart Card Research and Advanced Applications – CARDIS 2010*. Springer, Berlin, Heidelberg.

Hamburg, M., Tunstall, M., Xiao, Q. (2021). Improvements to RSA key generation and CRT on embedded devices. In *Topics in Cryptology – CT-RSA 2021*, Paterson, K.G. (ed.). Springer, Heidelberg.

Howgrave-Graham, N.A. and Smart, N.P. (2001). Lattice attacks on digital signature schemes. *Designs, Codes and Cryptography*, 23(3), 283–290.

Joye, M., Quisquater, J.-J., Bao, F., Deng, R. (1997). RSA-type signatures in the presence of transient faults. In *Cryptography and Coding*, Darnell, M. (ed.). Springer, Berlin, Heidelberg.

Joye, M., Lenstra, A.K., Quisquater, J.-J. (1999). Chinese remaindering based cryptosystems in the presence of faults. *Journal of Cryptology*, 12(4), 241–245.

Karabulut, E. and Aysu, A. (2021). Falcon down: Breaking falcon post-quantum signature scheme through side-channel attacks. In *2021 58th ACM/IEEE Design Automation Conference (DAC)*. IEEE, San Francisco.

Lomné, V., Roche, T., Thillard, A. (2012). On the need of randomness in fault attack countermeasures – Application to AES. In *FDTC 2012*, Bertoni, G. and Gierlichs, B. (eds). IEEE Computer Society.

Naccache, D., Nguyen, P.Q., Tunstall, M., Whelan, C. (2005). Experimenting with faults, lattices and the DSA. In *PKC 2005: 8th International Workshop on Theory and Practice in Public Key Cryptography*, Vaudenay, S. (ed.). Springer, Berlin, Heidelberg.

Nguyen, P.Q. and Shparlinski, I.E. (2003). The insecurity of the elliptic curve digital signature algorithm with partially known nonces. *Designs, Codes and Cryptography*, 30(2), 201–217.

Rauzy, P. and Guilley, S. (2014). Countermeasures against high-order fault-injection attacks on CRT-RSA. In *FDTC 2014*, Tria, A. and Choi, D. (eds). IEEE, Busan.

Ravi, P., Chattopadhyay, A., D'Anvers, J.P., Baksi, A. (2022). Side-channel and fault-injection attacks over lattice-based post-quantum schemes (Kyber, Dilithium): Survey and new results. Cryptology ePrint Archive, Paper 2022/737 [Online]. Available at: https://eprint.iacr.org/2022/737.

Ravi, P., Yang, B., Bhasin, S., Zhang, F., Chattopadhyay, A. (2023). Fiddling the twiddle constants – Fault injection analysis of the number theoretic transform. *IACR Transactions on Cryptographic Hardware and Embedded Systems*, 2, 447–481.

Schmidt, J.-M., Tunstall, M., Avanzi, R.M., Kizhvatov, I., Kasper, T., Oswald, D. (2010). Combined implementation attack resistant exponentiation. In *Progress in Cryptology – LATINCRYPT 2010: 1st International Conference on Cryptology and Information Security in Latin America*, Abdalla, M. and Barreto, P.S.L.M. (eds). Springer, Heidelberg.

SOG-IS Crypto Working Group (2023). SOG-IS crypto evaluation scheme agreed cryptographic mechanisms, version 1.3. Standard, Senior Officials Group – Information Systems Security [Online]. Available at: https://www.sogis.eu/documents/cc/crypto/SOGIS-Agreed-Cryptographic-Mechanisms-1.3.pdf.

Tupsamudre, H., Bisht, S., Mukhopadhyay, D. (2014). Destroying fault invariant with randomization – A countermeasure for AES against differential fault attacks. In *Cryptographic Hardware and Embedded Systems – CHES 2014*, Batina, L. and Robshaw, M. (eds). Springer, Heidelberg.

Wagner, D. (2004). Cryptanalysis of a provably secure CRT-RSA algorithm. In *ACM CCS 2004: 11th Conference on Computer and Communications Security*, Atluri, V., Pfitzmann, B. and McDaniel, P. (eds). ACM Press, New York.

Xagawa, K., Ito, A., Ueno, R., Takahashi, J., Homma, N. (2021). Fault-injection attacks against NIST's post-quantum cryptography round 3 KEM candidates. Cryptology ePrint Archive, Paper 2021/840 [Online]. Available at: https://eprint.iacr.org/2021/840.

Yen, S.-M. and Joye, M. (2000). Checking before output may not be enough against fault-based cryptanalysis. *IEEE Transactions on Computers*, 49(9), 967–970.

Yen, S.-M., Kim, S., Lim, S., Moon, S.-J. (2002). RSA speedup with residue number system immune against hardware fault cryptanalysis. In *ICISC 01: 4th International Conference on Information Security and Cryptology*, Kim, K. (ed.). Springer, Berlin, Heidelberg.

Yen, S.-M., Kim, D., Moon, S. (2006). Cryptanalysis of two protocols for RSA with CRT based on fault infection. In *FDTC*, Breveglieri, L., Koren, I., Naccache, D., Seifert, J.-P. (eds). Springer, Berlin, Heidelberg.

12

Fault Countermeasures

Patrick SCHAUMONT and Richa SINGH
Worcester Polytechnic Institute, Massachusetts, USA

A fault countermeasure is used to block a fault attack from reaching its objective. At high level, a fault countermeasure aims for the same objective as fault tolerant computing, namely to prevent an unpredictable fault causing a failure in the security objective of a design. However, fault countermeasures are fundamentally different from traditional fault-tolerant techniques that are designed to handle random faults. In a fault attack, faults are controlled by an intelligent attacker, who may search, adapt, or optimize the fault injection parameters toward a specific objective. Fault countermeasures are therefore optimized to protect the security objectives of a secure design, such as preventing information leakage or unauthorized access. The first half of the chapter develops a fault countermeasure taxonomy to describe the different design strategies. The second half of the chapter discusses various examples of fault countermeasures, organized according to design abstraction level.

12.1. Anatomy of a fault attack

A fault attack proceeds in five stages. A successful fault attack requires each of these five stages to be successfully completed. Hence, a fault countermeasure is effective if it can disable any single stage in the fault attack pipeline.

1) *Fault injection*: a fault attack starts by applying some form of electromagnetic or environmental stress on an electronic circuit. The fault injection will translate into an electrical effect in the circuit nodes, such as a temporary voltage excursion or a permanent short.

Embedded Cryptography 1,
coordinated by Emmanuel PROUFF, Guénaël RENAULT,
Matthieu RIVAIN and Colin O'FLYNN.

2) *Fault manifestation*: a fault becomes manifest when the voltage noise level created through fault injection is strong enough to change the logic level of a clock or data wire. A logic change over a clock cycle boundary is called a bit-flip; a temporary logic change is called a glitch. A fault may become manifest as a glitch on the power lines of a digital circuit, thereby affecting many different components at the same time. Most fault injection techniques cause temporary and reversible changes, but fault manifestation can also be permanent.

3) *Fault propagation*: a manifest fault resides deep inside the hardware belly of a secure system. The fault remains harmless unless it is able to propagate through different circuit nodes and across time in clock cycles. Analysis and control of the fault propagation path is an explicit requirement in many fault attacks.

4) *Fault observation*: eventually, a manifest fault and its propagated derivative will reach a primary output of the digital circuit where the fault effect can be observed. Simple suppression of faulty outputs may be sufficient to prevent fault attacks that require fault observation, such as differential fault analysis.

5) *Fault exploitation*: finally, an observed manifest fault must be exploitable, meaning that it must directly contribute to breaking the security objective of the design. Many fault attacks require precise faults, such as single bit-flips at a precise clock cycle. In typical fault attacks, where attacker control is much less accurate, the bulk of observable faults is not exploitable.

12.2. Understanding the attacker

The objectives and means of the attacker explain the "why" and "how" of a fault attack. In most cases, the attacker's goal is to remain unnoticed by the target, except for rare instances where the goal is to cause a denial-of-service. This is not always evident for the attacker, as fault exploitation always requires fault injection. On the other hand, only fully fault-tolerant targets will detect any fault injection at a significant cost and overhead of implementation. Practical, cost-effective real-world targets have limited fault coverage, and the attacker takes advantage of this gap between full fault-tolerance and cost-effectiveness. In the following, we summarize common fault attacker objectives and means.

12.2.1. *Fault attacker objectives*

An active fault attack gives the fault attacker control over the target. This opens up a diverse set of objectives.

– *Information leakage*: by analyzing the outcome of faulty processing, a fault attacker obtains information leakage on internal secret data items. Traditional DFA needs multiple observations of a faulty outcome, often while processing attacker-chosen input data. On the other hand, modern differential techniques no longer make use of the faulty outcome, but rather exploit the dependency between a fault detection and the internal secret data.

– *Tamper of internal data*: forcing the value of internal data allows an attacker to squash a secret from the system without learning it. Data tamper may also force pointer values in the target, leading to tampered control flow or unauthorized memory access.

– *Tamper of control flow*: the fault attacker may try to alter the sequence of operations executing on the target, for example, to prevent startup into a trusted system state. A successful fault attack does not need permanent, full control over the target system. For example, access controls often boil down to a single Boolean condition (access granted or not), which is tested by a conditional jump. That single instruction is an obvious target for the fault attack.

These objectives only list what an attacker *could* do and not what the attacker *will* do. During the design of a fault countermeasure, the attacker's objectives must be presumed based on the known security-critical operations of the target.

Additionally, there is no one-to-one correspondence between a fault attack objective and a fault countermeasure. A single fault attack objective may be achieved through various mechanisms, each requiring a different countermeasure. For instance, a random number generator is a crucial component in cryptography and even a slight bias in the random stream can cause problems. However, a small bias in the random number stream can be introduced in many ways, such as through excessive heat, suppressed voltage, data tampering with the internal random state, or control flow tampering with the computation.

12.2.2. *Fault attacker means*

To minimize the chance of detection, a fault attacker must complete the attack objective with a minimum of disturbance. An effective fault attacker will therefore carefully select the means of the attack.

– *Fault injection mechanism*: faults can be introduced into the electrical system of a target using techniques such as clock glitching and electromagnetic pulses. Despite requiring access to the target's low-level hardware, the attacker does not need to be close to the target. Some fault injection methods involve physical manipulation, while others only require access to the target's logical environment, such as via software on the same server. With the close relationship between software and hardware reliability in contemporary operating environments, remote fault injection is now a viable option.

– *Fault injection resolution*: every fault injection mechanism comes with a spatial and temporal resolution, reflecting the precision of the attacker's fault control. Fault injection methods with high spatial and temporal resolution are the best case scenario for the attacker, as they reduce the likelihood of detection. On the other hand, when fault countermeasures are absent, fault attacks remain possible at surprisingly low spatial and temporal resolution. The literature on fault attacks describes cases where automated setups have used thousands of fault injections to achieve a single, favorable outcome for the attacker.

– *Fault injection repetition*: most fault attacks are only effective when multiple fault injection trials are allowed. In typical fault attacks, there is an implicit assumption that the target is incapable of remembering past fault events. However, a fault countermeasure can (and should) take such fault history into account.

– *Fault attack observability*: the effectiveness of a fault attack depends on the level of detail the attacker must observe. The attacker must at least be able to confirm that a fault injection caused a fault manifestation. However, even if the fault manifestation is successful, it can still have undesirable outcomes for the attacker. For example, if the attacker observes the outcome of the fault attack through a data output, such as ciphertext, there are three possible outcomes: (a) the output remains unchanged; (b) the output is altered; or (c) the target becomes unresponsive. Only altered outputs (b) are useful for differential fault analysis.

12.3. Taxonomy of fault countermeasures

In Figure 12.1, we identify three principal axes to describe the construction and operation of fault countermeasures.

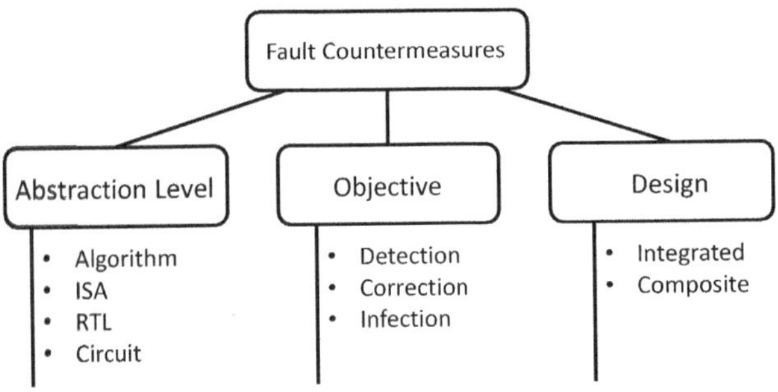

Figure 12.1. *Taxonomy of fault countermeasures along three dimensions*

1) *Countermeasure abstraction level*: the first axis identifies the principal level of computation abstraction of the countermeasure. The computation abstraction identifies the smallest computation step that is treated as faulty or correct by the the countermeasure. Fault countermeasures can be built at the circuit-level (lowest), the register-transfer level (RTL), the instruction-set architecture level (ISA), or the algorithm level. Correspondingly, the fault countermeasure will be expressed in terms of the correctness of individual circuit elements (transistors), register transfers, processor instructions, or high-level operations. A fault countermeasure can thwart a

fault attack if it can insert itself anywhere between the fault manifestation and the fault exploitation. Fault manifestation always occurs in hardware, at the lowest computation abstraction level. Fault exploitation, however, is often implemented at a higher level of computation abstraction. For example, DFA typically builds on the information flow in a cryptographic algorithm.

2) *Countermeasure objective*: the second axis describes what the fault countermeasure is aiming to do: detecting the fault, correcting the fault, or amplifying (infecting) the fault effect. A detection based countermeasure is able to flag the occurrence of a fault, but leaves the fault response to the system. Fault detection is appealing and often the easiest to implement, but it leaves the difficult design task of fault response open. An additional challenge is that fault response is also subject to fault injection. At the other end of the spectrum are fault correction countermeasures, which are essentially fault tolerant designs. A fault correction countermeasure complete removes the fault effect from the fault attack pipeline up to a given severity of fault effect. A third type of countermeasure, fault infection, does not prevent a fault from propagating, but aims directly at preventing fault exploitation. Such an infection-based countermeasure makes every fault result in a catastrophic failure of the computation, such that an adversary is denied the possibility of controlling the fault injection process.

3) *Countermeasure design*: the third axis describes how the fault countermeasure is realized at the selected abstraction level. We distinguish integrated countermeasures from composite countermeasures. An integrated countermeasure is one that transforms a given design into a different design that is able to detect or correct the fault. For example, an integrated countermeasure transforms an algorithm into a redundant algorithm. A composite countermeasure is a countermeasure that is created at a computation abstraction level above the design of interest. A composite countermeasure does not require redesign of algorithms. For example, a verify-after-sign protocol uses existing signature verification techniques. Detection-based countermeasures are always of the composite type, because they need to combine a fault response with a detection mechanism.

12.4. Fault countermeasure principles

This section enumerates several generic principle in fault countermeasures, which are then applied on specific cases in later sections.

12.4.1. *Redundancy*

Redundancy is the cornerstone of fault tolerant computing, and it is a basic building block in many fault countermeasures. Through redundant execution of the target application, followed by verification of the redundant outcome, the fault countermeasure aims to detect faults and possibly correct faults. Fault correction requires a higher level of redundancy than fault detection.

We distinguish several forms of redundancy.

– *Spatial redundancy*: eliminates fault attacks through the use of multiple parallel storage and computation elements in a secure design. The protection is achieved when the attacker is unable to simultaneously inject identical faults in each redundant element.

– *Temporal redundancy*: eliminates fault attacks through the repeated execution of a secure design. The protection is achieved when the attacker is unable to repeatedly inject identical faults in each redundant element.

– *Information redundancy*: eliminates fault attacks by redundantly encoding the values in a digital circuit. The protection is achieved when the attacker is unable to recreate valid codewords by fault injection.

The faults are detected or corrected when redundant results are merged and checked for consistency. However, the checking process itself can be subject to fault attacks. The solution to this challenge is known as the *Byzantine generals problem* in fault-tolerant computing. It states that at least $3m + 1$ redundant elements are needed to counteract the impact of m faulty elements.

Redundancy does not have to imply that the redundant copies must be identical. Indeed, diversity is an effective way to raise the difficulty of injection faults. For example, we may perform a forward operation $a = g(b)$, followed by an inverse operation $b = f(a)$, and then check that the final outcome is the same as the input.

12.4.2. *Randomness*

The most powerful adversary is one who is able to inject arbitrarily chosen faults over multiple clock cycles, and into multiple distinct circuit elements. Such an adversary can overpower redundancy because a matching fault can be injected in every redundant element. Of course, such a fault attack requires precise control of the fault injection hardware in terms of fault intensity, timing and location parameters.

By using randomness that cannot be anticipated by the attacker, fault countermeasures can counter such a strong adversary. The randomness eliminates the advantage of precise fault control. Randomness can be applied to the temporal variation of security-sensitive operations, to the values processed in security-sensitive operations or to the insertion of dummy operations. Randomness and redundancy also work well together, when the redundant elements each use randomness. For example, temporal redundancy with randomness will execute the same operation sequence twice but with a different timing.

12.4.3. *Detectors*

Fault detectors implement the principle of a trip-wire for fault injection. At the electrical level, sensors can monitor parameters such as supply voltage, light, clock frequency and timing for anomalies. At the logical level, the target application can be instrumented with dummy operations with a known outcome to detect fault injection attempts.

Fault detectors can be either in situ or else integrated. In-situ fault detectors are part of the target application. For example, shadow registers maintain a copy of a data register in the target. The fault detection works by comparing the shadow register value with the data register value. Integrated fault detectors are independent of the target application and merely reside in close physical proximity of the target. For example, a clock timing sensor measures the clock period of a hardware circuit, and flags when the period exceeds a predefined bound.

The major advantage of fault detectors is that they are independent of the application, and thus they are generally easy to add to the target. However, the use of fault detectors also brings specific challenges. First, fault detection is only half of the fault countermeasure, as a fault detector is only effective when paired with a proper fault response. Designing a good fault response is a challenge by itself, since the response is also subject to fault injection. Second, the faults picked up by a fault detector are not the faults experienced by the target application. A good fault countermeasure design would make the fault detector the most sensitive element of the target, so that any fault injection will trip the detector before anything else. However, the attacker may avoid the detector, for example, by localizing the fault injection process or by disabling the detector.

12.4.4. *Safe-error defense*

A safe-error is a fault manifestation that does not create a faulty result. Safe-errors are useful in a fault attack. For example, if a faulty operation has no impact on the result, then the attacker learns that there is no dependency from the faulty operation to the observable result. If that dependency happens to be secret, for example, because the faulty operation executes conditionally on the value of a secret bit, then the *absence* of faulty result leaks secret information. Safe-errors remind the fault countermeasure designer of a crucial insight, namely that the absence of fault effects can be as bad as the presence of a faculty effect. Historically, safe-errors came in two flavors, termed *C safe-errors* and *M safe-errors*, respectively. These refer to errors occurring during a computation (C) or storing (M) of in intermediate result. However, safe-errors are also used in biased fault attacks, which exploit the relation between an internal secret value and the onset of a fault.

The fault countermeasure against safe-errors is to ensure that no part of the application exclusively depends on internal secrets. For example, no part of an application's execution should execute conditionally on an internal secret bit. This is usually achieved by using Boolean expressions to compute conditional results. For example, an expression such as:

```
result = (secret & v1) | (!secret & v2)
```

will assign `v1` or `v2` to `result` without the use of conditional execution.

Identifying safe-error vulnerability requires careful information flow analysis of the application. In biased fault attacks, the defense is to eliminate the fault bias. For example, by tuning the internal timing a circuit, faults will either have no effect or else a catastrophic effect. This idea is also pursued in infective fault countermeasures.

12.5. Fault countermeasure examples

The remainder of the chapter presents a collection of fault countermeasures organized by design abstraction level.

12.5.1. *Algorithm level countermeasures*

In this section, we describe algorithmic countermeasures. Most algorithmic countermeasures are of the integrated type. They propose certain modifications to the algorithm design. We discuss techniques for symmetric-key designs and public-key designs.

– *Symmetric-key countermeasures*: the primary target for such fault attacks is retrieving the secret key by observing faulty ciphertexts. Symmetric-key ciphers are suited for integrated countermeasures in the form of dual modular redundancy. Such redundancy is desirable for designs that combine encryption and decryption, since the decryption can verify the following encryption and vice versa. The verification can execute at the algorithm level, round level, or even for individual round steps. The countermeasure also provides implicit randomization, provided that each input is unique and random.

By expressing the individual steps of a symmetric-key cipher in closed mathematical form, efficient information redundancy is possible using parity check bits or codeword bits. Such check bits predict the parity of the result. While parity check bits do not provide the same coverage as full modular redundancy, they enable a tradeoff between resource cost and fault countermeasure protection level.

In addition to dual modular redundancy and parity check bits, protocol-level countermeasures are also easy to implement. For example, fresh-rekeying schemes provide a deterministic yet unpredictable manner to change a cipher's key. Fresh-rekeying prevents the adversary from collecting more than a few faulty ciphertexts, much fewer than needed for a DFA.

More recent research results have shown infective countermeasures for symmetric-key designs, although their efficiency has yet to be conclusively demonstrated. One idea is fault-space transformation, which aims to create redundant designs with distinct fault injection behavior. This countermeasure aims at biased fault attacks.

– *Public-key countermeasures*: in public-key schemes, the primary fault attack target is the secret key of the design. Classic public-key cryptographic schemes, including RSA and ECC, have a solid connection to underlying mathematical structures, making them amendable to integrated countermeasures. On the other hand, public-key algorithms tend to be more challenging to protect than secret-key algorithms due to their higher computational complexity. For example, public-key algorithms often include conditional processing that depends on secret-key bits. There is a rich body of literature on techniques to protect the mathematical consistency of public-key algorithms and the storage and computations of public-key implementations. A classic example of the tight interaction between algorithm implementation and fault countermeasure design is the Montgomery powering ladder, which performs modular exponentiation. The Montgomery ladder avoids conditional processing and ensures that every intermediate result in the algorithm participates in computing the correct output, making safe-error attacks ineffective. However, it has proven very difficult to design countermeasures that can thwart multiple fault injection vectors at the same time. For example, the Montgomery power ladder does not protect against fault attacks on the public-key parameters, which can dramatically weaken the cryptographic strength of public-key structures. Hence, the assumed attacker's objectives play an important role in selecting the proper fault countermeasure for public-key cryptography.

Due to the difficulty in designing correct and complete integrated countermeasures, public-key algorithms are often protected using a composite countermeasure. For example, using verify-after-sign, the user of a signing algorithm can ensure the correctness of a signature by verifying the signature before release. This countermeasure is especially effective when the signature verification cost is much smaller than the signature generation cost.

Most recent work in fault countermeasures for public key schemes has focused on the post-quantum candidates proposed in the context of the competition run by the National Institute for Standards and Technology (NIST). The design challenge for these countermeasures is to ensure that the classic fault countermeasure techniques, such as randomization, recomputation, redundancy and verify-after-sign, can be applied efficiently to novel postquantum algorithms. Fault attacks and suitable countermeasures have been developed for NTRUEncrypt, lattice-based signatures and one-time hash-based signature schemes.

12.6. ISA level countermeasures

At the instruction-architecture level, fault attack countermeasures emphasize the correctness of instruction execution on a processor. These countermeasures are agnostic to a specific algorithm and are integrated as code transformations and compiler optimization steps. The general term for the transformation process is code hardening.

ISA-level countermeasures assume a fault model commensurate with the instruction level of computation. A common assumption is that a fault is observed as an instruction skip or as a random-register corruption. Of course, a fault model is an assumption on how the fault will become observable. However, the reality of fault injection at the ISA level of abstraction is much broader. Depending on the fault injection mechanism, a fault may cause arbitrary register corruption, including a hidden state. A fault may also cause faulty bits in instruction or data memory. Therefore, actual fault attacks on processors experience many effects that cannot be explained through the instruction-skip or random-register corruption alone, including, for example, processor exceptions and illegal instruction execution. An ISA-level countermeasure will rarely aim to address these unforeseen effects but rather concentrate on a more restricted fault model.

Many ISA-level countermeasures are integrated countermeasure techniques. Common protection techniques include instruction duplication, branch hardening, and testing of loop invariants. The protection offered by instruction duplication is that an attacker may not be able to inject the same fault during the back-to-back execution of the same instruction. For example, when a branch is replicated twice, a single instruction skip cannot prevent the branch execution. Duplication only applies to instructions without side effects. Stateful instructions require transformation into idempotent sequences. ISA-level countermeasures are appealing because their insertion can be automated as a code transformation. Hence, a compiler step can implement the fault countermeasure, and formal verification tools can evaluate the resulting code for correctness and consistency in the duplication model.

Usually, the redundancy at the ISA level is temporal, as redundant execution of instructions. However, the bits of a processor can be treated as parallel redundant elements. This parallel redundant form is created by capturing the target algorithm as a Boolean program, that is, using single-bit operations. Next, the Boolean program is rewritten using bitwise instructions, resulting in a bitslice-form program that can execute redundantly on a processor. With careful programming, redundant bitslicing protects against data corruption as well as instruction skip.

As with algorithmic countermeasures, most ISA-level countermeasures are of the integrated type, and they transform a program into a redundant protected program. However, a composite measure may be possible if the processor includes additional infrastructure to monitor the processor performance profile. For example, performance counters on specific events, such as the number of speculations of a given type, can be used to detect coarse-grain anomalies or subtle micro-architecture attacks such as RowHammer.

12.7. RTL-level countermeasures

RTL countermeasures include every technology-independent hardware fault countermeasure. The unit of computation in RTL is the register transfer. The fault model considered for a countermeasure is a corrupted register transfer that impacts the destination register of the transfer. A generic countermeasure at this level protects the register transfer using redundancy in time, space, or encoding. A large body of design techniques stems from fault-tolerant computing. Such methods use the redundant encoding of data, fine-state machine states, and temporal and spatial redundancy to enable fault detection. These classic fault protection techniques aim at fault detection and possible suppression of faulty output.

Biased-fault attacks measure the onset of faults in a design as a function of circuit stress. For example, a register transfer in a design becomes gradually corrupted when the implementation's clock period gradually decreases. As the onset of such faults, as a function of fault stress, is often data dependent, biased-fault attacks also work as side-channel attacks. Furthermore, when an attacker measures the absence of biased faults rather than their presence, biased-fault attacks become statistically ineffective fault attacks. For these more advanced attacks, fault detection alone is no longer sufficient. Recent work in RTL fault countermeasures emphasizes fault correction and methods to prevent faulty ciphertext from being produced. These countermeasures against biased fault attacks ensure fault correction for a limited number of simultaneous faults. Another strategy against biased fault attacks is to reduce fault bias from circuits. Reducing bias at the RTL is difficult because RTL is technology independent and thus oblivious to fault bias.

12.8. Circuit-level countermeasures

At the lowest level of abstraction, countermeasures aim at detecting the fault injection directly in terms of applied circuit stress.

Various sensors can detect the excursion of static and dynamic operating parameters, such as those caused by overclocking, undervolting, glitching and injection of electromagnetic pulses. Sensors can also detect the injection of photocurrent charges caused by light flashes, ionizing radiation or laser pulses. Sensor designs are challenging because they need to operate in a digital, noisy environment while performing an essentially analog measurement. In addition, the sensors must require minimal (or no) calibration and be autonomous.

Sensors detect fault injection indirectly through the effects of fault injection on the logical properties of a signal or directly by electrical measurements. Many all-digital stress sensors are based on the principle of timing fault detection. A timing fault detector compares a reference event to a variable event and triggers a fault when the timing difference between both events exceeds a predefined margin. Indeed, overclocking, undervolting, glitching and (to some extent) EM injection can all be detected at the digital level as a timing fault. Multiple sensors are needed when the fault injection is localized, such as when using EM injection probes or body-bias injection probes. Laser fault injection sensors aim to detect the photocurrent charges, which are known to cause transistors in the OFF state to become temporarily conducting. This photocurrent may generate a temporal short-circuit path in the transistor stack of CMOS gates, which in turn creates a local voltage drop. Photocurrents can also be detected directly using bulk current sensors.

Sensors become a single point of failure when they can be disabled. Therefore, sensors require careful integration and possibly shielding to prevent tamper at a low abstraction level. The shield is a conductive layer in the form of a mesh or a cover on the chip. Integrated circuits require shielding, depending on their mounting. For example, classic-mounted chips require front-side shielding to prevent probes and focus ion beam (FIB) attacks, while flip-chip-mounted chips require back-side shielding to prevent body bias or laser fault injection. Moreover, as shields can be mechanically removed by polishing or FIB, the countermeasure must actively monitor their integrity.

An alternative to fault sensing by sensors is to apply hardware redundancy at the circuit level, for example, by implementing regular logic as dual-rail complementary logic. Faults are then caught when the complementary rails hold inconsistent values. However, this technique comes at a high hardware cost and still requires the addition of a fault response after detection.

12.9. Design automation of fault countermeasures

In recent years, significant efforts have been invested in design automation techniques for the simulation and verification of fault countermeasures and the synthesis of fault countermeasures. However, the design of countermeasures for fault protection is challenging because the concerns of fault protection (such as redundant encoding) do not coincide with the functional requirements of the design.

Furthermore, inserting fault countermeasures into a design can be very tedious, such as with instruction duplication.

Design automation tools for fault countermeasures serve two main purposes. First, they verify the correctness of a given design with respect to a fault injection metric. Second, they provide a correct-by-construction mechanism to attach a fault countermeasure into a design.

Formal verification tools provide the substantial advantage of symbolically capturing the fault space. Formal fault verification can thus account for every possible fault occurrence within the model capabilities. Based on the symbolic representation of the fault design space, formal verification tools can then reason about possible outcomes and the correctness of a countermeasure. For example, formal tools can model an instruction sequence as an automaton. Next, the countermeasure-protected version can be captured using a similar automaton. Then, a solver will apply a fault model to the protected automaton and aim to demonstrate that the protected, faulted automaton is equivalent to the unprotected automaton. If the proof succeeds, a valid fault-attack path has been found. An example of this method is to verify the correctness of an instruction–duplication countermeasure under the fault model of a single instruction skip. As long as the fault model is comprehensive, formal tools are a powerful design space exploration mechanism for fault attacks. An alternate mechanism to fault countermeasure evaluation is the use of simulation. While simulation can only explore concrete fault injection cases, simulation is very good for testing fault injection cases for which no good fault model can be found.

12.10. Notes and further references

– Section 12.1. A detailed description of the anatomy of a fault attack for the case of a classic SoC is given by Yuce et al. (2020).

– Section 12.2. A standard reference of fault attacks on cryptography with the purpose of information leakage is the book by Joye and Tunstall (2012). Baksi et al. (2023) present an update for symmetric-key cryptography.

One of the most impressive achievements in modern fault attacks has been their adaption to remote targets. The fault attacker becomes a software program that can inject faults remotely. RowHammer by Kim et al. (2014) and CLKSCREW by Tang et al. (2017) demonstrate remote fault injection in dynamic memory and processor logic, respectively. Since then, remote fault injection has been repeatedly demonstrated, for example, on x86 CPUs (PlunderVolt by Murdock et al. (2020)), FPGA-SoCs (JackHammer by Weissman et al. (2020)) and FPGAs (FPGAHammer by Krautter et al. (2018); RAMJam by Alam et al. (2019)). A recent survey of the development of that field is presented by Mahmoud et al. (2023).

For every fault injection technique, there is a corresponding fault model. Richter-Brockmann et al. (2023) make a review of fault modeling techniques at the hardware level, and describe the fault types originating from each type of circuit stress. Proy et al. (2019) discuss the case of EM pulse injection on software execution. Explaining the effects of fault injection precisely is sometimes elusive. The case of EM pulse injection on hardware is a case in point. A recent summary of progress is presented by Dumont et al. (2021).

– Section 12.3. Bar-El et al. (2006) was among the first to systematically review fault attacks. Karaklajic et al. (2013) later refined the fault attack taxonomy from the hardware designers' perspective. Schmidt and Medwed (2012) describe a taxonomy for fault countermeasures in symmetric-key ciphers.

There is no universal agreement yet that infective countermeasures are effective. Battistello and Giraud (2015) showed that infective countermeasures for RSA were flawed. Battistello and Giraud (2016) broke infective countermeasures for AES.

– Section 12.4. A review of redundancy mechanisms for fault tolerant computing is covered in the book by Koren and Krishna (2020). The need for randomness in fault countermeasures was demonstrated by Lomné et al. (2012). Although randomness can be used to build a fault attack countermeasure, the random number generator itself is frequently the target of the attack. Some examples of such attacks are presented by Bayon et al. (2016), Madau et al. (2018) and Yao et al. (2018). Karaklajic et al. (2012) discusses the design of safe-error countermeasures.

– Section 12.5.1. While writing this chapter, we started collecting and classifying countermeasure papers according to the proposed taxonomy. The collection is listed on https://www.zotero.org/groups/4433035/faultcountermeasures.

Schmidt and Medwed (2012) provide a review of symmetric-key countermeasures with a taxonomy based on fault countermeasure kind. Bousselam et al. (2012) discuss a review of countermeasures specific for AES. Satoh et al. (2008) describe various redundancy based countermeasures for an AES hardware design. Patranabis et al. (2018) discuss an infective countermeasure for AES. The Montgomery powering ladder design is developed in Joye and Yen (2002).

Hariri and Reyhani-Masoleh (2012) present a set of countermeasures for elliptic curve cryptography. Fan et al. (2010) was one of the first to systematically compare attack vectors against countermeasures for the case of elliptic curve cryptography. This includes fault attacks. This research was later updated as Fan and Verbauwhede (2012).

– Section 12.6. Proy et al. (2017) describe techniques to harden code by compiler techniques. They give a good introduction to common fault models at ISA level. To study the fault model at ISA level on a new architecture, a benchmark such as Dureuil et al. (2016) can be helpful.

Breier et al. (2021) present a framework to evaluate redundant software encoding schemes. Patrick et al. (2016) present a redundant encoding scheme based on software bitslicing.

Kiaei et al. (2019) present a processor design with customized instruction set for redundant bitslicing. Gülmezoglu et al. (2019) show how subtle attacks (including Rowhammer) can be detected at ISA-level using performance counting infrastructure.

– Section 12.7. The classic work on redundant logic design is by Sellers et al. (1968). Wu and Karri (2004) describe techniques for redundant encoding during RTL design suited for fault detection and correction.

Countermeasures against biased fault attacks require a combination of fault encoding and correction. Meyer et al. (2019) and Daemen et al. (2020) explore techniques that serve simultaneously against fault injection and side-channel leakage. Other proposals for error-correcting encoding are by Breier et al. (2020, 2021). Ghalaty et al. (2014) describe a solution for removing fault bias from a circuit by balancing the propagation delays along combinational paths.

– Section 12.8. One of the early efforts at integrated (in-situ) timing fault detection is the timing sensor developed for Ernst et al. (2003). This work is based on so-called shadow-latches that can detect the onset of timing faults. Deshpande et al. (2016) use the principle of shadow latches being used to build a clock glitching sensor. Yuce et al. (2019) describe its integration in a microprocessor in order to detect fault attacks in software. Timing fault detectors are also presented by Zussa et al. (2014).

El-Baze et al. (2016) and Breier et al. (2017) describe all-digital sensors for EM injection, based on the observation that EM pulses create local timing faults. A different approach for EM detection is presented by Miura et al. (2016), which measures the impact of an EM pulse on the frequency of a carefully laid out ring oscillator.

Matsuda et al. (2020) describe a laser fault injection sensor based on bulk current measurement, while Viera et al. (2017) present a laser fault injection sensor based on sensing the effect of IR drop.

Cioranesco et al. (2014) and Wang et al. (2020) present designs of active frontside shields intended to block probing attempts. Borel et al. (2018) and Miki et al. (2020) describe backside shielding techniques. The latter is more challenging that the former because silicon processing steps do not provide metal on the chip backside, and because the active circuits required to sense the backside shields are located on the other side of the chip.

In recent years, a wealth of relatively low-cost techniques have been identified that offer attacker access to the physical layer of chip design. Nagata et al. (2022) make a comprehensive overview of the issues and the state-of-the-art in countermeasure techniques.

– Section 12.9. Formal verification techniques for fault vulnerability detection in software are proposed by Moro et al. (2013) and Goubet et al. (2015). Similar formal fault verification methods with hardware fault models are described by Arribas et al. (2020) and Richter-Brockmann et al. (2021).

Fault simulation techniques are studied by Dureuil et al. (2016) and Grycel and Schaumont (2021). Adhikary and Buhan (2022) make a review of standard tools for fault simulation at the instruction-set level.

Automated fault countermeasure insertion is investigated by Khairallah et al. (2018), Breier et al. (2018) and Aghaie et al. (2020).

12.11. References

Adhikary, A. and Buhan, I. (2022). Sok: Getting started with open-source fault simulation tools. Cryptology ePrint Archive, Paper 2022/1675 [Online]. Available at: https://eprint.iacr.org/2022/1675.

Aghaie, A., Moradi, A., Rasoolzadeh, S., Shahmirzadi, A.R., Schellenberg, F., Schneider, T. (2020). Impeccable circuits. *IEEE Trans. Computers*, 69(3), 361–376. doi: 10.1109/TC.2019.2948617.

Alam, M.M., Tajik, S., Ganji, F., Tehranipoor, M.M., Forte, D. (2019). RAM-Jam: Remote temperature and voltage fault attack on FPGAs using memory collisions. In *2019 Workshop on Fault Diagnosis and Tolerance in Cryptography, FDTC 2019*. IEEE, Atlanta. doi: 10.1109/FDTC.2019.00015.

Arribas, V., Wegener, F., Moradi, A., Nikova, S. (2020). Cryptographic fault diagnosis using VerFI. In *2020 IEEE International Symposium on Hardware Oriented Security and Trust (HOST)*, San Jose.

Baksi, A., Bhasin, S., Breier, J., Jap, D., Saha, D. (2023). A survey on fault attacks on symmetric key cryptosystems. *ACM Comput. Surv.*, 55(4), 86:1–86:34. doi: 10.1145/3530054.

Bar-El, H., Choukri, H., Naccache, D., Tunstall, M., Whelan, C. (2006). The sorcerer's apprentice guide to fault attacks. *Proceedings of the IEEE*, 94(2), 370–382.

Battistello, A. and Giraud, C. (2015). Lost in translation: Fault analysis of infective security proofs. In *2015 Workshop on Fault Diagnosis and Tolerance in Cryptography, FDTC 2015*, Homma, N. and Lomné, V. (eds). IEEE, Saint-Malo. doi: 10.1109/FDTC.2015.13.

Battistello, A. and Giraud, C. (2016). A note on the security of CHES 2014 symmetric infective countermeasure. In *Constructive Side-Channel Analysis and Secure Design*, Standaert, F.-X. and Oswald, E. (eds). Springer, Cham.

Bayon, P., Bossuet, L., Aubert, A., Fischer, V. (2016). Fault model of electromagnetic attacks targeting ring oscillator-based true random number generators. *J. Cryptogr. Eng.*, 6(1), 61–74. doi: 10.1007/s13389-015-0113-2.

Borel, S., Duperrex, L., Deschaseaux, E., Charbonnier, J., Cledière, J., Wacquez, R., Fournier, J., Souriau, J.-C., Simon, G., Merle, A. (2018). A novel structure for backside protection against physical attacks on secure chips or sip. In *2018 IEEE 68th Electronic Components and Technology Conference (ECTC)*, San Diego.

Bousselam, K., Natale, G.D., Flottes, M., Rouzeyre, B. (2012). On countermeasures against fault attacks on the advanced encryption standard. In *Fault Analysis in Cryptography, Information Security and Cryptography*, Joye, M. and Tunstall, M. (eds). Springer, Heidelberg. doi: 10.1007/978-3-642-29656-7_6.

Breier, J., Bhasin, S., He, W. (2017). An electromagnetic fault injection sensor using hogge phase-detector. In *2017 18th International Symposium on Quality Electronic Design (ISQED)*. IEEE, Piscataway.

Breier, J., Hou, X., Liu, Y. (2018). Fault attacks made easy: Differential fault analysis automation on assembly code. *IACR TCHES*, 2, 96–122.

Breier, J., Khairallah, M., Hou, X., Liu, Y. (2020). A countermeasure against statistical ineffective fault analysis. *IEEE Transactions on Circuits and Systems II: Express Briefs*, 67(12), 3322–3326.

Breier, J., Hou, X., Liu, Y. (2021). On evaluating fault resilient encoding schemes in software. *IEEE Trans. Dependable Secur. Comput.*, 18(3), 1065–1079. doi: 10.1109/TDSC.2019.2897663.

Cioranesco, J., Danger, J., Graba, T., Guilley, S., Mathieu, Y., Naccache, D., Ngo, X.T. (2014). Cryptographically secure shields. In *2014 IEEE International Symposium on Hardware-Oriented Security and Trust, HOST 2014*. Arlington.

Daemen, J., Dobraunig, C., Eichlseder, M., Gross, H., Mendel, F., Primas, R. (2020). Protecting against statistical ineffective fault attacks. *IACR TCHES*, 3, 508–543.

Deshpande, C., Yuce, B., Ghalaty, N.F., Ganta, D., Schaumont, P., Nazhandali, L. (2016). A configurable and lightweight timing monitor for fault attack detection. In *2016 IEEE Computer Society Annual Symposium on VLSI (ISVLSI)*. Pittsburgh.

Dumont, M., Lisart, M., Maurine, P. (2021). Modeling and simulating electromagnetic fault injection. *IEEE Trans. Comput. Aided Des. Integr. Circuits Syst.*, 40(4), 680–693. doi: 10.1109/TCAD.2020.3003287.

Dureuil, L., Petiot, G., Potet, M.-L., Le, T.-H., Crohen, A., de Choudens, P. (2016). Fissc: A fault injection and simulation secure collection. In *Computer Safety, Reliability, and Security*, Skavhaug, A., Guiochet, J., Bitsch, F. (eds). Springer, Cham.

El-Baze, D., Rigaud, J., Maurine, P. (2016). An embedded digital sensor against EM and BB fault injection. In *2016 Workshop on Fault Diagnosis and Tolerance in Cryptography, FDTC 2016*. IEEE, Santa Barbara. doi: 10.1109/FDTC.2016.14.

Ernst, D., Kim, N.S., Das, S., Pant, S., Rao, R.R., Pham, T., Ziesler, C.H., Blaauw, D.T., Austin, T.M., Flautner, K. et al. (2003). Razor: A low-power pipeline based on circuit-level timing speculation. In *Proceedings of the 36th Annual International Symposium on Microarchitecture*. IEEE, San Diego. doi: 10.1109/MICRO.2003.1253179.

Fan, J. and Verbauwhede, I. (2012). An updated survey on secure ECC implementations: Attacks, countermeasures and cost. In *Cryptography and Security: From Theory to Applications: Essays Dedicated to Jean-Jacques Quisquater on the Occasion of His 65th Birthday*, Naccache, D. (ed.). Springer, Cham. doi: 10.1007/978-3-642-28368-0_18.

Fan, J., Guo, X., Mulder, E.D., Schaumont, P., Preneel, B., Verbauwhede, I. (2010). State-of-the-art of secure ECC implementations: A survey on known side-channel attacks and countermeasures. In *HOST 2010, Proceedings of the 2010 IEEE International Symposium on Hardware-Oriented Security and Trust (HOST)*, Plusquellic, J. and Mai, K. (eds). IEEE, Anaheim. doi: 10.1109/HST.2010.5513110.

Ghalaty, N.F., Aysu, A., Schaumont, P. (2014). Analyzing and eliminating the causes of fault sensitivity analysis. In *Design, Automation & Test in Europe Conference & Exhibition, DATE 2014*, Fettweis, G.P. and Nebel, W. (eds). European Design and Automation Association. doi: 10.7873/DATE.2014.217.

Goubet, L., Heydemann, K., Encrenaz, E., Keulenaer, R. (2015). Efficient design and evaluation of countermeasures against fault attacks using formal verification. In *Revised Selected Papers of the 14th International Conference on Smart Card Research and Advanced Applications, CARDIS 2015*. Springer-Verlag, Heidelberg.

Grycel, J. and Schaumont, P. (2021). Simplifi: Hardware simulation of embedded software fault attacks. *Cryptography*, 5(2) [Online]. Available at: https://www.mdpi.com/2410-387X/5/2/15.

Gülmezoglu, B., Moghimi, A., Eisenbarth, T., Sunar, B. (2019). Fortuneteller: Predicting microarchitectural attacks via unsupervised deep learning. *CoRR* [Online]. Available at: http://arxiv.org/abs/1907.03651.

Hariri, A. and Reyhani-Masoleh, A. (2012). On countermeasures against fault attacks on elliptic curve cryptography using fault detection. In *Fault Analysis in Cryptography, Information Security and Cryptography*, Joye, M. and Tunstall, M. (eds). Springer, Heidelberg. doi: 10.1007/978-3-642-29656-7_10.

Joye, M. and Tunstall, M. (eds) (2012). *Fault Analysis in Cryptography*. Springer, Heidelberg. doi: 10.1007/978-3-642-29656-7.

Joye, M. and Yen, S. (2002). The montgomery powering ladder. In *Cryptographic Hardware and Embedded Systems - CHES 2002*, Kaliski, B.S., Koç, ç.K., Paar, C. (eds). Springer, Heidelberg. doi: 10.1007/3-540-36400-5_22.

Karaklajic, D., Fan, J., Verbauwhede, I. (2012). A systematic M safe-error detection in hardware implementations of cryptographic algorithms. In *2012 IEEE International Symposium on Hardware-Oriented Security and Trust, HOST 2012*. IEEE Computer Society. doi: 10.1109/HST.2012.6224327.

Karaklajic, D., Schmidt, J., Verbauwhede, I. (2013). Hardware designer's guide to fault attacks. *IEEE Transactions on Very Large Scale Integration (VLSI) Systems*, 21(12), 2295–2306.

Khairallah, M., Sadhukhan, R., Samanta, R., Breier, J., Bhasin, S., Chakraborty, R.S., Chattopadhyay, A., Mukhopadhyay, D. (2018). DFARPA: Differential fault attack resistant physical design automation. In *2018 Design, Automation Test in Europe Conference Exhibition (DATE)*. IEEE, Dresden.

Kiaei, P., Mercadier, D., Dagand, P.-E., Heydemann, K., Schaumont, P. (2019). SKIVA: Flexible and modular side-channel and fault countermeasures. Cryptology ePrint Archive, Report 2019/756 [Onilne]. Available at: https://eprint.iacr.org/2019/756.

Kim, Y., Daly, R., Kim, J., Fallin, C., Lee, J.H., Lee, D., Wilkerson, C., Lai, K., Mutlu, O. (2014). Flipping bits in memory without accessing them: An experimental study of dram disturbance errors. In *2014 ACM/IEEE 41st International Symposium on Computer Architecture (ISCA)*. IEEE, Minneapolis.

Koren, I. and Krishna, M.C. (2020). *Fault-Tolerant Systems*, 2nd edition. MKP, Hershey.

Krautter, J., Gnad, D.R.E., Tahoori, M.B. (2018). FPGAhammer: Remote voltage fault attacks on shared FPGAs, suitable for DFA on AES. *IACR Trans. Cryptogr. Hardw. Embed. Syst.*, 3, 44–68. doi: 10.13154/tches.v2018.i3.44-68.

Lomné, V., Roche, T., Thillard, A. (2012). On the need of randomness in fault attack countermeasures: Application to AES. In *2012 Workshop on Fault Diagnosis and Tolerance in Cryptography*. IEEE, Leuven.

Madau, M., Agoyan, M., Balasch, J., Grujic, M., Haddad, P., Maurine, P., Rozic, V., Singelée, D., Yang, B., Verbauwhede, I. (2018). The impact of pulsed electromagnetic fault injection on true random number generators. In *2018 Workshop on Fault Diagnosis and Tolerance in Cryptography (FDTC)*. IEEE, Amsterdam.

Mahmoud, D.G., Lenders, V., Stojilovic, M. (2023). Electrical-level attacks on CPUs, FPGAs, and GPUs: Survey and implications in the heterogeneous era. *ACM Comput. Surv.*, 55(3), 58:1–58:40. doi: 10.1145/3498337.

Matsuda, K., Tada, S., Nagata, M., Komano, Y., Li, Y., Sugawara, T., Iwamoto, M., Ohta, K., Sakiyama, K., Miura, N. (2020). An IC-level countermeasure against laser fault injection attack by information leakage sensing based on laser-induced opto-electric bulk current density. *Japanese Journal of Applied Physics*, 59(SG), SGGL02. doi: 10.7567/1347-4065/ab65d3.

Meyer, L.D., Arribas, V., Nikova, S., Nikov, V., Rijmen, V. (2019). M&M: Masks and macs against physical attacks. *IACR Trans. Cryptogr. Hardw. Embed. Syst.*, 1, 25–50. doi: 10.13154/tches.v2019.i1.25-50.

Miki, T., Nagata, M., Sonoda, H., Miura, N., Okidono, T., Araga, Y., Watanabe, N., Shimamoto, H., Kikuchi, K. (2020). Si-backside protection circuits against physical security attacks on flip-chip devices. *IEEE J. Solid State Circuits*, 55(10), 2747–2755.

Miura, N., Najm, Z., He, W., Bhasin, S., Ngo, X.T., Nagata, M., Danger, J. (2016). PLL to the rescue: A novel EM fault countermeasure. In *Proceedings of the 53rd Annual Design Automation Conference, DAC 2016*. ACM. doi: 10.1145/2897937.2898065.

Moro, N., Heydemann, K., Encrenaz, E., Robisson, B. (2013). Formal verification of a software countermeasure against instruction skip attacks. Cryptology ePrint Archive, Report 2013/679 [Online]. Available at: https://eprint.iacr.org/2013/679.

Murdock, K., Oswald, D.F., Garcia, F.D., Bulck, J.V., Piessens, F., Gruss, D. (2020). Plundervolt: How a little bit of undervolting can create a lot of trouble. *IEEE Secur. Priv.*, 18(5), 28–37. doi: 10.1109/MSEC.2020.2990495.

Nagata, M., Miki, T., Miura, N. (2022). Physical attack protection techniques for IC chip level hardware security. *IEEE Transactions on Very Large Scale Integration (VLSI) Systems*, 30(1), 5–14.

Patranabis, S., Chakraborty, A., Mukhopadhyay, D., Chakrabarti, P.P. (2018). *Fault Space Transformation: Countering Biased Fault Attacks*. Springer, Singapore.

Patrick, C., Yuce, B., Ghalaty, N.F., Schaumont, P. (2016). Lightweight fault attack resistance in software using intra-instruction redundancy. In *SAC 2016*, Avanzi, R. and Heys, H.M. (eds). Springer, Heidelberg.

Proy, J., Heydemann, K., Berzati, A., Cohen, A. (2017). Compiler-assisted loop hardening against fault attacks. *ACM Trans. Archit. Code Optim.*, 14(4). doi: 10.1145/3141234.

Proy, J., Heydemann, K., Berzati, A., Majéric, F., Cohen, A. (2019). A first ISA-level characterization of EM pulse effects on superscalar microarchitectures: A secure software perspective. In *Proceedings of the 14th International Conference on Availability, Reliability and Security, ARES '19*. Association for Computing Machinery, New York. doi: 10.1145/3339252.3339253.

Richter-Brockmann, J., Shahmirzadi, A.R., Sasdrich, P., Moradi, A., Güneysu, T. (2021). FIVER – robust verification of countermeasures against fault injections. *IACR Trans. Cryptogr. Hardw. Embed. Syst.*, 4, 447–473. doi: 10.46586/tches.v2021.i4.447-473.

Richter-Brockmann, J., Sasdrich, P., Güneysu, T. (2023). Revisiting fault adversary models: Hardware faults in theory and practice. *IEEE Trans. Computers*, 72(2), 572–585. doi: 10.1109/TC.2022.3164259.

Satoh, A., Sugawara, T., Homma, N., Aoki, T. (2008). High-performance concurrent error detection scheme for AES hardware. In *CHES 2008*, Oswald, E. and Rohatgi, P. (eds). Springer, Heidelberg.

Schmidt, J. and Medwed, M. (2012). Countermeasures for symmetric key ciphers. In *Fault Analysis in Cryptography, Information Security and Cryptography*, Joye, M. and Tunstall, M. (eds). Springer, Heidelberg. doi: 10.1007/978-3-642-29656-7_5.

Sellers, F.F., Hsiao, M.-Y., Bearnson, L.W. (1968). *Error Detecting Logic for Digital Computers*, 1st edition. McGraw-Hill Book Company, New York.

Tang, A., Sethumadhavan, S., Stolfo, S.J. (2017). CLKSCREW: Exposing the perils of security-oblivious energy management. In *26th USENIX Security Symposium, USENIX Security 2017*, Kirda, E. and Ristenpart, T. (eds). USENIX Association [Online]. Available at: https://www.usenix.org/conference/usenixsecurity17/technical-sessions/presentation/tang.

Viera, R.A.C., Maurine, P., Dutertre, J., Bastos, R.P. (2017). Importance of IR drops on the modeling of laser-induced transient faults. In *14th International Conference on Synthesis, Modeling, Analysis and Simulation Methods and Applications to Circuit Design, SMACD 2017*. IEEE. doi: 10.1109/SMACD.2017.7981593.

Wang, H., Shi, Q., Nahiyan, A., Forte, D., Tehranipoor, M.M. (2020). A physical design flow against front-side probing attacks by internal shielding. *IEEE Trans. Comput. Aided Des. Integr. Circuits Syst.*, 39(10), 2152–2165. doi: 10.1109/TCAD.2019.2952133.

Weissman, Z., Tiemann, T., Moghimi, D., Custodio, E., Eisenbarth, T., Sunar, B. (2020). Jackhammer: Efficient rowhammer on heterogeneous FPGA-CPU platforms. *IACR Trans. Cryptogr. Hardw. Embed. Syst.*, 3, 169–195. doi: 10.13154/tches.v2020.i3.169-195.

Wu, K. and Karri, R. (2004). Fault secure datapath synthesis using hybrid time and hardware redundancy. *IEEE Trans. Comput. Aided Des. Integr. Circuits Syst.*, 23(10), 1476–1485. doi: 10.1109/TCAD.2004.835132.

Yao, Y., Yang, M., Patrick, C., Yuce, B., Schaumont, P. (2018). Fault-assisted side-channel analysis of masked implementations. In *2018 IEEE International Symposium on Hardware Oriented Security and Trust, HOST 2018*. IEEE Computer Society. doi: 10.1109/HST.2018.8383891.

Yuce, B., Deshpande, C., Ghodrati, M., Bendre, A., Nazhandali, L., Schaumont, P. (2019). A secure exception mode for fault-attack-resistant processing. *IEEE Trans. Dependable Secur. Comput.*, 16(3), 388–401. doi: 10.1109/TDSC.2018.2823767.

Yuce, B., Schaumont, P., Witteman, M. (2020). Fault attacks on secure embedded software: Threats, design and evaluation. *CoRR* [Online]. Available at: https://arxiv.org/abs/2003.10513.

Zussa, L., Dehbaoui, A., Tobich, K., Dutertre, J., Maurine, P., Guillaume-Sage, L., Clédière, J., Tria, A. (2014). Efficiency of a glitch detector against electromagnetic fault injection. In *Design, Automation & Test in Europe Conference & Exhibition, DATE 2014*, Fettweis, G.P. and Nebel, W. (eds). European Design and Automation Association. doi: 10.7873/DATE.2014.216.

List of Authors

Guillaume BARBU
IDEMIA
Courbevoie
France

Davide BELLIZIA
Independent researcher
Italy

Eleonora CAGLI
CEA-Leti
Université Grenoble Alpes
France

Jessy CLÉDIÈRE
CEA-Leti
Université Grenoble Alpes
France

Brice COLOMBIER
Laboratoire Hubert Curien
UMR 5516, CNRS
Institut d'Optique Graduate School
Université Jean Monnet
Saint-Étienne
France

Cécile DUMAS
CEA-Leti
Université Grenoble Alpes
France

Jean-Max DUTERTRE
École des Mines de Saint-Étienne
France

Vincent GROSSO
Laboratoire Hubert Curien
UMR 5516, CNRS
Institut d'Optique Graduate School
Université Jean Monnet
Saint-Étienne
France

Loïc MASURE
LIRMM, CNRS
Université de Montpellier
France

Debdeep MUKHOPADHYAY
Indian Institute of Technology
Kharagpur
India

Colin O'FLYNN
Dalhousie University
and
NewAE Technology Inc
Halifax
Canada

Elisabeth OSWALD
University of Klagenfurt
Austria

Daniel PAGE
University of Bristol
United Kingdom

Olivier PEREIRA
Crypto Group
ICTEAM Institute
UCLouvain
Belgium

Thomas PETERS
Crypto Group
ICTEAM Institute
UCLouvain
Belgium

Emmanuel PROUFF
LIP6
Sorbonne Université
Paris
France

Guénaël RENAULT
Agence nationale de la sécurité des systèmes d'information
Paris
France

Matthieu RIVAIN
Crypto Experts
Paris
France

Sayandeep SAHA
Indian Institute of Technology
Kharagpur
India

Patrick SCHAUMONT
Worcester Polytechnic Institute
Massachusetts
USA

Richa SINGH
Worcester Polytechnic Institute
Massachusetts
USA

François-Xavier STANDAERT
Crypto Group
ICTEAM Institute
UCLouvain
Belgium

Adrian THILLARD
Ledger
Paris
France

Michael TUNSTALL
Google
Mountain View
United States

Yuval YAROM
Ruhr University Bochum
Germany

Index

B, C

D

E

N

O, P

Summary of Volume 2

Chapter 9. Protected RSA Implementations
Mylène ROUSSELLET, Yannick TEGLIA and David VIGILANT

Chapter 10. Protected ECC Implementations
Łukasz CHMIELEWSKI and Louiza PAPACHRISTODOULOU

Chapter 13. Gate-Level Protection
Sylvain GUILLEY and Jean-Luc DANGER

Chapter 14. Physically Unclonable Functions
Jean-Luc DANGER, Sylvain GUILLEY, Debdeep MUKHOPADHYAY and Ulrich RUHRMAIR

Summary of Volume 3

Chapter 4. Code Obfuscation

Sebastian SCHRITTWIESER and Stefan KATZENBEISSER

Part 2. Randomness and Key Generation

Chapter 5. True Random Number Generation

Viktor FISCHER, Florent BERNARD and Patrick HADDAD

Chapter 8. Nonce Generation for Discrete Logarithm-Based Signatures
Akira TAKAHASHI and Mehdi TIBOUCHI

Chapter 9. Random Error Distributions in Post-Quantum Schemes
Thomas PREST

Printed and bound by CPI Group (UK) Ltd, Croydon, CR0 4YY

13/09/2026

14961073-0006